Other Kaplan Books Related to Law School Admissions

LSAT 2006 Edition Premier Program

LSAT 2006 Edition Comprehensive Program

LSAT Logic Games Workbook

Get Into Law School: A Strategic Approach

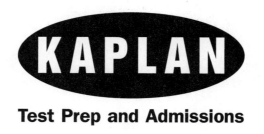

Test Prep and Admissions

LSAT® 180
2006–2007 Edition

Eric Goodman
and the Staff of Kaplan Test Prep and Admissions

Simon & Schuster

NEW YORK · LONDON · SYDNEY · TORONTO

Kaplan Publishing
Published by SIMON & SCHUSTER
Rockefeller Center
1230 Avenue of the Americas
New York, NY 10020

Materials in this book where adapted from the following sources:

Democracy and Education by John Dewey. New York, 1916.

"Women and Naturalization" in *Prologue: A Quarterly Journal of the National Archives and Records Administration*. Volume 3, Number 2, Summer 1998.

Teenage Brain: A Work in Progress, Bethesda (MD): National Institutes of Health, US Department of Health and Human Services; 2001 [updated 2004]. (NIH Publication Number: NIH 01-4929).

"Law and Liberty," Professor Roscoe Pound, Lectures on the Harvard Classics, *The Harvard Classics*. 1909–14.

"General Introduction," Professor Ralph Barton Perry, Lectures on the Harvard Classics, *The Harvard Classics*. 1909–14.

"Symbiotic Stars," by Minas Kafatos and Andrew G. Michalistisianos. Copyright © 1984 by Scientific American, Inc. All rights reserved.

"Must Virtue Be Taught?" by Thomas D. Eisele, *Journal of Legal Education*, volume 37, December 1987. Copyright © 1987. Reprinted by permission of the author and *Journal of Legal Education*.

"Mitochondrial DNA" by Leslie A. Grivell. Copyright © 1983 by Scientific American, Inc. All rights reserved.

Contributing Editor: Ben Baron
Editorial Director: Jennifer Farthing
Project Editor: Eileen McDonnell
Production Manager: Michael Shevlin
Content Manager: Patrick Kennedy
Interior Page Layout: Renée Mitchell
Cover Design: Mark Weaver

Manufactured in the United States of America.
Published simultaneously in Canada.

10 9 8 7 6 5 4 3 2 1

March 2006

ISBN-13: 978-0-7432-7936-9
ISBN-10:   0-7432-7936-0

For information regarding special discounts for bulk purchases, please contact Simon & Schuster Special Sales at 1-800-456-6798 or business@simonandschuster.com.

Table of Contents

kaptest.com/publishing

The material in this book is up-to-date at the time of publication. However, the LSAC may have instituted changes in the test or test registration process after this book was published. Be sure to carefully read the materials you receive when you register for the test.

If there are any important late breaking developments—or changes or corrections to the Kaplan test preparation materials in this book—we will post that information online at kaptest.com/publishing. Check to see if there is any information posted there regarding this book.

kaplansurveys.com/books

If you have comments and suggestions, we invite you to fill out our online form at **kaplansurveys.com/books**. Your feedback is extremely helpful as we continue to develop high-quality resources to meet your needs.

About the Author

Eric Goodman began teaching and writing for Kaplan two years after graduating from Cornell University. For over 12 years, Eric has written courses, software, and books that have helped thousands of test takers master the LSAT, GMAT, and GRE. As an instructional designer, he has also authored online courses and computer-based simulations in the fields of economics, corporate training, and e-commerce.

The Perfect Score

Ah, *perfection* . . .

We humans are a demanding bunch. We don't bound out of bed in the morning aspiring to mediocrity, but rather striving for *perfection*. The *perfect* job. The *perfect* shoes to go with the *perfect* outfit. We head to the beach on a *perfect* summer day to find the *perfect* spot to get the *perfect* tan.

Webster's defines perfection as "the quality or state of being complete and correct in every way, conforming to a standard or ideal with no omissions, errors, flaws or extraneous elements."

The LSAT test makers define perfection as a score of 180. If that's what you're after, then you've come to the right place. We at Kaplan have been training test takers to ace the LSAT for over 30 years. We understand your desire for the highest possible score. For those of you shooting for the moon, we salute your quest for perfection. The *perfect* LSAT score. The *perfect* law school. The *perfect* career.

WHAT IS THE LSAT AND HOW IS IT STRUCTURED

The LSAT is a half-day (205-minute) test designed to measure skills considered essential for success in law school: reading, organization and management of information, and reasoning. It consists of four scored 35-minute sections of multiple-choice questions and one unscored "variable" section used to pretest new test items. A 35-minute, unscored writing sample is administered at the end of the test.

The four scored sections include:
- One Reading Comprehension section (26–28 questions based on 4 passages, each about 450 words)
- One Analytical Reasoning or "Logic Games" section (23–24 questions based on 4 games)
- Two Logical Reasoning sections (24–26 questions each, consisting of short arguments followed by 1 or 2 questions)

The "variable" section will look like one of those other sections and have 24–28 questions. The number of scored questions you answered correctly is your "raw score." The score scale is 120 to 180.

Request the *LSAT/LSDAS Registration & Information Book* from LSAC by calling (215) 968-1001 for the most up-to-date information on the test. You must register in advance. The earlier you register, the better your chances of being assigned to your first or second choice test center.

Since you are aiming for a perfect score, we assume that you are familiar with the LSAT question types and believe you can already do well on the test—that you are looking for the tools to help you edge your score up from good to perfect.

WHO SHOULD USE THIS BOOK

We should warn you up front: This book is not for the faint of heart. It assumes you've already learned the basics, so it consists exclusively of examples of the toughest material you're likely to see on the LSAT (though we do define some basic terms.) No easy stuff, no run-of-the-mill strategies—just killer games, passages, and questions, complete with Kaplan's proven techniques to help you transcend "above average" and enter the rarefied arena of LSAT elite. If you're entertaining the notion of pulling off the perfect 180, then you're going to have to face down the most brutal material the LSAT test makers have to offer. Even if a perfect score is not your immediate goal, diligent practice with the difficult material in this book can help develop your skills and raise your score.

If you're looking for a more fundamental introduction to the LSAT, or practice with questions ranging from easy to difficult, then we recommend working through the traditional Kaplan LSAT Premier Program or Comprehensive Program as a prerequisite for the highly challenging material contained in this volume.

HOW TO USE THIS BOOK

This book is divided into three sections corresponding to the three question types: Logic Games, Logical Reasoning, and Reading Comprehension. (The Writing Sample is not included in this book because it doesn't contribute to your 120–180 score, and no Writing Sample prompt is written to be any more difficult than any other.)

Each section provides detailed guidelines on how to make the most of the material. Jump right to the section that gives you the most trouble, or work through the sections in the order presented—it's up to you. You'll notice that the habits and thought processes of top test takers are highlighted throughout the book. Study these thoroughly, and make these effective techniques your own.

No matter what you do, try not to overload; remember, this is dense, complicated material, and not representative of the range of difficulty you'll see on test day. One thing's for sure: If you can ace this stuff, the real thing will be a breeze.

Good luck!

section one

LOGIC GAMES

CHAPTER ONE

The Logic Games Challenge

Exactly five guests—August, Dasha, Henry, Memphis, and Nicholas—arrive at a Super Bowl party. No guest arrives at the same time as any other guest. Each guest brings exactly one of the following items to the party: beer, chicken wings, ice cream, pizza, or soda. Each guest brings a different item. Exactly two guests arrive between Henry's arrival and the arrival of the guest who brings chicken wings. The guest who brings the ice cream arrives fourth. Nicholas arrives after Dasha. Memphis is the only guest to arrive between the arrival of the guest who brings chicken wings and the arrival of the guest who brings beer.

1. If Memphis brings ice cream to the party, then the order of guest arrivals and the item each brings would be precisely determined if it were also known that . . .

Who knows? Who cares?

Well, for starters, the admission boards at most accredited law schools do—and if you're reading these words, chances are you're someone who's looking to impress that particular crowd. To most law school admission officers, the LSAT Logic Games section is not some arbitrary exercise in tortured logic (as it no doubt may seem to some test takers), but rather a realistic test of the kinds of reasoning skills necessary to think through complex legal issues and situations.

Above-average difficulty games appear often on the LSAT. Unfortunately, the advice to "just skip the tough ones and do the best you can on the others" simply won't cut it for those aspiring to enter 180 territory. If that's your quest, then you have no choice but to muster all your skill, speed, and stamina to face these killers head-on. For those of you simply interested in improving your gaming techniques, cutting your teeth on the hardest games will certainly help you to hone your skills and raise your score.

It is in this spirit, and with these objectives in mind, that we present the Logic Games in this book.

USING THE LOGIC GAMES IN THIS BOOK

The Logic Games in this book are broken up into four categories:

- Supercharged Standards
- Time Warps
- Volatile Mixtures
- Huh . . . ?

Together, these represent the full range of the types of difficult games you may encounter on your test. You'll find descriptions of these categories at the beginning of each chapter. You're probably best off working your way up to the games in the final chapter, which, as the name implies, are particularly nasty. You can do the games one at a time before reviewing the explanations, or plow through a bunch before coming up for air—really, it's up to you. A few suggestions, however:

Observe timing guidelines. You'll surely get the right answers eventually if you take an hour to do each game. The point, however, is how well you can handle the tough stuff under true LSAT conditions. You don't have to go so far as to hire a proctor to stand over you with a timepiece (although that probably couldn't hurt), but make sure you spend no more than nine and one-half minutes per game. Four games in 35 minutes allows for roughly eight and one-half minutes per game, but considering the difficulty level of these, it's reasonable to allow a little extra time.

Read the explanations. Review the keys to each game, comparing your own approach to the insights provided. Notice whether you are consistently coming up with the same deductions as us, and recognizing the same factors that cut these killers down to size. Take special note of the thought processes and habits of 180 test takers highlighted throughout the explanations.

Have fun. Remember, these are games. Games are meant to be fun.

A 180 test taker approaches the Logic Games section with good humor, a positive attitude, and enthusiasm for the challenge of facing the toughest material the test makers have to offer.

Oh, by the way: Regarding the Super Bowl feast, one way the arrival order and items brought by the guests would be fully known is if August shows up with the pizza.

But you already figured that out . . . right?

CHAPTER TWO

Supercharged Standards

What makes a Logic Game hard? Certainly games that contain very unusual game actions are difficult to manage. Games that consist of a mixture of multiple game actions can also be cumbersome and trying. Have no fear: You'll see plenty of examples of these later on. But some Logic Games that seem fairly straightforward at first glance, by virtue of complicating elements, must be counted among the killer elite as well.

Each of the games in this first Logic Games chapter involves one of three single standard game actions: Sequencing, Grouping, or Matching. For this reason, they may not seem as nasty as what's to come later, but beware: while these games represent standard LSAT fare, they are nonetheless deceptively difficult.

Keep your guard up.

LOGIC GAME 1

A college career counselor must schedule meetings with eight graduating seniors to discuss their plans. Of the eight students, four, Harmony, Ivy, Kawanna, and Laurita, are women, and four, Miguel, Nathaniel, Oliver, and Philippe, are men. She will meet one–on–one with each of these students over a period of five consecutive days, Monday through Friday. Her schedule permits her to meet with exactly one student each morning and with exactly one each evening; she meets students at no other times. The following conditions apply:

One of the women is scheduled for Monday morning.

Ivy is scheduled some time before Oliver.

Oliver is scheduled in the time slot immediately after Nathaniel's time slot.

The counselor will meet with no students on Wednesday.

Ivy cannot be scheduled on Monday.

Miguel is not last on the schedule.

Philippe is scheduled for Tuesday evening.

Laurita must follow Philippe but can neither immediately precede nor immediately follow Nathaniel.

1. Which one of the following could be a complete and accurate schedule of meetings?

    (A) Monday morning: Harmony; Monday evening: Kawanna; Tuesday morning: Ivy; Tuesday evening: Philippe; Thursday morning: Laurita; Thursday evening: Miguel; Friday morning: Nathaniel; Friday evening: Oliver

    (B) Monday morning: Harmony; Monday evening: Kawanna; Tuesday morning: Philippe; Tuesday evening: Laurita; Thursday morning: Ivy; Thursday evening: Miguel; Friday morning: Nathaniel; Friday evening: Oliver

    (C) Monday morning: Harmony; Monday evening: Kawanna; Tuesday morning: Laurita; Tuesday evening: Philippe; Thursday morning: Ivy; Thursday evening: Miguel; Friday morning: Nathaniel; Friday evening: Oliver

    (D) Monday morning: Miguel; Monday evening: Harmony; Tuesday morning: Ivy; Tuesday evening: Philippe; Thursday morning: Laurita; Thursday evening: Kawanna; Friday morning: Nathaniel; Friday evening: Oliver

    (E) Monday morning: Kawanna; Monday evening: Harmony; Tuesday morning: Ivy; Tuesday evening: Philippe; Thursday morning: Laurita; Thursday evening: Nathaniel; Friday morning: Oliver; Friday evening: Miguel

2. Which one of the following could be a complete and accurate list of the students scheduled for the morning meetings in order?

    (A) Kawanna, Harmony, Nathaniel, Oliver
    (B) Harmony, Miguel, Kawanna, Oliver
    (C) Kawanna, Harmony, Miguel, Oliver
    (D) Kawanna, Harmony, Miguel, Nathaniel
    (E) Harmony, Kawanna, Laurita, Nathaniel

3. Which one of the following must be true?

    (A) Harmony is scheduled for either Monday or Tuesday.
    (B) Kawanna is scheduled for either Monday or Tuesday.
    (C) Miguel is scheduled for either Tuesday or Thursday.
    (D) Ivy is scheduled for either Tuesday or Thursday.
    (E) Oliver is scheduled for either Tuesday or Thursday.

4. If Miguel is scheduled for Tuesday morning, then which one of the following could be true?

    (A) Philippe meets with the counselor immediately after Ivy does.
    (B) Kawanna meets with the counselor immediately after Harmony does.
    (C) Ivy meets with the counselor immediately after Miguel does.
    (D) Oliver meets with the counselor on Thursday.
    (E) Harmony meets with the counselor on Friday.

5. If Ivy is scheduled for Thursday evening, then each of the following must be true EXCEPT:

    (A) Miguel is scheduled for Monday afternoon.
    (B) Laurita is scheduled for Thursday morning.
    (C) Laurita is scheduled before Oliver.
    (D) Miguel is scheduled before Laurita.
    (E) Harmony is scheduled for Monday or else Tuesday.

6. Which one of the following must be false?

    (A) Ivy is scheduled for Tuesday.
    (B) Oliver is scheduled last.
    (C) Harmony is scheduled last.
    (D) Both Laurita and Miguel are scheduled for Friday.
    (E) Both Harmony and Nathaniel are scheduled for Friday.

LOGIC GAME 1: Meet the Counselor

What Makes It Difficult

The setup tells us we must schedule (or *sequence*) eight entities into a fairly standard calendar: five consecutive days, with two time slots each day, which on first glance gives us ten slots for eight entities.

Sequencing game
Ordering entities with respect to defined positions or with respect to each other.

If the test makers left it at that, then we'd need to list our entities out along with two Xs to represent the two empty slots we'd have. However, if you scanned through the rules before starting to sketch anything out, you noticed that Wednesday is off limits (Rule 4). That means we actually have only four days, with two slots each. There are thus only eight slots for the eight entities. Noticing this at the outset makes the game more manageable, but it's the interpretation required to get there that trips up even sharp test takers.

But, of course, that's not all there is to it. The setup is quite long, and there are eight rules to process—that's a lot of information to untangle, and a couple of the rules seem written deliberately to confuse test takers. Rule 3 is written in the opposite direction of Rule 2. Rules 2 and 3 both mention O, and because Rule 2 mentions O second, whereas Rule 3 talks about O first, some test takers will carelessly assume that O is in the middle of I and N. However, both rules put O *after* the other entity mentioned.

Rule 8 tells us that L "must follow" P. However, this does not mean "immediately" after. Many test takers will incorrectly think that L must appear on Thursday morning; however, that restriction is not implied. When the test makers mean "immediately," they say it (as they do in the second half of the rule, which helps clarify the issue for alert test takers).

The very last portion of Rule 8 also prohibits something that Rule 3 already made impossible: it tells us that L must "neither immediately precede nor immediately follow" N, whereas Rule 3 already makes it impossible for L to "immediately follow" N because O immediately follows N. Be careful of tricks like this. The test makers do this every so often, knowing that test takers will second-guess their previous assessments of the rules.

A 180 test taker knows that almost every Logic Game battle starts before the first question is read. Spending time up front making deductions and recognizing restrictions translates into quick points later on.

After going through all of the rules, take a look to see if anything else can come from them. You may have noticed some big deductions that made the game less unwieldy.

Keys to the Game

Only H and K are eligible for the first time slot. Rule 1 tells us that only women (H, I, K, and L) may occupy this slot. Because L must come after P and P is set in the fourth slot, we're down to H/I/K. However, Rule 5 tells us that we can't schedule I on Monday, so that leaves only H/K. Inserting an H/K placeholder in that first slot is an important reminder that the slot is occupied by one of these two.

I→NO is a set sequence. That's just a combination of Rules 2 and 3.

P→NO is also a set sequence. Rule 5 places I on Tuesday at the earliest, so the immediately adjacent pair NO cannot both fit before P's Tuesday evening timeslot. Therefore, NO must appear some time *after* P.

I is limited to one of three positions: Tuesday morning or one of the Thursday slots. Combining Rules 2 and 3, we have I→NO. That means I is never scheduled for Friday because two entities definitely must follow I. Rule 5, again, bars I from Monday, and P occupies Tuesday afternoon. That leaves only three slots for I.

I is a Key Player that allows us to set up limited options. A Key Player is an entity or set of entities that first, is limited to two or three slots, and second, substantially affects the placement of other entities (in a domino-effect manner), depending on its placement. Any time you realize an entity is limited to one of two or three locations, check to see whether it strongly impacts other entities. If so, then automatically presume it's worthwhile to map out both or all three possible configurations for that entity (we say "presume," because most test takers are intimidated by what they incorrectly imagine to be a nearly infinite set of options).

If I is on Tuesday morning, that doesn't tell us much that we don't already know—an unsatisfying start. But if I is on Thursday morning, then the sequence must be PINOL because Rule 8 puts L after P but never next to N. If I is on Thursday evening, the sequence must be PLINO because L still must follow P, and the NO pair have nowehere else to go. So our limited options look like this:

	Mon-a	Mon-p	Tue-a	Tue-p	Thu-a	Thu-p	Fri-a	Fri-p
Scenario 1	H/K		I	P				
Scenario 2	H/K			P	I	N	O	L
Scenario 3	H/K			P	L	I	N	O

Answers and Explanations

1. A   2. E   3. D   4. B   5. A   6. E

1. A

When they appear as the first question in a set, Acceptability questions are typically a quick tour through the rules. It turns out that (A) is an acceptable sequence. Rule 1 makes it impossible for Miguel to be on Monday morning, so (D) is incorrect. Rules 2, 3, 4, and 5 find no violators in this answer set. (E) is out of the question because of Rule 6. Phillipe should be scheduled for Tuesday evening, not morning, according to Rule 7, so that eliminates B. (C) places Laurita before Phillipe, which is a violation of Rule 8, so we can eliminate that choice, leaving only (A).

Acceptability questions
These ask which choice could be a possible sequence or arrangement
(that is, which doesn't break any of the rules).

---

2. E

This Acceptability question focuses only on the morning slots. Most of the time, questions that focus on only one half of the sketch rely heavily on what each choice forces into place in the other unseen half. When you've gone to the trouble of listing limited options, you get a big payoff with questions like these. (A) is unacceptable simply because it breaks up the NO pair. But each of (B), (C), and (D) are impossible because, by leaving no room for I in a morning slot, they force us into scenario 3, and the last two morning slots in this scenario must be L and N, in that order.

3. D

Our big deduction about I's limited options leads us straight to choice (D): we deduced that Ivy could appear only in the Tuesday morning slot or else in either of the Thursday slots—she cannot be scheduled for Monday (Rule 5), and putting I in a Friday slot leaves insufficient room for both of NO (Rules 2 and 3).

4. B

If M occupies the Tuesday morning slot, then we must be in either scenario 2 or 3. That leaves only two possible sequences for the last five slots and tells us that Monday afternoon is also occupied by H/K (whichever is not scheduled for the morning slot). These constraints rule out all but (B).

5. A

Ivy, our key player, carries a lot of weight. If she's scheduled for Thursday evening, that means we're in scenario 3, telling us the concrete positions of PLINO. The only entities with a little room to move around are H, K, and M. M could be scheduled either for Monday evening or Tuesday morning. That means (A) is correct. The other choices are set in stone in scenario 3.

6. E

Using our scenario list to search for an answer that is impossible, each of (A), (B), and (C) check out just fine—we've listed concrete situations in which these circumstances actually appear. That leaves us with (D) and (E). (D) seems possible in scenario 1—it would result in H/K, H/K, I, P, N, O, M, L. But by putting both H and N on Friday, we violate the NO requirement of Rule 3: if H is in the morning and N is in the afternoon, then there's no room for O to follow immediately after N. If it's the other way around, then H immediately follows N, which violates the same rule.

What's Next?

Pure Sequencing games (that is, those that don't involve other game actions) are generally the most straightforward games on the Logic Games section. Let's move on to see what kinds of challenges are presented in another standard Logic Game type, Grouping games of Distribution.

LOGIC GAME 2

Eight people—three adults, D, E, and F, and five children, M, N, O, P, and S—will caravan together to a concert in two cars: car 1 and car 2. Exactly four people, including the driver, ride in each car. The following conditions must be satisfied.

Each car must be driven by one of the three adults.
If D rides in car 1, then E must also ride in car 1.
If O rides in car 2, then S must ride in car 1.
M and N cannot ride together in the same car.

1. Which one of the following is an acceptable grouping of people to car 2?

    (A)   E, F, N, P
    (B)   D, E, F, M
    (C)   F, P, O, N
    (D)   F, P, M, N
    (E)   D, E, O, S

2. Which one of the following must be true?

    (A)   D rides in car 1.
    (B)   P rides in car 1.
    (C)   Three children ride in car 2.
    (D)   One or both of O and S ride in car 1.
    (E)   One or both of D and E ride in car 1.

3. If three of the children ride in car 2, then which one of the following is a pair of people who could both be assigned to car 1?

    (A)   E and P
    (B)   D and F
    (C)   F and S
    (D)   O and S
    (E)   P and S

4. If D rides in car 1, which one of the following is a pair of people who could ride together?

    (A)   E and F
    (B)   O and S
    (C)   E and P
    (D)   N and P
    (E)   D and P

5. If O and S ride together, which one of the following is a pair of people who must also ride together?

    (A)   M and S
    (B)   D and P
    (C)   D and E
    (D)   E and F
    (E)   S and P

6. If F rides in a different car than P, which one of the following must ride in car 2?

    (A)   D
    (B)   E
    (C)   P
    (D)   O
    (E)   S

Logic Game 2: Caravan to the Concert

What Makes It Difficult

The action in this game—*distributing* eight people into two *groups*—is straightforward.

Grouping: Distribution game
Forming several small groups out of a large group.

It's the interpretation of Rules 2 and 3 that causes most problems. Both rules are formal logic statements, and that alone makes them a challenge. But more importantly, these are classic formulations of the "if-then" constraint that appears on the LSAT frequently.

The test makers most likely use and re-use this formulation because so many people misinterpret these rules to mean that D and E must always ride together and that O and S can never ride together. Not so.

The game is also difficult for people who are not accustomed to using placeholder entities to remind themselves that slots are occupied by one of a select two or three entities. For example, the last rule tells us that each car has a seat that is definitely occupied by M or N. Most people don't think to indicate that positive aspect of the rule to themselves. Instead, they write only the negative aspect as "never M/N," which fails to capture the most significant aspect of the rule.

Keys to the Game

One slot in each car is occupied by D/E/F, and one is occupied by M/N. This is a more concrete way of stating the first and fourth rules. Writing "D/E/F" in one slot of your master sketch for each car gives the 180 test taker more information than most other students who simply write "at least 1 adult per car" off to the side. Likewise, fully occupying the last seat with M/N reminds us graphically that one of these kids is already in that seat.

Car 1	Car 2
D/E/F __ __ M/N	D/E/F __ __ M/N

Rule 2 does not mean D and E always ride together. The contrapositive of this if-then rule is 'If E is in 2, then D is in 2.' Together, these statements mean that any time D is in 1, the pair DE is in 1; any time E is in 2, the pair DE is in 2. But if E is in 1, that doesn't tell us about D; and if D is in 2, that doesn't tell us about E. So they can be separate, but only when E is in 1 and D is in 2.

A 180 test taker deals with the most concrete pieces of information first.

Rule 3 does not mean O and S are always separated, but they can't both be in 2. The contrapositive of this if-then rule is "If S is in 2, then O is in 1." These statements, taken together mean anytime either one of them is in 2, the other one must be in 1. They could both be together in 1, but they can never be together in 2. This means at least *one* of them must always be in car 1. 180 test takers use a placeholder, O/S, to occupy a spot in car 1 to remind them of this fact. (Remember that it's not accurate to place an O/S placeholder in 2 because O and S *could* be together in 1.)

	Car 1	Car 2
	D/E/F __ O/S M/N	D/E/F __ __ M/N

Limited options are available.

	Car 1	Car 2
Scenario 1	D/E/F __ O/S M/N	F P O/S M/N
Scenario 2	F O/S/P O/S M/N	D E O/S/P M/N
Scenario 3	E F O/S M/N	D P O/S M/N
Scenario 4	E O/S/P O/S M/N	D F O/S/P M/N

We already put an M/N placeholder in the last seat in each car to satisfy Rule 4. As we just saw, Rule 3 means car 1 has a seat occupied by one of O/S.

---

180 test takers are always on the lookout for key players that reduce the game to a few limited options.

Because D and E are a pair of entities that first, are limited to three configurations (both in car 1, both in car 2, or E in 1 and D in 2), and second, substantially affect the placement of other entities, that makes the pair DE a key player. So, the 180 test taker tries all three of these configurations.

If DE is in car 1, then 1 is full (we know this because we used placeholders to indicate that the other two spots are always occupied by O/S and M/N). So everything else dumps into car 2.

If DE is in car 2, then there's only one spot left in 2. It also means that adult F must drive car 1. Only two entities remain: P and whichever one of O/S isn't already in car 1. Any of these can fill the two remaining slots.

You've no doubt noticed that we've printed *four* scenarios, even though we only have three configurations for DE. If our key pair is separated, you might have noticed that we gain no additional concrete information; it just gives us car 1 containing E __ O/S M/N and car 2 containing D __ __ M/N. We could use that as scenario 3, but the 180 test taker in you just won't leave well enough alone. F, the other adult, is—like every other entity—limited to two locations, and F's placement substantially affects the remaining entities when D and E are separated. That makes F a key player within the final DE scenario. Lower-scoring test takers look at this and think "well, that's just way too much hassle for me—I've got questions to answer. I don't have *time* to think!" But the 180 test taker realizes that he will have to do this work at some point. He knows he has a choice: he can make these deductions now and make use of them with every question, or he can make them when the questions force him to and have access to them only for one or two questions.

ANSWERS AND EXPLANATIONS

1. C   2. D   3. C   4. D   5. B   6. A

1. C

The first Acceptability question is usually answerable by running through the rules and looking for violators, and this one is no exception. (B) places all of the adults in car 2, leaving no one to drive car 1, which is Rule 1, so we can eliminate that choice. (A) has D riding in car 1 with E in car 2, a violation of Rule 2. According to Rule 3, O and S cannot be in car 2 together, as in (E), and (D) places M and N both in car 2, which is a contradiction of Rule 4, so that leaves only (C).

2. D

A "must be true" rule with no "if" attached means at least one deduction is available from the setup alone. If you made a key deduction up front, scan the choices for this deduction or a direct implication of it. If you didn't make a deduction up front, use such a "must be true" question to help find it. Sure enough, one of our major deductions—that a seat in car 1 is occupied by O/S—leads us straight to (D). Each of the others is possible, but not necessary.

> A 180 test taker knows that a "must be true" question with no new information means that something may be deduced from the setup.

3. C

If three kids are in car 2, that means we're in scenario 1 or 3. In these scenarios, we never see E and P together in car 1; nor do we see D and F there. But we do have room in car 1 for F and S in scenario 3. That's our winner.

4. D

When D rides in car 1, that's scenario 1 only. In scenario 1, the only pair in the list that could be together is P and N in car 2. All the other pairs are separated.

> A 180 test taker never wastes time on other answer choices in Logic Games once she has found a choice that works.

5. B

If O and S ride together, that puts us in scenario 2 or 4, but it tells us a little more than that; it also tells us that O and S are in car 1, and that puts P in that O/S/P slot in car 2. Because D is in car 2 in both scenarios, it must be that D and P ride together in car 2. (C) is tempting, but remember, D and E do not have to ride in the same car.

6. A

The hypothetical tells us that we could be in any of scenarios 2, 3, or 4—only scenario 1 definitely puts F and P together. On first glance, that leaves open a lot of options. But the 180 test taker zeros in on what the question is looking for—namely, something that must be true no matter which one of these three scenarios we choose—and notices that the only constant among the three scenarios is that D is in car 2.

What's Next?

Now try your hand at another type of Grouping game. Instead of distributing items into subgroups, you'll have to select a group of items from a larger group. Sounds simple, right? Well, by now you know that if it was, it wouldn't be here.

LOGIC GAME 3

A zoo curator is selecting animals to import for the zoo's annual summer exhibit. Exactly one male and one female of each of the following types of animal are available: hippo, llama, monkey, ostrich, panther. The following restrictions apply:

If no panthers are selected, then both ostriches must be selected.

A male panther cannot be selected unless a female llama is selected.

If a male monkey is selected, then neither a female ostrich nor a female panther may be selected.

At least one hippo must be selected.

1. Which one of the following is an acceptable selection of animals for the exhibit?

   (A) Female hippo, female monkey, male monkey, male ostrich, male panther
   (B) Female hippo, male llama, female monkey, female ostrich, male ostrich
   (C) Male hippo, female llama, male llama, female monkey, female ostrich
   (D) Male hippo, female llama, male monkey, female panther, male panther
   (E) Female llama, male llama, male monkey, female ostrich, male panther

2. Which one of the following must be false?

   (A) Both a female hippo and male panther are selected.
   (B) Both a male monkey and a female llama are selected.
   (C) Both a female ostrich and a male hippo are selected.
   (D) All of the animals selected are female.
   (E) All of the animals selected are male.

3. If a male monkey is selected, then which one of the following animals must also be selected?

   (A) Female hippo
   (B) Male hippo
   (C) Female llama
   (D) Female monkey
   (E) Male ostrich

4. If the smallest number of animals is selected, then which one of the following animals must be selected?

   (A) Male hippo
   (B) Female llama
   (C) Male monkey
   (D) Female panther
   (E) Male panther

5. All of the following could be true EXCEPT

   (A) A female llama is the only female animal selected.
   (B) A female monkey is the only female animal selected.
   (C) A female ostrich is the only female animal selected.
   (D) A male ostrich is the only male animal selected.
   (E) A male panther is the only male animal selected.

6. If a female llama is not selected, then which one of the following is a pair of animals at least one of which must be selected?

   (A) Female hippo, female monkey
   (B) Male hippo, male llama
   (C) Female ostrich, male ostrich
   (D) Male ostrich, female panther
   (E) Female panther, male panther

Logic Game 3: Zoo Animals

What Makes It Difficult

Our mandate in this Grouping game is to select animals for an exhibit.

Grouping: Selection game
Choosing one small group out of a large one.

Difficulties abound. For one thing, there are 10 entities to manage—one male and one female of five different species. That alone makes the choices fairly cumbersome and forces us to come up with a convention to keep the animals straight. The ambiguity is heightened by what we're not told, namely: How many of these critters are we to take? It's always easier when we have an exact number to shoot for.

The rules offer an impressive array of formal logic. Rule 1 is an if-then statement presented in the negative, telling us what happens when no panthers are taken. Not fun. Surely it would be easier if they told us what happens if one were selected. Rule 2 is presented in a "cannot-unless" format, which requires a bit of translation, while Rule 3 is another if-then with negative shadings (although easier to handle than Rule 2). Rule 4 is the easiest of the bunch, but even that one doesn't give us anything definite—which hippo is it? Or maybe both? Can't tell. In a nutshell: heavy-duty formal logic, lots of entities with a troublesome male/female distinction, and nothing settled for sure.

What about the questions? Not much relief there: With all that's up in the air, we'd expect some comforting hypotheticals to set us on our way, but only two of the six question stems deal with specific animals, and one of them does so only in the negative, citing an animal that's not selected. That question, question 6, requires a fairly complex test of the choices. Even the Acceptability question, question 1, is made more difficult by the male/female distinction, which makes it hard to scan the choices as we prefer for this type. After all this trouble, this better be a darn good summer zoo exhibit. If not, we can always boycott it in favor of the summer festival from two games back. How did you do recognizing the keys to the game?

Keys to the Game

Settle on a convention for representing the entities. One way is to use a small letter "f" or "m" to signify gender followed by a capital letter representing animal type. That would give us a roster of fH, mH, fL, mL, fM, mM, fO, mO, fP, mP.

If both ostriches are not selected, then at least one panther must be selected. This is the proper interpretation of Rule 1. This can in turn be combined with Rule 3, as follows:

If a male monkey is selected, both a male panther and a female llama must also be selected. Rule 3 says that selecting a male monkey means not taking a female ostrich, but without both ostriches we're forced to choose a panther, as noted just above. But the other part of Rule 3 forbids a female panther with a male monkey. Therefore, the requisite panther under these circumstances must be male. Rule 2 further forces us to take the female llama.

A 180 test taker can draw the correct interpretations from formal logic statements and then combine those interpretations with other rules to form larger deductions.

KAPLAN

Answers and Explanations

1. B   2. E   3. C   4. D   5. B   6. D

1. B

We can use the standard method for Acceptability questions, checking the rules against the choices, crossing off those that don't conform, until only one choice is left standing. Rule 4 is the easiest to check—(E) is the only one without a hippo, so get rid of that one to start. Rule 3 provides a lot to go on: (D) violates Rule 3, attempting to pair a male monkey and female panther. (Choice (E) violates Rule 3 too, but we already eliminated that one using Rule 4.) (A) violates Rule 2, by including a male panther without also including a female llama, which leaves only Rule 1 left to check. Neither (B) nor (C) contains a panther, and according to Rule 1, that means that both ostriches must be selected. Only (B) meets this requirement; (C) falls one male ostrich short.

A 180 test taker breezes through Acceptability questions by using easier rules first to eliminate choices before handling the more complex rules.

---

2. E

No new information, so we have no recourse but to test the choices. However, we need not test them in order. We're looking for a statement that cannot be true. Choices (A) through (C) each contain a single pairing of animals, which doesn't seem too restrictive; whereas (D) and (E) seem to be much more inclusive: all males, all females. Moreover, (A) and (C) involve hippos, which are fairly unrestricted. (Sure, we need one of them, but which one we don't know.) All in all, the sharp test taker would probably find (D) and (E) more likely to lead to a violation, and would check those first.

(D) It is possible to select only females: The twosome fH and fP readily attests to this, so (D) is not the answer we seek.

(E) It is impossible to select only males. If we tried, then we'd have to leave out the female ostrich, but we know from our analysis of Rule 1 what happens then: Without both ostriches, we'll need at least one panther. Sticking to the all-male mandate of the choice means we'd have to select the male panther, not the female one, but that would lead us down a dead end, as the male panther requires the female llama. No simple matter, but either way we slice it, we can't get away with a strictly male roster, so (E) is correct. As for the others:

(A) It's eminently possible to include a female hippo and male panther—just be sure to add a female llama (Rule 2). Rule 4 is taken care of by the selection of fH, and Rules 1 and 3 don't even apply.

(B) In this one we're looking to pair a male monkey and female llama in the same selection. First thing we need to add is a hippo—got to have one of those according to Rule 4, and either one is fine for now. We know that a male monkey precludes the selection of a female ostrich and female panther, and we deduced above that any selection including a male monkey must include a male panther. There you have it; this rounds out an acceptable list: mM, fL, mP, and either hippo will do just fine, so it is possible to select the pair in (B), which is why (B) is wrong.

(C) A female ostrich and male hippo can be chosen together, although we'll need either to select the male ostrich, allowing us to leave out the panthers, or else leave out the male ostrich, in which case we'll have to take one of the panthers. Either way, (C) is possible.

3. C

Our key deduction from above: A male monkey means no female ostrich. Without both ostriches, we're forced by Rule 1 to choose a panther. But Rule 3 forbids a female panther with a male monkey, so the panther we select must be male. A hop, skip, and a jump to Rule 2 forces us to select the female llama to go with the male panther; thus, choice (C).

(A), (D), (E) The acceptable group mM, mP, fL, and mH demonstrates that if a male monkey is selected, we can do without the animals in all three of these choices.

(B) Substitute the female hippo for the male hippo in the group listed above and we see that the male hippo is expendable as well.

4. D

We're looking for the smallest group possible, and we know that at least one hippo must be selected, so let's start there. Either a male one or female one will do. Can that be an entire acceptable group? Well, no; Rule 1 won't allow it. If only a single hippo were selected, then certainly both ostriches wouldn't be taken, and Rule 1 would therefore force us to take at least one panther. We can avoid a panther altogether by selecting both ostriches, but that would give us three animals. Can we do better? Yup—we can leave out the pair of ostriches and take a single panther. But which one? Not the male panther, because then we'd have to take the female llama as well, and remember, we're looking to take the minimum number of animals. The female panther comes with no additional baggage, so taking her, along with either hippo, results in the smallest group possible, a group of two.

Notice that we've seen this group before: In question 2, we eliminated choice (D) by choosing a twosome of females: the female hippo and the female panther. The work you did in that question could have helped you in this question as well.

(A), (B), (C), (E) No need to belabor these choices once we've seen that the smallest group possible is the female panther and either one of the hippos.

5. B

Again, no new information in the stem, so we need to work efficiently through the choices, eliminating the ones that could be true and choosing the one that proves to be impossible. Notice that the choices all involve the selection of a single animal in a particular gender. Since we're looking for the case where this can't be true, it makes sense to gravitate toward the animals with more restrictions; that is, the ones who rely on other animals to be selected. In fact, the only dependent animal in the list is the male panther in (E), and as it turns out, a group consisting of mP, fL, fH proves that (E) is possible. This type of proactive thinking is still strongly encouraged, even though it didn't pan out here.

A 180 test taker doesn't sour on strategies that are generally effective when they don't yield benefits in a particular case.

We'll simply test the other choices.

(A) A group consisting of the female llama, the male panther, and the male hippo works just fine, proving that the female llama can be the only female animal selected, so we can cross off (A).

(B) Nope; can't do it. It all comes back to Rule 1 again: We can't take the female ostrich, because we're testing to see if the female monkey can be the only female selected. Therefore, according to the implication of Rule 1, we must take a panther. But again, we are trying not to select the female in this choice, so we have to take the male, which ultimately brings us back to selecting a female after all: the female llama mandated by Rule 2. In the end (B) is impossible, and is therefore the choice we seek.

The following acceptable selections show how the remaining choices are possible:
(C) fO, mO, mH
(D) mO, fO, fH

6. D

No female llama means no male panther (Rule 2). Any situation involving panthers always brings us back to Rule 1: With the male panther out of the picture, there's a choice: take the female panther, and then we can do anything we want about the ostriches. But if we leave out the female panther, then Rule 1 kicks in and we have to select both ostriches. This is why (D) is correct: Of the pair "male ostrich"/"female panther," it is necessary to take at least one. Female ostrich could substitute for male ostrich and the choice would still be correct. As for the others:

(A), (C) The acceptable group made up of the male hippo and female panther that we've seen a number of times throughout the game proves that both members of the pairs listed in (A) and (C) can be left out without a problem.

(B) Female hippo/female panther is but one acceptable group that demonstrates that both members of this pair are expendable under these circumstances.

(E) We can do without the female panther if we take both ostriches (remember, the male panther is already out of commission thanks to the stem), and throw in a male or female hippo and we're good to go.

What's Next?

Had enough of hippos, panthers, monkeys, and the rest? Or are you sorry this game is over, just getting the hang of manipulating these complex entities and daunting formal logic rules? Then rejoice! Next up is another grouping game of selection that presents similar challenges.

LOGIC GAME 4

A bank manager selects at least four, and no more than six, new employees to attend a regional training event. Each new employee is either a loan officer or a teller, and each works either part time or full time. Of the eight new employees, three are part-time loan officers, two are full-time loan officers, two are part-time tellers, and one is a full-time teller. The manager selects the attendees according to the following conditions:

No other employees are eligible to attend the event.
At least three loan officers are selected.
At least two full-time employees are selected.
If the full-time teller is selected, then at least one part-time teller is also selected.

1. Which one of the following is an acceptable group of employees that can attend the event?

    (A) Two full-time loan officers, one full-time teller, two part-time tellers
    (B) One full-time loan officer, one full-time teller, two part-time loan officers, one part-time teller
    (C) One full-time loan officer, two part-time loan officers, two part-time tellers
    (D) Two full-time loan officers, one full-time teller, three part-time loan officers, one part-time teller
    (E) One full-time loan officer, one full-time teller, three part-time loan officers

2. If not all of the new full-time loan officers are selected, then which one of the following must be true?

    (A) At least one part-time teller is selected.
    (B) Exactly one part-time teller is selected.
    (C) No full-time tellers are selected.
    (D) Exactly two part-time loan officers are selected.
    (E) Exactly three part-time loan officers are selected.

3. If the maximum number of loan officers is selected, then which one of the following must be true?

    (A) Exactly five employees are selected.
    (B) Exactly six employees are selected.
    (C) No part-time tellers are selected.
    (D) At least one part-time teller is selected.
    (E) No full-time tellers are selected.

4. Which one of the following CANNOT be true?

    (A) More full-time loan officers than part-time loan officers are selected.
    (B) More part-time tellers than full-time loan officers are selected.
    (C) More full-time tellers than part-time loan officers are selected.
    (D) An equal number of part-time tellers and full-time tellers are selected.
    (E) An equal number of part-time loan officers and full-time loan officers are selected.

5. If an equal number of part-time loan officers and full-time tellers is selected, then which one of the following must be false?

    (A) More part-time employees than full-time employees are selected.
    (B) More full-time employees than part-time employees are selected.
    (C) Exactly five employees are selected.
    (D) An equal number of part-time tellers and full-time tellers are selected.
    (E) Exactly six employees are selected.

6. If the minimum number of employees is selected, then each of the following must be true EXCEPT:

    (A) No more than two part-time loan officers are selected.
    (B) Exactly two full-time loan officers are selected.
    (C) No full-time tellers are selected.
    (D) No part-time tellers are selected.
    (E) No more than one part-time teller is selected.

Logic Game 4: Bank Employees

What Makes It Difficult

We said in the previous game that in Grouping games of Selection it's easier when we have an exact number to shoot for. On that count, we're better off in Bank Employees than in Zoo Animals, as the limitation of 4–6 entities selected is set from the start. But the test maker that giveth, also taketh away: The entities are even more difficult to distinguish, falling into four very similar-sounding categories; and a strict number element pervades the entire game, which complicates matters even further.

The rules aren't so bad: The first is what we at Kaplan call a "loophole closer." It ties up a possible loose end but offers no real additional information.

So there are functionally only three rules to deal with in the game. Rules 2 and 3 deal with number considerations, and may be slightly confusing to some because one concerns employee type (loan officer) while the other speaks of employee status (full time). Rule 4 offers a fairly straightforward formal logic if-then statement—mild, in fact, in comparison to those offered in the previous game.

The questions pose the same kind of wording difficulty posed in Zoo Animals, only worse: the eye simply has trouble distinguishing "part-time loan officers," "full-time loan officers," "part-time tellers," and "full-time tellers" on the page. It's fairly easy to confuse them. Finally, the test makers play up the numbers element to the hilt: "more of these than those, an equal number of these and those, exactly this many of these and that many of those . . . ." Ugh! Combine that with trying to keep the employee types straight, and it gets mind-numbing after a while.

In the real world, a bank manager, presumably trained in numerical operations, might be the perfect person to sort through all of this nonsense. Unfortunately, on the LSAT it's your job to stand in for the manager and make the selections. Here are some points that significantly simplify your task. Did you see them yourself?

Keys to the Game

Settle on a convention for representing the entities. Same advice as in the previous game. You absolutely need a way to represent the entities that's both clear and easily accessible. How's about using uppercase for full time, and lowercase for part time? That way the entities will be lll / LL / tt / T. Then you can simply circle or cross off employees as need be.

A 180 test taker doesn't balk at recopying an initial setup when necessary.

At least one part-time loan officer will always be selected. This is due to Rule 2's mandate for at least three loan officers, combined with the fact that there are only two full-time loan officers. Circle one l.

At least one full-time loan officer will always be selected. That's because we need at least two full-time employees according to Rule 3, but there's only one full-time teller. Circle one L. These two deductions in effect simplify the game down to a selection of two to four employees from the remaining six.

If no part-time teller is selected, then the full-time teller is not selected, and both full-time loan officers are selected. This is the implication of Rule 4, and this implication combined with Rule 3

Answers and Explanations

1. B   2. A   3. E   4. C   5. A   6. D

1. B

A standard Acceptability question, but one made more difficult by the wordy entities. The usual strategy for these applies; use the rules to eliminate choices. (D), which lists seven employees selected for training, directly contradicts the condition in the first sentence of the game requiring four to six employees for the event. Rule 2 kills (A), which has only two loan officers. Rule 3 eliminates (C), which has just one full-time employee, and Rule 4 gets rid of (E), which has a full-time teller, but no part-time teller. (B) is the only one left, so it's correct.

A 180 test taker does not lose sight of rules that are buried in the scenario.

---

2. A

If not all of the full-time loan officers are selected, then exactly one full-time loan officer is (the one we deduced above). Then we have to add another part-time loan officer to the one we already deduced above, in order to satisfy Rule 2, not to mention the full-time teller to take care of Rule 3. Since the full-time teller is selected, Rule 4 requires a part-time teller to be selected. (A) is thus the winner: At least one part-time teller must be selected. (C) is impossible, while the other choices are possible only.

3. E

Next we're instructed to select the maximum number of loan officers. Might as well shoot for the moon: Since no rule specifically prevents us from choosing all five loan officers, let's see what follows if we do.

A 180 test taker knows how to test for maximums and minimums.

When looking for a maximum, choose the largest number possible to test and work your way down. That way, when a scenario works out, you have the answer. Selecting all five loan officers violates no rules, but we have to examine what else is possible in order to test the choices. One more employee can join them to give us six total, but need not. However, selecting the full-time teller would mess things up, since that would force us to add a part-time teller, giving us a grand total of seven—no good. So (E) must be true. Since we could add one part-time teller to the mix, but don't have to, (A), (B), (C), and (D) all could be true, but need not be.

4. C

No new information, and we're looking for an impossibility. As it turns out, our deduction regarding the necessity for at least one part-time teller helps us cut right to the chase: Since there is only one full-time teller, and at least one part-time loan officer is always selected, there's no way for full-time tellers to outnumber part-time loan officers. At best, they're even. (C) is the impossibility we seek.

(A) is wrong because we can select two full-time loan officers, one part-time loan officer, and one part-time teller.

(B) is out because we can select two part-time tellers, one full-time teller, one part-time loan officer, and one full-time loan officer.

(D) The correct choice for question 1 demonstrates that it's quite possible for the number of part-time tellers selected to equal the number of full-time tellers selected.

A 180 test taker uses the right answer to Acceptability questions to test choices in later questions whenever possible.

(E) is no good because we can choose two full-time loan officers and two part-time loan officers.

5. A

Selecting an equal number of part-time loan officers and full-time tellers means one of each. Selecting the full-time teller means that at least one part-time teller is selected as well. Additionally, since at least three loan officers must be selected, both full-time loan officers will be selected. The only variable is the second part-time teller; maybe she's in, maybe she's out—no way to tell. Testing the choices against this nearly completed arrangement, we don't have to look far: (A) must be false. With all three full-time employees selected and only one part-time loan officer eligible, the best that can happen is that the part-timers tie the score with the variable part-time teller. But there's no way to get more part-timers than full-timers under these circumstances.

(B), (C), and (D) are all possible. All we'd have to do is leave out that final part-time teller.

(E) Put that second part-time teller in, however, and there will be exactly six employees selected.

6. D

The minimum number of employees is four. To satisfy Rules 2 and 3, three of them must be loan officers and two must be full-time employees. We can do this in two ways: We can select one part-time loan officer, two full-time loan officers, and one part-time teller; or we can take two part-time loan officers and two full-time loan officers. Any other scenario will force us to choose at least five employees. (A), (B), (C) and (E) all conform to both scenarios, and are therefore wrong. (D) need not be true because the first scenario includes the selection of a part-time teller.

What's Next?

Well, enough of Selection chores for now. Don't worry—we'll see more of this game action coupled with others later on in the more complex Hybrid game types. For now, let's move on to the final type of standard single game action that may just cause you trouble all by itself. We call these Matching games, and as the name implies, they require you to match up different elements with one another according to strict conditions.

LOGIC GAME 5

A warehousing company owns exactly four large refrigerated warehouses numbered one through four. All four warehouses are located on a single pier. Each is divided equally into two separate units, a West unit and an East unit, and each unit supplies its own loading dock. The company stores only dairy products and meat products at its warehouses. The following rules control assignment of food products to the warehouse units.

Each unit stores either dairy products or else meat products.

Exactly three units store meat products.

1-West and 2-West store dairy products.

If a warehouse stores meat products in either of its units, then the other unit in that warehouse stores dairy products.

If meat products are assigned to 3-East, then 4-West stores meat.

1. Which one of the following is an acceptable assignment of products to warehouse units?

   (A) 1-West: Meat, 1-East: Dairy; 2-West: Dairy, 2-East: Meat; 3-West: Dairy, 3-East: Meat; 4-West: Dairy, 4-East: Dairy
   (B) 1-West: Dairy, 1-East: Meat; 2-West: Dairy, 2-East: Meat; 3-West: Dairy, 3-East: Dairy; 4-West: Dairy, 4-East: Dairy
   (C) 1-West: Dairy, 1-East: Meat; 2-West: Dairy, 2-East: Meat; 3-West: Dairy, 3-East: Dairy; 4-West: Meat, 4-East: Dairy
   (D) 1-West: Dairy, 1-East: Dairy; 2-West: Dairy, 2-East: Meat; 3-West: Meat, 3-East: Meat; 4-West: Dairy, 4-East: Dairy
   (E) 1-West: Dairy, 1-East: Meat; 2-West: Dairy, 2-East: Meat; 3-West: Dairy, 3-East: Meat; 4-West: Dairy, 4-East: Dairy

2. If 4-West stores dairy, then dairy must also be stored in which one of the following?

   (A) 1-East
   (B) 4-East
   (C) 2-East
   (D) 3-East
   (E) 3-West

3. If meat is stored in 3-East, which one of the following is a complete and accurate list of the units in which meat CANNOT be stored?

   (A) 1-West, 2-West
   (B) 1-West, 2-West, 3-West
   (C) 1-West, 2-West, 4-East
   (D) 1-West, 2-West, 3-West, 4-East
   (E) 1-West, 1-East, 2-West, 3-West, 4-East

4. If 2-East stores dairy, then it could be true that dairy is also assigned to both

   (A) 1-East and 4-West
   (B) 1-East and 4-East
   (C) 3-East and 3-West
   (D) 3-West and 4-West
   (E) 3-East and 4-East

5. If warehouse 2 stores only dairy, which one of the following, if true, would be sufficient to establish the assignments of all of the units?

   (A) 1-East stores meat.
   (B) 3-West stores meat.
   (C) 4-West stores meat.
   (D) 4-West stores dairy.
   (E) Warehouse 4 stores both meat and dairy.

6. If dairy is stored in 3-East, and dairy is also stored in 3-West, then there are exactly how many possible distinct configurations for product storage at the warehouses?

   (A) 2
   (B) 3
   (C) 4
   (D) 5
   (E) 6

Logic Game 5: Meat and Dairy Warehouses

What Makes it Difficult

Like most of the other games in this Supercharged Standards chapter, the real-life situation depicted in this game is hardly difficult to comprehend—we're just talking about meat and dairy, after all. The game includes what is essentially a baby red herring: the setup tells us that "each unit supplies its own loading dock," but the game never mentions loading docks again. Test takers who scanned over the entire game at the outset to form a solid overview noticed this and did not become distracted by the loading dock language.

Matching game

Matching two kinds of entities to each other.

But this game's main challenges come from the unwieldy construction of eight units all identified as West and East and from a few of the questions themselves. In particular, question 3, which asks which units CANNOT be assigned meat, is actually asking for the list of units that must store dairy, and if the test makers had chosen to phrase the question in the positive, it would be easier to grapple with. Matching games typically require us to link up entities with other entities or with entity characteristics, and this game is true to form: we must match up each unit with the food type it stores.

Keys to the Game

No unit is empty. That first rule isn't just a repeat of the information in the paragraph that tells us the company doesn't deal in products other than meat and dairy. Rule 1 tells us that each unit is *full* and that it holds only one of the two kinds of products.

Three warehouses are split meat/dairy or dairy/meat; the other warehouse holds all dairy. This is the deduction we make when we consider what Rule 2 says and implies (three meat units means the other five are dairy) and combine it with Rule 4, which tells us that each meat unit is paired up with a dairy.

Either warehouse 1 or 2 (or both) is dairy-West, meat-East. Because we have three warehouses with a meat and a dairy, we can't have both 1 and 2 all dairy—at least one of them must have meat, and it will have to be in the East unit of that warehouse because Rule 3 puts dairy in the West unit of each.

If 4-West is dairy, then so is 3-East. This is the proper contraposition of Rule 5. However, don't forget that these two units could end up with different products if 4-West is meat and 3-East is dairy.

Answers and Explanations

1. C   2. D   3. D   4. E   5. D   6. A

1. C

As we've seen before, and will see again, Acceptability questions that appear first in the set are best solved by using individual rules to knock out wrong choices. Rule 1 doesn't help us. Rule 2 eliminates (B), which has only two meat units. (A) puts meat in 1-West, which we know from Rule 3 has to be dairy, so we can eliminate that choice. Rule 4 eliminates (D) because warehouse 3 has meat on both sides. Finally, (E) violates Rule 5. That leaves (C).

2. D

This question has a limited focus: it is testing your comprehension of how an if-then statement works and, in particular, how to form a contrapositive.

> **"contrapositive"**
> To contrapose an if-then statement, you flip the sides around and negate both sides. "IF A, THEN B" becomes "IF NOT B, THEN NOT A."

As we noted above, Rule 5 says "If 3-East is meat, then 4-West is meat"; its contrapositive then is "If 4-West is dairy (i.e., it is NOT meat), then 3-East is dairy." That's choice (D).

3. D

The question is in CANNOT form, but it is actually asking us for a complete list of all the units that absolutely *must* store dairy. It would help a lot if we could use the Rule 3 requirement that 1-West and 2-West both store dairy to eliminate choices. But, of course, every choice contains these two units, so we're back to square one. If we re-sketch this scenario, we start with dairy in 1-West and 2-West. Then, according to the question's hypothetical, we add meat to 3-East. The first thing we might notice is that Rule 5 mandates meat in 4-West. Then Rule 4 tells us that these meat units must pair up with dairy in their opposite units (3-West and 4-East). Only 1-East and 2-East are unassigned. So, the correct answer—the one that lists all the units to which dairy *must* be assigned—is the West units of 1, 2, and 3, and 4-East.

> A 180 test taker milks the game's most influential rule or entity for all it's worth. He turns to it when he gets stuck or is forced to try out choices.

4. E

Another re-sketch is valuable here, starting as always with the information in the master sketch, namely, that 1-West and 2-West are dairy. Add the question's information: 2-East stores dairy. That means warehouse 2 is our all-dairy warehouse. So, as we deduced before, warehouses 1, 3, and 4 must each contain meat, and the meat in warehouse 1 must be in 1-East, which rules out (A) and (B).

The correct answer is a pair that "could" both contain dairy. We could get into trouble in a couple of ways: first, by creating another all-dairy warehouse (as in (C)), and second, by violating Rule 5's contrapositive, which is a violation we see in (D). If 4-West is dairy, then 3-East must be, too; however, (D) makes 3-West dairy, which would make warehouse 3 another all-dairy warehouse. That means (E) must be our winner.

5. D

This one is a zinger because it requires clear command of not only what both the if-then and contrapositive mean, but also what they don't mean. If 2 is our all-dairy warehouse, then, as we've discussed previously, we know that 1 must have meat in the East unit. So, adding that statement, as in (A), is useless.

(B) and (C) function in the same way: they complete only the warehouse they mention, and they don't complete the remaining warehouses. Here's why: putting meat in 3-West guarantees that 3-East must contain dairy (Rule 4). But Rule 5's if-then statement only gets triggered by 3-East containing meat. So, warehouse 4, which definitely contains one of each, can flip-flop.

By the same token, if 4-West contains meat, then 4-East must be dairy. But the contrapositive of Rule 5 only triggers if 4-West contains dairy, which, you've no doubt noticed, is precisely what choice (D) gives us, thereby locking in dairy for 3-East, meat for the remaining units in 3 and 4, and of course, meat in 1-East. That's everything.

By the way, (E), like (A), must be true based on the question's hypothetical—if warehouse 2 is the all-dairy warehouse, then the others must each contain both meat and dairy. So (E) adds no new information.

6. A

Making warehouse 3 the all-dairy warehouse forces meat into the East units of 1 and 2. That locks up everything but warehouse 4, which contains both meat and dairy but could flip-flop their arrangement. The flip-flop option means exactly two configurations are possible.

What's Next?

If you're in the top tier of test takers, then you no doubt already have many clever strategies under your belt. If, however, you're still making that climb to join the elite, you'll need to start using a few tricks of your own. What better opportunity to work your magic than another game? See what you can make of this next Matching game, "Show Riders."

LOGIC GAME 6

Three show riders—Art, Brenda, and Chaz—perform in all three of the Rosstown Rodeo's daily performances. Each rider rides one of the rodeo's horses—Nutmeg, Oz, and Paint—for the duration of an entire show, one rider per horse. The daily shows consist of a morning show, an afternoon show, and an evening show. The following is known about the riders and their mounts:

   Brenda does not ride Oz in any of the shows.
   Chaz rides Paint in at least one of the three shows, but not in the afternoon show.
   Art rides the same horse in the afternoon and evening shows.
   Chaz does not ride Oz in the morning show.

1. Which one of the following must be true?

   (A)   Art rides Oz in the morning show.
   (B)   Brenda rides Nutmeg in the morning show.
   (C)   Chaz rides Oz in the afternoon show.
   (D)   Art rides Paint in the evening show.
   (E)   Chaz rides Nutmeg in the evening show.

2. If Art rides Oz in the evening show, then which one of the following must be true of Brenda?

   (A)   She rides Nutmeg in the morning show.
   (B)   She rides Paint in the morning show.
   (C)   She rides Nutmeg in the afternoon show.
   (D)   She rides Paint in the afternoon show.
   (E)   She rides Paint in the evening show.

3. If Brenda rides Paint in the afternoon show, then which one of the following must be false?

   (A)   Art rides Oz in the morning show and Brenda rides Paint in the evening show.
   (B)   Art rides Nutmeg in the afternoon show and Chaz rides Paint in the morning show.
   (C)   Art rides Nutmeg in the evening show and Brenda rides Paint in the evening show.
   (D)   Brenda rides Paint in the morning show and Brenda rides Nutmeg in the evening show.
   (E)   Brenda rides Nutmeg in the evening show and Chaz rides Oz in the evening show.

4. If Chaz rides the same horse in the morning and afternoon shows, then all of the following must be true EXCEPT:

   (A)   Art rides Oz in all three shows.
   (B)   Brenda rides Paint in exactly two of the shows.
   (C)   Brenda rides Nutmeg in the afternoon show.
   (D)   Chaz rides Nutmeg in the morning show.
   (E)   Chaz rides Paint in the evening show.

5. Which one of the following must be true?

   (A)   If Art rides Paint in the afternoon show, then Chaz rides Paint in the evening show.
   (B)   If Chaz rides Nutmeg in the morning show, then Chaz rides Oz in the afternoon show.
   (C)   If Brenda rides Paint in the evening show, then Art rides Nutmeg in the afternoon show.
   (D)   If Brenda rides Nutmeg in the afternoon show, then Chaz rides Paint in the morning show.
   (E)   If Chaz rides Paint in the evening show, then Brenda rides Nutmeg in the morning show.

6. If Chaz rides Nutmeg in the afternoon show only, then which one of the following must be true?

   (A)   Art rides Oz in as many shows as he rides Paint.
   (B)   Brenda rides Nutmeg in as many shows as she rides Paint.
   (C)   Chaz rides Nutmeg in as many shows as he rides Oz.
   (D)   Art rides Nutmeg in as many shows as he rides Paint.
   (E)   Brenda rides Oz in as many shows as she rides Paint.

Logic Game 6: Show Riders

What Makes It Difficult

The intro paragraph of this Matching game is a bit cumbersome, but cutting through the wordiness reveals a fairly straightforward game action: pairing up three riders to three horses in three time slots—morning, afternoon, and evening. The game requires a great deal of elimination strategy, since once a rider is pegged for a horse, no one else can ride that horse during that show. Sounds easy enough, but lose sight of this fact and the questions are simply unworkable.

The rules are not very helpful. No definite match-up is stated; mostly what we get is information on pairings that can't exist. And the last four questions of the set are downright unfriendly, most requiring numerous steps. Question 3 has a lot of nerve following up a "must be false" question stem with choices containing two match-ups each. That's possibly a lot of testing to do for each choice. Question 5 contains hypotheticals (if-then statements) in the choices themselves—never a sunny prospect. And question 6 introduces a numerical element into the pairing scenarios, requiring us to compare the number of times a rider rides one horse with the number he or she rides another.

As usual, there are a few things to do and/or notice that help turn this potential killer into a manageable experience.

Keys to the Game

Settle on a convention to represent the action. Matching games are usually amenable to lists and grids; some prefer one, some the other. If you sketch a 3×3 table, and put the time slots across the top (morn, aft, and eve) and the riders down the side (A, B, and C), then you can simply fill in the horses in the nine boxes as needed.

Brenda rides Nutmeg or Paint in all three shows. Chaz rides Nutmeg or Oz in the afternoon, and rides Nutmeg or Paint in the morning. These are Rules 1, 2, and 4 stated positively. Get that info into your sketch.

A 180 test taker turns negative statements into positive ones.

Art rides Oz in the morning. Our big deduction, derived from the fact that both Brenda and Chaz must ride Nutmeg or Paint in the morning show. The only rider eligible for Oz in the morning show is therefore Art, so we can build that right into the sketch.

Yee-ha! Saddle 'em up—we're ready to ride.

Answers and Explanations

1. A   2. D   3. E   4. C   5. D   6. D

Putting all of our insights together into one grid, here's what we have going into the questions:

	morn	aft	eve
A	O		
B	N or P	N or P	N or P
C	N or P	N or O	

1. A

Just as we deduced. The other four choices are possibilities only.

2. D

The if-clause plus Rule 3 tells us that Art rides Oz in the afternoon and evening. Looking over our afternoon list, we see that Chaz can ride only Nutmeg or Oz, and since Oz is taken, Chaz must ride Nutmeg in the afternoon, leaving Paint for Brenda, choice (D). This is a taste of the process of elimination element that we're faced with in most questions. (C) is flat-out false, while the other choices are possibilities only. Not so bad so far, right? Well, the honeymoon's pretty much over, as the next four take a turn for the worse.

3. E

This question begins where we ended in the last question, with Brenda riding Paint in the afternoon; but that doesn't mean that everything has to fall out the same way. With Brenda taking Paint in the afternoon, all we know for sure is that Art and Chaz between them will ride Nutmeg and Oz in that show. We're looking for something that can't be true. There's no real way to avoid testing out some choices here, but perhaps you prephrased something concrete to look for?

A 180 test taker is proactive. She gives some thought to what the right answer might look like or do.

With Paint taken by Brenda in the afternoon, Paint can't be ridden by Art or Chaz during that show. Either of those things would make for a fine answer choice, but of course that would be too simple, right? Well, what about a scenario that forces one of those things to happen? It's a bit more roundabout, but that's exactly what we get in (E). If Nutmeg and Oz are ridden in the evening show by Brenda and Chaz, Art must ride Paint in the evening. But Rule 3 would then force Art to ride Paint in the afternoon as well . . . and there you have it—a conflict with the mandate in the stem. (E) must be false. The rest could be true.

4. C

If Chaz rides the same horse in the first two shows, what horse would that be? A quick glance at our sketch reveals that only Nutmeg qualifies. That assignment makes everything else fall into place. To wit: Brenda needs to ride Paint in the morning and afternoon (Rule 1); Art is left with Oz in the afternoon and (Rule 3) the evening; and Chaz has to ride Paint (Rule 2) in the evening, leaving Nutmeg for Brenda in the evening. There are lots of steps here, but ultimately every slot is filled:

	morn	aft	eve
A	O	O	O
B	P	P	N
C	N	N	P

The only choice that doesn't correspond to the correct assignments is (C): Brenda rides Paint, not Nutmeg, in the afternoon.

5. D

Yipes! If-then statements in the choices give us little alternative but to try out each choice. However, as usual there's a shortcut, and it involves using previous work.

(A) is flat-out false. Art riding Paint in the afternoon means he rides Paint in the evening as well, so can't have that horse in the evening show.

(B), (E) If Chaz gets Nutmeg in the morning, must Chaz ride Oz in the afternoon? Let's try giving him a horse other than Oz—for example, his other possibility for that time slot, Nutmeg. Can that work? Well, it just did work above in question 4, as the diagram above indicates, so (B) need not be true. And wait a minute: The same scenario proves that (E) need not be true, either.

> A 180 test taker always looks for shortcuts. When given no new information to work with, and forced to simply test out choices, she asks herself: "Have I seen this situation somewhere before?"

(C) If Brenda rides Paint in the evening, does that require Art to ride Nutmeg in the afternoon? Try the "proving the exception" strategy just discussed—see if Art can ride some other horse instead. The following arrangement shows that this is possible, allowing us to kill (C):

	morn	aft	eve
A	O	O	O
B	N	P	P
C	P	N	N

(D) must be correct, since we've eliminated all the others, but for the record: If Brenda rides Nutmeg in the afternoon, then Chaz rides Oz in the afternoon. Consequently, Art has to ride Paint in the afternoon show and (Rule 3) in the evening as well. And with Paint ridden by Art in the evening, Chaz's required ride on Paint (Rule 2) will have to take place in the morning. No exceptions possible here, so (D) gets the point.

A 180 test taker is adept at eliminating answer choices containing hypotheticals by "proving the exception."

---

6. D

If you miss the "only" here, it's fairly hopeless. Otherwise, it's not so tough: If Chaz's one and only ride on Nutmeg is in the afternoon, then he'll have to ride Paint in the morning, leaving Nutmeg as Brenda's morning horse. Meanwhile, Brenda will have to ride Paint in the afternoon, leaving Oz for Art in the afternoon and (Rule 3) the evening as well. Remaining are Brenda and Chaz's evening assignments; and because of the question stem's "only," it'll be Nutmeg for Brenda and Paint for Chaz in the evening. The entire roster is complete, and only (D) has it right: For Art, zero Nutmeg rides does equal zero Paint rides.

A 180 test taker takes careful notice of "keywords"—structural signals that authors employ in order to help convey their ideas.

What's Next?

Without further ado, let's move on to another matching game and the last of our Supercharged Standards, "University Course Assignments."

LOGIC GAME 7

A university is arranging five new advanced-level courses, one each in Anthropology, Botany, Chemistry, Drama, and Economics. To teach the five courses, the university has hired three new professors, Karanoff, Largent, and Marakowski, who teach no other courses at the university. Each professor will teach at least one course. The courses will be held in exactly five rooms in the same building, numbered consecutively 101 through 105, each of which will accommodate one and only one of the courses. No course is taught by a professor lacking training in that subject, and none of the three professors is trained in any subject in which one of the other two is trained. The following conditions must be met:

Karanoff is trained in Anthropology.
Any professor who is trained in Botany is also trained in Chemistry.
Economics must be held in room 104.
Chemistry must be held in either room 101 or 102.
Marakowski will teach in room 102.

1. Which one of the following could be a complete and accurate list of the assignments of professors to courses?

   (A) Karanoff: Anthropology and Economics; Largent: Drama; Marakowski: Chemistry and Botany
   (B) Karanoff: Anthropology and Botany; Largent: Economics; Marakowski: Chemistry and Drama
   (C) Karanoff: Botany and Chemistry; Largent: Economics; Marakowski: Anthropology and Drama
   (D) Karanoff: Anthropology; Largent: Drama, Botany, and Chemistry; Marakowski: Economics
   (E) Karanoff: Anthropology, Botany, and Chemistry; Largent: does not teach; Marakowski: Drama and Economics

2. Each of the following is a pair of courses both of which Marakowski could teach EXCEPT:

   (A) Botany in Room 101 and Drama in Room 102
   (B) Botany in Room 101 and Drama in Room 105
   (C) Chemistry in Room 102 and Economics in Room 104
   (D) Botany in Room 102 and Economics in Room 104
   (E) Drama in Room 102 and Economics in Room 104

3. If Karanoff teaches Anthropology and exactly two other courses, which one of the following could be false?

   (A) Karanoff teaches in Room 101.
   (B) Karanoff does not teach Economics.
   (C) Largent teaches exactly one course.
   (D) Marakowski teaches Botany.
   (E) Marakowski does not teach Economics.

4. If Botany is held in Room 102, which one of the following must be true?

   (A) Karanoff teaches in Room 101.
   (B) Largent does not teach in Room 101.
   (C) Karanoff teaches Chemistry.
   (D) Largent teaches Economics.
   (E) Marakowski teaches Economics.

5. Assume the rule that Karanoff is trained in Anthropology is revoked but all other rules still apply; if Marakowski teaches exactly one course and Largent teaches Economics and at most one other course, each of the following could be false EXCEPT:

   (A) Karanoff teaches in Room 101.
   (B) Largent teaches Anthropology.
   (C) Karanoff teaches exactly two courses.
   (D) Karanoff teaches Drama.
   (E) Marakowski teaches Drama.

6. Which of the following is the complete and accurate list of all of the courses that could be held in Room 102?

   (A) Botany
   (B) Drama
   (C) Botany and Chemistry
   (D) Botany, Chemistry, and Drama
   (E) Anthropology, Botany, Chemistry, and Drama

Logic Game 7: University Course Assignments

What Makes it Difficult

Once again, the general, real-life situation is easy to grasp: we need to *match* up teachers to courses, teachers to rooms, and courses to rooms. One of the biggest challenges in this game is the density of the opening paragraph. It's a tough one to get through. First, the length of the paragraph and the amount of information in it are a challenge. We seem to have three kinds of entities (courses, professors, and rooms) of which we have to keep track.

Second, the paragraph presents its information in a needlessly complicated way. The language about *training* is pointless—why not just say the professor teaches that course? The test makers do this routinely to see whether you are able to distill complicated presentations down to their essential information. Here, *training* in a course simply means the professor teaches the course.

Third, the game gives us room numbers in consecutive order, which makes most people think of sequencing. But it's not until you have grappled with the mechanics of the entire game that you see that sequencing isn't a relevant task—this game is just about matching the three entity types up with each other.

A 180 test taker is not intimidated by complex or wordy choices; he keeps his focus and confidently marches ahead.

The questions also pose some severe challenges. Making a question an EXCEPT question always adds difficulty. Question 3 poses a serious challenge with choice (B) because the question is asking a negative, the answer also provides a negative, and it's one that must be true, which makes it incorrect! Suspending a rule, as in question 6, creates a significant distraction because the test taker must reassess her setup to be sure she does not continue to apply any deductions she derived from the combination of that rule with others.

Keys to the Game

The complicated language of the game boils down to a simple situation: We've got five courses, five rooms (that's a one-to-one match-up—easy to understand), and three professors to teach these courses (a three-to-five match-up, which seems a little less friendly, but actually becomes our best friend once we see how the mechanism works). The statements about training mean that any time a professor has training in a subject, he or she teaches that subject. It's a longer way of making a simple assignment of professor to course. We have to remember that each professor gets matched up with at least one course.

Botany and Chem always go together. Alone, this would be an improper deduction from this "IF Botany, THEN Chem" statement, the contrapositive of which is "IF NOT Chem, THEN NOT Botany." However, unlike other games, the IF side of this formal logic statement will definitely happen because all five courses must be taught (in other words, *someone* is teaching Botany, so we know that this hypothetical rule will definitely apply to exactly one professor). Whoever teaches Botany will definitely have to teach Chem. Therefore, whenever we determine the assignment of either of these courses, the same professor must also teach the other course or else the two would be taught by separate professors, violating the rule.

KAPLAN

If M only teaches one course, it's Drama. M can't teach Anthro because K teaches that course. Because M has to teach in 102, M cannot *only* teach Econ because Econ is in 104. Finally, no one can teach *only* Botany or *only* Chem because they always go together.

Answers and Explanations

1. A   2. A   3. D   4. B   5. A   6. D

1. A

As with most Acceptability questions that appear first in the set, we start by using the rules individually to eliminate the wrong choices. Rule 1 eliminates (C) because K isn't teaching Anthropology. Rule 2 knocks out (B) because Botany and Chemistry are split up. The opening paragraph itself eliminates (E), which has L teaching nothing despite the paragraph's statement that each professor will teach at least one course (middle of the paragraph).

But that's where the fun ends: the question asks about teacher-course assignments, but the rest of the rules are about room assignments. So now we'll have to use deduction to eliminate the last wrong choice. Rule 3 says Economics is in 104; (D) violates this rule by putting M in 104 as her only course, but Rule 5 says she teaches in 102. Only (A) remains.

2. A

EXCEPT questions
These are really "which of the following must be false" questions.

The correct answer is a pair that violates at least one rule if M teaches both. Choice (A) is impossible because if M is teaching Botany in 101 and Drama in 102, then, because she teaches Botany, she must also teach Chemistry (Rule 2), but she won't be able to teach Chemistry in 101 or 102 as required by Rule 4 as both rooms are aready taken. That's our choice. Choices (B), (C), and (D) are all fine because she'll be able to teach Chem in 101 or 102. Choice (E) would mean she wouldn't be teaching Botany or Chem because she'd have to teach both, and the question says she teaches only one course; in this case, L would teach both, and L can teach Chem in 101.

3. D

If K teaches three courses, then we know that, in addition to Anthro (Rule 1), she must also teach Botany and Chem: if she taught both Drama and Econ, then one of the other two teachers would be left with nothing to teach. Right off the bat this tells us that (B) is necessarily true, which makes it a wrong choice, but it also tells us that (D) must be false, which is even more than what we're looking for. Incidentally, (A) must be true because Chem must be in 101 or 102, and M, who is not teaching Chem, is taking up room 102. (C) must be true because, with K teaching three, that leaves only two left—one each for M and L. (E) must be true because M has to teach in 102, and Econ is in 104 (which means L is teaching Econ in this scenario).

4. B

This question requires several steps of deduction. If Botany is in room 102, then that must mean M teaches Botany because (Rule 5) M teaches in room 102. Then, according to Rule 2, M must also teach Chemistry. Rule 4 tells us that Chemistry must be taught in 101 or 102, but because Botany is in 102, that leaves only 101. Because M teaches Chemistry in 101, that must mean that neither K nor L teaches in that room.

5. A

Many test takers will overlook the fact that our earlier deduction—if M teaches only one course, it's Drama—is undone by this question stem because that deduction was based, in part, on the fact that M could never teach Anthro. This makes (E) a wrong answer but a very tempting one. Here, M could teach either Drama *or* Anthro but still not Botany or Chem because Rule 2 is still in play. The question tells us that L teaches Econ in 104 and might teach Anthro or Drama, but he cannot teach Botany or Chem, each of which requires the other. That means K teaches Botany and Chem, and because Chem must be in 101 or 102 and M teaches either Drama or Anthro in 102, K will have to teach Chem in 101. So, (A) can't be false—it's definitely true.

6. D

The test makers occasionally ask questions designed to cause you to doubt your original assessment of the game. Questions like this one tend to raise the hair on the back of most test takers' necks—their immediate response is to think, "well, it can't just be the whole list of courses minus the one explicitly excluded by the rule (here, Rule 3)!" Sometimes, that *is*, in fact, exactly the case. Here, however, there's an additional deduction that applies: the combination of Rule 1 and Rule 5 means Anthro cannot be held in 102 because K teaches Anthro, but M teaches in 102.

What's Next?

This concludes our Logic Games warm-up, as we move on to more challenging material. Perhaps you found these to be pretty tough already. Tough, maybe. But not quite brutal. Despite some complexities, all the games in this chapter revolve around a single game action, which is almost always easier than handling multiple tasks at once. Furthermore, all are amenable to a few key deductions and a little cleverness.

But perhaps you breezed through the games in this chapter, wondering to yourself, "I thought these were going to be difficult? What gives?" Have no fear. It gets worse. Much worse.

CHAPTER THREE

Time Warps

Once upon a time the LSAT test makers introduced aspiring law students to the wonderful world of what we at Kaplan call Process games.

Process, or Time Warp, game
Fit behavior to a prearranged plan or pattern.

Since a key skill tested in this game type is your ability to think forward and backward in time, we also call then "Time Warps."

Games fitting this definition appeared regularly from LSAT PrepTest X through LSAT PrepTest XVI (1994–1995). They've been pretty much absent since then, but there are a few good reasons to wrack your brain on this game type. First, there's no guarantee that they won't appear again; in fact, one *did* appear on an undisclosed test in 1998. Secondly, there's always a chance that you'll see a game on your test that doesn't fit into the standard categories—so pitting your wits against games that are *unusual* can't hurt, and will almost certainly help prepare you for any type of oddball that you may encounter.

Before you begin, here are some useful questions to think through when faced with a Time Warp game:

- What is the situation at the start?
- How often do changes occur?
- What specifically happens during a change?
- How is the situation different after the change?
- Hypothesize: What could happen? Go through some "what ifs" about the game to get a feel for how the process works.

LOGIC GAME 8

A botanist is testing the effects of sunlight on four plants. At the beginning of the first month of the experiment, the plants—F, G, H, and I—are in front of the north window, the east window, the south window, and the west window, respectively. The botanist will rotate the plants exactly once a month, at the end of each month, in one of the following two ways:

Rotation 1: The plant in front of the north window will be moved to the east window. The plant in front of the east window will be moved to the south window. The plant in front of the south window will be moved to the west window. The plant in front of the west window will be moved to the north window.

Rotation 2: Plant F will be moved to the window that H was in front of during the previous month. Plant H will be moved to the window that Plant I was in front of during the previous month. Plant I will be moved to the window that G was in front of during the previous month. Plant G will be moved to the window that F was in front of during the previous month.

1. Which one of the following could be the window locations for the four plants at the beginning of the second month?

	north	east	south	west
(A)	F	G	H	I
(B)	F	I	H	G
(C)	G	F	I	H
(D)	I	F	G	H
(E)	I	G	F	H

2. If G is in front of the north window at the beginning of the second month, which one of the following must be true?

    (A) F is in front of the east window.
    (B) F is in front of the west window.
    (C) H is in front of the east window.
    (D) I is in front of the east window.
    (E) I is in front of the west window.

3. If F is in front of the east window at the beginning of the second month, which one of the following is a complete and accurate list of the windows that F could be in front of at the beginning of the third month?

    (A) north
    (B) west
    (C) south, west
    (D) east, south
    (E) north, east, south, west

4. Which one of the following CANNOT be true at the beginning of the third month?

    (A) Plant F is in front of the west window.
    (B) Plant G is in front of the east window.
    (C) Plant H is in front of the east window.
    (D) Plant I is in front of the east window.
    (E) Plant I is in front of the west window.

5. If, at the beginning of the third month, G is in front of the south window, which one of the following must be true?

    (A) Plant F was in front of the east window at the beginning of the second month.
    (B) Plant G was in front of the east window at the beginning of the second month.
    (C) Plant I was in front of the east window at the beginning of the second month.
    (D) The botanist used Rotation 1 to rotate the plants at the end of the first month.
    (E) The botanist used Rotation 1 to rotate the plants at the end of the second month.

6. If, at the beginning of the second month, I is in front of the north window, which one of the following could be true at the beginning of the third month?

    (A) Plant F is in front of the east window.
    (B) Plant F is in front of the north window.
    (C) Plant G is in front of the north window.
    (D) Plant H is in front of the west window.
    (E) Plant I is in front of the south window.

7. Which one of the following CANNOT be true at the beginning of the third month if the botanist rotated the plants according to Rotation 1 at least once during the first two months?

    (A) F is in front of the south window.
    (B) G is in front of the east window.
    (C) H is in front of the east window.
    (D) I is in front of the east window.
    (E) I is in front of the south window.

Logic Game 8: Plant Rotations

What Makes It Difficult

The presentation of an initial situation, followed by a description of how things change over time, are the sure giveaways that we have a Time Warp game on our hands. The rules are long and intimidating. However, once you get past the initial shock, you'll find that they simply describe the mechanics of two possible rotation methods. You're best served spending a bit of extra time to make sure you get them right and find a reasonable way to represent the action.

The questions pose the usual difficulties found in these kinds of games. Some questions ask you to look forward in the process and follow the steps through to a result, while others—generally the tougher ones—tell you what the result of the process was, and ask you to work backward to reconstruct the situation that made this result possible. Another difficulty is that there are no big deductions to make up front. We simply have to bang out the questions one by one (seven, no less), following the rotations wherever they may lead.

There really isn't much to draw for this kind of game, but you have to compensate for this lack of pencil work with extra brainwork. As always, there are still a few key things you can do that should ease your brain's burden a bit.

Keys to the Game

Anticipate the relevant issues that will be tested. Namely, what can, cannot, or must be the plants' locations after one, two, or more rotations? What window can each plant be rotated to from their previous month's position? Based on the plants' locations after a certain number of rotations, what locations were possible in the previous months?

Simplify Rotation 1: Think of it simply as each plant moving one space clockwise. You may wish to indicate this visually on the page. Unfortunately, there's no analogous method to make Rotation 2 easier to handle. You simply have to note those switches on the page and refer to them when necessary.

Use your work on previous questions to help you with later ones. This is always a good strategy, but turns out to be especially helpful here.

Answers and Explanations

1. D   2. D   3. C   4. E   5. C   6. E   7. C

1. D

What does "at the beginning of the second month" mean? Since the plants are rotated exactly once a month, at the end of each month, this means that at the beginning of the second month the plants have gone through one rotation from their initial placements. So pick a rotation and set 'em in motion. Enacting Rotation 1 sends each plant one space clockwise, giving us:

north	east	south	west
I	F	G	H

Is that a choice? Yup, (D). Easy enough.

A 180 test taker uses Acceptability questions as tools to help cement the game's workings.

---

2. D

The plants have undergone one rotation, and G is at the north window. G starts at the east. If Rotation 1 was used, G would go south, so Rotation 2 must have been used. Using Rotation 2 on the initial setup, we see that G goes to the north (F's previous location), F goes to the south (H's old home), H goes to the west (I's last spot), and I goes to the east (G's old location). I at the east window is choice (D), the answer.

3. C

After one rotation F is at the east window. F starts up north. The only way for F to get to the east after one move is by way of Rotation 1, which puts F east, G south, H west, and I north. Where could F go next? Under Rotation 1, the east plant goes to the south. Under Rotation 2, F goes to H's previous location, so F would go to the west. South and west are the only two possibilities, choice (C).

A 180 test taker keeps asking himself the relevant questions, in this case: "How could this happen?" and "Where can or must the other entities be?"

---

4. E

Now we're entering pretty abstract territory: We're given no new information, and are asked about what can't be true at the beginning of month 3. First we have to translate what "the beginning of the third month" means: it means after two rotations.

So we need to take the entities through two rotations. From the initial setup, the plants could move to the following positions:

Rotation 1

north	east	south	west
I	F	G	H

Rotation 2

north	east	south	west
G	I	F	H

Now, begin with each of these new positionings and see where the plants could go next. After Rotation 1, if Rotation 1 is used again, I would go east, F would go south, G would go west, and H would go north, giving us:

north	east	south	west
H	I	F	G

Checking this against the choices, we see that I could be at the east window after two rotations, so we can cross off choice (D) since we're looking for something that *cannot* be true.

After Rotation 1, if Rotation 2 is used, F would go west, G would go east, H would go north, and I would go south, yielding:

north	east	south	west
H	G	I	F

We see from this that F could be at the west window and G could be at the east window after two rotations, which allows us to axe both (A) and (B).

After Rotation 2, if Rotation 1 is used, F would go to the west, G would go to the east, I would go to the south, and H would go to the north, giving us the same arrangement as the previous one. It therefore doesn't allow us to eliminate any of the remaining choices, so we press on.

After Rotation 2, if Rotation 2 is used, again F would go to the west, G would go to the south, H would go to the east, and I would go to the north.

north	east	south	west
I	H	G	F

This arrangement proves that H could be at the east window after two rotations, so axe choice (C). We're left with (E), the answer.

Takes a bit of work, doesn't it? But as you'll see, it turns out to be well worth the effort.

A 180 test taker often finds clever ways to cut questions down to size, but can force his way through a tough question, too.

---

5. C

This potentially nightmarish question can be discarded quickly and painlessly if you handled question 4 in the manner described above, and you remembered to make use of that previous work here. We just went through the process of plotting out all the possibilities leading up to the month 3 arrangement, so we can just check the question stem against those. From them, we see that the only way for G to land at the south window at the beginning of month 3 is if Rotation 2 is performed consecutively. 1-1 puts G in the west, while 1-2 and 2-1 lands G in the east. Now it's simply a matter of scanning the choices for the one that accords with a double shot of Rotation 2.

(A) No, Rotation 2 sends F from north to south for the beginning of the second month.

(B) No, Rotation 2 sends G from east to north for the beginning of the second month.

(C) Yup: Rotation 2 sends I from west to east. (C) must be true and is the answer we seek.

(D), (E) No. We already decided that Rotation 2 must be used at the end of the first and second months in order for G to face south at the beginning of month 3.

A 180 test taker knows that long and difficult games must be written in such a way as to make at least a few shortcuts possible.

---

6. E

If I is at the north window after one rotation, Rotation 1 must have been used on the initial arrangement. You've seen this before; this places F at the east, G at the south, H at the west, and I at the north. Where could the plants go from there? Again, use your previous work in question 4. Starting with the ordering just listed for the beginning of the second month, the plants could go to the following positions based on which rotation method is used next:

Rotation 1

north	east	south	west
H	I	F	G

Rotation 2

north	east	south	west
H	G	I	F

From there it's a simple matter of checking the choices against these two possibilities. I could be in front of the south window; choice (E) could be true and is the answer.

7. C

Now we're looking for what can't be true after two rotations if Rotation 1 was used for at least one of those rotations. This leads to three possibilities: Rotation 1 then Rotation 1; Rotation 1 then Rotation 2; and Rotation 2 then Rotation 1. Once again, we worked through each of these possibilities back in question 4:

Rotation 1 followed by Rotation 1

north	east	south	west
H	I	F	G

Rotation 1 followed by Rotation 2 and Rotation 2 followed by Rotation 1

north	east	south	west
H	G	I	F

Once again, all we have to do to find the choice that can't be true is match the choices against these possibilities. H is never at the east window, so (C) can't be true and is therefore the correct answer.

What's Next?

Notice how question 4 was the turning point of the game. Fighting your way through the hardest question of the set in fact made the following three questions much easier to handle. Here's a case in which what seemed to be a curse turned out to be a blessing in disguise. But don't expect such kind treatment from every Process game.

LOGIC GAME 9

Four astronauts aboard a space shuttle—Dalton, Ellis, Ford, and Gunther—are assigned the following responsibilities on the first day of a three-day space mission: monitoring communications, walking in space, taking photos, and making repairs, respectively. At the beginning of each subsequent day of the mission, the astronauts' responsibilities are rotated, in accordance with exactly one of the following scenarios:

Scenario 1: Ford and Gunther are assigned to switch responsibilities.

Scenario 2: The astronaut last assigned the responsibility of walking in space is assigned the responsibility of making repairs, and the astronaut last assigned the responsibility of making repairs is assigned the responsibility of walking in space.

Scenario 3: Dalton and Gunther are assigned to switch responsibilities, and Ellis and Ford are assigned to switch responsibilities.

1. Each one of the following could be the assignment of astronaut to responsibility on the second day of the mission EXCEPT:

    (A) Dalton; monitoring communications
    (B) Ford; making repairs
    (C) Dalton; making repairs
    (D) Ellis; monitoring communications
    (E) Gunther; walking in space

2. Which one of the following is a complete and accurate list of astronauts whose responsibility on the second day of the mission could be the same as their responsibility on the first day of the mission?

    (A) Dalton, Ellis, Ford
    (B) Dalton, Ford, Gunther
    (C) Dalton, Ellis, Ford, Gunther
    (D) Dalton, Ellis
    (E) Ellis, Ford

3. If Ford's responsibilities remain constant throughout the mission, all of the following must be true EXCEPT:

    (A) Dalton's responsibilities remain constant throughout the mission.
    (B) Gunther is assigned to walk in space on the second day of the mission.
    (C) Ellis is assigned to walk in space on the third day of the mission.
    (D) The responsibilities are not rotated according to scenario 3 on the second day of the mission.
    (E) Ellis's responsibilities remain constant throughout the mission.

4. If no scenario is repeated and if responsibilities are rotated according to scenario 3 on the second day of the mission, then which one of the following could be true on the third day of the mission?

    (A) Ellis is assigned to monitor communications.
    (B) Ford is assigned to make repairs.
    (C) Dalton is assigned to take photos.
    (D) Ellis is assigned to walk in space.
    (E) Gunther is assigned to take photos.

5. If Ellis is assigned to make repairs on the third day of the mission, which one of the following CANNOT be true?

    (A) The responsibilities are rotated according to scenario 1 on the second day of the mission.
    (B) The responsibilities are rotated according to scenario 1 on the third day of the mission.
    (C) The responsibilities are rotated according to scenario 2 on the second day of the mission.
    (D) The responsibilities are rotated according to scenario 3 on the second day of the mission.
    (E) The responsibilities are rotated according to scenario 3 on the third day of the mission.

6. If at some point during the mission Dalton is assigned to take photos, which one of the following must be true on the second day of the mission?

    (A) Ellis is assigned to walk in space.
    (B) The responsibilities were rotated according to scenario 2.
    (C) Gunther is assigned to walk in space.
    (D) The responsibilities were rotated according to scenario 3.
    (E) Ford is assigned to monitor communications.

Logic Game 9: Space Mission

What Makes It Difficult

Dalton, Ford, Ellis, and Gunther have a pretty cool mission. Your mission, however, is pretty mundane: figuring out who does what on each day.

We're up against the same basic thing as in the previous game. It's hard because it's a bit unusual and the switches described are fairly wordy. "Scenarios" labeled 1, 2, and 3 may jut up against "days" one, two, and three in your head. As always, thinking backward in time requires mental agility, and what complicates things further is the fact that the switches take place on both the astronaut level (as per scenarios 1 and 3) and on the responsibility level (scenario 2). Not a big deal, but something we have to keep track of.

There are no deductions to blow the game wide open, which is par for the course in these Process types. But that doesn't mean there's nothing that can help you get through in one piece. Here are the keys:

Keys to the Game

Anticipate the relevant issues that will be tested. Same as before. Here, we need to focus on who's doing what on each of the three days, and what assignments on one day make it possible for specific assignments to arise on other days.

Responsibilities are changed exactly twice. This is a helpful thing to notice. Day one is set, and the mission is only three days total. It's good to have an upward limit in place.

In scenarios 1 and 2, two astronauts switch tasks, and two stay the same. In scenario 3, all four switch. Not a major revelation, but again, anything that we can latch onto that places some restrictions on the action should help us in the long run.

> A 180 test taker sees a Logic Game from all possible angles, noticing everything from big deductions down to small observations.

Don't assume anything that you're not explicitly told. Do the intro or the rules specify that each person must do a different job each day? No. Do they specify that no scenario can be repeated? No. Unless we're told otherwise, jobs can be repeated and any scenario can be executed twice.

> A 180 test taker remains open to all possible game actions that are not explicitly forbidden.

Answers and Explanations

1. D   2. A   3. E   4. B   5. D   6. A

1. D

If the four wrong choices are possible assignments for the second day, then simply thinking through what could happen on day two—that is, after the enactment of exactly one scenario—should allow us to throw out those choices in fairly short order.

A 180 test taker is not thrown by a variation on an Acceptability question.

If scenario 1 is enacted on day two, Ford takes Gunther's repair job (B) while Gunther becomes the photographer (not a choice). Meanwhile, Dalton (A) and Ellis retain their previous jobs.

If scenario 2 is enacted, then Ellis and Gunther switch; Ellis does repairs (not a choice) while Gunther walks in space (E). Finally, scenario 3 sees Dalton take over Gunther's repair job (C), while Gunther monitors communications, Ellis takes over the photos, and Ford walks in space. Ellis must be the noncommunicative one of the bunch; we'll never see him monitoring communications, choice (D).

2. A

We got something of a head start on this question during question 1, where we saw (using scenario 1) that both Dalton and Ellis could retain their previous jobs on day two. Only choices (A), (C), and (D) mention both of those astronauts, so the other two must be tossed out. Under scenario 2, Dalton and Ford retain the same jobs while Ellis (the initial walker) and Gunther (the initial repairperson) switch. So Ford has to be included in the right answer too. But that's the lot: Everyone changes with scenario 3, so no matter what happens on day two, Gunther will have to change jobs. Dalton, Ellis, and Ford represent the "complete and accurate list" sought here.

3. E

If, as we're told, Ford never switches jobs over the entire three-day mission, then it has to be true that neither scenario 1 (where Ford switches with Gunther) nor scenario 3 (where everyone switches) can be executed. Which in turn means that scenario 2 must take place on both the second and third day. On day 2, Ellis the walker and Gunther the repairperson must switch, and on day three, they must switch back. Choices (A) through (D) all point to specific elements of the process just described. (E), however, is false: Ellis does a stint as repairperson on day two before resuming his space walk on the final day of the mission.

4. B

According to this if-clause, what just happened in question 3 cannot happen here; no scenario can be repeated. Then we're told to apply scenario 3 on day two, so during that day the assignments become:

D	E	F	G
repairs	photos	walking	comm

Given the prohibition against repetition, scenario 1 or 2 must be enacted on day three. If scenario 1 happens, Dalton and Ellis retain their jobs while Ford and Gunther switch. Since we're looking for something that could be true, it makes sense to take a quick peek at the choices to see if we can stop here.

A 180 test taker avails himself of every opportunity to work faster.

Unfortunately, none of the choices corresponds to that state of affairs, so we'll have to press on. The only remaining possibility is that day three sees scenario 2 take place, in which case Ellis and Gunther retain their jobs while Dalton and Ford (currently repairperson and walker, respectively) switch. At the end of that process, Ford is the repairperson, as (B) has it.

5. D

Ouch. This question ups the ante even higher, taking us further into "backward reasoning" than we've gone up to now. Think about our ultimate goal: Ellis making repairs on day three. So Ellis, who starts day one walking in space, has to end up in repairs, the job that Gunther starts out with. Now scan the scenarios, and notice that scenario 2 seems to do what we need: switching Ellis the walker with Gunther the repairperson. Clearly we cannot execute scenario 2 twice, because Ellis and Gunther would begin day three in the same jobs they began with. But if scenario 2 were executed (giving Ellis the repair job), and another scenario could then take place that would *leave Ellis in that job* . . . well, that would be what we'd need. And, of course, scenario 1 is available for that very purpose. If scenario 2 is executed on day two and scenario 1 on day three, then Ellis ends up as repairperson and we see that (B) and (C) are true. Since we're looking for something that cannot be true, we can cross those off and move on.

Meanwhile, scenario 1 has another use, in tandem with scenario 3. Scenario 1 gives Gunther's job to Ford, while scenario 3 sees Ford exchange jobs with Ellis. Executed in that order, the repair job will go from Gunther on day one, to Ford on day two, to Ellis on day 3. And that demonstrates the possibility of (A) and (E) being true. What cannot happen is scenario 3 on day two, for that would bestow Gunther's repair job on Dalton, and there'd be no way for Ellis to inherit the repairs from Dalton on day three—no scenario allows for that.

6. A

This one has the vaguest opening of any question on this game ("If at some point . . . "), but it does give us a definite starting point: Dalton, who begins day one monitoring communications, must at some point take photos, the job Ford begins with. (And notice that the question leads to some kind of definition: The right answer is something that must be true on day two.) No scenario sees Dalton and Ford switch directly, so the "some point" must be day three. Our job therefore is to get Dalton in position to snag the photo gig, and one glance at the scenarios tells us that scenario 3 must be involved. Why? Because that's the only one in which Dalton makes a direct switch, and scenario 2 won't help because although Dalton may be involved there, it deals with walking and repairs only, while the stem is trying to get a camera into Dalton's hands.

It takes a little forward vision, but perhaps you noticed that if scenarios 1 and 3 were executed in that order, then Ford's initial photo job would go to Gunther on day two, and finally to Dalton on day three. In the process, as (A) has it, Ellis would indeed continue to walk in space on day two as he did on day one. As it happens, and as trial and error (if nothing else) might reveal, the process described is the *only* way to get the photo job to Dalton, so only (A) is true; the other choices either describe something that happens on day three (D) or that never happens at all: (B), (C), and (E).

What's Next?

The next Time Warp introduces a new element not seen in these first two.

LOGIC GAME 10

Promotions within a university's physics department are determined by a system involving an annual vote of the department's Promotions Committee. In January of the first year of the system, the faculty members of the department are as follows:

Full Professors: Kraft, Leon, Marko
Associate Professor: Norman
Assistant Professors: Oscar, Powell, Quinn
Lecturers: Rose, Stuart, Tower

Under the system, in June of each year at least one lecturer must be promoted to assistant professor, at least one assistant professor must be promoted to associate professor, and at least one associate professor must be promoted to full professor. The Promotions Committee consists of only the current full professors, and no one abstains on any promotion vote.

Everyone below the rank of full professor is voted on by each member of the Promotions Committee.
A faculty member is promoted upon receiving three or more Yes votes from the Promotions Committee.
Leon always votes No to Rose.
Kraft always votes No to Rose and Yes to Powell.
Marko always votes Yes to Powell.
During the first three years of the system, no faculty members leave the department and no new members are hired.

1. Which one of the following must be true?

    (A) Powell is promoted to associate professor in the second year of the system.
    (B) Norman is promoted to full professor in the first year of the system.
    (C) Rose is promoted to full professor in the third year of the system.
    (D) Quinn is promoted to associate professor in the first year of the system.
    (E) Tower is promoted to assistant professor in the second year of the system.

2. Which one of the following must be false?

    (A) Stuart and Tower are promoted to assistant professor in the first year of the system.
    (B) Oscar, Powell, and Quinn are promoted to associate professor in the first year of the system.
    (C) Neither Rose nor Quinn is promoted in the second year of the system.
    (D) Neither Tower nor Oscar is promoted in the first year of the system.
    (E) Either Stuart or Tower is promoted to assistant professor in the second year of the system.

3. Which one of the following must be true about the third year of the system?

    (A) Powell is promoted to full professor.
    (B) Stuart is promoted to associate professor.
    (C) Tower is promoted to assistant professor.
    (D) Oscar is promoted to full professor.
    (E) Rose is promoted to assistant professor.

4. If Leon and Kraft always cast exactly the same votes, then which one of the following must be true?

    (A) Rose is promoted to assistant professor in the second year of the system.
    (B) Powell is promoted to full professor in the second year of the system.
    (C) Oscar is promoted to associate professor in the second year of the system.
    (D) Norman is promoted to full professor in the second year of the system.
    (E) Tower is promoted to assistant professor in the second year of the system.

5. What is the maximum possible number of full professors following the vote in the second year of the system?

    (A) 4
    (B) 5
    (C) 6
    (D) 7
    (E) 8

6. If Powell is an associate professor for the entire second year of the system, then all of the following must be true EXCEPT:

    (A) Leon voted Yes to Powell in the first year of the system.
    (B) Leon voted No to Powell in the second year of the system.
    (C) Leon voted Yes to Quinn in the second year of the system.
    (D) At least two assistant professors are promoted in the first year of the system.
    (E) Oscar or Quinn or both are promoted to full professor in the second year of the system.

Logic Game 10: University Promotions

What Makes It Difficult

The process element is of course a complexity to reckon with in this one, much as it was in the previous two games. We have to think flexibly, applying much mental dexterity working out the usual situations, continually asking ourselves such things as: "If this happens, what will be the case later on?" Or "if this is the case later on, what must have happened earlier?" But this one has a few added complications. The game is long and intimidating on the page. We begin with a given hierarchy, and then have changes determined by votes. Three positive votes result in a promotion; anything less and the faculty member in question stays where he or she is for another year. So we have to count votes, but that's not all: The people casting the votes changes over time also, as more people attain the rank of full professor each year.

And speaking of years, the time element is a bit confusing, what with the program beginning in January of Year 1, but the first vote taking place in June of that year, and in June of each subsequent year. Your understanding of this is certainly put to the test in the confusing question 6.

It's a good thing these people are in academia, considering that a Ph.D. may be needed to figure out this promotion scheme. Let's see how we can make this thing more manageable. In fact, there are many deductions to be made, which is actually suggested by the open-ended structure of the first three questions.

A 180 test taker knows that "must be true" and "must be false" questions with no new information mean something can be deduced up front.

Keys to the Game

Streamline the action. Condense it in your mind to "at least one person in each category gets bumped up each year."

Norman is promoted to full professor in Year 1's vote. He's the only eligible associate that year, and the requirement is clear: " . . . at least one associate professor must be promoted to full professor." Take it one step further:

Kraft, Leon, and Marko all voted for Norman in Year 1. Three votes are needed for promotion, and they're the only ones voting that year.

Rose is not promoted to assistant professor in Years 1 or 2. Two of the three original full professors are anti-Rose, so there's no way she's going anywhere until new blood joins the rank of full professor. The real clever among you probably sniffed out the further consequence of this:

Rose must be promoted to assistant professor in Year 3. The instructions are clear: Someone gets bumped from lecturer to assistant each year, and if Rose can't go in Years 1 or 2, then she'll be the only one left to go in Year 3. Wait, there's more:

Stuart and Tower must be promoted in Years 1 and 2, one in Year 1, the other in Year 2. If they both got bumped up in the first year, then no lecturer would be available for promotion in Year 2, as we've seen that Rose ain't moving on that soon.

Answers and Explanations

1. B   2. A   3. E   4. B   5. D   6. C

Well, it seems like we've answered a number of questions already, and in fact, we have. That's the whole point of thinking through the initial setup, looking for things that can be determined in advance. As far as process games are concerned, this was heavily stocked with possible deductions. If you didn't notice these things up front, that's okay, but you'd still be called upon to notice them in the course of answering the questions.

A 180 test taker nails down all that she can during the setup stage.

---

1. B

Even in hard games we should anticipate a "gimme" or two—questions that reward us directly for our deductive work (or for simply hanging in there). We've just seen that (B) must be true: Norman must be promoted in Year 1.

(A) could be true but need not be: Powell could easily move from assistant to associate in Year 1.

(C) is impossible: Rose is simply not rising that high that fast, with Leon and Kraft's thumbs down.

(D) and (E) are also possible only, and easiest to spot since we know so little about Quinn and Tower.

2. A

Another of our deductions above: Once we noticed that Rose was mired in Lecturer Land for the first two years, we saw that one of Stuart and Tower must make the jump in each of the first two years. If *both* Stuart and Tower move up in Year 1, then they leave Rose behind; but Rose (as we've seen) cannot possibly move up in Year 2, because two of the four full professors voting that year, Leon and Kraft, will vote her down. And even if Rose *could* move up in Year 2, no lecturers would be left to be promoted in Year 3. No way around it: (A) is impossible.

(B) No problem. It's "at least one," remember. All three assistants can move up, because either Stuart or Tower (not, as we've just seen, both) will move up to take their place.

(C) Certainly Rose is going nowhere in Year 2, and Quinn could stay put as well.

(D) If true, then Stuart would move up to Assistant, and either Powell or Quinn to associate. Eminently possible.

(E) must be true. Some lecturer has to be promoted to assistant in Year 2; Rose is staying put, so of Stuart and Tower, whichever stays back in Year 1 will go forward in Year 2.

If you didn't make the deductions discussed above, then this is a good question to come back to after learning more about the game and seeing possible promotions in action. But a 180 test taker is armed with many strategies. Failing to notice a deduction in a Logic Game need not be disastrous; you can find others ways to streamline your work and get through the question set.

3. E

Perhaps a tough question to figure out on the fly, thinking three years into the future. But if you interrogated the situation as we did above, then this thinking is already done. As we've seen, Rose cannot move up until at least three full profs are willing to vote for her and outvote perennial naysayers Leon and Kraft. That cannot happen before the Year 3 vote; and since in Year 3 Rose will be the only lecturer left, she will have to move up after that vote. As for the others:

(A) and (D) could happen as early as Year 2; on the other hand, either Oscar or Powell could get no higher than associate.

(B) could happen as early as Year 2, but need not happen at all.

(C) could happen as early as Year 1, and *must* happen by Year 2. So (C) would be a perfectly good answer to the question of what *cannot* be true in the third year of the system.

4. B

What does it mean that Kraft and Leon always vote in lockstep? It means that Leon must always vote for Powell, which in turn means that Powell is always assured of three yes votes and hence will advance until achieving full professorship in Year 2. (B) is correct.

A 180 test taker transforms abstract "if" statements into concrete realities whenever possible.

(A) The stem doesn't change Rose's situation; she still cannot do any better than reach the assistant level in Year 3.

(C) and (E) are only possibly true, while (D) we've known to be false all along—Norman's on the Year 1 promotion plan.

5. D

Here's one that scratchwork can help with, since the movement of a maximum number of entities is concrete; we can plot it. Let's try to get as many as possible up to full status following Year 2's vote, which also means putting as many as possible in position Year 1 to get promoted to full professor in Year 2. At best, Year 1's vote could see N moving to full professor, all three assistants (O, P, and Q) becoming associates, and either Stuart or Tower becoming an assistant. Then, in Year 2's vote, O, P, and Q could all become full professors, while of S and T, one moves to associate and the other moves up to assistant. Those movements are all copacetic, so seven can be on the top rung of the academic ladder after Year 2's vote.

6. C

Here's the one that harps on the time element, as mentioned above. It's strangely worded, and difficult to decipher. At least we have only a single faculty member to deal with: Powell. So let's track her plight starting at the beginning of the system so that we can work in this "entire second year" business.

In January of Year 1, Powell was an assistant professor. If she became an associate professor by Year 2, then she must have won promotion in the vote in June of Year 1, getting three thumbs-ups from Kraft, Leon, and Marko. (A) is proven true right there, so we can cross if off. During the entire length of Year 2, however, Powell remained in that same job, which means that she must have been voted down in Year 2. If she were promoted, then she would be an associate for only half of Year 2. Powell always gets solid votes from Kraft and Marko, so Norman and Leon—choice (B)—must have voted thumbs-down; a yes from either would turn Powell into a full professor in June of Year 2. The kicker is that in Year 1, someone else besides Powell must have been promoted from assistant to associate—that's because *somebody* has to be promoted to full professor in Year 2, and we've just seen that it isn't Powell. Therefore (D) and (E) must be true: Powell and at least one other (O or Q, maybe both) must be promoted to associate in Year 1, and O or Q or both must have made it to Full Prof in Year 2. (C) is only possibly true, and hence correct.

What's Next?

Things sure took a turn for the worse there at the end, huh? This game is generally pretty nasty, deductions or no deductions. And speaking of generals, we have one coming up next in our final Time Warp challenge. This one harks back to "Plant Rotations," involving a similar north, south, east, west configuration. Of course, "Regiments and Areas" will pose its own unique difficulties, although thankfully we can leave this university-voting thing behind. There's only one decision maker in "Regiments and Areas": a general directing troops in the defense of a city.

LOGIC GAME 11

Four regiments—A, B, C, and D—are positioned to defend the areas to the north, south, east, and west of a city, respectively. At their general's command, exactly two of the regiments will join forces to form one large regiment, in accordance with the following conditions:

No regiment will be commanded to join forces with any other regiment more than once.

No regiment will defend two areas simultaneously.

If Regiment A joins forces with Regiments B or C, the resulting regiment will defend the west.

If Regiment B joins forces with Regiment D, the resulting regiment will defend the south.

If Regiment C joins forces with Regiments B or D, the resulting regiment will defend the north.

If Regiment D joins forces with Regiment A, the resulting regiment will defend the east.

1. If the only areas defended are the south and east, then which one of the following pairs of regiments must have joined forces?

    (A) A and B
    (B) B and D
    (C) C and D
    (D) A and D
    (E) B and C

2. If the general issues exactly one command, then which one of the following CANNOT be the areas defended by regiments?

    (A) East, west
    (B) North, south
    (C) North, south, east
    (D) North, south, east, west
    (E) South, west

3. If exactly one area is not defended by a regiment, then each of the following must be true EXCEPT:

    (A) Regiment A did not join forces with another regiment.
    (B) The west is not defended by a regiment.
    (C) Regiment B did not join forces with another regiment.
    (D) The general issued exactly one command.
    (E) Regiment D joined forces with another regiment.

4. If none of the original regiments is defending its original area, then which one of the following must be true?

    (A) Regiment A joined forces with another regiment to defend the west.
    (B) Regiment B joined forces with another regiment to defend the west.
    (C) Regiment C joined forces with another regiment to defend the north.
    (D) Regiment D joined forces with another regiment to defend the east.
    (E) Regiment A joined forces with another regiment to defend the east.

5. If the general's second command results in two regiments joining forces to defend the north, then which one of the following must be false?

    (A) The east is not defended after the general's first command.
    (B) The west is not defended after the general's first command.
    (C) The east is defended after the general's first command.
    (D) The west is defended after the general's first command.
    (E) The south is not defended after the general's first command.

6. If at some point exactly three regiments are defending their original areas, and the general issues the maximum number of commands, which one of the following must be true?

    (A) Regiment A joined forces with another regiment to defend the east.
    (B) Regiment B joined forces with another regiment to defend the north.
    (C) Regiment B joined forces with another regiment to defend the west.
    (D) Regiment C joined forces with another regiment to defend the north.
    (E) Regiment C joined forces with another regiment to defend the west.

Logic Game 11: Regiments and Areas

What Makes It Difficult

The action is a bit more straightforward than that of the previous game. It may remind you a bit of the Plant Rotations game, although there's a new wrinkle we need to consider—this business of *combining* the regiments. How does that happen? It's left kind of vague in the introductory paragraph, and we need the first two indented rules to fully understand the game's action. The last four rules set out the consequences of the various combinations, and we have no choice but to get them down on the page, while of course noting the regiments' initial positions. There's nothing more to sketch.

Unlike in the previous game, there's also not much in the way of deductions, so you simply have to rely on your ability to power through the questions. And those are no picnic, either. There's the usual amount of backward thinking involved in these process games, and a number of questions contain multiple possibilities that simply need to be plotted out before an answer can be determined.

Here are a few things that you may have noticed that make the game a bit easier to handle.

Keys to the Game

When two regiments combine, they go where the rules take them, and then they're done. Also, regiments never split up. These are the correct interpretations of Rules 1 and 2.

After an initial command, one or two areas will be left undefended. A second command is possible after the first switch—the two regiments not involved in the first command can combine, leaving two definite areas undefended.

The general issues a maximum of two commands. After two commands, all four regiments will have been involved in a combination, meaning that nothing further is possible.

A 180 test taker looks to establish numerical parameters in games that don't explicitly set them out.

The scenario set out in Rule 4 is unique. It's the only case in which a regiment (B, to be precise) combines with another regiment but stays to defend its original area. Noticing this is the key to a few of the more difficult questions.

Answers and Explanations

1. D   2. D   3. C   4. C   5. A   6. E

1. D

For the south and east to be the only defended areas, regiments must disappear from the north and west. Regiments A and D are in those areas initially, and if they join forces, the combined new regiment would join C in the east, which fits perfectly with the stem. In fact, that's the only way to satisfy the stem: If the general issues two commands, then somehow the four regiments would have to form two pairs that would end up in the south and east only. But the only combo that ends up in the south is B + D, and the only one that ends up in the east is A + D. So that doesn't work. A + D heading east must be the command here, so (D) is correct.

> A 180 test taker uses the first few questions of a difficult game to confirm that he fully understands the game action and rules. If he encounters problems, he may have missed something in the game intro.

2. D

Not so difficult for those who keep the big picture in mind. Recall the earlier observations regarding the consequences of commands. After one command either one area (if Rule 4 is enacted) or two areas (if Rules 3, 5, or 6 are enacted) will be undefended, so the clever test taker speeds down to and marks off choice (D) without much ado, or much time spent, for that matter. The following actions prove that the other choices are all possible:

(A) A + B → west

(B) C + D → north

(C) B + D → south

(E) A + C → west

> A 180 test taker looks for shortcuts to rack up as many 10-second points as possible, and resorts to brute force only when necessary.

3. C

Here's the first place where our analysis of Rule 4 comes in handy. There's only one way for exactly one area to be left undefended, and that's if B joins with D to defend the south. As we saw, B begins in the south, so the result looks like this:

north	south	east	west
A	B	C	
	D		

All other combinations entail both regiments traveling to new territory, which would immediately leave two areas undefended. But maybe a second command could remedy that situation, enabling the defense of three areas so that only one would be undefended? No way. No matter what successive combos the general picks, two commands would mean two conglomerate regiments defending two areas, leaving two open for attack. So in order to satisfy the stem, we need exactly one command sending Regiment D to join B in the south, leaving the west as the single undefended area. Every choice accords precisely with this scenario except for (C), which in fact must be false under these circumstances.

4. C

Every regiment moves in this one, which should immediately suggest two things: First, having just dealt with a B + D → south scenario in the previous question, we know that this command is verboten, since B would stay at home in the south, in violation of the stem. Secondly, the general must have issued two commands; if only one command is issued, at least some regiments will remain where they are. Now perhaps this is a simple question buried within a difficult question set, in which case one of those deductions would be listed as a choice. No such luck. Based on the nature of the choices, we're forced to examine the more complicated question—where do they go? Let's power through the choices:

(A) Must Regiment A head west? Let's try to send A somewhere else in order to prove that choice (A) need not be true. The only other option for A is joining up with D (which starts out west) to defend the east. So far so good. Then B and C can merge and head north, new territory for both of those regiments. Since we've shown that Regiment A need not go east, choice (A) need not be true. Applying the same method to the other choices:

(B) B + C → north, A + D → east proves (B) need not be true.

(C) Regiment C's only other possible destination besides north is west, which it defends in conjunction with A. That leaves B and D, and the problem discussed above: When these two hook up, B stays put in the south, and that violates the stem. Regiment C therefore must, as this choice maintains, hook up and head north.

(D) C + D → north, A + B → west proves (D) need not be true.

(E) A + B → west, C + D → north proves (E) need not be true.

A 180 test taker is adept at eliminating choices in "must be true" questions by finding exceptions to the assertions in the wrong choices.

---

5. A

Question 5 takes us to a predictable place in Process games—beyond the first step to a later stage in the process. We're told that the second command results in forces combining to march north, so we need to work backward to infer what might have or must have happened before that. Only a limited number of commands send regiments north: C + B and C + D. If C and B join to head north after command 2, then A + D → east would be the necessary combination in command 1. Here's what that would look like. Let's call it Option 1:

after one command

north	south	east	west
	B	C	
		A/D	

after two commands

north	south	east	west
B/C		A/D	

If, however, C and D join to head north after command 2, then A + B → west would be the necessary combination in command 1. Option 2 would therefore look like this:

after one command

north	south	east	west
		C	D
			A/B

after two commands

north	south	east	west
C/D			A/B

Now that we've covered all possibilities, we can check our scenarios against the choices, looking for the one that must be false. And we don't have to look far: The east is defended after command 1 in both options, so (A) must be false and (C) must be true. (A) is therefore the correct answer. As for the others, Option 1 shows that (B) could be true, while Option 2 shows that both (D) and (E) are possible.

A 180 test taker is not afraid to plot out multiple options when necessary, and does so quickly and confidently.

---

6. E

This one is the flip side of question 3, and in fact we can use the same reasoning to speed us on our way. We saw in the earlier question that in order for exactly one area to be undefended, D must have joined with B to defend the south as a result of the general's first command. That way, B stays in the south, leaving the west as the only undefended area. If any other command is issued first, then two regiments will head to new territory, and there will never be a point at which three regiments are defending their original areas, as required by the stem. "Exactly three regiments defending their original areas" here in question 6 is functionally identical to question 3's "exactly one area is not defended," so as in the earlier question, B + D → south must be the general's first command here.

A 180 test taker recognizes questions that employ different wording, but actually mean the same thing or hinge on the same concept.

That takes care of the "at some point" part of the question stem, but wait, there's more: The general issues the maximum number of commands, which we know to be two. So after B and D combine, A and C must get together and head west.

after one command

north	south	east	west
A	B/D	C	

after two commands

north	south	east	west
	B/D		A/C

Now it's a simple matter of scoping out the truism. (E) has it right for this final question of the game.

What's Next?

You've now seen examples of Sequencing, Grouping, Matching, and Process game actions playing out individually in various games. Now let's turn to chapter 4 and see what happens when these actions are combined *within* single games.

CHAPTER FOUR

Volatile Mixtures

The plot thickens, as we move now from single-action games to multiple-action—or Hybrid—games.

Hybrid, or Mixture, game
Performing two or more of the other actions.

What does that mean, exactly? Well, remember "Caravan to the Concert" in chapter 2, the game in which we had to distribute eight people into two groups? Not a simple task, was it? Well, now imagine that we also had to determine which children were male and which were female. That certainly complicates matters, doesn't it? Or how about chapter 2's "Show Riders"? Instead of Art, Brenda, and Chaz magically appearing as the stars of the show, what if we had to first select the three lucky showpeople from a pool of seven eligible riders? That would, annoyingly, add a grouping element to the game's basic matching action.

And that's essentially what these Hybrid games do: add one game action on top of another. They're complicated because they require us to handle many things at once. As the games in previous chapters aptly illustrate, managing a single game action can be daunting enough; now we have to become jugglers.

So, what can you do? A few pointers:

- Keep your focus as you scope out the various challenges presented by Hybrid games. It's easy to get distracted.
- Think in terms of active verbs when decoding the game introductions. For example, say to yourself: "My job is to *select*; to *match*; to *order*"—and so on.
- Determine which action if any, is the primary driver of each game. In one game, sequencing may dominate, while a grouping element may be secondary. In another game, these may be reversed.
- When answering individual questions, focus on the action that's tested. Even when multiple game actions are present, some questions focus on only one.

Enough said—let's get at 'em.

LOGIC GAME 12

Wendell, a messenger, makes exactly six deliveries during the course of a five-day work week, from Monday to Friday. He makes no more than two deliveries on any given day. Each delivery consists of exactly one item, either a single package or a single document. The six items delivered are selected from the following items: packages A, B, C, D, and E, and documents F, G, H, J, and K.

If Wendell delivers C, then he delivers K the very next day.

If Wendell delivers B, then he does not deliver E.

If Wendell delivers F, then he delivers G.

If Wendell delivers G, then he delivers F.

If Wendell delivers K, then he delivers A on a later day of the week than K.

Wendell delivers D on Thursday.

The number of packages and the number of documents Wendell delivers during the week are not equal.

1. Which one of the following is impossible?

    (A)   Wendell makes one delivery on each of exactly two days during the week.
    (B)   Wendell makes one delivery on each of exactly three days during the week.
    (C)   Wendell makes two deliveries on exactly one day during the week.
    (D)   Wendell makes two deliveries on each of exactly two days during the week.
    (E)   Wendell makes two deliveries on each of exactly three days during the week.

2. Wendell CANNOT deliver which one of the following pairs of items on the same day?

    (A)   A and H
    (B)   C and D
    (C)   D and E
    (D)   F and J
    (E)   G and K

3. The delivery of which one of the following items would make it impossible for Wendell to deliver G?

    (A)   A
    (B)   C
    (C)   E
    (D)   H
    (E)   K

4. If Wendell delivers E exactly two days before he delivers C, then all of the following could be true EXCEPT:

    (A)   Wendell delivers C the day after H and the day before D.
    (B)   Wendell delivers D the day after C and the day before H.
    (C)   Wendell delivers H the day after E and the day before C.
    (D)   Wendell delivers J the day after C and the day before A.
    (E)   Wendell delivers K the day after J and the day before A.

5. Which one of the following could be true?

    (A)   A and E are the only packages Wendell delivers.
    (B)   C and D are the only packages Wendell delivers.
    (C)   F and G are the only documents Wendell delivers.
    (D)   H and J are the only documents Wendell delivers.
    (E)   J and K are the only documents Wendell delivers.

6. If Wendell delivers more documents than packages, then Wendell CANNOT deliver which one of the following pairs of items?

    (A)   A and D
    (B)   B and D
    (C)   E and K
    (D)   F and H
    (E)   H and J

7. If Wendell makes deliveries on the fewest number of days possible, and if he delivers C on Monday, then which one of the following must be false?

    (A)   Wendell delivers C on an earlier day of the week than J.
    (B)   Wendell delivers E on the same day of the week as K.
    (C)   Wendell delivers H on a later day of the week than E.
    (D)   Wendell delivers K on an earlier day of the week than B.
    (E)   Wendell delivers C on the same day of the week as H.

KAPLAN

Logic Game 12: Wendell's Deliveries

What Makes It Difficult

Our first game is a fairly common Hybrid variety: a mixture of Sequencing and Grouping. Six items need to be selected for delivery from a group of 10 items total. Complicating this is the fact that the available items themselves are broken up into two categories: packages and documents. This sequence element involves a straightforward calendar schedule; once the items for delivery are selected, Wendell delivers them in some order during the five days of a single week. So we need to worry about not only which items are in play, but also standard sequencing concerns such as which items are delivered before and after which others.

There are as many rules as questions—and only one concrete piece of information among them. Rule 7 is particularly troublesome, compounding the numbers element introduced in the introductory paragraph. There are exactly six deliveries, with no more than two on any given day, but now we have to also make sure that Wendell deliver an unequal number of packages and documents.

The question set is fairly difficult, containing a large number of abstract stems with no new information as well as an unusually large number of questions phrased in the negative; that is, looking for things that *cannot* be true, are *impossible*, and must be *false*. The choices in question 1 take a certain amount of deciphering. The questions involving sequencing all contain shades of the grouping element, since there's no way to order the deliveries without first knowing which items are delivered. All in all, a very complex treatment of a fairly straightforward scenario. Luckily there are a few key deductions that simplify things for us. Did you notice them?

Keys to the Game

Wendell delivers either four packages and two documents or two packages and four documents. There are only two ways to get to six without selecting an equal number of each type: one and five or two and four. But Rule 2 forbids us to select all five packages, and taking all five documents doesn't work either: Since K requires A, and D is always selected, that would be seven items selected. So a 4/2 breakdown it is. And we can be more specific . . . .

If four packages and two documents are delivered, A and C must be delivered. D is always taken, and only one of B and E is eligible (Rule 2). **K must also be delivered (Rule 1), which means F and G cannot be,** since choosing one means choosing the other and in this 4/2 breakdown only two documents can be delivered.

If two packages and four documents are delivered, F and G must be selected. That's because leaving out one means leaving out the other, and there would be no way to select four documents. **And in this scenario, C cannot be delivered,** since choosing C means choosing K, and by extension, choosing A, which, including the omnipresent D, would put us over the top on the package front.

A 180 test taker scopes out all of the possibilities in games that are heavily invested in numerical restrictions.

These deductions don't blow the game wide open, but they do give the clever test taker a way in to each question that others may not have at their disposal. And any advantage is significant on the difficult, time-pressured Logic Games section.

Answers and Explanations

1. B   2. B   3. B   4. D   5. E   6. C   7. D

1. B

We're looking for an impossibility, given no new information, and perhaps you noticed that each choice deals with the number of deliveries on different number of days during the week. That means that the test makers are simply interested in seeing if we understand how six entities can be distributed among five days when the maximum per day is two.

A 180 test taker uses the nature of the answer choices in abstract questions to help direct her attack on the question.

Here are the possibilities:

2, 1, 1, 1, 1

2, 2, 1, 1, 0

2, 2, 2, 0, 0

Checking these against the choices, (A) and (D) conform to the second option, (C) matches the first scenario, and (E) pegs the third possible breakdown of items per day. (B) is the impossibility: Having exactly one delivery on each of exactly three days would require scheduling a three-delivery day, which isn't allowed, so (B) is correct.

2. B

Since the correct answer is a pair that *cannot* be chosen together on the same day, the four wrong choices will be pairs that *can* (or must) be. This question might be profitably postponed until later in the game, since in the course of the questions, we're bound to see lots of pairs of items chosen together on the same day; in other words, more than one wrong answer for question 2 is likely to emerge as we go along. If you answered it right off, however, you'd see it's not very difficult. Rule 6 tells us a fact (our one single concrete fact at this point) about a day late in the week, and Rules 1 and 5 deal with entities later in the week than other entities, so chances are a combination of these rules will lead to the impossible pair of items we seek.

A 180 test taker zeros in on what appear to be the heaviest restrictions when faced with a "CANNOT be true" question.

If, as (B) has it, C and D are delivered on the same day, that day would of course be Thursday; K would have to be delivered on Friday (Rule 1), but then there would be no place to put A as mandated by Rule 5. All of the other choices are perfectly possible—no need to run through them.

3. B

Which item is incompatible with G? All we know about G from the rules is that the delivery of document G requires the delivery of document F, but a combination of two of our deductions above tells us right off the bat that G and C can never be a part of an acceptable group. If there are four packages and two documents delivered, A and C must be delivered, because D is always taken, and only one of B and E is allowed. Since C is taken, K must also be delivered, which means F and G cannot be, because this 4/2 breakdown allows for only two documents. So the only way that Wendell can deliver F and G is if he delivers four documents and two packages, in which case choosing C would lead to a violation since C requires K which in turn requires A. That's too many packages. Definitely not an easy question, and another which may have benefited from your skipping and returning to after more acceptable orderings were in the books.

A 180 test taker senses when to postpone a question.

---

4. D

The relevant question to work our way into this one is: "Where could C be?" Well, begin with where C *can't* be—Thursday or Friday—since if C is delivered, K must be delivered on a later day and A on an even later day than K. So the latest C can be delivered is Wednesday, lest we run out of room for K and A. Taking into account the requirement in the stem, it turns out C in fact *must* be delivered on Wednesday, resulting in the arrangement:

Mon	Tues	Wed	Thurs	Fri
E		C	D/K	A

With A, C, D, and E already present, we know we're in the four packages, two documents world, which means the final item must be document H or J, since the FG pair would put us over the limit. With that in mind, we can test the choices, in search of the one that can't be true:

(A), (C) Pop H into Tuesday and we can cross off (A) and (C) as eminently possible.

(B) However, maybe H is on Friday, in which case (B) would work.

(D) would require putting J on Thursday, which would result in three items delivered on Thursday, a definite no-no according to the "two max per day" numbers rule in the intro. (D) is what we want.

For the record, (E) works just fine as long as J joins C on Wednesday.

5. E

Another vague question offering no new information, so we have two choices: We can try the choices out one by one, or we can look to see if any of the choices conform to an arrangement already seen. Well, the previous question resulted in a nearly full ordering, and lo and behold, in the 4/2 packages-to-documents breakdown depicted, J and K could be the only documents delivered, as choice (E) maintains. We can see this as well from our earlier deduction that in the four packages, two documents scenario, one of the documents selected must be K, with the other being H or J. This, incidentally, eliminates (C) and (D) from consideration.

(A) is easy to kill on account of Rule 6: D is an omnipresent package in this game.

(B) C requires K, and K requires package A, so C and D can't be the only two packages taken.

6. C

"More documents than packages" may not mean a lot to someone who didn't put any effort into forming deductions, but for those who saw the kinds of keys discussed above, and especially the numbers breakdown, know this immediately puts us into the four documents, two packages world. And we also know exactly what that entails: F and G are delivered, but C cannot be. With that in mind, let's find our illegal pairing:

(A) AD / FGHK works fine, so (A) is out.

(B), (D), (E) BD / FGHJ works fine, so we can kill (B), (D), and (E) from that delivery roster alone.

A 180 test taker is adept at using a single valid scenario to eliminate a number of choices. Her goal is to do no more work than necessary.

(C) K requires the delivery of A, and D is always delivered, so throwing E in as well would give us three packages right there. But then there would be no way for more documents than packages to be delivered, so the pair in (C) is the one that doesn't work.

7. D

Sequencing makes a reappearance after a brief hiatus over the last two questions; we can tell by the stem's requirement that C must be dropped off on Monday, and also by the "earlier, later, same day" wording of the choices. But grouping is never far behind in this game, and, in fact, we can hark all the way back to our work in question 1 to get a leg up here. There, we decided that the only possible number distributions of items to days of the week are:

$$2, 1, 1, 1, 1$$
$$2, 2, 1, 1, 0$$
$$2, 2, 2, 0, 0$$

The fewest number of possible delivery days is therefore three, as long as two packages are delivered on each of the three days. Back to the sequencing element: C on Monday means K on Tuesday and A sometime after that. But to keep with the three-delivery-days requirement, we'll have to pair A up with D on Thursday, giving us:

Mon	Tues	Wed	Thurs	Fri
C	K		D/A	

Furthermore, with three packages already, there must be one more package and one more document added to the roster. B or E must be the other package, and H or J will do it for the documents. We don't know which of these will be delivered, but we do know that one will have to be delivered on Monday and the other on Tuesday to give us the 2/2/2 breakdown. And that's what allows us to single out (D) as the choice that must be false: For K to be delivered on an earlier day of the week than B, B will have to either be delivered on Thursday, which already has two deliveries, or Wednesday or Friday, in violation of the mandate in the stem. Various ways of inserting B or E and H or J into the first two days of the week show the remaining choices to be possible.

What's Next?

As you can see, there's a lot going on in these Mixture games, but the upside is that they usually provide fertile ground for deductions. So keep your eyes open for opportunities to combine the rules. "Wendell's Deliveries" combines a time sequence with a grouping aspect. The following game, "Wax Statues," combines a basic linear Sequencing arrangement with a Matching element.

LOGIC GAME 13

Exactly four statues stand in line on the floor of a wax museum, numbered 1 through 4 from left to right. Two of the statues are male figures and the other two are female figures. Two of the statues represent athletes, one represents a gangster, and the other represents an inventor. Exactly one of the four statues glows in the dark.

The statue that glows in the dark is either statue 1 or statue 4.

Statue 2 represents an athlete.

At least one male figure stands in line between the two female figures.

One of the statues representing an athlete glows in the dark.

1. Which one of the following must be true of statue 3?

   (A) It represents either the gangster or an athlete.
   (B) It is either a male figure or it represents the inventor.
   (C) It stands in line immediately adjacent to a statue that glows in the dark.
   (D) It is either a male figure or it stands in line immediately adjacent to a female figure.
   (E) It stands in line immediately adjacent to two statues representing athletes or immediately adjacent to two statues that do not glow in the dark.

2. If statue 4 is a male figure that glows in the dark, then all of the following must be true EXCEPT:

   (A) Statue 1 is a female figure.
   (B) Statue 2 is a male figure.
   (C) Statue 3 represents the gangster.
   (D) Statue 4 represents an athlete.
   (E) Exactly one statue stands in line between the two statues representing athletes.

3. If the two male figures stand in line immediately adjacent to each other, then which one of the following must be false?

   (A) A female figure glows in the dark.
   (B) The statue representing the inventor is a female figure.
   (C) Statue 3 is a male figure.
   (D) Both statues representing athletes are male figures.
   (E) The statue representing the gangster is a female figure.

4. If the two statues representing athletes stand in line immediately adjacent to each other, then which one of the following would make it possible to precisely determine every characteristic of the four statues in line?

   (A) A statue representing a female inventor stands in line immediately adjacent to a statue representing the gangster.
   (B) A statue representing a male gangster stands in line immediately adjacent to a statue representing an athlete.
   (C) A statue representing a male athlete stands in line immediately adjacent to a statue representing the other athlete.
   (D) A statue representing a female gangster stands in line immediately adjacent to a statue representing an athlete.
   (E) A statue representing a male inventor stands in line immediately adjacent to a statue representing an athlete.

5. If statue 3 represents a female gangster, then all of the following must be true EXCEPT:

   (A) If statue 1 represents the inventor, then statue 4 glows in the dark.
   (B) If the statue that glows in the dark is a female figure, then the statue representing the inventor is a male figure.
   (C) If statue 1 glows in the dark, then only one statue representing an athlete is a male figure.
   (D) If the statue representing the inventor is a female figure, then both male figures represent athletes.
   (E) If statue 2 is a male figure, then statue 4 glows in the dark.

6. If the statue representing the inventor is a male figure, and if it stands at some distance to the left of the statue representing the gangster, then which one of the following must be true?

   (A) Statue 1 is a male figure.
   (B) Statue 1 glows in the dark.
   (C) Statue 2 is a female figure.
   (D) Statue 3 represents the inventor.
   (E) Statue 3 is a male figure.

KAPLAN

Logic Game 13: Wax Statues

What Makes It Difficult

The Sequencing element isn't so bad here—only four statues standing in a row. But the Matching part is a little involved, what with three types of statues of various genders, one glowing in the dark. We have to keep tabs on three things about four statues, and combining all that with the 1–4 sequencing element makes for a somewhat complicated mixture. There is a heavy number dimension to incorporate as well: exactly two males, two females, two athletes, one gangster, and one inventor grace the floor of the museum. Rule 3 is less definite, requiring at least one male standing between two females.

Despite these complexities, the setup is really not so bad. The questions, however, make up for that, containing a usual mix of difficulties: "EXCEPT" questions that require you to weed out things that cannot or need not be true; a question with hypotheticals (if-statements) in the answer choices; and long-winded questions containing wordy answer choices that require extra concentration to keep the entities and match-ups straight.

As usual, a little insight up front goes a long way toward making your task much more manageable. How did you do pinpointing the keys to the game?

Keys to the Game

Either statue 1 or 4 must be a glowing athlete. This deduction results from combining Rule 1, Rule 4, and the last line of the intro.

A 180 test taker knows that not every rule is indented. Often, important rules (especially ones regarding the numbers that govern the game) appear in the opening paragraph.

Statue 3 must be the gangster or the inventor. Since Rule 2 locates an athlete in space 2, and we've narrowed the second athlete's position to 1 or 4, statue 3 must be G or I.

The two female statues cannot stand next to one another. This is the simplest and most efficient understanding of Rule 3. As long as we never order adjacent females, this rule will be satisfied.

A 180 test taker thinks of the rules in terms that will be easy to apply in the context of the game.

Answers and Explanations

1. E   2. C   3. D   4. D   5. E   6. E

1. E

We deduced that statue 3 must be the gangster or inventor, and it pays to scan for that. Unfortunately, the test makers will have none of making things that easy for us. We have here examples of the complex and wordy choices alluded to above. Let's simply go about eliminating the ones that need not be true.

(A) At least our deduction above allows us to kill this one quickly: Statue 3 could be the inventor.

(B) What's wrong with female gangster for statue 3? Nothing, as the following arrangement clearly shows.

1	2	3	4
female inventor	male athlete	female gangster	male athlete (glow)

This scenario eliminates choice (D) as well.

(C) need not be true. The glowing athlete could line up in spot 1.

That leaves (E), which you could (and should!) circle with no further fanfare.

A 180 test taker has confidence in his work. When he has eliminated all but one choice, he marks down the remaining one without bothering to check it.

For the sake of completeness, we'll treat choice (E) here, even though the advice above should prompt you not to do so on test day. If the second glowing athlete takes spot 4 in line, as indicated in the sequence above, then the first part of (E) is true. If, however, the second glowing athlete stands in space 1, then the second part of (E) is true as well. Either way you slice it, (E) must be true.

2. C

We can use the arrangement created in choice (B) above as our base. The figure that glows in the dark is an athlete, so the male glower in spot 4 must be an athlete, and the females must alternate in 1 and 3 in order to satisfy Rule 3. The only thing left unresolved is whether the gangster is first and the inventor third, or the other way around. All of the choices conform to this state of affairs except for (C): Statue 3 could be the inventor.

3. D

There's only one way for the male statues to stand next to each other and still maintain the integrity of Rule 3, and that's if the male statues are 2 and 3, leaving the female statues as 1 and 4. (A) and (C) are therefore statements that must be true—a male is third in line; and the glowing statue, whether it's first or fourth, must be female. The statement that must be false is (D). The athlete that's second in line must be male, but the other athlete, the glowing one, is either statue 1 or 4, and in this situation those statues are female. As for the others: If the male in the third space is a gangster, then (B) would be true, but if the male in the third space is an inventor, then (E) would be true. The only statement that cannot be true, and therefore must be false, is (D).

4. D

First off, we have to deal with the sequencing concern in the stem and get those athletes next to each other. It turns out there's only one way to do that: Since one of the athletes is in space 2, the other one must be standing in 1 or 3. But one of those athletes must glow, and of 1 and 3 only space 1 allows for this, so the glowing athlete must be first in line, next to the other athlete in spot 2. In a simpler game, this realization might be enough to answer the question. As if! Here, the question itself is complex, and the choices no picnic, either. We're looking for a piece of information that would solidify the entire ordering; that is, one that make it possible to know every attribute of every statue in line. That means that the wrong choices all leave at least one thing up for grabs. Let's see what effect each one has on the situation.

(A) If the athletes are in spaces 1 and 2, the inventor and the gangster must take 3 and 4, in some order. Can we tell which statue is in which spot? Nope. Either way works fine, so this isn't the choice that squares everything away.

(B) What if a male gangster stands next to an athlete? Well, that tells us something helpful. With athletes in 1 and 2, the only open space adjacent to an athlete is space 3, so we can fill that slot with a male gangster, resulting in:

1	2	3	4
athlete (glow)	athlete	male gangster	inventor

The inventor must be in the last slot, but now we have the male/female aspect to deal with. Can we settle that issue as well? Well, we can't place a male statue in spot 4, because then the females would be adjacent in 1 and 2, in violation of Rule 3. So 4 must be female. But what about 1 and 2? Male in 1 and female in 2 would satisfy Rule 3 as well as the other way around, so we can't say that everything is precisely determined.

(B) must be axed, but it got us so close that it points the way to correct choice (D), which is identical to (B) except for making the gangster in 3 female, which *does* fully determine the sex of each statue. A female in 3 means a female in 1 and males in 2 and 4. And that's the whole shebang.

> A 180 test taker uses what was learned in eliminating one choice to zero in on the right choice.

(C) tells us the least of all: We already know the two athletes are next to each other. Knowing that one is male doesn't tell us *which* one, nor does it solidify the gangster/inventor placements in spots 3 and 4.

(E) Since the gangster and inventor are functionally identical in this game, this choice has the same exact consequences as choice (B)—we'd still be up in the air regarding the sex of statues 1 and 2.

5. E

With all those if-statements in the answer choices, this one looks to be a horror show, but it's manageable if you use your pencil and your head, in either order. If statue 3 is a female gangster, then the other female statue must be statue 1, in order to satisfy Rule 3. That means statues 2 (which we know is an athlete) and 4 are male. All that's up for grabs is which of the second athlete and the inventor is in 1 and which is in 4. If the athlete takes spot 1, then we'd have:

1	2	3	4
female athlete (glow)	male athlete	female gangster	male inventor

Choices (B) and (C) pertain to this state of affairs, and indeed, in this ordering the inventor is male (B) and only one athlete is male (C). So these two can be crossed off.

However, if the inventor takes spot 1, then the ordering would look like this:

1	2	3	4
female inventor	male athlete	female gangster	male athlete (glow)

(A) and (D) conform to this arrangement, and yes, statue 4 is glowing (A) and both males are athletes (D). But (E)—well, (E)'s if-clause is true in *both* options (we deduced that from the get-go), but only in the latter arrangement does statue 4 glow. (E) is therefore only possibly true, so it's correct here.

A 180 test taker quickly plots out a few possible arrangements when necessary, especially when testing out complex choices.

---

6. E

Next we get multiple pieces of hypothetical information in the stem. We're told that the inventor is male and is also ahead of the gangster in line. We deduced up front that the third statue has to be a gangster or an inventor, so let's try out each scenario.

If statue 3 is the gangster, then the male inventor would have to be statue 1; statue 4 would therefore be an athlete, and a glowing one at that. As for gender, given that statue 1 is male, statue 3 would have to be male as well, or else the females would be adjacent in violation of Rule 3. Here's this possibility:

1	2	3	4
male inventor	female athlete	male gangster	female athlete (glow)

We can see from this arrangement that (B) and (D) need not be true. As for the other possibility, the inventor can be statue 3 and still satisfy the mandate in the stem. That would result in this arrangement:

1	2	3	4
athlete (glow)	athlete	male inventor	female gangster

In this scenario, statue 4 would have to be female, and 3 is male due to the stem, but we cannot be sure about the gender of 1 and 2. One of them is male and the other female, but Rule 3 will stand no matter which way we assign them. The upshot is that in both scenarios above, statue 3 is male, making (E) the correct answer. We can see from this latter ordering that (A) and (C), the remaining two choices, are only possibly true.

What's Next?

Are you getting the hang of these mixture types? As involved as this game is, the sequencing element—ordering four statues in a line—is still fairly straightforward. The following game, "Locker Room," illustrates what happens when a more complicated spatial sequence is combined with a matching task.

LOGIC GAME 14

One wall of a locker room contains exactly eight lockers, arranged in two rows of four lockers each. The top row of lockers is numbered 1, 3, 5, and 7, from left to right, and the bottom row is numbered 2, 4, 6, and 8, from left to right. The lockers are arranged such that locker 1 is positioned directly above locker 2, locker 3 directly above locker 4, locker 5 directly above locker 6, and locker 7 directly above locker 8. Each locker is either small, medium, or large, and each locker is either empty or full.

No large locker can be arranged directly above another large locker.

Each medium locker must be arranged either directly above or directly below another medium locker.

All medium lockers are empty.

The top row contains exactly two empty lockers.

Locker 5 is small.

Locker 4 is large and empty.

No more than four lockers are empty.

In the bottom row, exactly one large locker is adjacent to a medium locker.

1. Which one of the following must be true?

    (A) Locker 3 is small.
    (B) Locker 2 is empty.
    (C) Locker 7 is medium.
    (D) Locker 5 is empty.
    (E) Locker 8 is large.

2. Which one of the following is impossible?

    (A) a large, empty locker in the top row
    (B) a small, full locker in the bottom row
    (C) a medium, empty locker in the top row
    (D) a small, empty locker in the bottom row
    (E) a large, full locker in the top row

3. All of the following could be true EXCEPT:

    (A) Locker 1 is large.
    (B) Locker 2 is small.
    (C) Locker 3 is empty.
    (D) Locker 6 is empty.
    (E) Locker 7 is full.

4. If locker 2 is large, then all of the following must be true EXCEPT:

    (A) Locker 2 is full.
    (B) Locker 8 is medium.
    (C) Locker 5 is empty.
    (D) Locker 6 is large.
    (E) Locker 7 is empty.

5. The maximum number of small, medium, and large lockers, respectively, is which one of the following?

    (A) 5, 4, 4
    (B) 5, 2, 3
    (C) 4, 3, 4
    (D) 4, 2, 3
    (E) 5, 3, 3

6. If as few of the lockers as possible are large, which one of the following could be false?

    (A) Exactly one of the empty lockers is small.
    (B) The bottom row contains more large lockers than the top row.
    (C) The top row contains more small lockers than the bottom row.
    (D) The bottom row contains adjacent empty lockers.
    (E) The top row contains adjacent empty lockers.

Logic Game 14: Locker Room

What Makes It Difficult

This one's a sequencing/matching mixture, but the sequencing element is spatial as opposed to the usual linear variety, an example of which being the statues standing in a row in the previous game. Sure, there's a row of entities here, but then there's *another* row as well. We need to be cognizant of which lockers are next to which others, as well as which ones are *on top of* which others. This requires a bit of visualization, and a sketch that accurately reflects the sequencing action while allowing you to incorporate the matching element too.

A 180 test taker learns to come up with the sketch that works best for her.

The description of the lockers is fairly wordy, and there's a decent amount to keep track of: the location and size of each locker, and the status of each one's contents (empty or full). There are a ton of rules (eight), and they take all different forms. Some deal with the physical layout of the lockers (Rules 1, 2, 4, and 8) while Rule 3 involves the more abstract matching aspect. Three rules set out the number specs for the game (Rules 4, 7, and 8), while two are thankfully concrete (Rules 5 and 6).

At first glance it may seem as if the large number of rules adds to the game's complexity, and perhaps it does until you wrestle them to the ground. But once you do, you'll see that deductions abound which greatly simplify your work with the questions.

Keys to the Game

Start with the information in Rules 5 and 6 and build from there.

Locker 3 must be small. Since locker 4 is large, locker 3 cannot be large (Rule 1), and cannot be medium either, since it isn't above another medium locker (Rule 2). Since locker 3 cannot be large or medium, it must be small.

There will be exactly one more empty locker in the bottom row, besides locker 4, making exactly four empties altogether. That's because there must be no more than four empty lockers, and there are exactly two in the top row and one so far in the bottom row (locker 4). So at most there can be one more empty locker, but Rules 3 and 8, taken together, tell us that there must be exactly one more, since there must be at least one medium locker in the bottom row (Rule 8), and all medium lockers are empty. This realization, finally, enables one more deduction:

There must be exactly two medium lockers total—either 1 and 2, or 7 and 8. We definitely need at least one medium locker in the bottom row to satisfy Rule 8, but more than one would violate Rule 7. So there must be one medium empty locker in the bottom row, and it must be directly under a medium empty locker in the top row. 3 and 5 are both small, so 1 and 2 or 7 and 8 it is for the mediums.

Answers and Explanations

1. A   2. D   3. D   4. C   5. B   6. E

1. A

A "must be true" question with no new information is normally testing for a key deduction. We deduced above that locker 3 must be small, and there it is as choice (A).

2. D

With no new information, you have to tackle this question choice-by-choice, but this task is significantly easier with all of the information above at our disposal. Could we have a large empty locker in the top row, as in (A)? Sure, either locker 1 or locker 7 could be large and empty. Either locker 2, locker 6, or locker 8 could be small and full, which kills (B). As for (C), we deduced that either locker 1 or locker 7 must be medium and empty, so there must be a medium empty locker in the top row. (D) asks if we can have a small, empty locker in the bottom row. Since there can be no more than four empty lockers (Rule 7), and exactly two of them are in the top row (Rule 4), the bottom row can contain no more than two empty lockers. One of those is locker 4 (Rule 6), which is large, and we deduced that one empty locker in the bottom row will be medium. Therefore, we cannot have a small, empty locker in the bottom row, so (D) is impossible. On test day, you wouldn't even check choice (E). For the record, however, either locker 1 or locker 7 could be large and full.

> A 180 test taker moves on as soon as he finds a Logic Games answer that works. That's one of the reasons he can finish the section and often have time to double-check his work.

3. D

Again, you have to tackle this question choice-by-choice, but we can use our previous work to speed things up a bit. In the last question, we saw that locker 1 can be large, which knocks off (A). As for (B), locker 2 could be small as long as locker 7 and locker 8 are medium and locker 6 is large, to satisfy Rule 8. Locker 3 could be empty without causing any problems, so (C) is wrong. Next, we have to see whether locker 6 could be empty, and our work on the previous question comes into play again. We know that there are no more than two empty lockers in the bottom row, that locker 4 will be one of the empties, and that either locker 2 or 8 will be both medium and empty. Therefore, if locker 6 is empty, then there would be three empty lockers in the bottom row, which is impossible. So, (D) cannot be true. Again, you wouldn't need to check (E), but locker 7 could be full as long as both locker 1 and locker 2 are medium and empty.

4. C

Locker 2 is large (and full, because we'd have too many empties otherwise). We still need a medium locker adjacent to a large one in the bottom row, so locker 8 must be medium (and therefore empty), locker 6 must be large (Rule 8), and locker 7 must be medium and empty. The only choice that need not be true is (C): Locker 5 can be empty or full.

KAPLAN

5. B

We deduced above that there must be exactly two medium lockers in the game at all times, which immediately narrows our search to choices (B) and (D).

Both choices indicate three large lockers max, so we'll take that for granted and simply check out the small situation.

A 180 test taker uses elimination strategy, always looking for the quick and easy ways to test out choices.

It's possible for lockers 3, 5, 6, 7, and 8 to all be small, so (B) with five small lockers is correct.

6. E

The fewest number of large lockers occurs if lockers 1 and 2 are medium and 3, 5, 6, 7, and 8 are small (if the mediums were 7 and 8, then 6 would need to be large to satisfy Rule 8). In fact, we employed this arrangement when maximizing the number of small lockers. Notice how maximizing the number of one set of entities minimizes the number of another set—this is often the case. So much is determined, but there's still the matter of answering the question, which is of the tricky "could be false" variety. Let's discard the choices that must be true.

(A) must be true because the top lockers consist of one medium and three small, and exactly two of them must be empty—the medium and one of the small lockers.

(B) is true; the bottom row has one large locker, the top row zero.

(C) is true, by a count of three to two.

(D) is true: 2 is a medium (and therefore empty), and 4 is always empty from Rule 6.

(E) That leaves (E): Locker 1 is empty (medium), but locker 3 need not be the other empty one. Either locker 5 or locker 7 could do the honors.

What's Next?

As you've seen, Hybrid games are often amenable to some big deductions that effectively cut them down to size. Without the kinds of realizations discussed above, this game takes on a nightmarish tinge. With them, it's just another game, "ripe for the pickings."

Our next offering, "Dogs on Podiums," presents another opportunity for you to practice with Hybrids.

LOGIC GAME 15

A dog groomer displays dogs on two different podiums, Podium 1 and Podium 2. Each podium contains exactly three dogs: one on the left, one in the middle, and one on the right. Only dogs displayed in adjacent spaces on the same podium are considered "next to" each other. The dogs available for display are BJ, Doozi, Ivory, Nutley, Pepper, Quest, and Shamash. The dogs are displayed according to the following conditions:

Nutley and Pepper cannot be displayed on the left side of either podium.

BJ and Ivory cannot be displayed in the middle of either podium.

Nutley and Quest cannot be displayed on the right side of either podium.

If Shamash is displayed on Podium 1, then Doozi is displayed on Podium 1.

If Quest is displayed on Podium 2, then BJ is displayed on Podium 2.

If BJ is displayed on Podium 1, then Nutley is displayed on Podium 2.

Doozi and Pepper cannot be displayed on the same podium.

1. If BJ is displayed on Podium 1, which one of the following must be true?

   (A) Quest is displayed on Podium 1.
   (B) Quest is not displayed next to Doozi.
   (C) Quest is displayed on one of the two podiums.
   (D) Quest is not displayed on Podium 2.
   (E) Quest is displayed next to Pepper.

2. If Pepper is displayed in the middle of Podium 1, and Ivory is not displayed on either podium, then all of the following must be true EXCEPT:

   (A) Quest is displayed on the left side of Podium 1.
   (B) Shamash is displayed on the left side of Podium 2.
   (C) Pepper is displayed next to BJ.
   (D) Doozi is displayed next to Nutley.
   (E) BJ is displayed on the right side of Podium 1.

3. If BJ and Shamash are displayed on Podium 1, which one of the following must be false?

   (A) Pepper is displayed on the right side of Podium 2.
   (B) BJ is displayed next to Doozi.
   (C) Quest is displayed next to Nutley.
   (D) Doozi is displayed next to Shamash.
   (E) Ivory is displayed on the left side of Podium 2.

4. If Pepper is displayed next to Shamash, which one of the following could be true?

   (A) BJ is displayed on Podium 1.
   (B) Nutley is displayed on Podium 2.
   (C) Shamash is displayed on Podium 1.
   (D) Quest is displayed on Podium 2.
   (E) Ivory is displayed on Podium 1.

5. If Nutley is not displayed on either podium, and Doozi and Shamash are displayed on different podiums, then how many different displays of dogs are possible for Podium 2?

   (A) 1
   (B) 2
   (C) 3
   (D) 4
   (E) 5

6. Which one of the following is impossible?

   (A) Quest is displayed next to both Ivory and Shamash.
   (B) Nutley is displayed next to both Doozi and Shamash.
   (C) Doozi is displayed next to both Ivory and Quest.
   (D) Shamash is displayed next to both BJ and Pepper.
   (E) Pepper is displayed next to both BJ and Quest.

Logic Game 15: Dogs on Podiums

What Makes It Difficult

The phrase "next to" in quotes in the introduction suggests the sequencing element here: a mini left-middle-right exercise to perform for each podium. So first we have to figure out which dogs are on which podiums, and then we have to determine *where* on the podium each is displayed. Not too tough on the face of it, but the rules are many and involved. The first three are stated in the negative, telling us what parts of the podiums certain dogs *can't* be; while the rest have to do with the grouping element, dealing with the podiums on which the dogs can appear.

There's a subtle complexity that involves the numbers that govern the game: There are six spots, but seven dogs, and you have to figure out just how to handle that wrinkle. The kicker is that the kinds of deductions we can usually make from the type of if-then statements in this game are thwarted by the fact that one dog will not be chosen. That makes it hard to combine the rules. Finally, many of the questions require multiple steps. The game's involved enough; the questions are simply tough. A "Doozi," indeed. But a few key interpretations speed us on our way.

Keys to the Game

Make use of the fact that one dog must be left off the podiums. While appearing to make the game more difficult, this wrinkle actually gives the clever test taker an additional way into the questions. In order to figure out who's where, one can begin by asking "which dog is left out?"

A 180 test taker turns even the game's complexities to her advantage.

Nutley, if displayed, must be in the center of one of the podiums. That's the upshot of Rules 1 and 3.

Pepper, if displayed, must be middle or right. BJ and Ivory, if displayed, must be left or right. Q, if displayed, must be middle or left. Not great revelations, perhaps, but it's always easier to think in terms of where entities could be than where they cannot be.

Work out and be crystal clear about the implications of if-then Rules 4–6:

Rule 4: If D2, then if S is displayed, S2. The implication is tricky here, since we also have to account for the possibility that D is not displayed at all. Since only one dog will not be displayed, we also know that if D is not displayed, S must be displayed, and cannot be displayed on Podium 1 (or else D would have to be there as well). Therefore, if D is not displayed, then S2.

Rule 5: If B1, then if Q is displayed Q1; and, as with rule 4, if B is not displayed, then Q1.

Rule 6: If N1, then if B is displayed, B2; and, as above, if N is not displayed, then B2.

Answers and Explanations

1. D   2. B   3. C   4. E   5. C   6. A

1. D

Rule 6 says that if B is on 1, N must be on 2. That's not a choice, so we have to keep looking. Rule 5 involves BJ as well, and thinking through its implication: If B is on Podium 1, then Q, if displayed, must be on 1. Either way, that means that Quest is not on 2, so (D) is correct.

> A 180 test taker remembers that even hard games usually have some easy questions.

2. B

Once we know which dog sits out, we also know the six dogs that must be displayed, and that, of course, is powerful information. If I isn't displayed, and P is in the middle of Podium 1, then N must be displayed in the middle of 2. D must be on 2 (Rule 7), which means S must be on 2 as well (the implication of Rule 4). That leaves B and Q for Podium 1, with Q on the left (Rule 3), and B on the right. The choice that need not be true is (B); Shamash could be displayed on the left *or* right side of Podium 2.

Lots of steps, huh? Some involve the rules directly, some the *implications* of the rules we discussed above. Either way, this is what we're in for in this game: much step-by-step deductive work requiring a fair amount of concentration and precision.

3. C

What happens if B and S are on 1? D must be on 1 (Rule 4). N must be displayed on Podium 2 (Rule 6), and in the middle of that podium, thanks to our combination of Rules 1 and 3. The implication of Rule 5 dictates that if B is on 1, then Q, if displayed, must be on 1 also. Since that's impossible here (Podium 1 is already full), Quest must sit this one out, and (C) must be false. (A), (D), and (E) must be true, while (B) could be true but need not be.

4. E

P next to S can't happen on Podium 1; D would have to be there also (Rule 4), but that would violate Rule 7. So we should place P and S on 2, which eliminates choice (C). If they're to be next to one another, then N can't be on that podium because N, as we've seen, must always be in the middle, which would separate P and S and violate the question stem. So N can't be on 2, which means that B can't be on 1 due to the implication of Rule 6. That kills choices (A) and (B). (D) is no good—Q on 2 means B on 2, which would give us four dogs on Podium 2, so (E) turns out to be the only statement that could be true under these circumstances. Whew! Not fun, but doable.

> A 180 test taker is skilled at ferreting out the rules that are relevant to each new situation.

5. C

S must be on 2 and D on 1 in order for S and D to be on different podiums (if S were on 1, then D would have to be there too, according to Rule 4). Without N, every other dog must be placed somewhere. Rule 7 forces P onto Podium 2, while the implication of Rule 6 places B on 2 as well. That leaves I and Q for Podium 1, but those who took in the rest of the question stem can dismiss Podium 1 altogether now, since the question centers on Podium 2 and all the dogs for that podium have been determined.

> A 180 test taker stays focused on the question that's asked to avoid wasting time on determinations that yield no reward.

Now that we know *which* dogs are on 2, we can figure out how many arrangements are possible for that podium by taking Rules 1 and 2 into account: BSP, BPS, and SPB are the only possible orderings, from left to right, which gives us three possible Podium 2 displays, choice (C).

6. A

With no new information to go on, there's no real way to go about this one other than to try out each choice. In this case, we luck out because the answer happens to be (A). QIS can't be displayed on Podium 1, because then D would have to join them according to Rule 4, and QIS can't go on Podium 2 because then B would have to join them, thanks to Rule 5. But even if the answer wasn't located so conveniently in (A), trying out these choices turns out to be not nearly as difficult as it seems—in fact, not difficult at all, considering that each one corresponds to a situation we've already seen. (B) and (E) describe the exact podiums we formulated back in question 2, while (C) and (D) represent two of the possible orderings we just uncovered in question 5.

What's Next?

That does it for the dog show. Let's move on to the final Hybrid game of this chapter, and a deceptive game at that.

LOGIC GAME 16

A car dealer orders seven new cars. Each car consists of a single model and a single color. The models that the dealer can choose from are the Puma, the Radon, the Swan, the Tutu, and the Universe. The colors that the dealer can choose from are black, green, maroon, and yellow. The dealer orders in accordance with the following guidelines:

At least three black cars are ordered.

If one or more black Tutus are ordered, then any and all Radons ordered will be green.

If one or more maroon Pumas are ordered, then any and all Universes ordered will be black.

If a maroon Tutu is ordered, then exactly six of the cars ordered will be black.

If no yellow Universes are ordered, then any and all Radons ordered will be yellow.

1. Which one of the following is an acceptable list of cars ordered by the car dealer?

   (A) Three black Radons, one maroon Tutu, three black Swans
   (B) Three black Pumas, three yellow Universes, one green Radon
   (C) Four black Tutus, two maroon Swans, one yellow Radon
   (D) Three yellow Radons, two maroon Pumas, two black Swans
   (E) Five black Pumas, one maroon Tutu, one green Universe

2. What is the maximum number of black cars the dealer can order?

   (A) 3
   (B) 4
   (C) 5
   (D) 6
   (E) 7

3. If the dealer orders four green Swans, which one of the following must be true?

   (A) At least one maroon Puma is ordered.
   (B) At least one yellow Radon is ordered.
   (C) At least one black Swan is ordered.
   (D) No Pumas are ordered.
   (E) No Radons are ordered.

4. If the dealer orders a green Radon, which one of the following CANNOT be included in the order?

   (A) A yellow Universe
   (B) A green Swan
   (C) A maroon Puma
   (D) A black Tutu
   (E) A yellow Swan

5. If the dealer orders at least one car of each model, and the Radon is the only yellow car ordered, which one of the following must be included in the order?

   (A) A green Tutu
   (B) A maroon Puma
   (C) A black Swan
   (D) A black Puma
   (E) A black Universe

Logic Game 16: Seven Cars on Order

What Makes It Difficult

The Radon? The Tutu? What kind of cars are these? A better question is: What kind of *rules* are these? Nasty Formal Logic ones, to be sure. As we indicated at the end of "Dogs on Podiums," this game is a hybrid game, but a deceptive one. After all, the matching aspect seems clear—we have to link up cars and colors—but what's the other game action? In a standard matching game, the entities to be matched are given; in this one, however, we have to *select* the models and colors from a list of possibilities, so there's a grouping element present as well.

The rules, simply put, are the real killers here. The "any and all" formulation found in three of the five rules is ripe for misinterpretation, and the negatively stated Rule 5 has been known to give people fits. Other than suggesting that you find a convenient way to distinguish the models from the colors (e.g., capital and lowercase abbreviations), the major key to the game is nothing more complicated than understanding the rules and their implications, so let's spell those out here.

Keys to the Game

Rule 1: There are at least three black cars. This is the only simple rule of the bunch.

Rule 2: If bT, then all R's are g. Get this "any and all" business straight from the outset: If a black Tutu is ordered, that doesn't necessarily mean that a green Radon must be ordered—there could be NO Radons ordered at all. The correct interpretation is that IF a Radon is ordered along with a black Tutu, then it must be green. Once you understand this correctly, you can and should think through its implication, namely: If R not g, then no bT. In other words, if a Radon is ordered in any color besides green, then no black Tutus can be ordered. Applying this line of thinking to the rest of the rules:

Rule 3: If mP, then all U's are b. Implication: If U not b, then no mP.

Rule 4: If mT, then six b. Implication: If there are not six b, then no mT. Take a moment to think through the further implications of this rule. Since seven cars are ordered, this means that at most one maroon Tutu may be ordered. If another Tutu is in the order, it (along with all of the other cars) must be black.

Rule 5: If no yU, then all R's are y. Implication: If R not y, then there must be a yU. If a Radon's ordered that's not yellow, then a yellow Universe must be ordered.

If a maroon Tutu is ordered, then no Radons can be ordered. This can be deduced from combining Rules 4 and 5. It's not crucial, but if you can pick up on subtle and tricky deductions like this, then you're definitely on the right track.

These rules and their implications are quite complex and easily confused, but you should have no problem, right?

A 180 test taker can think through, combine, and apply the toughest Formal Logic rules that appear on the LSAT.

Answers and Explanations

1. **B**   2. **E**   3. **E**   4. **C**   5. **A**

1. B

There are only five questions in the set—a minor blessing—and the first two simply test your basic understanding of the game. The normal technique for Acceptability questions works fine here: testing each rule against each choice. Rule 1 kills (D), which doesn't have the requisite three black cars. Rule 2 axes (C), which contains black Tutus but a Radon that's not green. Rule 4 eliminates (E): a maroon Tutu can't be part of an order containing a green car. Finally, Rule 5 takes care of (A), which has no yellow Universe and non-yellow Radons. (B) remains as the acceptable list.

2. E

In questions seeking maximums, the best strategy is to shoot for the moon; in other words, to try out the highest number and work your way down from there. We know there must be at least three black cars, but can all seven be black? Why not? There are no rules restricting Swans, so the dealer could easily order seven black Swans. There's no need to find other possible groups of seven black cars to conclude that seven works, so (E) is the answer.

A 180 test taker recognizes the "floaters" or "free agents" in a game, and gravitates toward those in situations calling for the least restrictions.

---

3. E

What does four green Swans mean? Well, Swans are our floaters, so no rules directly come into play based on their inclusion. But what about the numbers game? We have to have three black cars, and in this question four of the seven are green Swans, so the other three remaining must be black. Therefore, there can't be any yellow Universes ordered, which triggers Rule 5: any Radons ordered will have to be yellow. But that's impossible: Since the other cars ordered are all black, we know that no Radons can be included in the order, choice (E).

4. C

Inclusion of a green Radon leads us to Rules 2, 4, and 5. It meets the requirements of Rule 2, so a black Tutu could be ordered, eliminating (D). According to Rule 4, a maroon Tutu cannot be ordered when a green car is included, but unfortunately, that's not a choice. But Rule 5 tells us that a yellow Universe *must* be included in the order, since leaving one out forces all Radons to be yellow, and here we have a green one. This is seemingly no help, since we're trying to *eliminate* a choice. But all that means is that we have to go one step further to see where this new information leads. A yellow Universe leads us to Rule 3, the implication of which gives us our answer, (C). Since the order must include a yellow Universe, then there's no way for all Universes ordered to be black, which means that a maroon Puma cannot be included in the order.

Lots of steps are required, much like the more involved questions in "Dogs on Podiums." What makes these questions difficult is not necessarily the difficulty level of each step, but simply the number of steps required and therefore the number of possible places to slip up. Note that if you were running out of time, and had to guess on a question like this, you could still narrow down the choices at a glance by eliminating (B) and (E). Why? Because these involve Swans, our floater model, which means that unless Rule 4 is invoked, we can probably slip any color Swan into the order.

KAPLAN

5. A

One complex question to go, and this one offers two pieces of information. It's a particularly tough question because in order to figure out what car must be included, we have to eliminate color options for a certain model until only one color remains. Unfortunately, there's nothing to suggest that this is the way to go, so either you saw this intuitively, or had enough time to work out enough possibilities until this "process of elimination" idea struck you. In any event, the reasoning goes like this: The fact that a Radon is the only yellow car leads us to Rule 2, and tells us that a black Tutu can't be ordered. It also points to Rule 4—a maroon Tutu is out of the question as well. And guess what? Since the Radon is the *only* yellow car, any Tutus ordered can't be yellow, and we just saw that they can't be black or maroon. Since, according to the stem, at least one car of each model is ordered, at least one Tutu must be included, and since it can't be yellow, black, or maroon, a green Tutu (or Tutus) must be ordered. That's choice (A).

A 180 test taker understands that sometimes the only way into a difficult matching question is elimination.

What's Next?

All right then—we're four-fifths of the way through this Logic Games section, and if you've gotten this far you're probably ready for the final four killer games.

CHAPTER FIVE

Huh…?

The title of this chapter reflects the response most test takers have upon encountering the kind of games you're about to see: "Games That Make You Reconsider Your Decision to Go to Law School."

So far, in chapters 2–4, you've done battle with individual Sequencing, Grouping, Matching, and Process games, as well as Hybrid games that combine these game actions in various ways. What more is there, you ask? What can possibly be even harder than these first 16 games?

Well, the games in this chapter all involve and combine these same types of game actions, but they do so in particularly novel (read: "brutal") ways. As usual, we'll touch on the specific difficulties of each in the individual game explanations. For now, suffice it to say that these final four games represent the toughest of the tough, the scariest of the scary—to put it bluntly, the nastiest possible material you may encounter on the LSAT Logic Games section.

Good luck.

LOGIC GAME 17

Five chests are numbered 1 through 5 from left to right, and a monarch is filling each with treasure. Each chest will contain at least one, but not more than two of the following types of treasure: gold, opals, platinum, rubies, silver, and topaz. Each type of treasure will be placed in at least one chest. Each chest will be secured by exactly one mechanism—bolt, chain, or lock. The monarch fills the chests according to the following conditions:

At least two chests must contain rubies.

Exactly two chests must contain opals, and these chests cannot be adjacent to each other.

Both chests that contain opals must be to the left of any chests that contain gold.

Chests 2, 3, and 4 cannot contain silver.

Any chest that contains rubies must be secured by a chain.

Any chest that contains opals must be secured by a bolt.

Chest 2 is secured by a chain.

1. Which one of the following CANNOT be true?

    (A) Chest 1 is secured by a lock.
    (B) Chest 2 contains topaz.
    (C) Chest 3 is secured by a lock.
    (D) Chest 4 contains opals.
    (E) Chest 5 is secured by a chain.

2. If a chest containing treasure and secured by a lock is not adjacent to a chest secured by a bolt, then which one of the following must be true?

    (A) Chest 1 contains platinum.
    (B) Chest 4 contains opals.
    (C) Chest 4 contains rubies.
    (D) Chest 5 contains gold.
    (E) Chest 5 contains silver.

3. If rubies are contained in the maximum number of chests, which one of the following must be true?

    (A) Chest 3 is secured by a bolt.
    (B) Chest 4 is secured by a bolt.
    (C) A chest containing silver is secured by a bolt.
    (D) A chest containing gold is secured by a chain.
    (E) A chest containing platinum is secured by a lock.

4. Which one of the following must be true?

    (A) At least one chest containing gold is adjacent to a chest containing opals.
    (B) At least one chest containing platinum is adjacent to a chest containing silver.
    (C) At least one chest containing rubies is adjacent to a chest containing topaz.
    (D) At least one chest containing gold is adjacent to a chest containing topaz.
    (E) At least one chest containing opals is adjacent to a chest containing rubies.

5. If chest 4 contains platinum and topaz, which one of the following pairs of treasures must be contained in the same chest as each other?

    (A) opals and silver
    (B) gold and platinum
    (C) rubies and topaz
    (D) gold and silver
    (E) opals and platinum

6. If chest 3 is secured by a lock, which one of the following could be false?

    (A) Chest 1 contains silver.
    (B) Chest 2 contains rubies.
    (C) Chest 3 contains topaz.
    (D) Chest 4 is secured by a bolt.
    (E) Chest 5 is secured by a chain.

Logic Game 17: Treasure Chests

What Makes It Difficult

Well, at least there's one thing in our favor: the action of this game is not too difficult to understand. A greedy monarch filling up treasure chests with loot—nothing fancy about that. Each chest secured by a single mechanism? Sure, makes sense. After all, we don't expect the king to just let his treasures stand around unguarded. Essentially we have a Hybrid game on our hands. "Numbered 1 through 5 from left to right" is a big hint that sequencing is involved, and in fact, we later find that the issues of adjacency and order are relevant. The fact that each chest will contain *at least one, but not more than two* types of treasure also suggests a distribution element; each chest can be thought of as a "group" containing up to two different treasure types. But wait, there's more: A whole different set of entities must also be doled out to the chests; namely, the type of fastening mechanism—bolt, chain, or lock. So there's a matching element as well: We have to match the chests to the treasures contained inside to the mechanism that secures it. Surely a lot to keep track of.

The number conditions stated in the intro are also a bit wordy. "At least one, but not more than two types of treasure" in each chest that each chest must contain exactly one or two treasure types.

A 180 test taker drives numerical information to its most definite conclusion.

Moreover, "each type will be placed in at least one chest" means we can't leave out any of the five types entirely; every type must appear somewhere.

All that to assimilate and we haven't even gotten to the rules yet. There are a lot of them to work with, although there's no rule that's particularly hard to understand. However, if you don't put them together and nail down a few important things up front, the game is nearly impossible (at least in the time you're allotted on the test). The keys to the game are therefore a few major deductions. Did you see them?

Keys to the Game

Any chest not secured by a chain cannot contain rubies. Likewise, any chest not secured by a bolt cannot contain opals. These are the correct, and very important, implications of Rules 5 and 6.

Rubies and opals cannot be contained in the same chest, since one must be contained in chain-secured chests, the other in bolt-secured chests. These chests are mutually exclusive, since each chest is secured by exactly one kind of mechanism.

Opals cannot be contained in chest 2, because chest 2 is secured by a chain, and opals must go in chests secured by a bolt. **Opals also can't be in chest 5**, because there would be no room for the required gold chest (Rule 3). With those two chests off limits to opals, there's only one way to place the two opals chests nonconsecutively: **Chest 1 must contain opals, and the other chest containing opals must be either chest 3 or chest 4.** Furthermore, since chest 1 contains opals, **chest 1 must be secured by a bolt.**

That's a lot of ammunition. And we certainly need it to get through the questions. It's even helpful to check out a few possibilities based on this state of affairs. If the second opals chest is chest 3, then gold can be in chest 4 or 5, or both. If the second opals chest is chest 4, gold can be only in chest 5.

Answers and Explanations

1. A   2. C   3. D   4. E   5. A   6. C

1. A

We're given no new information and asked to find the statement that cannot be true. Normally, we may think of holding off on such a question until various scenarios are revealed in the later questions, but having made so many deductions up front, it's worth at least scanning the choices to see if there's an easy point to be had. And indeed, correct choice (A) is simply an extension of one of our deductions. We saw that chest 1 must contain opals; this was because chest 2, secured by a chain, can't have opals, and there's no way to fit both nonconsecutive opals chests between 3 and 5 while still leaving room for the chest containing gold. That means that opals is a definite for chest 1, which further means that chest 1 must be secured by a bolt, not a lock as stated in (A).

2. C

Without the deductions above, there's virtually no way into a question like this; if everything's wide open, then the information in the stem barely tells us anything. But knowing what we know, it tells us plenty. A locked chest can't be chest 1, which we deduced is bolted, or chest 2, which we're told is chained. Furthermore, we deduced that opals must be in chest 3 or chest 4, secured by a bolt. If the opals are in 4, then the locked chest required by the stem must be in 3 or 5, which would make it adjacent to bolted chest 4. So the bolted opals chest in this case must be chest 3, and the locked chest must therefore be far away in chest 5:

1	2	3	4	5
bolt		bolt		lock
opals		opals		

We can kill choice (B) at this point, but that's all, so we need to press on. What about the rubies?

A 180 test taker gravitates toward the game's most "influential" entities—the ones that take up the most space in the arrangement or that we know the most about.

Those who overlook the implication of Rules 5 and 6 are stuck at this point, but for the rest it's a simple matter to recognize that chests 1, 3, and 5 are not secured by chains, and therefore aren't suitable for the rubies. The two rubies chests must therefore be 2 and 4, which means that (C) is correct. (B), as we saw, must be false, while the rest could be true, but need not be.

KAPLAN

3. D

In this one we need to place rubies in as many chests as possible. Chest 1 is off limits, since we know by now that opals are for sure contained there, and no chest with opals can also contain rubies. Chest 2 is wide open for rubies; it's even secured by a chain, the requisite mechanism for a rubies chest, so we can place R in 2. Now we have a choice: As we saw earlier in the keys to the game, the second opals chest will be either chest 3 or 4, and depending on which it is, we can then figure out how to place the maximum number of R's. No sense trying to psychically intuit the whole thing; work out on paper what happens in each case, remembering that you want to maximize the occurrence of rubies.

A 180 test taker is not afraid to use his pencil when necessary to chart out multiple possibilities.

If opals (with a bolt) are in chest 3, then rubies (with chains) can be placed into chests 4 and 5:

1	2	3	4	5
bolt	chain	bolt	chain	chain
opals		opals	rubies	rubies

In this scenario, gold, always to the right of opals, must be in chest 4 or 5 or both. On the other hand, if the opals are placed in chest 4, then rubies can be placed in chests 3 and 5:

1	2	3	4	5
bolt	chain	chain	bolt	chain
opals		rubies	opals	rubies

In this scenario, gold would have to be in chest 5. Either way, it will share a chest with rubies. And since rubies are always in a chest with a chain, (D) is correct. One way or another, gold will be in a chain-secured chest. Now that's a long chain of deduction—even using our key deductions as a starting point.

(A) is true only in scenario one above; in scenario two, chest 3 contains rubies and is therefore secured by a chain.

(B) is the opposite of (A): It's true for scenario two above, but not for scenario one.

(C) is true only in scenario two, when silver (always restricted by Rule 4 to chests 1 and 5) would have to be forced into bolted chest 1, since chest 5 would be filled up with rubies and gold. However, in scenario 1, silver could end up only in chest 5 along with rubies, nicely secured by a chain.

(E) Platinum is a total free agent here; in either scenario we could place platinum in chest 2 with rubies, secured by a chain, which is enough to kill choice (E).

4. E

Another not-if question testing our basic understanding of the game. All of the choices are in the same format, each dealing with the notion of adjacency. In other words, the correct answer pairs up two chests that must be right next to one another. We have no other option but to work through the choices, eliminating the bad ones by coming up with exceptions to them.

However, a little cleverness is in order. It stands to reason that the treasures that must be next to one another will likely be the ones that with the severest restrictions. Platinum and topaz, for example, our "free agents" here, don't really *need* to go anywhere in particular; they just need to be included somewhere. So while (B), (C), or (D) could theoretically be the right answer, they aren't the best candidates, and we're better off trying the other two first.

A 180 test taker pays attention to "free agents," the entities least restricted by the rules.

(A) No, we can place opals in chests 1 and 3 and gold only in 5, filling in the other treasures around them.

(E) must be true: At least one opals chest must be next to a rubies chest. Again we begin from our big deductions: Chest 1 contains opals, while the other opals chest is either chest 3 or chest 4. But we need at least two rubies chests. If opals are in 1 and 3, then rubies must be in chests 2 and 4, 2 and 5, or 3 and 5 (or all three—2, 3, and 5). If, however, opals are in 1 and 4, then rubies must be in chests 2 and 3, 2 and 5, 3 and 5, or 2, 3 and 5. No matter what, at least one opals chest must be next to a rubies chest, and (E) is therefore correct. And notice how, true to the strategy cited above, the right answer involves the two most influential, that is, the two most restricted entities in the game.

(B), (C), (D) There are many ways to split up the treasures in these choices. As we mentioned above, platinum and topaz are restricted so little in this game that it's not a problem separating each from just about any other treasure type. If you noticed that these choices all try to place severe restrictions on entities that are essentially "free agents," then the right thing to do is look elsewhere.

5. A

And speaking of our "free agents," they're highlighted in this question. A simple case of one thing leading to another: If P and T occupy chest 4, then the second opals chest must be chest 3 (and of course we deduced earlier that chest 1 *always* contains opals). Gold must therefore be contained in chest 5 (Rule 3). Now we need to include at least two rubies chests, but two is actually all we have room for: Rubies can't go in the chests containing opals (because these treasures must be in chests secured by different mechanisms), and chest 4 is maxed out, so rubies must therefore be placed in chests 2 and 5. Now chest 5 is maxed out also, since it contains both rubies and gold; so silver, which we haven't used yet and which can be placed only in chests 1 or 5, must be placed in chest 1, joining the opals that are always there. This lengthy chain of deduction explains why "opals and silver," choice (A), must be together under these circumstances.

(B), (D) Neither of these choices can be true. The only chest containing gold in this question is chest 5, which also contains rubies. Silver, as we saw while deriving the correct answer, can only be in chest 1, along with opals.

(C) and (E) both could be true, but need not be: We *could* place topaz in chest 2 along with rubies, but we need not do so, because topaz is already assigned to chest 4. Similarly, platinum could join opals in chest 3, but the platinum requirement is also taken care of by the question stem.

6. C

If chest 3 is secured by a lock, then clearly chest 3 can contain neither rubies (Rule 5) nor opals (Rule 6). We deduced that opals are always in chest 1, and in either 3 or 4, so now we know that the second opals chest—always secured by a bolt—must be chest 4. This, in turn, means that gold must be contained in chest 5 and *only* in chest 5 (Rule 3). Now for the rubies: Chests 1, 3, and 4 are off limits to rubies because they're all secured by mechanisms other than chains; thus we can satisfy Rule 1 only by placing rubies in chests 2 and 5. Of course, that means chest 5 gets a chain. Finally, just like in question 5, chest 5 is now full, which forces silver into chest 1.

1	2	3	4	5
bolt	chain	lock	bolt	chain
opals	rubies		opals	gold
silver				rubies

In a question looking for what "could be false," the wrong choices all *must* be true.

A 180 test taker is able to characterize in every case what the right answer and the wrong choices will be like.

(A), (B), (D), and (E) all conform perfectly to this arrangement, so we can cross those off.

(C) must therefore be the choice that could be false. We know that locked chest 3 doesn't have opals or rubies, and it *never* contains silver or gold, so it must contain platinum and/or topaz. Chest 3 could contain just platinum instead of the topaz listed in the choice, so (C) is indeed what the test makers are after here.

What's Next?

Did this one drive you nuts? If so, you must not have made the deductions discussed above, because, as you can see from the explanations, these deductions really make the questions much more manageable. The game is very difficult to handle without them.

Big deductions, however, won't save you in the following game. In "Children's Questions," you'll revisit the Time Warp game type that you saw in chapter 3. But this time, it's mixed with a definite Sequencing element, making it all the more annoying. Rev up your forward and backward thinking skills and see what you can make of this game within a game.

LOGIC GAME 18

A teacher is organizing a game of "Questions" to be played by the five children in her class. The game begins with the children standing in five adjacent spaces, numbered 1 to 5 from front to back. As the game begins, the children are standing in the following order, from front to back: Kim, Ho, Mal, Quincy, Fahroud.

In each round of the game, the teacher calls out one of two colors, either red or blue.

If red is called, then exactly two questions will be asked: The child in space 3 will ask a question of the child in space 2, and the child in space 5 will ask a question of the child in space 4.

If blue is called, then exactly two questions will be asked: The child in space 2 will ask a question of the child in space 1, and the child in space 4 will ask a question of the child in space 3.

When a child who has been asked a question does not answer correctly, he or she changes places in line with the asker. When a child who has been asked a question answers correctly, he or she does not change places with the asker.

The teacher never calls the same color in two consecutive rounds of the game.

1. Which one of the following could be the order of children, listed from front to back, after exactly one round of the game in which the teacher called red?

    (A) Quincy, Ho, Mal, Kim, Fahroud
    (B) Ho, Kim, Mal, Fahroud, Quincy
    (C) Kim, Mal, Ho, Quincy, Fahroud
    (D) Ho, Kim, Mal, Quincy, Fahroud
    (E) Kim, Mal Quincy, Fahroud, Ho

2. Which one of the following could be the order of children, listed from front to back, after exactly one round of the game in which the teacher called blue?

    (A) Ho, Mal, Kim, Quincy, Fahroud
    (B) Kim, Mal, Ho, Fahroud, Quincy
    (C) Ho, Kim, Mal, Fahroud, Quincy
    (D) Ho, Kim, Quincy, Fahroud, Mal
    (E) Kim, Ho, Mal, Quincy, Fahroud

3. Which one of the following could be true after the first two rounds of the game?

    (A) Fahroud has answered one question.
    (B) Ho has asked two questions.
    (C) Kim has asked one question.
    (D) Mal has answered two questions.
    (E) Quincy has answered two questions.

4. If after three rounds of the game Ho and Fahroud have advanced as far to the front of the line as possible, then all of the following pairs of children could be standing in adjacent spaces after the third round of the game EXCEPT

    (A) Fahroud and Ho
    (B) Fahroud and Mal
    (C) Kim and Mal
    (D) Kim and Quincy
    (E) Mal and Quincy

5. If, after three rounds of the game, Quincy has advanced as far to the front of the line as possible, and if the other four children are still in the same positions relative to each other, then which one of the following must be true?

    (A) After three rounds of the game, Fahroud stands in the space in which Mal was standing after two rounds of the game.
    (B) After two rounds of the game, Ho stands in the space in which Quincy was standing after one round of the game.
    (C) After two rounds of the game, Kim stands in the space in which Ho was standing after one round of the game.
    (D) After three rounds of the game, Kim stands in the space in which Mal was standing at the beginning of the game.
    (E) After two rounds of the game, Mal stands in the space in which Quincy was standing after one round of the game.

6. If, after four rounds of the game, the order of children from front to back is Fahroud, Ho, Quincy, Kim, Mal, then which one of the following must be false?

    (A) Ho answered a question correctly in round 1.
    (B) Ho answered a question incorrectly in round 4.
    (C) Kim answered a question correctly in round 2.
    (D) Mal answered a question incorrectly in round 2.
    (E) Mal answered a question incorrectly in round 3.

Logic Game 18: Children's Questions

What Makes It Difficult

A quick scan of the game—with its references to things like "if blue is called" and "if after three rounds"—suggests that this is a Process game, but it also contains a strong Sequencing element: five students lined up from front to back, 1 through 5. Our main job—keeping track of the changes in position that result from questions being answered correctly or incorrectly—doesn't become fully clear until the fourth indented rule, and that's disconcerting to some.

A 180 test taker perseveres and doesn't get flustered if the full dimensions of the game aren't revealed immediately.

As mentioned earlier, Process games are generally not very ripe for big deductions, and this one is no exception. The rules speak to the question-answer and switching mechanisms in general, but you need to wait for the questions to provide concrete information that put the rules into action. That means that you simply have to find a reasonable way to represent the action so that it's accessible to you, and then power through the questions. And there are some truly nasty ones in this set. For example, in this game type we expect the test makers to ask us to think forward and backward in time—but four rounds out (question 6)?! That's just mean. And in question 5, the choices are almost as long as the wordy stem, requiring us to perform mental gymnastics to work through the question *and* to decipher the choices.

There's not much you can do up front other than understand the general situation, work through each rule, and settle on a means of sketching the action that will help you through the questions. From there, it's simply a matter of execution, although as always there are a few points that will aid you in your attack on the game.

Keys to the Game

Red and blue rounds must alternate (Rule 5), and it's crucial that you keep track of the colors of each round. Some early questions explicitly indicate which colors are called out; others will strongly imply it; and the hardest questions force you to figure out in what order the colors are called out based on the ordering of the children in later rounds.

Stay focused on the key issues governing the game, namely: What happens when a color is called out? What happens when a question is answered correctly? What happens when a question is answered incorrectly? And most importantly: What must have happened in earlier rounds to put the children into position to end up where we find them later on?

Hypothesize: What *could* happen? Go through some "what ifs" about the game to get a feel for how the process works. There's no need to go crazy working out scenarios to get your feet wet, since the first question or two in process games usually tests your basic understanding of the game. But it's still good to do a quick warm-up for those.

Answers and Explanations

1. C   2. E   3. D   4. B   5. B   6. C

1. C

The first question, as is often the case in Process games, tests nothing more than a most rudimentary understanding of the game action and rules. We're asked to project just one round out, and we're told explicitly that it's a red round. When red is called, child 3 asks child 2 a question, 5 asks 4, and 1 is uninvolved. This last bit means that after this round the original child 1, Kim, will remain in her original place. So the best way to begin is by immediately rejecting (A), (B), and (D), the choices that shift Kim's position.

> A 180 test taker relies on effective answer choice strategies to eliminate choices in bulk whenever possible.

Of the remaining choices, (C) reflects the outcome if Quincy in space 4 answers correctly but Ho in space 2 does not: Fahroud and Quincy would stay put, while Ho and Mal would exchange spaces 2 and 3.

2. E

In the same vein, and even easier. In a "blue" round, child 5 (Fahroud, to begin with) is inactive, so the three choices that displace Fahroud, (B), (C), and (D), bite the dust immediately. If answerers 1 (Kim) and 3 (Mal) are both correct, then no one will move from the opening position, which just happens to be the scenario reflected in choice (E). The only possible difficulty here is if you assumed that the order must change. But then this question would in fact be a blessing in disguise, since it would eventually force you to abandon that notion. For the record, Kim can't possibly move back two places in line after only one round, so (A) can't possibly be the acceptable ordering we seek.

It was very generous of the test makers to begin the game with two basic questions testing the fundamentals. Things, however, get a bit more difficult from here.

3. D

We're given no new information, and need to find something that could be true after two rounds of the game. There's really no other option but to test the choices.

(A) Fahroud is all the way down in space 5 to begin with. If the game starts out with a blue round, Fahroud sits out round 1, and then asks a question in round 2. If red begins the game, then Fahroud asks Quincy a question in round 1. If Quincy answers correctly, Fahroud stays in space 5 and sits out blue round 2. If, however, Quincy answers Fahroud's question incorrectly in red round 1, they swap, and then Fahroud will have to ask the child in space 3 a question in blue round 2. No matter how we slice it, there's no way for Fahroud to have answered a question after the first two rounds, so (A) is incorrect.

(B) Can Ho ask two questions in the first two rounds? Well, we better start with a blue round, so that Ho in space 2 can present a question to Kim in space 1 (if we started with red, Ho would begin by answering a question, which isn't what we want). Again, there are two choices. If Kim answers

Ho's question correctly, then Ho stays in space 2 and would be forced to answer a question in red round 2. If Kim botches the question, then Ho moves up to space 1, and then neither asks nor answers a question in red round 2. No good.

(C) If red-blue is the order of the first two rounds, then Kim is idle in round 1 and answers a question in round 2. If blue-red is the order, then Kim would answer a question in round 1 and could possibly move down to space 2, but then would have to answer another question in red round 2. The bottom line is that Kim can't ask a single question in the first two rounds, so we have to press on.

(D) If we start off with a blue round, Mal in space 3 would answer a question addressed by Quincy in space 4. If Mal fumbles it, he would drop down to space 4, and then would answer a question from Fahroud in red round 2. (D) is therefore possible, and correct. For the record:

(E) Quincy can answer a question in round 1 if red is called out first, but cannot answer a second question in round 2. That's because if he answers correctly, he stays in space 4 and then must ask a question in blue round 2. And if he answers incorrectly, then he drops down to space 5 where he'd have to sit out blue round 2.

Notice that there's really nothing to draw here; you simply need to run through the first two rounds in your head to see whether each choice is possible.

4. B

A complex challenge, considering that we must deduce the colors called out, and the switches that must occur, to get Ho and Fahroud as far to the front as possible by the end of the third round. Then we need to evaluate the ordering at the end. Now Ho, beginning in space 2, is pretty close to the front as is. Three rounds is plenty of time to get him up to the front of the line, and that could happen whether red-blue-red is called or blue-red-blue. Fahroud, however, begins way down in the cellar, so the operative question concerns what must happen to enable him to cover the most distance.

A 180 test taker focuses on the operative questions; that is, the ones that immediately help him drive the action forward.

In order for Fahroud to get as far as possible, the order of the rounds must be red-blue-red; if blue was first, then Fahroud would sit out the entire first round, contrary to our cause. Meanwhile, as long as Ho answers Mal's opening question correctly and stumps Kim in blue round 2, he could get to No.1 and keep that position after round 3. So here's what must be the case following red round 1:

intial order	after round 1
K	K
H	H
M	M
Q	F
F	Q

In blue round 2, Fahroud continues his advance, while Ho captures the No. 1 space:

intial order	after round 1	after round 2
K	K	H
H	H	K
M	M	F
Q	F	M
F	Q	Q

In red round 3, Fahroud must advance yet again by stumping Kim, as the stem requires, and Quincy in 5 poses a question to Mal in 4. The mandate in the stem, however, says nothing about this interaction, so Mal may get it right, and stay put, or may bobble it, and slip into last place:

intial order	after round 1	after round 2	after round 3
K	K	H	H
H	H	K	F
M	M	F	K
Q	F	M	M or Q
F	Q	Q	M or Q

Finally we're in a position to answer the question: After round 3, Fahroud and Mal can't be next to each other in line, which makes (B) correct. (A) and (E) list children that must be adjacent (notice that no matter what happens between Mal and Quincy in the last round, they'll still be adjacent), while (C) and (D) contain kids that merely could be neighbors, depending on Mal's answer in round 3.

5. B

This time it's Quincy who moves "as far to the front of the line as possible," but the investigation works the same way: How far can he get in three rounds? Given a "blue" round 1, which of course is possible, he can stump Mal, move to position No. 3, stump the No. 2 kid, take over position No. 2, and then stump the No. 1 kid and move into first place. This is the only way Quincy can move that far front, so blue-red-blue must be the order of the rounds. But wait—there's another piece of hypothetical info: At the end of the third round, the other four kids must still be "in the same positions relative to each other." So with Quincy in space 1 after round 3, Kim, Ho, Mal, and Fahroud must bring up the rear in that order.

intial order	after round 3
K	Q
H	K
M	H
Q	M
F	F

So figuring out the shape of things after three rounds isn't so difficult, but the choices pose new problems, comparing, as they do, the positions after round 3 with positions earlier in the game. We can dispose of (D) quickly: We know that Kim is in second place after round 3, while Mal started the game in third. The rest, however, deal with interim rounds 1 and 2, which are a bit hard to visualize without officially plotting them out. If you can handle all that in your head, fantastic, but if not, it's not unreasonable to quickly fill in the gaps between the beginning and round 3.

In blue round 1, we know Quincy must begin his ascent by switching with Mal, but what happens between Kim and Ho? A little analysis reveals that Kim must answer correctly, because if she doesn't, she'll slip into space 2, which will make her Quincy's next victim in round 2. That's too much space lost for Kim; she'll never be able to get back to space 2 by the end of round 3. So here's what we now know:

intial order	after round 1	after round 2	after round 3
K	K		Q
H	H		K
M	Q		H
Q	M		M
F	F		F

All of the remaining choices involve round 2, so we'll have to press on and fill in the final empty column. Start with the obvious: Quincy continues to climb, stumping Ho, so switch those. In this red round, Fahroud in 5 interrogates Mal in 4, but knowing that after round 3 they remain in that order, it's impossible for them to switch and then immediately switch back a round later. So Mal will have to get it right, keeping those two where they are:

intial order	after round 1	after round 2	after round 3
K	K	K	Q
H	H	Q	K
M	Q	H	H
Q	M	M	M
F	F	F	F

This is the only way the children can be in a position to produce the ordering that we know results from round 3. In round 3, Quincy completes his journey to the top, satisfying one condition in the stem, while Ho in 3 holds off Mal in 4, satisfying the other requirement. Now we can see for sure that (B) has it right while the others are off base.

That's a decent amount of work, but still, it's feasible if you maintain your focus and follow through the necessary steps in an efficient and orderly manner.

A 180 test taker creates the time needed to work out the tough questions by effective time-management in the rest of the section.

---

6. C

One final question, and there's no relief in sight—in fact, this one's even worse, if possible, since it appears we have to go out four rounds in search of something that *must* be false. How can we possibly know what happens between the initial ordering and the one we're told is in effect after round 4? A little cleverness is required here. Does anything in particular strike you about the ordering given in the stem? Fahroud's performance should stand out; he started the game in the basement, and is now proudly standing in first place. How could that have happened? There's only one way: red-blue-red-blue must be the four rounds, since starting with blue wouldn't give Fahroud enough time to capture first place. So once again, we know the colors of each round, and thanks to our work in the previous questions it might now be obvious that Fahroud must advance through a string of stumpers that allow him to move ahead one space at a time. The difficulty, again, will be to figure out what happens in the other question asked in each round in order to make the ordering listed in the stem possible. We'll just have to plot out the rounds.

We know the initial ordering, of course; we know that red is called in round 1; and we know that F and Q must switch places. The issue is the other question, in this case, Mal asking Ho. If Ho gets it wrong, then Mal will take over second place; but since Mal needs to end up in the cellar after round 4, this can't be—it would put Mal too far up after round 1 to get down to space 5 by the end of round 4. So Ho must have met the challenge.

intial order	after round 1	after round 2	after round 3	after round 4
K	K			F
H	H			H
M	M			Q
Q	F			K
F	Q			M

You can (or perhaps you already did) fill in the remaining two rounds in similar fashion, keeping in mind Fahroud's steady and relentless advance, and the other correct or incorrect answers that must be given in order for round 4 to turn out as it does. Here's the complete picture:

intial order	after round 1	after round 2	after round 3	after round 4
K	K	H	H	F
H	H	K	F	H
M	M	F	K	Q
Q	F	M	Q	K
F	Q	Q	M	M

Now we can determine that (C) must be false: Kim must have fumbled her question in round 2, or else she wouldn't be able to get down to fourth place by the end of round 4.

What's Next?

The good news is that this game is finally over. The bad news is that there are two left that are just as bad, maybe worse. (But you *are* enjoying these, right?)

LOGIC GAME 19

An automobile dealership displays its cars for sale in eight adjacent showrooms numbered 1 through 8 from left to right. On display are cars of each of four body styles: coupe, hatchback, sedan, and wagon. Five of the models displayed come with the base options package; three come with the performance options package. All cars are painted one of three colors: lime, maroon, or orange. In each showroom are cars of exactly one style, one options package, and one color, in accordance with the following conditions:

At most, three of any body style is displayed.

Sedans are exhibited in more showrooms than any other body style and are always displayed adjacent to coupes.

Exactly one showroom exhibits wagons, which are maroon and come with the base options package.

If any showroom has lime colored cars, those cars are performance-package coupes.

Showroom 1 contains coupes.

The cars in Showroom 3 are orange and have the performance package.

1. Which one of the following could be a complete and accurate arrangement of the body styles in showrooms 1 through 8, respectively?

    (A) coupe, wagon, sedan, coupe, sedan, sedan, hatchback, hatchback
    (B) coupe, sedan, hatchback, wagon, hatchback, coupe, sedan, hatchback
    (C) coupe, sedan, hatchback, sedan, coupe, sedan, hatchback, hatchback
    (D) coupe, sedan, hatchback, sedan, coupe, sedan, wagon, hatchback
    (E) sedan, coupe, wagon, sedan, coupe, sedan, hatchback, hatchback

2. Each of the following statements could be true EXCEPT:

    (A) Cars in showroom 1 are painted lime.
    (B) Cars in showroom 2 are painted lime.
    (C) Cars in showroom 4 are painted lime.
    (D) Maroon wagons cannot occupy showroom 3.
    (E) Three showrooms display sedans.

3. If the cars in showroom 5 are painted lime, which one of the following must be true?

    (A) Hatchbacks are on display in showroom 3.
    (B) Hatchbacks are on display in showroom 4.
    (C) Wagons are on display in showroom 4.
    (D) The showroom exhibiting wagons is adjacent to a showroom exhibiting sedans.
    (E) Showroom 1 exhibits performance-package cars.

4. Which one of the following statements about the cars on display could be true?

    (A) Three showrooms contain cars painted lime.
    (B) Two showrooms contain lime coupes, and two showrooms contain performance-package hatchbacks.
    (C) Every orange car on display is a performance-package hatchback.
    (D) The maroon wagons are not displayed adjacent to either sedans or hatchbacks.
    (E) All hatchbacks and wagons are displayed in odd-numbered showrooms.

5. At most, how many orange cars can be displayed with the base option package?

    (A) 2
    (B) 3
    (C) 4
    (D) 5
    (E) 6

6. Which one of the following must be true?

    (A) If there are no lime cars, then at least one showroom must display maroon coupes.
    (B) If only one showroom displays orange cars, then exactly two showrooms display lime cars.
    (C) If exactly two rooms contain performance-package maroon cars, then one of them contains coupes.
    (D) If there are no performance-package sedans, then there must be a room with orange performance-package coupes.
    (E) If showroom 4 displays the only maroon cars, then showroom 3 displays performance-package hatchbacks.

Logic Game 19: Car Dealership

What Makes it Difficult

The situation is fairly straightforward: a car dealership has 8 rooms full of cars of differing styles, options, and colors. Our job is to *Group* them (we're selecting a certain number of each body style, options level, and color), *Match* them up with each other, and also *Sequence* them left to right according to their showroom number. So this is essentially a triple-skill Hybrid game. Whereas they've done a little of the grouping for us (3 performance and 5 base options packages), we will still have to answer questions about how many of each body style and how many of each color can be present.

We also have to track how each entity type constrains not only entities of the same type, but also entities of the other two types. For example, the lime color goes with coupe and performance only. Wagon goes with maroon and basic only.

The test makers also hit us with five questions in one with question 6: all of the choices begin with a hypothetical, requiring you to try each answer on its own. It's a classic time wasting tactic that we see in every LSAT.

Keys to the Game

Of the 8 rooms, 1 has wagons, 2 have coupes, 2 have hatchbacks, and 3 have sedans. Test takers who didn't do this math at the outset suffered terribly during this game, because the other major deductions—not to mention most of the questions—were based on this inference.

The paragraph says "On display are cars of each of four body styles...." The *are* in this sentence guarantees that each style is used at least once. Next, Rule 1 tells us the styles can't be used more than three times, meaning it's either 1, 2, or 3 of each style. With four styles and only eight slots, the combinations are already limited. Rule 2 limits them further by telling us that sedans occur more often than any other style. That means sedans must occur 3 times, and all others must occur either twice or once. Finally, Rule 3 tells us that it's the wagons that occur one time. For the styles to add up to 8, we've got to have 2 of each of the coupes and the hatchbacks.

> A 180 test taker attempts to define the entities as clearly as possible before launching into the question set.

Slot 2 must be sedans, and the coupe that isn't room 1 is surrounded by sedans: CS...SCS.... Now that we know there are 3 sedans and 2 coupes, the second half of Rule 2 is very important, especially because Rule 5 tells us that one of the coupes is in room 1. To have all of the sedans adjacent to the coupes, room 2 must be one of the sedans, and the remaining coupe must be surrounded by sedans. Note, also, that all sedans (as well as all hatchbacks) are either orange or maroon—Rule 4 makes any lime car a coupe.

Slot 3 is a sedan or a hatchback. Because slot 2 is a sedan, we can't put the second coupe in slot 3—that wouldn't leave room to place all 3 sedans adjacent to coupes. Also, because the only wagon is a maroon wagon (Rule 3), slot 3 can't contain the wagon. So, only sedans or hatchbacks could occupy slot 3.

Answers and Explanations

1. D   2. B   3. A   4. C   5. C   6. E

1. D

We start by using the rules individually to eliminate the wrong choices. Rule 1 doesn't help us. Rule 2 eliminates (B) because we've got more hatchbacks than sedans and (A) because the last sedan, in slot 6, isn't next to a coupe. (C) does not contain any wagons, which is in complete contrast to Rule 3. Rule 4 is about colors, so it doesn't help us here. Rule 5 invalidates (E), leaving only (D).

2. B

This EXCEPT question is asking us for an answer that must be false. The others are answers that could be true or must be true (remember that a statement that must be true is certainly something that *could* be true). Choice (B) is the one that's impossible because of this chain of logic: (1) we have to display three rooms of sedans (Rules 1 and 2); (2) all three sedan rooms must be adjacent to a coupe room (Rule 2); (3) we can only have 2 coupe rooms (Rules 1 and 2), and one is in slot 1 (Rule 5); THEREFORE, slot 2 must be one of the three sedans, and the other two sedan rooms will surround the remaining coupe room. That means slot 2 can't be lime because lime guarantees coupe (Rule 4). Choice (E) is a must-be-true statement based on Rules 1 and 2; the others are merely possible.

3. A

If room 5 is lime, then according to Rule 4, it is a lime performance coupe. Because coupes are adjacent only to sedans (see earlier deductions), rooms 4 and 6 are sedans, as is room 2. That accounts for all three of our rooms with sedans, which means room 3 must be either hatchbacks or wagons. Because the only wagons room will contain maroon and base-model wagons, room 3 must contain hatchbacks. That's (A).

4. C

This question functions just like an Acceptability question. Four choices will create violations. (A) is a problem because it means we'd have three coupe rooms (Rule 4), but we deduced earlier that exactly two rooms would be coupes. (B) would mean we'd have four performance car rooms: two lime rooms would be two lime/performance/coupe rooms (Rule 4) added to the two performance hatchback rooms, but the paragraph states that we have five base-model cars and three performance cars. (C) is acceptable—we could, for example, have orange cars only in room 3—and is therefore our answer. (D) is impossible because the wagons would then have to be adjacent to coupes, and as we inferred earlier, the coupes are adjacent only to sedans. Finally, (E) is incorrect because putting hatchbacks and the wagons in the remaining odd-numbered rooms (3, 5, and 7) would prevent two of the three sedans from being adjacent to coupes.

5. C

Usually, we'd expect to have to make a deduction to answer a question like this. Many test takers, when they don't see any relevant deduction, second-guess their understanding of the game and waste time spinning their wheels. This question is deceptively simple. It's actually just a math problem: we've got to have exactly five rooms with base-option cars. One of them is the maroon-wagon room. All four others could be orange, as in:

1	2	3	4	5	6	7	9
C	**S**	S	C	**S**	**H**	**H**	W
O	**O**	O	O	**O**	**O**	**O**	M
P	**B**	P	P	**B**	**B**	**B**	B

The 180 test taker simply tries a possible combination or two instead of wasting time second-guessing his understanding of the game.

---

6. E

Here's a five-question question: any time you see all five answers start with "If," you're looking at a good question to leave for later, because the test makers are trying to force you to try as many as five separate hypotheticals. They use this device regularly to consume time. The 180 test taker recognizes that this question is designed to consume time and starts working backward from choice (E), because the correct answers to these time-consuming questions are statistically skewed toward (D) and (E).

Sure enough, (E) must be true: if the only maroon cars are in room 4, that makes them wagons. This, in turn, means room 3 cannot contain either sedans or coupes because Rule 2 puts sedans in room 2 and requires that the second coupe room be surrounded by the remaining two sedan rooms. Therefore, room 3 must display hatchbacks.

Incidentally, (D) would mean that room 3 contains hatchbacks because it has to be either sedans or hatchbacks; these performance-package maroon cars could be any of coupes, sedans, or hatchbacks in (C). Also, if (B)'s hypothetical were true, we could have one orange and seven maroon cars, and all the coupes could be orange, making (A) unnecessary.

A 180 test taker carries information to its logical, and relevant, conclusions.

What's Next?

Things got a bit nasty at the end there, big deductions and all. But that is, after all, what we'd expect from the toughest of the tough. Next up is our final Logic Game, and of course it wouldn't be right if we didn't end with another real killer. It's the story of a small town as submitted by town residents and compiled into a documentary by a video editor.

LOGIC GAME 20

A video editor is assembling a single documentary of a small town from five reels of footage submitted by town residents. Exactly three reels—R, S, and T—contain town events, and exactly two reels—M and N—contain landscapes. Each reel arrives at the editor's studio separately. Immediately upon receipt, each reel is used in exactly one of two ways:

    Either the reel, by itself, forms a single scene of the documentary, or the reel is combined with one or more reels to form a single scene of the documentary.

    The documentary is assembled according to the following restrictions:

    Any reel that is not combined with another reel forms a single scene bearing the name of that reel.

    If either landscape reel is received immediately before or immediately after reel R, then the footage on that landscape reel will be combined with the footage on reel R to form a single scene R.

    If either landscape reel is received immediately before or immediately after reel S, then the footage on that landscape reel will be combined with the footage on reel S to form a single scene S.

    Reel N is received before reel R.

    Scenes will appear in the completed documentary in the order in which they are formed.

1. Which one of the following could be the ordering of scenes, from first to last, contained in the completed documentary after all of the reels have been received?

    (A)   N, R, S, T, M
    (B)   R, S, T, M, N
    (C)   N, T, M, S, R
    (D)   N, M, T, S, R
    (E)   M, T, S, T, N

2. What is the minimum number of scenes that the documentary must contain after all of the reels have been received?

    (A)   1
    (B)   2
    (C)   3
    (D)   4
    (E)   5

3. If the unfinished documentary consists of exactly two scenes, and reel S is the only reel yet to be received, then all of the following could be true EXCEPT

    (A)   Reel T was received second.
    (B)   Reel N was received second.
    (C)   Reel T was received first.
    (D)   Reel M was received third.
    (E)   Reel R was received third.

4. Which one of the following must be true of a completed documentary that consists of exactly five scenes?

    (A)   Reel M was received second.
    (B)   Reel N was received first.
    (C)   Reel R was received third.
    (D)   Reel S was received fifth.
    (E)   Reel T was received third.

5. If the completed documentary consists of exactly four scenes, then the first four reels can have been received in which one of the following orders?

    (A)   N, S, T, R
    (B)   N, M, T, S
    (C)   S, M, R, T
    (D)   M, T, N, R
    (E)   T, N, S, M

6. If the completed documentary consists of scenes R, T, and S, in order from first to last, then which one of the following must be true?

    (A)   Reel N was received first.
    (B)   Reel R was received third.
    (C)   Reel T was received third.
    (D)   Reel T was received fourth.
    (E)   Reel S was received fifth.

7. If, after all the reels are received, no two reels have been combined to form a scene, then which one of the following CANNOT be true?

    (A)   Reel N was received before reel T.
    (B)   Reel S was received before reel M.
    (C)   Reel S was received before reel R.
    (D)   Reel M was received before reel N.
    (E)   Reel T was received before reel S.

Logic Game 20: The Video of a Small Town

What Makes It Difficult

What *doesn't* make it difficult? We trust that you found enough to give you a real headache in this one to safely skip this formality and move right to the keys to the game.

Keys to the Game

Get a grasp of the unusual game action. As unusual as the game is, it consists of game actions you've seen before. Footage reels are received in order, no two reels at the same time, which suggests sequencing. And the reels and scenes change over time, which suggests a process element. A tough combo, no doubt, but if you rely on your skills in each individual area, you should be okay.

> A 180 test taker breaks down even an "oddball" game into its most familiar elements.

Get a grasp of the key issues that govern the game, namely: In what order are the reels received? What happens when a reel arrives? Based on the order of reels received, what scenes, in what order, will make up the documentary?

Distinguish between the different types of reels to keep them straight. Using uppercase for town events (R, S, T) and lowercase for landscapes (m, n) works fine.

Perform a few run-throughs to make sure you understand how the rules work. It pays to even use an extreme example to illustrate. If the first three scenes to arrive are m, R, and n, in that order, then both m and n will be consumed by R, resulting in one scene entitled R, containing the footage from m, n, and R combined.

> A 180 test taker makes sure she understands how complicated rules work before wading into the questions.

Each town events reel (R, S, and T) will end up in the completed documentary as a scene bearing its name; that's because no rules allow for the renaming of R, S, and T. The only question is whether m and n, the landscape reels, will make it unscathed into the big show, or if (depending on the order in which the reels are received) they'll get eaten and incorporated into R and/or S. This leads to a numbers deduction:

The completed documentary will consist of a minimum of three scenes (if both m and n disappear) or a maximum of five scenes (if both m and n survive).

The only entity that has no part in the combination rules is town events reel T. As the free agent in this game, T has the ability to get between R and S and the vulnerable landscape reels, and will therefore most likely play a large role in determining the fate of m and n.

Answers and Explanations

1. D   2. C   3. A   4. E   5. D   6. A   7. B

1. D

This Acceptability question provides a welcome chance to test your understanding of the game. Rule 4 is the easiest to check, and it clearly eliminates (B), which has reel n received way after reel R. Choice (A) is no good because it features n next to R; but R would swallow up n and n would disappear, according to Rule 2. Similarly, (C) is out thanks to Rule 3: S would modify scene m to create a new scene S. (E) is out of the question: As we saw above, scenes R, S, and T must be part of the completed documentary, but in (E), R has inexplicably disappeared and T has been used twice. No good; only one appearance per reel, and only m and n can disappear. That leaves (D), and it's okay: If the reels came in in that order, none would be eaten by any of the others and no rules would be violated.

2. C

We already considered this issue in our dissection of the game above, so this question is a breeze. We saw that the completed documentary must consist of a minimum of three scenes, if both m and n disappear, or a maximum of five scenes if both m and n survive.

3. A

The second part of the if-clause is a good place to start: S is the only reel not yet received, meaning that R, T, m, and n have been received.

A 180 test taker always strives to turn negative statements into positive ones.

But wait: Even having received all four of these reels, the unfinished documentary, we're told, contains only two scenes so far. That can only mean that m and n have been eaten up; that they've disappeared. Well, who could have done such a thing? It's pretty clear by now: The only reels that swallow up other reels in this game are R and S, but S hasn't showed up yet, so we're forced to conclude that the reels must have been received in such a way as to allow R to swallow up both m and n. R, therefore, must have been received right in between m and n.

The only choice not consistent with this state of affairs is choice (A): If reel T were received second, then there'd be no way for R to be in position to eat both m and n. Receiving reels m-T-n-R, in that order, would lead to an unfinished piece with three scenes: m, T, and R. Similarly, n-T-m-R or n-T-R-m would also give us three scenes. R can't be received before n, so these are the only possibilities under (A)'s circumstances; and since none of them result in only two scenes, (A) cannot be true and is therefore the correct answer.

(B), (C), and (E) are all shown to be possible by this ordering of received reels: T-n-R-m. In this case, reel n is received immediately before R, and reel m is received immediately after R, which means both would be combined with R and would therefore disappear, leaving exactly two scenes (T and R) awaiting S's arrival.

(D) If the first four reels are received in the order n-R-m-T, then n and m will again disappear into R, and only R and T will be left, so it is possible for m to have been received third in this situation.

4. E

"Completed documentary" means that all five reels have been received, and " . . . consisting of five scenes" means that no reel got swallowed up by another; in other words, both m and n must have survived.

> A 180 test taker has the ability to see past the wording the test makers give him, and recognize the more specific and helpful implications of that wording.

How can this be? Well, m and n can survive only if they both keep plenty of distance from the landscape-reel eaters, R and S. In fact, the only way that m and n aren't received at some point consecutively with R and S is if neutral reel T breaks the two groups up. If T is received third, then it's possible to place the two landscape reels m and n on one side of T, and the other two events reels R and S on the other side of T. Thanks to Rule 4, we can't have n coming after R, so this situation further breaks down to this: Reels m and n, in either order, are received first and second; T is received third; R and S, in either order, come in fourth and fifth. There's no other way to protect m and n from being consumed by R or S. T must be received right in the middle in order to allow the documentary to have the full five scenes, so (E) is the correct answer here.

(A), (B), and (D) are all possible based on the ordering discussed above—there's flexibility as to the order of m in relation to n in the first two slots, and R in relation to S in the last two. But none of these must be true.

(C) No way: T is received third, as discussed above.

5. D

Don't be fooled—the answer choices list only the first four reels received, but the question is about the *completed* documentary, which means that we have to take into consideration the fifth reel received as well. (That might not be a bad way to start—add the missing reel to each of the choices: (A) m; (B) R; (C) n; (D) S; (E) R.) We're trying to find the ordering of received reels (including the fifth reel that we just indicated) that will result in a *four*-scene documentary. Let's see what happens.

(A) Follow the action from the beginning: n forms a scene, S swallows up the n scene to form a single S scene, T and R follow with their own scenes . . . but then m, as the fifth reel received, will be combined with scene R, leaving only three scenes in the final documentary: S, T, and R.

(B) We just saw in the previous question that if T is third, no reels get combined and the completed documentary will contain five scenes, not the four we're going for here.

(C) Rule 4 kills this one immediately—n can't be the last reel received, since it can never be received after R.

(D) does the trick: If the first four reels received are m, T, n, and R, in that order, then up to that point, reel m will stay intact but reel n will be absorbed by reel R, and the documentary scenes will look like this: m, T, R. The scene yet to be received in this scenario is S, and after receipt it will form its own scene after R, giving us the requisite four-scene documentary (m, T, R, S).

(E) Same logic here as in (A) above: S would swallow up both n and m, even before reel R was received, again resulting in a three-scene documentary (T, S, and R).

6. A

The stem, once translated, tells us that both reels m and n have been swallowed up—the only question is *when*. Rule 4 specifies that n must be received before R. Beginning then with n—R—T—S as the partial order of reels received, our only task is to fit m into this order in such a way as to result in a completed documentary made up of scenes R, T, and S. Under these circumstances m can't come right before n, because if that happened, m would survive, and the completed piece would consist of scenes m, R, T, and S. And that's enough to get us to the right answer: No matter where we end up working m into the ordering, n must be the first reel received, choice (A). Note that m cannot be received second, immediately after n, because then n would not combine with R and scene n would be the first scene of the documentary.

(B) is impossible: If R is received third, and T and S come after it in the finished documentary, then both m and n must have been received before R, in which case one of those reels would have been converted into its own scene.

(C) is possible, but not necessary; the order of reels received could have been n-R-m-T-S, in which case m, rather than T, would be received third.

(D) and (E) are both invalidated by this ordering of reels received: n-R-T-S-m. Both m and n would drop out as scheduled, leaving us with the completed documentary listed in the stem.

> A 180 test taker gets stronger as she progresses through a game thanks to her increased familiarity with it, which makes questions late in the set a bit more manageable.

7. B

If this sounds familiar, there's a good reason: it's just question 4 all over again. " . . . no two reels were combined to form a scene . . . " is the same thing as " . . . completed documentary consisting of five scenes."

And we saw in question 4 how this must come about: m and n, in either order, are received first and second; T is received third; R and S, in either order, must come in fourth and fifth. Simplified: m/n-T-R/S. From this it's simple to see that S cannot be received before m, and that choice (B) is correct.

(A) and (E) both must be true, according to the ordering listed above.

(C) and (D) both could be true, as the acceptable ordering m-n-T-S-R shows.

A 180 test taker is often rewarded with a "gimme" simply for making it to the end of a difficult game.

---

section two

LOGICAL REASONING

CHAPTER SIX

The Logical Reasoning Challenge

Do you like to point out the unwarranted assumptions in others' arguments? Do you like to home in on logical flaws like a detective, and analyze precisely how arguments could be made better or worse? Then LSAT Logical Reasoning, which accounts for not one, but two of the four scored sections of the LSAT, is for you. So start dissecting op-ed pieces and cutting the contestants on television debates down to size. When you see your LSAT score, you'll be glad you did!

1. If all of the statements in the passage are true, each of the following must also be true EXCEPT:

(A) Op-ed pieces and television debates contain content that is related in some way to material tested in the Logical Reasoning sections of the LSAT.
(B) No other LSAT question type appears in more sections of the LSAT than Logical Reasoning.
(C) Mastering the Logical Reasoning question type will ensure an excellent LSAT score.
(D) Logical flaws and assumptions are among the topics tested on the LSAT.
(E) Thinking like a detective can favorably affect one's LSAT score.

Choice (C) is correct. Mastering Logical Reasoning is *necessary* to achieve a top LSAT score, but not *sufficient;* one must ace the other two sections on the test as well. You'll be hearing more about this distinction between necessary and sufficient conditions later on. (A) is valid: The instructor strongly implies that dissecting op-eds and debates will lead to a higher score, which, in fact, it certainly can. (B) plays off the numbers in the text. Since two of the four sections on the LSAT consist of Logical Reasoning questions, you don't have to know anything else about the test to deduce that no other question type could possibly take up more than two sections of the test. (D) legitimately ties the first two sentences to the first part of the third, and (E) is strongly suggested by the fact that the proclivity for playing detective inferably bodes well for one's Logical Reasoning performance.

So win arguments! Prove people wrong! Amaze your friends! Be the life of the party! Get a score of 180 on the LSAT! . . . Just a few of the many and varied uses of the ability to master the subtle art of Logical Reasoning.

Disclaimer: Hacking through the bogus arguments of others and/or demonstrating superior logical acumen in everyday conversation will NOT make you the most popular person in town.

The purpose of this chapter is to help you hone your critical thinking skills through practice on some of the toughest Logical Reasoning material around. The following offers some guidelines on how to get the most out of the Logical Reasoning material in this book.

USING THE LOGICAL REASONING QUESTIONS IN THIS BOOK

This section is broken up into a number of chapters each detailing various difficulties commonly encountered in LSAT Logical Reasoning. It is designed to allow you to learn as you go and to apply your learning to subsequent questions as you progress through the section.

- First, we introduce you to the five major categories of difficult Logical Reasoning questions.
- Then we offer in-depth practice with tough questions in each of these five major categories.
- After that, nine other common but often difficult Logical Reasoning features or structural elements are presented, each highlighted by an example.
- Finally, 38 additional questions representative of all the elements and forms discussed are served up for your practicing pleasure.

Instructions are provided throughout intended to lead you through the various sections. Here are a few general pointers to keep in mind when tackling all Logical Reasoning questions, but especially challenge questions like the ones you're about to see:

Keep your eye out for the author's evidence, conclusion, and any assumptions relied upon in the argument. The wordiness and logical subtlety of the questions that follow often cause test takers to lose sight of what's actually being said, and it's nearly impossible to answer questions like these correctly when one is foggy about the specifics. The conclusion is the "what" of the matter; the evidence is the reasons "why" the author feels entitled to make that particular claim; and assumptions are any missing premises that are nonetheless needed in order for the conclusion to stand.

Paraphrase the text. We include the same advice later on for the longer Reading Comprehension passages. You can get a leg up on tough text by simplifying the passage's ideas and translating them into your own words.

Observe timing guidelines. On the real test, 24–26 questions in 35 minutes works out roughly to a minute and a quarter per question. Try to answer the questions in this section in about that time, but you can certainly cut yourself a little slack considering the high level of difficulty of the questions in this section.

Familiarize yourself with the common Logical Reasoning concepts tested. Review the logical elements and structures discussed throughout the chapter, and look to recognize which of them are present in each Logical Reasoning question you encounter in this book as well as in any other questions you practice with during your LSAT preparation. While the specific subject matter (names, places, scenarios, etc.) changes from question to question and test to test, the underlying logical patterns remain incredibly consistent. Get to know them.

CHAPTER SEVEN

Types of Challenging Logical Reasoning Questions

You should already be aware that common Logical Reasoning questions ask about:
Assumptions
Methods of argument
Inferences
Roles of statements in an argument
Parallel reasoning
Logical flaws
Strengthening/Weakening an argument

Less common questions ask about:
Paradoxes
Points at issue between two different arguments
Application of a principle to a new situation

A few of these are inherently difficult question types, but most of them can be easy or difficult depending on other factors that we'll be analyzing for you in the next few chapters.

In this chapter, we'll take a brief look at the five categories of difficult Logical Reasoning questions: Formal Logic, Parallel Reasoning, Numbers and Statistics, Surveys and Studies, and Just Plain Tough. Chapter 8 will provide you with additional, in-depth practice with these categories, but first you need to familiarize yourself with the types of tough Logical Reasoning questions you're likely to see on test day.

FORMAL LOGIC

Formal Logic questions
These involve formal logic elements like inference or assumption, or use words and phrases like *if/then, only if, all, some, none, no , unless, most, every, always,* and *never.*

When a stimulus contains these words, translations and deductions are often possible, which in a way brings us into Logic Games territory. For some, this is good news. For others, the appearance of such Logic Games elements on the Logical Reasoning sections is an unmitigated disaster.

Let's try a Formal Logic example.

1. Kurtis wants to repair his vintage guitar. Only an experienced craftsperson can repair a vintage guitar, but no craftsperson has a chance of becoming a virtuoso guitar player.

   Which one of the following can be properly inferred from the passage?

   (A) Kurtis will be able to repair his vintage guitar.
   (B) Kurtis is not an experienced craftsperson.
   (C) Kurtis has no chance of becoming a virtuoso guitar player.
   (D) If Reed is an experienced craftsperson, then he will be able to repair Kurtis's vintage guitar.
   (E) If Reed has a chance to become a virtuoso guitar player, then Reed cannot repair Kurtis's vintage guitar.

Explanation: Kurtis's Guitar

Poor Kurtis is in a jam. His vintage guitar is on the blink and he needs to have it repaired. The "only" statement can be translated into a simple "if/then" statement: If someone can repair a vintage guitar, then that person is an experienced craftsperson. But (and here's the proper translation of the next clause) if someone has a chance at becoming a virtuoso, then that person is not a craftsperson. (Evidently, life's too short to master both.) Putting those together—which is essentially what we need to do in all Formal Logic questions—we see that repairing a vintage guitar and being a virtuoso are mutually exclusive, since the first requires a craftsperson and the second excludes all craftspeople.

Assumptions and Inferences
In a deductive argument, an assumption is a piece of necessary, but unstated, evidence. An inference is a necessary, but unstated, conclusion.

Not terrible tricky, but we're not out of the woods yet; the test makers have one last curve to throw us. Reed in choices (D) and (E) appears to pop out of nowhere, and normally in such cases we say that such characters are outside the scope. But Reed, while not mentioned in the stimulus, is actually *within* the scope since (D) and (E) contain hypotheticals. And (E) is simply an extension of what we just deduced: If Reed has a chance to become a virtuoso, then he can't be a craftsperson. And since only a craftsperson can repair a vintage guitar, noncraftsperson Reed can't help Kurtis out.

(A), (B), (C) All we know about Kurtis is what he *wants* to do: repair his guitar. And none of the statements tells us what that want leads to, so we can deduce nothing from it. We don't know whether Kurtis is an experienced craftsperson, or has a shot at virtuosity, so none of these can be inferred here.

(D) Did you get tricked by this one? The second clause translates to "If one can repair a vintage guitar, then one is an experienced craftsperson." That doesn't mean that any old experienced craftsperson can make the repairs—other skills might be needed that Reed doesn't possess. Stated another way: Being an experienced craftsperson is a *necessary,* but not *sufficient* trait of anyone who can repair a vintage guitar. (Remember those words—you'll be seeing them again.) In (D), Reed makes the cut on that account, but may fail in other ways.

PARALLEL REASONING

Parallel Reasoning is a perennial LSAT question type. Since time immemorial (well, at least since the early '90s) there have been two Parallel Reasoning questions on every LSAT Logical Reasoning section (occasionally just one, but almost always two per section). So on test day you can just about count on seeing four questions that ask you to find the choice that mirrors the logic of a stimulus. Test takers generally find these difficult because they're fairly lengthy and involved, and each choice tells a different story, making it hard to focus on the underlying logic of the original.

Parallel Reasoning questions
These identify an argument that uses the same kind of evidence to draw the same kind of conclusion.

Question 2 is a Parallel Reasoning question.

2. The only vehicles that have come across the bridge since dusk have been tanks. All of the tanks that came across the bridge since dusk were light tanks. Thus, all of the vehicles that have come across the bridge since dusk have been light.

    Which one of the following exhibits faulty reasoning most similar to the faulty reasoning exhibited in the passage above?

    (A) The only flowers in the garden are roses, and all of the roses in the garden are red. Therefore, all of the flowers in the garden are red flowers.
    (B) All of the bears in the zoo are carnivores. All of the bears in the zoo are also large. So all carnivores are large.
    (C) The only objects on the showroom floor are kitchen appliances. All of the kitchen appliances on the showroom floor come with two-year warranties. Therefore, all of the objects on the showroom floor come with two-year warranties.
    (D) All of the objects that spilled out upon the counter were rocks from Professor Wainright's collection. Professor Wainright's collection is exclusively made up of soft rocks. Thus, all of the objects that spilled out upon the counter were soft.
    (E) All of the paintings hanging in the gallery are oil paintings. The only paintings in the gallery are still-lifes and portraits. So all of the portraits hanging in the gallery are oil paintings.

Explanation: *Light* Tanks?

The flaw in the logic of the stimulus argument is suggested in its title: Can a tank be considered a *light* vehicle? A tank can certainly be light relative to other tanks; those are the kind we find here crossing the bridge since dusk. But a tank, by its very definition, cannot be considered a light *vehicle*; in fact, common sense would dictate otherwise. A tank is, by definition, a big, heavy, armor-plated vehicle, and so even the lightest tank is a heavy vehicle. The qualifier "light" is thus a relative term, and can't be automatically transferred from one class of objects to another class. A light elephant, for instance, is not a light animal.

Which one of the choices makes the same mistake of misapplying a relative qualifier? (D), the correct choice, copies the flaw exactly; the objects in Professor Wainright's collection may have been soft rocks (say shale or sandstone), but that doesn't mean they can be described as soft *objects*. Even a soft rock is a hard object, just as even a light tank is a heavy vehicle. And indeed, the chance of coming upon a light tank is just about as good as the chance of finding a soft rock. Note how the flaw here is based on a misunderstanding of sets. We'll be seeing that again later on.

(A) does not use a relative qualifier: red is red. Thus, (A) is perfectly right in saying that if all the flowers are red roses, then they all must be red flowers.

(B) makes a different kind of mistake: All X is Y, all X is Z; therefore, all Y is Z. Basically, (B) says that because the property of being a carnivore happens to coincide with the property of being large in this particular collection of zoo bears, therefore the property of being a carnivore must always be accompanied by the property of being large. There's no parallel to the misuse of a relative term in this one.

(C), like (A), does not use a relative qualifier. A "two-year warranty" means the same thing when applied to a "kitchen appliance" as it does when applied to "object" in general. So (C)'s argument is sound.

(E) follows suit; if all the paintings in the gallery are oil paintings, then any subset of the paintings in the gallery, such as the portraits in the gallery, must also be oil paintings. The term "oil painting" doesn't change its meaning when applied to "portrait" and to "painting."

NUMBERS AND STATISTICS

The LSAT test makers just *love* their statistics. Perhaps that's because statistics are used these days—often fallaciously—to supposedly "prove" or justify just about anything. That makes numbers and statistics a particularly fertile ground for Logical Flaw and Weaken the Argument questions, or, as in the case of question 3 below, a plain old inference question that requires us to simply interpret the stats.

3. The poems of Irish author Kieran Malloy sold most successfully in the period directly after Malloy received the O'Donovan Award, one of his country's highest literary honors, upon the release of his new book *Sea and Sky*. In the six-month period before Malloy received the award, 63% of the poems he sent out were accepted for publication, a far greater percentage than in the preceding years. In the six-month period directly following the award and a great deal of publicity, however, 91% of the poems Malloy submitted for publication were accepted. Interestingly, Malloy's revenue from publications was about the same in both periods, since he published the same number of poems in the six months before the release of *Sea and Sky* as he did in the six months following its release.

Which of the following statements can be properly concluded from the passage, if the information above is true?

(A) The O'Donovan Award brought Malloy's writing to the attention of more editors than had previously been aware of his work.

(B) Malloy was more interested in competing for literary awards than in increasing the amount he was paid for the publication of his poems.

(C) Malloy produced fewer poems in the six-month period following the publication of *Sea and Sky* than he had in the six-month period preceding its release.

(D) Malloy paid more attention to marketing his work after *Sea and Sky* received such a prestigious award.

(E) Due to his increased exposure after receiving the O'Donovan Award, Malloy was able to ask substantially more for the poems produced after the release of *Sea and Sky* than for the poems produced before its publication.

Explanation: The Poems of Kieran Malloy

Kieran Malloy's poems sold best after he received the O'Donovan Award. We are told 63% of the poems he submitted for publication were accepted during the six months before he received the award, while in the six months following the award, 91% of his poems were accepted for publication. On the other hand, in both periods, the same total number of Malloy's poems was accepted for publication.

A 180 test taker knows that often the test makers are testing her ability to distinguish between rates and raw numbers.

Consider what conclusion this evidence will support. If 63% equals the same number of poems before the award as 91% equals after the award, then Malloy must have produced more poems in the period before he received the award—that's the only way that the numbers can work out. (C) states this conclusion from the opposite angle: Malloy must have produced fewer poems in the six months after he received the O'Donovan Award. So, (C) is our correct answer choice.

(A), if anything, suggests that Malloy published more poems in the period after he received the award, which the stimulus tells us is not the case. Additionally, the stimulus doesn't give us any information about how editors might have responded to *Sea and Sky*, giving us no basis to form a conclusion about these editors.

(B) The information we're given pertains only to the hard facts of the matter: the number of poems Malloy produced and the revenue he gained during two periods of time. (B) is thus outside of the scope of the stimulus, since the author never tells us anything about Malloy's motivations for writing. There's no way to make a reasonable conclusion about his "interests" here.

(D) might suggest, like (C), that Malloy's revenue from publishing his poems would be higher in the second period, but we know that the revenue was the same. However, it's not even necessary to look so deeply into this choice. The primary reason we know (E) is incorrect is that marketing is never discussed in the stimulus.

A 180 test taker does not read more into a stimulus than is warranted.

(E) The author tells us that revenue from both periods is equal, since Malloy publishes the same number of poems in both. It follows, then, that if he had charged more money for his poems in the second period, he would have made more money than he did in the first period, which contradicts the information we're given in the stimulus. Because this choice is inconsistent with the passage, it certainly can't be inferred from it.

SURVEYS AND STUDIES

This category is related to the previous one. More often than not, the surveys, studies, and occasional experiments that show up in Logical Reasoning questions are backed by numbers and percentages, and we can almost consider these two types as one big category. However, it's worth breaking them up because 1) surveys and studies have their own predictable patterns on the LSAT, and 2) they don't always involve numbers or percentages, and sometimes, when they do, as is the case in question 4 below, the numerical info is secondary to the mechanisms of the study itself. You'll be seeing quite a few surveys and studies in this book.

A 180 test taker approaches with skepticism any survey, study, or experiment described in a LR stimulus. Often what's tested is how these surveys went awry.

Here is an example of a question that falls into the Surveys and Studies category.

4. High blood pressure, or hypertension, is a medical condition that puts strain on the heart, increasing the risk of stroke and heart disease, and is more likely to develop in people over 40 than in those aged 40 and under. The many risk factors for hypertension may include obesity, stress, and alcoholism. A recent study asked executives who have high blood pressure, and are over the age of 40, to gauge their level of stress on a scale of one (very low) to ten (very high). 87 percent of respondents rated their stress levels at eight or higher. It is therefore very likely that Jeanne, a 46-year-old advertising vice-president, has high blood pressure, since she rates her stress level at a nine.

The argument above is flawed because it

(A) disregards genetic predisposition and other lifestyle factors

(B) cites as a partial cause a factor that is a direct causal mechanism for the condition in question

(C) ignores the possibility that Jeanne may be among the 13 percent of executives who rate their stress levels at a seven or lower

(D) limits the dangers of high blood pressure to stroke and heart disease.

(E) fails to indicate the possibility of hypertension among executives aged 40 and older who rate their stress levels at a level of eight or higher

Explanation: High Blood Pressure and Stress

The author's conclusion is apparent at the end of the passage, where she states that Jeanne likely has high blood pressure, since she is an executive over 40 who has high stress levels. The main piece of evidence is the recent study cited by the author, which states that 87% of executives over 40 with high blood pressure have levels of stress that are rated eight or higher. The study addresses only the stress levels of executives over 40 *who have high blood pressure*. Therefore, the author's claim is flawed because it draws a conclusion about a 45-year-old executive based on a study about executives over 40 *with hypertension*.

In other words, there is a scope shift (another term you will see more of later on) between the evidence the author presents and the conclusion she reaches. The author's mistake is that she accepts the study as being applicable to Jeanne. (E) captures this mistake most clearly: To come to a conclusion about whether Jeanne has high blood pressure, the author must provide evidence that is relevant to Jeanne, since the evidence in the passage does not. She needs a statistic that gives the likelihood that an executive over 40 who rates her stress level at eight or higher would have high blood pressure. The evidence that's provided might look like that, but it isn't, and (E) shows the discrepancy between the two, making it the best choice.

(A) may be true, but it doesn't address the problem at hand. A doctor might say that a family history of high blood pressure is a more significant risk factor than a stressful lifestyle, but that conclusion is not the issue here. Rather, the argument concerns Jeanne's chances of having high blood pressure based on the information in the study the author cites.

(B) might be confusing, but the argument really isn't about degrees of causation. The passage does cite stress as a partial cause of high blood pressure, but this choice is saying that stress is in fact a direct (primary) cause of the condition. There's no evidence at all in the stimulus to back up that conclusion.

(C) is the easiest choice to eliminate; it contradicts the stimulus, where we see that Jeanne rates her stress level at a nine, not a seven or lower. (You might also notice that the 13% statistic isn't accurate; it comes from the 87% figure from the study in the stimulus, but that figure refers to the percentage of executives over 40 who have already been diagnosed with hypertension. You can therefore infer that 13% of executives over 40 with hypertension rate their stress level at a seven or lower, but we can't extrapolate this to mean that 13% of *all* executives over 40, as (C) is attempting to do.)

(D), like choice (A), could be true, but this isn't where the flaw in the argument lies. Even if the passage gave a more comprehensive description of high blood pressure's effects, it is still attempting to draw a conclusion about Jeanne based on evidence that isn't relevant to her case.

JUST PLAIN TOUGH

Not every difficult Logical Reasoning question is distinguished by a common logical feature—some are "just plain tough." These are akin to the Supercharged Standards of the Logic Games section, and foreshadow the "Just Plain Tough" Reading Comprehension passages you'll see later on. These general killers come in all varieties: standard question types like Assumption, Inference, and Strengthen/Weaken an argument, as well as less common types such as Paradox questions like the example below. If you're shooting for that elusive 180, you simply have to be prepared to face down the tough stuff no matter what form it takes.

Give this tough question a shot:

5. In the last two centuries, the Spanish-speaking immigrant population in the city of Cerez grew dramatically. As the population increased, the number of citizens who spoke both English and Spanish fluently grew proportionately because children from ages 5 to 16 were required by law to enroll in school and all students in the Cerez district were required to pass proficiency examinations in English. What has puzzled language experts, however, is a recent sharp decrease in English language fluency among Spanish-speaking high school graduates in Cerez.

Which one of the following, if true, best helps to resolve the discrepancy mentioned above?

(A) Modern Spanish-speaking citizens of Cerez display personality characteristics that resemble those of Spanish speakers from the last century more closely than they resemble those of modern bilingual citizens of Cerez.

(B) Modern Spanish-speaking citizens of Cerez participate in more traditional gatherings than most bilingual residents of Cerez, but they participate in fewer traditional gatherings than did Spanish speakers in the last century.

(C) Modern Spanish-speaking citizens of Cerez are recently descended from long-time bilingual families that failed to maintain English language skills due to a new Spanish immersion school opening in Cerez.

(D) The celebrations of modern Spanish-speaking communities in Cerez involve a great deal of public speaking, and children are taught to write and perform speeches from a very young age.

(E) The traditions of modern Spanish-speaking communities in Cerez are an amalgamation of the cumulative experiences of previous generations plus innovations to the heritage added by the current generation of Spanish speakers.

Explanation: The Spanish Speakers of Cerez

The author clearly identifies the source of the confusion when he mentions what puzzles language experts. They're perplexed by two facts that seem inconsistent with each other. First, the mandatory enrollment of Cerez children in English-language schools seems to have caused an increase in the number of bilingual citizens. Second, the rate of bilingualism within the Spanish-speaking population has now decreased sharply. The basic question is: Why do the present-day Spanish speakers in Cerez lack English skills, when earlier Spanish speakers necessarily acquired English skills through mandatory schooling? Let's look to the answer choices and find one that specifically answers this question.

A 180 test taker rephrases a paradox as a question and looks for the answer choice that answers it.

(A) does nothing to explain why the modern Spanish speaker lacks English language skills. Personality similarities don't have any clear relationship to language acquisition.

(B) A comparison of the frequency of community gatherings does not in any way explain why the current Spanish-speaking population lacks English skills.

(C) would explain the discrepancy and is therefore the correct answer. If it were true, the population did acquire English skills through schooling, but subsequently lost those skills when they began attending a school that didn't require them to speak English. Thus the modern Spanish speakers could both have graduated high school and lack English fluency. The inconsistency is no longer an inconsistency—all the pieces of the puzzle find a home in this explanation.

(D) again touches on the issue of modern Spanish-speaking traditions without referring to English fluency, the central element of the argument's paradox.

(E) is too broad to resolve this discrepancy. It might give you the room to start making assumptions, but it doesn't specifically resolve the issue of English fluency. Regardless of the sentiments in (E), the fact remains that English fluency is decreasing in Cerez when the evidence suggests that it should not be.

NOW TRY THESE . . .

Next, try your hand at the following five questions. Each question represents one of the categories just discussed. See if you can pick out the logical element operating in each.

6. Choi: All other factors being equal, children whose parents earned doctorates are more likely to earn a doctorate than children whose parents did not earn doctorates.

   Hart: But consider this: Over 70 percent of all doctorate holders do not have a parent that also holds a doctorate.

   Which one of the following is the most accurate evaluation of Hart's reply?

   (A) It establishes that Choi's claim is an exaggeration.
   (B) If true, it effectively demonstrates that Choi's claim cannot be accurate.
   (C) It is consistent with Choi's claim.
   (D) It provides alternative reasons for accepting Choi's claim.
   (E) It mistakes what is necessary for an event with what is sufficient to determine that the event will occur.

7. Relocation after the takeover of a small company by a larger corporation can lead to a downturn in employee morale, which is often followed by instances of increased absenteeism. In many cases, the employees of the smaller company are retained in their previous locations and positions rather than integrated into the physical and corporate structure of the larger company, thereby helping to avoid a decrease in morale. However, the habitual absenteeism exhibited by certain employees in large corporations generally has nothing to do with a decreased sense of morale, but rather is a consequence of a lack of motivation and limited sense of possibility both within and outside the workplace.

   If all of the statements above are true, which one of the following statements must be true?

   (A) It is easier to avoid problems stemming from relocations after corporate takeovers than it is to solve the motivational issues of chronically absent employees.
   (B) In all corporations, retention of a smaller company structure cannot completely diffuse behavioral problems resulting from a relocation after a corporate takeover.
   (C) Relocations after corporate takeovers do not lead to any of the instances of absenteeism that occur within large corporations.
   (D) The effect that the retention of a smaller company structure has in minimizing absenteeism is primarily limited to its ability to restore employees' trust in their supervisors.
   (E) To the extent that retention of a smaller company structure may help to minimize absenteeism after a corporate takeover and relocation, it is probably not the result of changing the morale levels of employees in the larger corporation.

8. A computer crash has occurred when a computer's central processing unit "freezes up" and cannot respond to further commands or perform additional functions. In the split second during a computer crash, however, certain functions are still possible. When Cindy's Micron 401 computer crashed, she suspected it was due to an electrical power surge to the computer. The Micron 401 processor usually does not work fast enough during a crash to produce an error message on the screen before the computer "freezes." However, an error message can be triggered by an electrical power surge to the computer. Whenever a Micron 401 computer crashes without producing an error message on the screen, the computer's hard drive is damaged. Upon restarting her computer, Cindy determined that its hard drive was not damaged.

Which one of the following must be true on the basis of the information above?

(A) If the Micron 401's processor worked faster during the crash, the computer's hard drive would have been damaged.

(B) The Micron 401's hard drive is specially suited to withstand computer crashes.

(C) If the Micron 401's crash was not due to an electrical power surge, the computer's processor worked unusually fast during the crash.

(D) The Micron 401 computer is built to withstand electrical power surges.

(E) If an error message appeared on the screen of the Micron 401, it did so only after the computer crashed.

9. A social worker surveyed 200 women who recently had given birth to their first child. Half of these women had chosen to have their children in a hospital or obstetric clinic; the other half had chosen to give birth at home under the care of certified midwives. Of the 100 births that occurred at home, only five had presented any substantial complications, whereas 17 of the hospital births had required extra attention because of complications during delivery. The social worker concluded from this survey that the home is actually a safer environment in which to give birth than is a hospital or clinic.

Which one of the following, if true, most seriously calls the social worker's conclusion above into question?

(A) All of the women in the study who were diagnosed as having a high possibility of delivery complications elected to give birth in a hospital.

(B) Many obstetricians discourage their patients from giving birth in their own homes.

(C) Women who give birth in their own homes tend to experience less stress during labor and delivery than do those who deliver in hospitals.

(D) Women who give birth in hospitals and clinics often have shorter periods of labor than do those who give birth at home.

(E) Pregnant doctors prefer giving birth in a hospital.

10. Mitchell will play basketball tomorrow only if Allyson takes the day off. Allyson will not take the day off unless Lisa borrows a car. Since Lisa has not borrowed a car, Mitchell will not play basketball tomorrow.

The pattern of reasoning displayed above is most closely paralleled in which one of the following?

(A) Jeannie will not go out to dinner unless Sheila also goes out to dinner. Kurt will travel upstate tomorrow only if Jeannie goes out to dinner. However, since Sheila cannot go out to dinner, Kurt will not travel upstate tomorrow.

(B) Ashley will run the race this weekend only if Jon or Randi also runs. Jon will not run the race, but Randi will. So Ashley will run the race this weekend.

(C) Matthew will go to the amusement park next weekend only if Jack agrees to go. Jack will not go to the amusement park unless the admission fee is inexpensive. Since the admission fee is expensive, Jack will not go to the amusement park next weekend.

(D) Sean will go bowling tonight if he finishes his work and there is no league play scheduled at his local bowling alley. Although he has confirmed that no league play is scheduled, Sean has not finished his work, and therefore will not go bowling tonight.

(E) If Karen gets baseball tickets, Ira will not wash the car tomorrow. Karen will not get baseball tickets unless Jimmy goes out of town. However, since Jimmy has gone out of town, Karen will get baseball tickets.

ANSWERS AND EXPLANATIONS

Explanation: Doctorate Children

6. C

Hart's 70 percent figure pretty much tells us that Numbers and Statistics is the name of the game here. We're asked to evaluate Hart's response to Choi, so let's see what Choi has in mind. Choi's statement is a comparison among individuals: If my parents have earned doctorates and yours didn't, then Choi says that the odds are better that I will earn a doctorate than that you will. Choi's claim goes no further. He doesn't claim that children of doctors are *guaranteed* to earn doctorates, and he doesn't even claim that they are *likely* to earn doctorates. He merely claims that these children are *more likely* to earn doctorates than their counterparts who do not have a parent that earned a doctorate. So even if only 5 percent of doctors' children earn doctorates themselves, Choi's claim is still correct as long as fewer than 5 percent of children whose parents didn't earn a doctorate went on to earn a doctorate themselves.

Thus the irrelevancy of Hart's 70 percent figure, which gives us information on a different group—*those who already earned their doctoral degree.* So the data Hart presents can be true and yet have no bearing on Choi's claim. An example: Suppose that there are 10 people in the world with doctorates. Choi merely claims that children of these people are more likely to get doctorates than children of other people. Hart comes along and says that of the 10 people, say, 8 of them (over 70%) come from doctorate-less parents. Does that alter Choi's claim in any way? No. All other factors being equal, the children of those doctors could still be more likely to earn doctorates, even if most doctorate holders don't have that particular heritage. Because of this, Hart's consideration doesn't contradict Choi's claim in any way, and we can therefore say that Hart's is consistent with it (C).

(A), (B), and (D) are all off the mark in that they require a connection between Hart and Choi that simply isn't there. Because the speakers' target groups are different, no positive or negative connection can be made between the two claims, and so we therefore cannot say that one shows the other to be exaggerated (A) or false (B), or that one helps the other (D).

(E) The concept of necessity vs. sufficiency cannot be invoked against Hart because Hart's statement is merely the presentation of a statistic. As such, in this case there is no "event" to which this common type of LSAT mistake could apply. (More about necessary and sufficient conditions later.)

Explanation: Corporate Takeovers

7. E

This is the one that's just plain tough, although there is an element of causation present, an issue we'll be taking up later. The argument begins with a chain of causality: A corporate takeover (step 1) can lead to a decrease in employee morale (step 2), which can in turn lead to increased absenteeism (step 3). Retention of the structure of the company that's been taken over keeps people from having to change positions or locations, thereby keeping the first domino from falling, and therefore positively influencing at least the second step in the chain. This is the author's first explanation for increased absenteeism, and the structure-retention solution refers only to it. The author then gives an entirely different explanation for absenteeism, this time more specifically explaining its appearance among employees of the *larger* company. Accordingly, absenteeism in these employees is caused by a lack of motivation and a limited sense of possibility, both at and away from work. We have two paths explaining absenteeism, and the answer to this inference question will test our ability to distinguish between them. Let's evaluate the answer choices, keeping these distinctions in mind.

(A) While the author offers us one potential antidote to the first type of absenteeism issue without making any such reference in regard to the second, that doesn't mean that there is no solution for the second type. The fact that something is not mentioned can't be taken to mean that it does not exist, so we have no information about solving the second type of problem, and thus no way of inferring which type of absenteeism issue is easier to solve. When you see answer choices that include words like "easier" and "than," the test makers want you to make a comparison between two things in the stimulus. You must remember to hold the test makers accountable for the terms they use and check to see if you know what makes the problem of absenteeism easier to solve.

(B) For all we know, retention of a smaller structure alone may be enough to avoid absenteeism issues in some corporations, perhaps those that had no such issues before the takeover, or even those with employees who are simply not driven to show their discontent by missing work.

(C) is too extreme and distorts the argument. The author writes that relocation after a corporate takeover leads to absenteeism among some employees, which may include those in the larger corporation; the author certainly doesn't rule out the possibility. Furthermore, the author's statement that a lack of motivation leads to absenteeism doesn't imply that a lack in motivation is the *only* cause of the problem. The two explanations aren't mutually exclusive.

(D) also goes too far out on a limb. The author mentions that one effect of retention of a smaller company structure is that people aren't forced to move or change positions within the company, and therefore are less likely to react by missing work. However, we don't know that a restored trust in their supervisors is inherent in this case; we know only that the retention of the smaller structure has an effect on their actions at the time of the takeover. The word "primary" is an extreme word and you should never choose a choice that is more extreme than the stimulus it is based on.

A 180 test taker is wary of extreme answer choices. The right answer to an inference question doesn't intensify the argument.

(E) does the trick: The author does not create a link implying that habitual absenteeism is caused only by relocation after a corporate takeover or by the downturn in morale that the relocation creates, so it follows that retention of a smaller structure probably doesn't decrease the incidence of the problem. The author says that habitual absenteeism is not caused by a sudden downturn in morale, so a change in morale levels within the company probably wouldn't help matters any. If the retention of the smaller structure helps to reduce absenteeism, then it probably does so in some other way.

Explanation: Computer Crash

8. C

The computer in this one does a crash and burn, as do many test takers faced with this question. Formal Logic is the name of the game here, if you hadn't guessed. This question is a good example of a Formal Logic question that requires you to combine many statements, which makes it among the most difficult and time-consuming questions on the exam.

A 180 test taker begins a tough Formal Logic question by scoping out the concrete information and using it to set off a chain of deductions.

What's the most concrete info here? It's the fact that the hard drive was not damaged. What other formal logic statements tell us something about the hard drive? Well, if there's no error message, then the hard drive *is* damaged. The correct implication of this statement is that if the hard drive is NOT damaged, then there cannot be "no error message," which means that there *is* an error message. So since we know the hard drive was not damaged, we know there must have been an error message. This would make for a fine choice, were it not for the further information at the end regarding the particulars of error messages. We're told that usually, the processor doesn't work quickly enough to produce an error message, and that such a message could instead result from an electrical surge. But what if there was no surge? Since we've deduced already that an error message must have appeared, we can further deduce that in the absence of an electrical surge, the processor must have worked unusually fast during the crash, choice (C). This is a particularly tough question because the formal logic statements combine to lead to a nice deduction, but that deduction isn't the answer; it only *leads* to the answer.

(A) There's no stated connection between the speed of the processor and the hard drive, so we can eliminate (A).

(B), (D) Even if the passage blew you away, you should still be able to eliminate these two fairly quickly. The intention behind the 401's construction is never addressed; it's way outside the scope.

A 180 test taker uses every method at her disposal to increase her odds of getting the point.

(E) is impossible. A crash is characterized by a "freeze," so after a crash no additional functions can be performed.

Explanation: Home Births

9. A

Here's a very typical example of how surveys appear in LSAT Logical Reasoning. A social worker surveys 100 women who chose to give birth in a hospital, and 100 who chose to have their babies at home. The social worker concludes that the home is the safer environment in which to give birth, based entirely on the fact that in the sample studied, there were more cases of complications in the hospital. She assumes that the environment was responsible for the number of complications, and overlooks any other possible reason for the survey results. (A) weakens the argument by providing such an alternative reason for the statistical disparity: Women who were at high risk for complications all decided to give birth in a hospital. In other words, the study was skewed; the women in the two groups (the 100 who gave birth in the home and the 100 who gave birth in the hospital) were not equally likely to have complications to begin with.

A 180 test taker scrutinizes the sample groups used in surveys looking for disparities in their data or characteristics that may invalidate the survey.

(B) and (E) both make inappropriate appeals to authority—the fact that many doctors prefer hospital births alters neither the results of the study nor the conclusion drawn from these results.

(C) provides the opposite of what we're looking for—it strengthens the argument by providing a possible reason why home births are safer.

(D) The point at issue is where it's safer to give birth, not the respective labor times. Since there's no evidence that *shorter* labors are *safer* labors, (D) doesn't weaken the argument. Later on we'll refer to such slight deviations as "scope shifts."

Explanation: Mitchell and Basketball

10. A

Poor Mitchell. Seems as if he's all ready to play, but Allyson and Lisa are standing in his way. Obviously this is our Parallel Reasoning question of the bunch, and as you'll see, there are generally two varieties: ones that ask you to mirror the logic of an argument, and ones that ask you to mirror the *flawed* logic of an argument. If the stem doesn't designate the reasoning in the original as flawed, then we can safely assume that the logic is valid and that the logic of the right answer will be valid in the same way. And there's nothing wrong with the conclusion here: Since Lisa has *not* borrowed a car, Allyson will *not* take the day off, and therefore Mitchell *cannot* play basketball.

Notice the Formal Logic element present here; in fact, it's extremely common to find Formal Logic constructions in Parallel Reasoning questions. When the statements are linked as closely as these, it's possible, and often helpful, to represent them algebraically.

This pattern of reasoning breaks down to:

If A (Mitchell plays) → then B (Allyson takes off)

If B (Allyson takes off) → then C (Lisa borrows car)

Since NOT C (Lisa does NOT borrow car) → then NOT A (Mitchell does NOT play)

It's fairly linear and perfectly logical, as we noted above. Let's attack the choices, in search of the same pattern.

(A) If A (Kurt will travel upstate) then B (Jeannie goes out to dinner). If B (Jeannie goes out to dinner) then C (Sheila goes out to dinner). Since NOT C (Sheila cannot go out) therefore NOT A (Kurt will not travel upstate). No problem. We have a winner.

A 180 test taker knows that statements in the correct answer to a Parallel Reasoning question need not be in the same order as those in the original.

(B) Comparing conclusions is enough to eliminate (B). The original predicts that something will not happen, but (B) indicates that something will happen. Also, there is no "or" scenario present in the original, so this can't be parallel.

(C) Close, but no cigar: If A (Matthew goes to amusement park) then B (Jack goes). If B (Jack goes) then C (fee is inexpensive). Since NOT C (fee is NOT inexpensive), NOT B (Jack will NOT go). The conclusion doubles back on Jack, instead of coming full circle to Matthew, as it should.

(D) cites *two* conditions which together would be sufficient for Sean to go bowling. There's nothing parallel to this in the original.

(E), like (B), predicts that something *will* happen.

What's Next?

Need more practice with these types of Logical Reasoning questions? We've got just the thing for you—in the very next chapter.

CHAPTER EIGHT

A Closer Look

Now it's time to really dig in and drill on the common types of tough Logical Reasoning questions we touched upon in chapter 7. We'll begin with five straight Formal Logic challenges, then move on to Parallel Reasoning, Numbers and Statistics, Surveys and Studies, and Just Plain Tough questions. Enjoy!

PRACTICE SET 1: FORMAL LOGIC

1. In ancient Mondavia, only members of the ruling council had access to classified information, and only people born into the elite class were members of the ruling council. Although some historians believe that a Mondavian peasant uprising was solely responsible for overthrowing the ancient Mondavian regime, the perpetrators of the successful coup must have known the location of the state's armament supplies as well as the inner layout of Mondavia's fortresses and strategic strongholds. This information was classified.

   The argument is structured to lead to the conclusion that

   (A) Mondavian peasants in the ancient Mondavian regime knew as much about the state's classified security information as did members of the Mondavian elite

   (B) all members of the Mondavian elite class had access to the state's classified security information before the overthrow of the ancient Mondavian regime

   (C) the accidental discovery of state secrets allowed the Mondavian peasants to overcome great odds in overthrowing the ancient Mondavian regime

   (D) at least one member of the Mondavian elite class helped in the overthrow of the ancient Mondavian regime

   (E) the ancient Mondavian regime could not be overthrown by people lacking knowledge of armament locations and the design of strategic strongholds

2. If the average cumulative grade in Biology 214 has increased in March, then either participation in lab sessions has increased or absenteeism in lectures has decreased during the month, but not both. If participation in lab sessions has increased in March, then the students will be given an optional research paper for extra credit. If the average cumulative grade has not increased in March, then the students will not be given an optional research paper for extra credit.

   If all of the above statements are true, which one of the following can be concluded from the fact that the students in Biology 214 will not be given an optional research paper for extra credit?

   (A) The average cumulative grade has not increased in March.

   (B) Participation in lab sessions has not increased in March.

   (C) Absenteeism in lectures has not decreased in March.

   (D) Participation in lab sessions has increased in March.

   (E) The average cumulative grade has increased in March.

3. Garden City's police department has an extremely competitive recruiting process. Candidates must satisfy a strenuous physical fitness requirement, and must also pass a comprehensive written examination that tests memorization and requires no background knowledge of the test subjects. The only way to pass the written exam is by preparing with a study guide that is distributed by the city's department of human services. If every candidate receives a complete study guide, then no candidate will have any more information than any other candidate regarding the content of the examination. If no candidate has any more information than any other candidate, then no candidate has a better chance of passing the examination. However, the department of human services did not provide a complete study guide to every candidate. Therefore, some candidate has a better chance of passing the examination than all of the other candidates.

The reasoning in this argument is flawed because it overlooks the possibility that

(A) even if one candidate received a more extensive study guide than all of the other candidates, that candidate might not necessarily pass the examination
(B) some candidates who did not receive a complete study guide will nonetheless be able to pass the examination
(C) all of the candidates received identical study guides for the written test
(D) some candidate may share a particular section of the study guide with other participants who did not receive that section
(E) none of the candidates received a complete study guide for the written examination

Questions 4–5

Unless public transportation becomes much more popular, traffic will become more congested and pollution from cars will get worse. Yet public transportation will only become much more popular when the railway system is modernized and expanded. Such modernization and expansion, however, will take place only when the state becomes convinced of the importance of improved public transportation, or when rail technology improves to the point that high-speed railroads become profitable for private investors.

4. Which one of the following can be properly inferred from the passage?

(A) If the state becomes convinced of the importance of improved public transportation, then high-speed railroads will become profitable for private investors.
(B) If rail technology does not improve enough for high-speed railroads to become profitable for private investors, then traffic will become more congested.
(C) If public transportation has gotten much more popular, then the railway system has been expanded.
(D) If the railway system is modernized and expanded, public transportation will become much more popular.
(E) If public transportation does not become more popular, then the railway system either has not been modernized or has not been expanded.

5. If all the statements in the passage are true, and if it is also true that rail technology will not improve to the point that high-speed railroads will become profitable for private investors, then which one of the following CANNOT be true?

(A) Either the state will become convinced of the importance of improved public transportation, or traffic will become more congested and pollution from cars will get worse.
(B) The railway system is modernized and as a result traffic congestion is reduced.
(C) The railway system will be modernized and expanded, but traffic congestion will continue to get worse.
(D) The state is not convinced of the importance of improved transportation, but traffic congestion and pollution from cars will be reduced.
(E) Although traffic congestion continues to get worse, public transportation does not become more popular, and the state is not convinced of the importance of improved public transportation.

PRACTICE SET 1: ANSWERS AND EXPLANATIONS

Explanation: Mondavian Uprising

1. D

In chapter 7's "Computer Crash," we advised that in tough Formal Logic problems it often pays to begin with the most concrete piece of information. Here, that honor goes to the last sentence of the stimulus, specifically the notion that Mondavian supply locations and fortress layouts were classified. We can combine this with the sentence immediately before to reasonably infer than the perpetrators of the coup must have known classified information, which then relates back to the first sentence: Only the members of the ruling council had access to classified info, which means that the rebels must have had help from the ruling council. Perhaps at this point you feel like the restless kid in the back seat—"*are we there yet*?" Not quite; one final step. Since only members of the elite class are on the ruling council, the rebels must have had help from at least one member of the elite class. It's a bit windy, but the deductions here eventually bring us to (D).

(A) is contradicted by the passage, since only those born into the ruling class had access to classified information.

(B) Being in the ruling class is necessary, but not *sufficient*, for access to classified info.

(C) The "accidental discovery" in (C) is neither stated nor implied.

(E) is quite close, but fails on one particular count. The perpetrators *of this particular peasant coup* needed such strategic info, but that doesn't imply that it's impossible in another situation (such as attack from a much stronger empire) for the regime to be toppled without knowledge of armament locations and strongholds.

A 180 test taker develops a knack for finding the flaw in even the most tempting wrong answers, knowing that there is no "second best" choice.

Explanation: Biology 214 and Extra Credit

2. B

This one might look like a Logic Game at first, but it does give you a fairly helpful question stem, letting you know which part of the argument the inference will apply to. Since there are several formal logic statements to work with here, knowing which one to choose will let you start out ahead.

The question stem provides us with the first part of an "if-then" statement, so it follows that the correct answer choice will probably be the second half of the statement. Since the students are not given an optional paper for extra credit, what do we know? Reading the part of the stimulus that deals with the extra credit assignment, we come to sentences 2 and 3. See if sentence 2 is helpful: If participation in lab sessions has increased in March, then the students will be given an optional research paper for extra credit. The correct implication of this is that is students *do not* receive an extra credit paper, then participation in lab sessions has *not* increased. You've already been given the first half of this statement, the "if" clause in the question stem. The second half, the "then" clause that follows, is found in correct choice (B).

(A) offers an option in regard to the class's average cumulative grade, but according to what we know, the average grade could have increased or not. (For example, the class could have had perfect attendance in lectures, raising the average grade, but not said a word in any of their lab sessions, losing the opportunity for that extra credit paper.) There's no accurate inference we can draw here based on the information we're given.

(C) deals with absenteeism in lectures, about which we can make no inferences based on the information we've been given regarding the extra credit paper.

(D) As we saw above, under these circumstances, participation in lab sessions has not increased in March.

(E) deals with the class's cumulative grade, but as we saw in (A), there is no way to draw an accurate inference about the cumulative grade based on the information we have.

Explanation: Garden City Police Department

3. C

The author describes the department's recruiting efforts and challenging written test, and informs us that one can pass the examination *only* with the help of the city's study guide. It follows, therefore, that if every candidate has the same information about the content of the test, then every candidate has an equal chance to pass the exam. So far, so good. Next, the author moves away from the hypothetical situation to describe what really happened. The city's department of human services didn't give every candidate a complete study guide, but that doesn't necessarily mean that one candidate has more information than the others do. Just because the city didn't give a complete guide to everyone, it doesn't mean that they gave *more* complete guides to some people than to others.

Our formal logic skills come into play here: We are told that if everyone is fully informed, then no one has an advantage. It doesn't follow that if everyone is not fully informed, then someone does *have* an advantage. That's a very common formal logic error, and since the author commits it, the correct choice should identify this as the flaw in the argument. (C) does this by stating what could still be true given the argument: Every candidate could have received the same incomplete study guide. In concluding categorically that some lucky candidate has an advantage over the others, the author doesn't allow for the possibility in (C), and so this is the choice that legitimately points to the flaw in the argument.

(A) Probably the easiest way to eliminate (A) is to recognize that the author is discussing who has the best *chance* of passing the examination. The author never suggests that having a better change at passing the exam means actually passing the exam. If the author had made such a suggestion, this choice would be a flaw—but since the author never did, it isn't.

(B) takes this issue from another angle by suggesting that people with incomplete study guides might still pass the examination. The author never suggests otherwise, since again the stimulus discusses solely who has the best chance of passing the exam, not who will therefore actually pass it. While this choice and (A) are consistent with the stimulus, neither one points to a logical flaw in the argument.

A 180 test taker notices small shifts in scope between the information in a stimulus and the focus of the corresponding choices.

(D) simply states one possible consequence of handing out different study guides. The scenario here is consistent with the facts of the stimulus, so it's okay on that count, but it allows for the possibility that some candidate has a better chance than the others, as the author maintains. In other words, it doesn't point to a flaw in the argument. Only the plausible possibility that's stated in (C), and which is overlooked by the author, would show the author's conclusion to be unwarranted.

(E) is close, but not quite there. Even if no candidate receives a complete study guide (which is possible), there still exists the possibility that some candidates receive more complete guides than others, a situation that wouldn't by itself expose a flaw in the argument.

Explanation: Railway System

4. C

Translating (and abridging) the "unless" statement in the first sentence, we get: "If public transport isn't more popular, then we'll have more traffic and pollution." We can make this translation because the formal logic statement "X unless Y" is really just another way of saying "if not Y, then X." The next two sentences present two complicated "only if" statements: Public transport will become more popular only when (that means "only if") the railways are both modernized and expanded. The modernization and expansion, then, are prerequisites for increased popularity.

A 180 test taker knows that the easiest way to handle an "only if" statement is to turn it into a straightforward "if-then" statement.

In this case, turning the statement into "if-then" language yields: "If public transport is much more popular, then the railways were modernized and expanded." The last statement links right up. The only way the railways will get modernized and expanded is if . . . actually, there are two possible ways these results could occur—either the state becomes convinced of the importance of improved public transportation, or technology improves so that high speed railroads become profitable. Turning that into a regular "if-then," we get: "If the railways are modernized and expanded, then either the state has been convinced of the importance of improved public transport, or high speed railways have become profitable investments." Let's go to the choices, looking for the one that's inferable based on this mess of information.

(A) We're told only that the two ways in which the railways can become modernized and expanded are the state's being convinced and high-speed railways becoming profitable. There isn't, however, any causal connection between the two, as (A) would have it.

(B)'s pessimism is likewise unfounded. Even if high-speed railways don't become profitable investments, the state could become convinced of the importance of improving public transport. That would, ultimately, allow traffic to not become more congested.

(C) is inferable; in fact, it's nothing more than the basic if-then rewrite we formed from the second sentence. That's very LSAT-like. One of the test makers' favorite tricks in questions like this one is to hound us with a lot of statements and implications, and then present a correct choice that's a mere rewrite of one of them.

(D), (E) (D) confuses "if-then" and "only-if" statements. We're told that public transport can grow more popular only if the railways are modernized and expanded. This doesn't mean that it *will* grow more popular simply because the railways have been modernized and expanded—there may be other factors involved. (E) is just another way of stating the sentiment in (D): Since it means exactly the same thing, it's wrong in exactly the same way.

A 180 test taker recognizes what are essentially identical choices, and eliminates both on the grounds that there can be only one right answer.

---

5. D

No sense allowing such a plethora of information to go to waste—may as well squeeze another question out of this maze of formal logic statements. The stem effectively kills one of the only two possible ways that modernization and expansion can occur; namely, technology improving so that high-speed railroads become profitable. With that possibility nixed, we can deduce that modernization and expansion depend solely on the other factor: the state's becoming convinced of the importance of improved public transportation. If, as (D) has it, the state *doesn't* come around on this issue, then we can work backward from there. Coupled with the info in the stem, we can now conclusively infer that modernization and expansion won't happen, which, in turn means that public transportation will *not* become more popular. Relating this new fact back to the first sentence, we can deduce that traffic and pollution will both increase. Remember, as we noted in the previous question, the "unless" statement in the first sentence translates as "If public transport isn't more popular, then we'll have more traffic and pollution." So under these circumstances set forth in the stimulus, the question stem, and choice (D), the upshot for sure is an increase in traffic and pollution. Since the second part of (D) comes to the opposite conclusion, (D) is the statement that can't be true.

A 180 test taker meticulously analyzes formal logic statements and can identify what must, can, and cannot be true based on them.

(A) could be true. If the state is not convinced of the importance of improved transportation, then the results will follow as stated above and pollution will get worse.

(B) Modernization is a prerequisite for popularity, so if we throw in expansion as well, it's possible that public transportation will get more popular, which in turn makes a reduction in traffic congestion possible as well. So (B) could be true.

(C) Modernization and expansion are necessary for increased popularity, but don't guarantee it. (We'll deal with this issue of necessary and sufficient conditions more extensively a little later in the book.) So (C) is possible as well.

(E) All of these things can happen without violating any conditions. In fact, working backward, if the state is not convinced, then that will cause the other things in the choice to occur (in conjunction, of course, with the condition in the question stem).

PRACTICE SET 2: PARALLEL REASONING

6. Lisa runs four miles each day and usually experiences no pain or discomfort afterward. Therefore, it is unreasonable to conclude that Lisa has a knee injury based solely on the fact that she has had aches in her shins and knees after running on several occasions.

   The argument above is most similar in reasoning to which one of the arguments below?

   (A) On some occasions, a leak inside a chemical plant can escape and prove harmful to people in the surrounding area. However, it is unreasonable to conclude on this basis that all leaks inside chemical plants are dangerous to people outside of the plant because in the majority of cases, leaks are contained and neutralized before they can escape, or are not large enough to pose a threat

   (B) Of state laws that are repealed, most are on the books for over ten years before they are challenged. So it is unreasonable to believe that a law will not be challenged after five years, even if it has not been challenged up to that point.

   (C) Some school systems that have fine arts programs produce high-achieving students. However, schools without fine arts programs have also produced high-achieving students. Therefore, it is unreasonable to believe that fine arts education affects students' level of achievement.

   (D) A large number of attorneys who do pro bono work report a higher level of job satisfaction than their counterparts who do not do pro bono work. It is therefore unreasonable to conclude that there is no connection between doing pro bono work and having a higher level of job satisfaction, even though many other attorneys who do pro bono work do not report a higher level of job satisfaction.

   (E) Some households that participate in fund-raising garage sales made little or no money for charity. So it is unreasonable to believe that the garage sale is an effective way to raise money for charity, even though some households did raise larger sums of money.

7. Most of the office complexes designed by Valentine Brown have a central open area around which the buildings are grouped. But it is also true that most of the office complexes designed by Mr. Brown have underground walkways between the buildings. So most of the office complexes designed by Valentine Brown combine a central space around which the buildings are grouped with a system of underground walkways between the buildings.

   Which one of the following arguments contains flawed reasoning most similar to the flawed reasoning in the argument above?

   (A) Most of the children in class say that dessert is their favorite meal, and that pecan pie is their favorite dessert. So the favorite food of most children in class is pecan pie.

   (B) Excessive reading can weaken a person's eyesight. Excessive reading can also make a person round-shouldered. Excessive reading, therefore, can make a person round-shouldered and near-sighted.

   (C) The majority of customers at Torrance Autos wish to buy a four-door sedan. But the majority of customers at Torrance Autos also wish to purchase a red car. So the majority of customers at Torrance Autos wish to purchase a red, four-door sedan.

   (D) People who spend the most time watching television say they most prefer to watch sports programs and situation comedies. Thus, sports and situation comedies are probably the most frequently watched varieties of programming on television.

   (E) Constance will live only in an apartment that has a playground attached. Philip will live only in an apartment that allows pets. Therefore, if Constance and Philip live together, they will live only in an apartment that has a playground attached and allows pets.

8. One morning, George Petersen of Petersen's Garage watches as a 1995 Da Volo station wagon is towed onto his lot. Because he knows that nearly 90% of the 1995 Da Volo station wagons brought to his garage for work in the past were brought in because of malfunctioning power windows, he reasons that there is an almost 9 to 1 chance that the car he saw this morning has also been brought in to correct its faulty power windows.

Which one of the following employs flawed reasoning most similar to that employed by George Petersen?

(A) Mayor Lieberman was re-elected by a majority of almost 75%. Since Janine Davis voted in that mayoral election, the chances are almost 3 to 1 that she voted for Mayor Lieberman.

(B) Each week nine out of 10 best-selling paperback books at The Reader's Nook are works of fiction. Since Nash's history of World War II was among the ten best-selling paperback books at The Reader's Nook this week, the chances are 9 to 1 that it is a work of fiction.

(C) 90% of those who attempt to get into Myrmidon Military Academy are turned down. Since the previous 10 candidates to the academy were not accepted, Vladimir's application will almost certainly be approved.

(D) Only one out of 50 applications to bypass zoning regulations and establish a new business in the Gedford residential district is accepted. Since only 12 such applications were made last month, there is virtually no chance that any of them will be accepted.

(E) Nearly 95% of last year's Borough High School graduating class went on to some type of further schooling. Since only a little more than 5% of that graduating class took longer than the usual four years to graduate, it is probable that everyone who did graduate within four years went on to further schooling.

9. Although striped bandicoots and bilbies are very similar in appearance, their diets come from entirely different sources. Since the bilby does not eat plants, the striped bandicoot's diet must include plants.

Which one of the following is an argument that contains flawed reasoning most similar to the flawed reasoning in the argument above?

(A) Only currently enrolled students may use the athletic facilities at the Appleton school. Since Patricia does not use the athletic facilities at the Appleton school, she cannot be a currently enrolled student.

(B) Diaz and Freund never play tennis at the community center on the same day. Since Diaz played tennis at the community center on Sunday, Freund could not have played tennis at the community center on Sunday.

(C) Although they are both respected scientists in the field of physical chemistry, Chatterjee and Myers have never served on the same peer review panel. This is hardly surprising, however, given that Myers only serves on peer review panels during the month of August, when Chatterjee is on vacation.

(D) Rob and Janet always go to the movies each week, but never to the same movie as each other. It is certain that Janet sometimes sees comedies, since Rob never sees comedies.

(E) All of the marbles in this bag have the same weight. Therefore, if a single marble were removed and weighed, it would be possible to determine the total weight of all the marbles in the bag.

10. National voter-registration drives aim to help disenfranchised sections of the population to participate in elections, but the drives are led by groups that are not based in the communities where they work. Disenfranchised groups will participate in the democratic process only if members of their own communities recruit them. Therefore, national voter-registration drives are ineffective and should be discontinued.

Which one of the following exhibits reasoning most similar to the reasoning displayed in the argument above?

(A) Most candidates for teaching positions must pass a state teacher certification test. Many people who would otherwise pursue a career in education are unable to pass the test. Therefore, state teacher certification tests narrow the pool of teachers and should be abolished.

(B) A college program for returning students over age 30 attempts to integrate them into the younger student population by placing a maximum of one returning student in each class. In order to be successful, returning students must not feel isolated from their peers. Therefore, the practice of separating returning students undermines their success and should be abandoned.

(C) A proposed smoking ban would outlaw cigarette, cigar, and pipe smoking inside any building other than a private home. People who smoke are more likely to spend money at bars and restaurants, but polls indicate that many smokers would stop going out if the ban took effect. Thus, the smoking ban will be harmful to local businesses and should not be passed into law.

(D) Automotive emissions laws are intended to reduce the pollution released from existing cars and to create more fuel-efficient cars in the future. People will not support stringent emissions laws that will require them to make costly upgrades to their vehicles. Thus, the emissions laws are self-defeating and should be repealed.

(E) School uniform policies in public schools are intended to reduce the visible signs of economic disparities in the student population. However, even families without much money can often find ways to buy fashionable clothing for their children. Thus, uniform policies in public schools are unnecessary, and should be discontinued.

PRACTICE SET 2: ANSWERS AND EXPLANATIONS

Explanation: Lisa's Knees

6. A

The author argues that Lisa doesn't usually have any pain in her shins and knees after running. Therefore, she doesn't have a knee injury, even though she has sometimes had aches in her shins and knees after running. To sum up the structure of the argument, then, the author states that something (running) doesn't usually create a certain result (pain in shins and knees), and then concludes that something which might explain a causal relationship between the two (a knee injury) is not present. In other words, if a causal relationship isn't usually present, then it isn't present at all.

A 180 test taker abstracts arguments, rephrasing them in general terms, particularly in Parallel Reasoning questions.

Looking for another choice that demonstrates the same structure, we find (A), where the author states that a leak in a chemical plant does not usually indicate the presence of danger, and therefore argues against a causal relationship between the two. The last sentence begins, "in the majority of cases," paralleling the "usually" of the stimulus. It matches the original in all the major elements.

(B) presents a different argument altogether, arguing that the fact that something hasn't created a result is not an indication of whether it will create that result in the future. The original argument says that something doesn't create a result, so a causal relationship is not present.

(C) argues against a causal relationship, but it doesn't parallel the original evidence because it cites what "some" school systems do, not what "most" do. Additionally, the structure of the argument differs from that of the stimulus; (C) states that an outcome (high-achieving students) is sometimes produced by one thing (fine arts) and sometimes by another (no fine arts), and concludes that there is therefore no relationship. The stimulus argues against a relationship by saying that an outcome (pain in knees) is usually *not* produced.

(D) is incorrect because its conclusion argues *for* a correlation between two occurrences (pro bono work and job satisfaction), while the stimulus argues *against* a correlation (between running and pain in the knees).

(E) begins by saying that something (garage sale) sometimes doesn't create a certain result (raising money). This choice is already not parallel, since the evidence in the stimulus states that something doesn't create a certain result *most of the time*. "Some households" in (E) doesn't parallel "usually" in the stimulus. Additionally, (C) is concerned with the outcome of an event, whereas the stimulus and correct choice (A) argue about the relationship between two events.

Explanation: Office Complexes

7. C

Remember "*Light* Tanks" in chapter 7? In that one, we said that the author misunderstood the sets involved. The author of this stimulus simply doesn't understand sets either. Just because most of Brown's office complexes have underground walkways, and most of Brown's office complexes have a central space, doesn't mean that most of Brown's office complexes have *both* of these features. Perhaps most of those office blocks that have underground walkways do not have central spaces. For instance, say Brown put up 10 office complexes. Six of them have central spaces; six of them have underground walkways. It's then fair to say that most (six out of 10) have walkways and most (six out of 10) have central space. But it's still entirely possible that only two complexes have both features; there might be four complexes with walkways only and four with central spaces only. (C) makes the same mistake of not seeing that the overlap of two large sets might be a much smaller set. It's possible that few of those Torrance Auto customers who want four-door sedans want them red, and that most of the customers who want red cars are among those who don't want four-door autos.

A 180 test taker has a solid grasp on the nature of sets.

(A) doesn't work the same way. What we get here is a narrowing of sets; the set of desserts exists *within* the set of meals. There is no overlap of two different sets as there is in the stimulus.

(B), (E) Nothing wrong with the logic in these two: (B) simply describes two possible effects of excessive reading, and then says that it's possible for both of these effects to follow from excessive reading at the same time. There's no claim that this happens in the majority of cases. There's nothing intrinsically flawed about this reasoning, which disqualifies this choice immediately. (E) deals with absolute conditions, and also draws a valid conclusion. *Every* place Constance will live must have a playground; *every* place Philip will live must allow pets. So any place they both live must fulfill both conditions.

(D) is a simple, and *tentative* conclusion, that doesn't require figuring out the overlap of two sets as does the original argument in the stimulus. (D) simply says: TV addicts like these types of programs, so these programs are probably watched the most—not parallel.

Explanation: Petersen's Garage

8. B

Given this kind of reasoning, Petersen's garage must be an interesting place to work. Think about it this way: If 90% of a particular doctor's patients go to the doctor for treatment of strep throat, and Joe arrives with blood gushing out of his head, would the doctor figure that the odds are overwhelming that Joe is suffering from strep throat? We hope not; after all, one has to take some form of statistics course en route to becoming a doctor.

Evidently, George Petersen missed that course. In fact, Petersen gives us a little lesson on how *not* to use statistics. He knows that 9 out of 10 Da Volos are brought to his shop because of malfunctioning windows, so he reasons that this particular Da Volo, which is being *towed in*, has probably also been brought in for malfunctioning windows. Surely the fact that the car is being towed indicates that there must be some more serious problem. Petersen has mindlessly applied a numerical formula while ignoring additional information. Where else, besides the doctor example above, do we see such reasoning? Why, in choice (B), of course. (B) uses previous figures to conclude that there's a 9 to 1 chance that Nash's history of World War II is a work of fiction. (B) ignores the compelling contrary evidence (namely, that this book is a *history*) and mindlessly applies a numerical formula where it clearly shouldn't be applied. The author of (B) would no doubt feel right at home at Petersen's Garage.

You'll notice that we don't include this one in the Numbers and Stats section. While you might have been led to think that numbers are the key, the fact is that the actual numbers don't matter in this particular case; the flaw is one of ignoring pertinent information when formulating a statistical conclusion. The key to this question is therefore non-numerical.

A 180 test taker gets to the heart of the matter, recognizing which logical elements are most likely to be relevant to the right answer.

(A)'s use of statistics is reasonable. We don't know anything special about Janine Davis; she's just a voter. Therefore, since almost 3 out of 4 voters chose Lieberman, there's an almost 3 out of 4 (or 3 to 1) chance that Janine voted for Lieberman.

(C) reasons that Vladimir's chances of being admitted into the academy have been improved by the rejection of the previous candidates. That's not a persuasive line of argumentation, but it's nothing like the stimulus.

(D) is a straight numerical argument. The conclusion seems overstated (even 1 out of 50 isn't "virtually no chance"), but it's not at all like the stimulus; we're not shown a particular case with special information that goes against the numbers.

(E)'s mistake is to assume that all those who took more than four years to graduate did not go on to further schooling; this allows (E) to conclude that the 95% who graduated in four years did go on. It's statistically flawed, certainly, but no special case is discussed, and therefore there's no similarity to the stimulus.

Explanation: Bandicoots and Bilbies

9. D

Bandicoots? Bilbies? No matter: Exotic names aside, in the world of Parallel Reasoning they could just as easily be widgets or geraniums, for all we care. The key in this question type is to paraphrase the situation in general terms. Here, the problem with both the stimulus and choice (D) is the assumption that because two things differ in some fundamental way, they must differ in some other fundamental way. Just because the two creatures in the stimulus have different diets, and one of them never eats plants, doesn't mean that the other one *does* eat plants. It's equally possible that both creatures eschew plants in their two, very different, diets. By the same token, just because Rob and Janet go to different movies, and one of them never attends comedies, doesn't mean that the other person *does* attend comedies. For all we know, neither Rob nor Janet ever attends comedies in their different moviegoing experiences.

(A)'s conclusion is a statement of that which cannot be true—not so in the stimulus—and includes a necessary condition ("only") that the stimulus lacks.

(B), like (A), is a statement of that which cannot have been true, so it's not parallel to the stimulus. Also, (B)'s conclusion can be properly drawn from its evidence, so (B) doesn't qualify as "flawed reasoning." If a Parallel Reasoning question asks for a parallel flaw, then the first requirement of the right answer is that it be flawed. If the logic is sound, dismiss such choices immediately in Parallel Flaw questions.

(C) is an explanation of a phenomenon ("This is hardly surprising . . . given . . . "). The stimulus argument is not.

(E)'s conclusion is conditional (If so and so occurred, then such and such would be possible . . .), but the conclusion in the stimulus is not.

Explanation: Voter Registration

10. B

The "only-if" in the second sentence denotes Formal Logic, which we've seen is a common component of Parallel Reasoning questions. The stimulus starts off by telling us that voter registration drives attempt to reach disenfranchised groups but are led by people from other communities. Then comes the "only-if" statement, which, when properly translated, means that *if* disenfranchised people participate in the democratic process, *then* they have been recruited by members of their own communities. The author concludes that the national voter-registration drives should be discontinued. As with all Parallel Reasoning questions, it will be helpful to get a better sense of the structure of the passage. The author shows that a certain program has a goal and an unintended negative side effect. The author then explains that the goal can't be met if the side effect exists (which we're told it does), and concludes therefore that the program isn't effective and should be terminated. It's a pretty solid argument, and we can see these same elements in (B): goal (assimilate older students), negative side effect (isolating older students from one another), conclusion (stop separating older students).

(A) never explains the goal of teacher certification tests, and so does not survive past consideration of the very first element of the stimulus.

(C) never discusses the goal of the smoking ban, so you must eliminate it. Don't be fooled by the fact that it does include what could be called a side effect and a negative consequence of it. If every element of the stimulus is not present, it's not the correct choice.

A 180 test taker spends only as much time as is necessary to eliminate a choice.

(D) identifies the goal of a program (here, emissions laws) and explains a negative side effect. But in the second sentence, the issue shifts away from the success of the emissions laws to their ability to get support. The original argument stays focused only on the program's potential for success.

(E) identifies the goal of a certain program (here, uniform policies), but never identifies an unintended negative side effect. We can stop right there.

PRACTICE SET 3: NUMBERS AND STATISTICS

11. In the years 1971 to 1980, the population of the state prison system was, on average, about 82 percent of maximum occupancy. During those years, the average number of prisoners entering the system each year was equivalent to 9.1 percent of maximum occupancy. From the years 1981 to 1984, the average number of prisoners entering the system each year fell to 7.3 percent of maximum occupancy, yet the population of the state prison system rose to almost 89 percent of maximum occupancy.

    Which one of the following, if true, helps to resolve the apparent discrepancy?

    (A) The average sentence of a prisoner in the state system increased from 1981 to 1984.
    (B) Beginning in 1981, many of those entering the state prison system had been transferred from prisons in other states.
    (C) Between 1981 and 1984, the percentage of prisoners incarcerated for violent crimes increased by 26 percent.
    (D) In 1981, a legislative fact-finding committee proposed a revision of the state's parole and work release programs.
    (E) Between 1971 and 1984, the proportion of active criminals actually caught and incarcerated in the state prison system has steadily increased.

12. A local department store hires college students for one month every spring to audit its unsold inventory. It costs the department store 20 percent less to pay wages to students than it would cost to hire outside auditors from a temporary service. Even after factoring in the costs of training and insuring the students against work-related injury, the department store spends less money by hiring the student auditors than it would by hiring auditors from the temporary service.

    The statements above, if true, best support which of the following assertions?

    (A) The amount spent on insurance for college-student auditors is more than 20 percent of the cost of paying the college students' basic wages.
    (B) It takes 20 percent less time for the college students to audit the unsold inventory than it does for the outside auditors.
    (C) The department store pays its college-student auditors 20 percent less than the temporary service pays its auditors.
    (D) By hiring college students, the department store will cause 20 percent of the auditors at the temporary service to lose their jobs.
    (E) The cost of training its own college-student auditors is less than 20 percent of the cost of hiring auditors from the temporary service.

13. In order to promote off-season business, Mt. Dunmore Lodge made the following "Welcome Back" offer to their winter guests: Guests who rent a room for at least a week during ski season can come back during the summer and get 25% off the standard summer price of any room they rent. After the summer passed, the owners of the lodge determined that the majority of their guests had taken advantage of the "Welcome Back" offer and paid the reduced rates. However, they were surprised to find they still managed to rent more rooms at full price than they did at the discount rate.

Which one of the following, if true, most helps to explain the apparent discrepancy in the passage?

(A) Most of the guests who stayed at Mt. Dunmore Lodge during the winter did not stay for a full week.

(B) Those guests taking advantage of the "Welcome Back" discount were more likely to bring their families with them than were those guests who were paying full price.

(C) Some of the guests who received the "Welcome Back" discount also received a 10% rate reduction through their auto club.

(D) In order to pay for the construction of a new gymnasium and a new pool, the owners of the lodge raised their summer prices considerably.

(E) On average, guests who took advantage of the "Welcome Back" discount spent more money at the hotel on additional goods and services than guests who paid full price for their rooms.

Questions 14-15

The occurrence of sports-related injuries at Mercer High School has increased sharply in the last four years, as evidenced by the fact that since the school instituted a new physical education requirement for all of its students, the number of students injured in physical education classes alone has nearly doubled. However, certain types of injuries have actually decreased in number during this period. It is true that foot and leg injuries have increased by more than 40 percent, but head injuries now account for only 25 percent of all sports-related injuries in school. This is a significant drop from five years ago, when head injuries made up 55 percent of all sports-related injuries in school.

14. The argument above is most vulnerable to criticism on the grounds that it does which one of the following?

(A) It overlooks the possibility that the total number of injuries occurring within the school has increased in the last four years.

(B) It relies on evidence that contradicts its conclusion.

(C) It fails to discuss the possibility of students receiving injuries other than those to their heads, feet, or legs.

(D) It assumes that a decrease in the percentage of head injuries necessarily signifies a decrease in the number of head injuries.

(E) It takes for granted that the new physical education requirement is equally responsible for the two different types of injuries.

15. The assertion that sports injuries at Mercer High are increasing is most justified if which one of the following is assumed?

(A) Sports-related injury was not the most common type of injury among students ten years ago.

(B) Prior to the implementation of mandatory physical education classes, less than ten percent of students at Mercer were not enrolled in these classes.

(C) The number of non-sports injuries at Mercer High has decreased in the last four years as enrollment in physical education classes has increased.

(D) The majority of injuries in the mandatory physical education class have been foot and leg injuries, while head injuries have occurred primarily during team practices.

(E) Mercer High's sports injury rate is higher than the average sports injury rate in the rest of the city's schools.

PRACTICE SET 3: ANSWERS AND EXPLANATIONS

Explanation: Prison Paradox

11. A

Here we have a case in which an apparent paradox stems from a misunderstanding of statistics. Clear up the misunderstanding, and the paradox vanishes—that is, the rise described at the end no longer seems surprising.

> A 180 test taker knows that the way in which numbers and percentages are used or misused is key to answering many questions.

Here are the facts: In the early years, the prisons were 82% full, and just over 9% of the total possible occupancy arrived each year in the form of new prisoners. Now that the latter figure is down to 7.3%, the author is surprised that the prisons are more full: 89% full. She evidently expects that as one figure drops, so should the other. The key is seeing that she is focusing on the trend in incoming prisoners only, when the totals take into account all prisoners. Consider the long-termers. If the average length of sentences of all prisoners is increasing, then it's small wonder that the prisons are more crowded now, even if a smaller percentage of the inmates are newcomers. That's what (A) is all about.

(B) Where the prisoners came from has no impact on how many are, or should be, here in this state.

(C) Nothing in the evidence concerns the nature of crime, so no information about the nature of the crimes that land these people in jail in the first place can resolve the paradox.

(D) A "proposed revision" is way too weak. Was it instituted? And even if it was, what effect would it have? There's no way to know, so (D) is irrelevant and does nothing to clear up what the author considers to be a surprising result.

(E), even if true, begs the question of why the percentage of the prison total entering the system is lower than years ago, but the prisons are fuller. All (E) says is that fewer criminals are getting off scot-free.

Explanation: Student Auditors

12. E

The question stem directs us to find the assertion best supported by the evidence in the stimulus. All we have given here is evidence: The department store pays college students 20 percent less than it would pay employees from a temporary service. Add the costs of training and insurance, and the store *still* pays less for college students. The correct answer must arise from the facts: college students cost the store up to 20 percent less than do employees from a temporary service—even after training and insurance. Prephrasing an answer would be tough, so we should move right to testing the choices.

(A) attempts to relate the amount spent on insurance for student auditors to the total amount of their wages, but we have no basis for which to make this comparison. The amount spent on insurance for college-student auditors can be more, less, or equal to 20 percent of their basic wages without violating the numerical facts presented.

(B) and (D) should have been fairly easy kills. (B) involves time, a subject not included in the stimulus, while (D) mentions the loss of jobs at the temporary service, even though we know nothing about the overall demand for their auditors.

(C) is a little more subtle, but it involves how much the temporary service pays its auditors, not how much it charges the store for them. A classic "scope shift," something we'll be talking more about later.

A 180 test taker always pays attention to the scope of the argument, which helps him to axe easy and difficult choices alike.

(E) fits, and one way we can verify that it's correct is to see what happens if it's *not* true. If the cost of training college students is *more* than 20 percent of the cost of hiring auditors from the temporary service, the overall cost of college students must be higher than the cost of temporary-service auditors. That would contradict the stimulus, so (E) must be true.

A 180 test taker knows that one way to verify an answer in an assumption or inference question is to see what happens when she denies or negates the choice.

Explanation: Mt. Dunmore Lodge

13. B

One of the toughest things about this question is fully understanding the puzzling phenomenon described. Here's the discrepancy we're asked to resolve: How can it be that most winter guests availed themselves of discounted pricing, yet the lodge nevertheless rented more rooms at full price? Clearly it's a numerical mystery, which will require a numerical solution. (B) provides such an answer: If the discounted folks were mainly families, packing in more guests per room, while the full-price guests tended to come solo with fewer guests per room, then it's easier to explain how there could be lots of discounted guests wandering around the hotel but more rooms rented at full price.

Notice that the solution to the paradox hinges on the recognition that elements in the evidence and conclusion that appear to be similar are in fact totally different things (number of guests vs. number of rooms). This question furnishes another example of what we'll cover more fully later on as a "scope shift."

(A) These guests aren't even eligible for the summer discount, so they play no part in the argument or the confusing result.

(C) That some people got an added discount doesn't serve to explain the paradox. The relevant comparison is between discounted guests and non-discounted guests, so the fact that some discounted guests are enjoying even larger discounts doesn't change a thing.

(D) The argument centers on a full vs. discounted rate. What that rate is is irrelevant; it does nothing to explain why more rooms were rented at full rate in light of the evidence.

(E) goes beyond the scope of the passage. Other charges above and beyond room rates are never discussed and are therefore not an issue.

A 180 test taker doesn't hesitate to work out actual examples to clarify her understanding of a numerical concept.

Here, imagine, for instance, that the hotel has 10 rooms, and rents three at a discount and seven at full price. Now suppose that the discounted rooms contain five people per room, while the full-price rooms each contain one person. Voilà! More full-priced rooms than discounted, but more discounted guests than full-priced ones.

Explanation: Sports Injuries at Mercer High

14. D

The author states that the number of sports-related injuries in school has increased, citing a rise in two types of injuries following the implementation of a new physical education requirement for all students. Getting to the heart of the argument, the author then asserts that certain types of injuries have not increased in number, conceding that the percentage of foot and leg injuries has increased but noting that the percentage of head injuries has decreased. The latter statement sounds like good news initially, but it's tempered by the fact that the author blurs the distinction between numbers and percentages. Head injuries represent a decreased percentage of total injuries; that doesn't mean that fewer students have received head injuries. A decreased percentage doesn't necessarily imply a decreased number of head injuries, and the author's flaw lies in failing to recognize this, as (D) expresses.

(A) The total number of injuries occurring inside the school is outside of the scope of this argument, which deals specifically with sports injuries to the feet, legs, and head. The author doesn't need to consider the overall injury rates in school in order to make this argument.

(B) is too vaguely worded, and when we reread the passage, we see that it's not accurate. The evidence about percentages doesn't directly contradict the author's conclusion; it simply doesn't necessarily support it in the way the author intended.

(C) The argument doesn't explicitly discuss other types of sports injuries, so we don't really know where they fall. However, this omission certainly doesn't negate the possibility that other groups might exist.

(E) Not really, since the author doesn't link the physical education requirement to either type of injury.

15. B

Now for part 2 of "Sports Injuries at Mercer High." Re-evaluating the argument, we can see that the author presents one piece of evidence in support of his assertion: The number of students injured in physical education classes has nearly doubled since the classes became mandatory for all students. In order to use this evidence to support the assertion that injuries have increased dramatically, the author must assume that the increase in the number of injuries is greater than the increase in the number of students. (B) clearly expresses this assumption: If only 10% of Mercer students were not enrolled in physical education classes, then 90% of students were already taking the classes before they became mandatory. That would mean that the enrollment of the classes increased by only 10%, but injuries went up nearly 50%—a dramatic increase.

(A) Knowing what types of injuries were common among students 10 years ago doesn't have any real bearing on the claim in the first sentence of the passage. Maybe sports injuries were common at that time, and maybe not. Either way, this doesn't help justify the assertion that recent injuries are up.

(C) is far outside the scope. Injuries from causes other than sports have no relevance to this argument about sports-related injuries.

(D) attempts to make connections that the author hasn't made for us, and doesn't address the question at hand. The passage is talking about whether the number of injuries has, in fact, increased. Knowing where the different types of injuries occurred doesn't get us any closer to answering that question.

(E) compares Mercer High's injury rate to the city's—which isn't relevant to the assertion in question. The author asserts only that sports injuries at Mercer have increased; there is no mention of their relative increase or of the injury rates at other schools.

PRACTICE SET 4: SURVEYS AND STUDIES

Questions 16-17

A survey of registered voters in the Ninth Ward revealed that the percentage of Yellow Party council members who received the highest satisfaction rating was greater than the percentage of Orange Party council members who received the highest rating. Yet, the survey organizers were probably erroneous in their conclusion that political party affiliation determines voters' satisfaction with a council member, since the Yellow Party council members in the survey all had six or more years of experience in politics, whereas the Orange Party council members were newer to politics, and many of them were serving their first terms.

16. The statements above, if true, support which of the following statements?

(A) Fewer Orange Party council members than Yellow Party council members received the survey's highest rating.

(B) There is no relationship between the popular appeal of the council members evaluated in the survey and any previous political experience on the part of those council members.

(C) If voters were surveyed regarding their impressions of state senators, the percentage of Orange Party senators who would receive the survey's highest rating would be lower than the percentage of Yellow Party senators who would receive the highest rating.

(D) Experienced politicians are more likely to receive high ratings in voter satisfaction surveys than are new politicians.

(E) Among council members with the same amount of experience, differences in political party affiliation may not affect the way their constituents' satisfaction is rated.

17. Each of the following statements, if true, supports the author's contention that the organizers misinterpreted the survey data EXCEPT:

(A) The fact that one has five or more years of experience in politics is a positive indicator of that person's popularity with the voting public.

(B) Voter satisfaction ratings of a council member are influenced by the council member's level of experience in politics.

(C) The Yellow Party is made up primarily of middle-aged voters and is thus more likely than the Orange Party to select older candidates to run under its banner.

(D) It is rare for new politicians to attain the voter appeal of politicians who have been in the public eye for three or more years.

(E) Politicians who have served in public office for several years are generally able to obtain larger donations and a greater number of staff than those who are new to politics.

18. For the past several years the university film society has shown classic European and Hollywood films. Faced with declining attendance, the society recently changed its policy and now screens primarily contemporary Hollywood films, with classics being shown once per month at most. Last week's attendees were asked to respond to a survey about the change in policy. As only 8 of 150 people surveyed said they preferred classic films, the society has decided that the change to a contemporary focus was in the best interests of its members.

    The society's conclusion is most vulnerable to criticism on the ground that it ignores the possibility that

    (A) members are likely to become more disenchanted with the policy change as time goes on
    (B) those members most likely to be unhappy with the change did not respond at all to the survey
    (C) members would understand that their reaction to the change in the society's screening policy was the intended primary focus of the survey
    (D) the film being shown the night the survey conducted was a classic film
    (E) members of a university film society are more likely to be interested in European films

19. In a recent election, Jones won over Smith by a small margin after the Jones campaign ran an advertisement criticizing Smith's voting record in the state legislature. Exit polls showed that seventy percent of those who had intended to vote for Smith and had seen the advertisement cast their votes for Jones. Ninety percent of those who voted for Jones, however, had not seen the advertisement.

    Which one of the following would provide an explanation for the exit poll results above?

    (A) Only a small percentage of people who voted for Jones were influenced by the anti-Smith advertisement.
    (B) Political advertising has little or no effect on voter behavior.
    (C) It is impossible to determine the influence of negative advertising on voter behavior.
    (D) Most Jones supporters were uninformed voters.
    (E) Political advertising is ineffective because it fails to reach likely voters.

20. Researchers, perplexed by the development of measles immunity in children who were not given the measles vaccination, believe that they now understand this phenomenon. The children in question were all raised from birth on a baby formula produced by the manufacturer Dihydro. The Dihydro formula contains a synthetic chemical known as dihydron-X, which has been shown in lab tests to rapidly destroy cells infected with measles. Researchers have concluded that those children who ingest the Dihydro formula maintain dihydron-X in their bloodstreams indefinitely. When measles-infected cells proliferate in the child's body, the dihydron-X responds to the invasion by quickly killing off all infected cells, thus arresting the progress of the disease so rapidly that the child is perceived to have a measles immunity.

    Which one of the following most accurately characterizes the role played in the passage by the unstated assumption that some children who receive measles vaccinations develop an immunity to measles?

    (A) It is a point that, taken together with the fact that some children who do not receive the measles vaccine develop an immunity to measles, generates the problem that motivated the research described in the passage.
    (B) It is a generalization assumed by the researchers to prove that the explanation of their puzzling case must involve a reference to the chemical composition of measles-resistant cells.
    (C) It is a generalization that, if true, makes impossible the notion that some children who do not receive a measles vaccine develop an immunity to measles.
    (D) It is a hypothesis that the researchers take to be proven conclusively by the findings put forth in the passage.
    (E) It is a conclusion that is overturned by the researchers' discovery that some children who do not receive vaccines nonetheless develop a measles immunity.

PRACTICE SET 4: ANSWERS AND EXPLANATIONS

Explanations: Ninth Ward Council

16. E

Here we have two opposing views presented within a single argument. A survey showed that as a group, Yellow Party council members were rated more highly than Orange Party members. The first viewpoint is that of the survey organizers, who concluded from this that the political party of a council member must determine how satisfied voters are with his or her job performance. This might seem reasonable, but then the author, using the contrast Keyword "yet," states that this conclusion is probably wrong and offers an alternative explanation. He notes that the Yellow Party members who received higher ratings are more experienced politicians than their counterparts in the Orange Party. Notice that the author doesn't disagree that Yellow Party members receive higher ratings, but rather supports a different explanation for those ratings; the effect is the same in both viewpoints, but the causes differ. We're looking for an inference based on this argument, so once we have a firm grasp of the content, it's time to move on to the answer choices.

(A) confuses percentages and numbers. The survey results are based on the percentage of council members in each party to receive the highest rating, not on the actual number of council members to receive the top rating. For example, according to the stimulus, it could be possible that 50% of 20 Orange Party members receive the high rating, and 75% of 12 Yellow Party members receive the high rating, in which case fewer Yellow Party members receive the highest rating, despite the Yellow Party members receiving the higher percentage of top ratings. As we've just seen quite clearly in "Sports Injuries at Mercer High," question 14, a lower percentage does not necessarily mean a lower number.

(B) On the contrary: The author *does* suggest that there is a relationship between previous experience in politics and high satisfaction ratings from voters, so this answer choice contradicts the author's argument.

(C) The argument is about voters' satisfaction ratings with council members in the Ninth Ward. Based on that argument, we cannot infer anything about how voters would respond in a survey about state senators.

(D) distorts the information in the stimulus. Certainly, of the council members who were named in this particular survey, some have several years of experience in politics, while others are serving their first terms. Does that allow us to conclude who's "more likely" to receive high voter satisfaction ratings? For all we know, the Yellow Party members with high ratings were just as popular with voters during their first terms in office. The absolute statement here is not inferable from the information in the stimulus.

(E) is the only choice that's left. The author suggests that having experience in politics is more important than political party affiliation in determining voter satisfaction, so it logically follows that political party affiliation may not be a significant factor in voters' ratings of council members with an equal number of years of experience. By positing another factor (besides political party affiliation) to account for the survey results, the author's argument certainly allows for the possibility that political party affiliation *may* have no effect on voter satisfaction ratings.

Note that the incorrect choices here contain some common wrong answer types: confusing numbers and percentages (A); a choice that suggests the opposite of what's in the passage (B); a choice that strays outside the scope of the argument (C); and a classic distortion (D).

A 180 test taker recognizes the kinds of wrong choices that appear again and again on the LSAT.

---

17. C

The second question based on this stimulus asks us to locate the one answer choice that *doesn't* strengthen the author's argument. We therefore want to eliminate the four choices that support the connection between a council member's voter satisfaction rating and her level of experience in politics. The correct choice will be the one that *doesn't* support the author's causal link between previous political experience and higher voter ratings in the Ninth Ward.

(A) If previous experience in politics indicates greater popularity with voters, then the author's proposed link between experience and voter satisfaction seems more plausible, and we are more likely to believe that the organizers are wrong (as the author maintains) about the effects of party affiliation.

(B), (D), and (E) all strengthen the author's argument by tying past experience in politics to present popularity with voters. (B) links previous experience directly to ratings. (D) takes it from another angle, explaining that new politicians do not often achieve the same popularity with voters as that attained by more experienced politicians. It still strengthens the argument by offering a direct relationship between length of experience and level of popularity. (E) links prior experience in politics to the ability to obtain greater financial and human resources, offering another benefit available to experienced politicians that gives them an advantage in popularity with voters. Like (A), all of these choices make it seem more reasonable to argue that the organizers have misunderstood the role of political party affiliation in the survey results. That is, they all support the author's alternative explanation.

(C) *Why* a party selects its candidates has no impact on this argument. The fact remains that of council members in this particular survey, the Yellow Party members were all relatively experienced in politics while the Orange Party members were not, and the author uses this fact to counter a previous conclusion. (C) gives us one possible explanation for this fact, but it has no effect on *how* the fact is used by the author—and that's really what constitutes the crux of her argument. This is the one choice that does not strengthen (or, for that matter, even affect) the author's argument, so it is the right answer.

Explanation: University Film Society

18. B

There is considerable danger in drawing conclusions from a survey when the survey sample may be self-selecting. In this example, attendees of a single film screening were asked about their preferences. Although 8 out of 150 is indeed a small percentage, it's likely that anyone disenchanted with the society's new policy just didn't attend this screening.

A 180 test taker, when presented with a survey, asks whether the results accurately represent the views of the whole group targeted.

Only (B) picks up on this problem in the argument—that the sample for this survey may have been greatly skewed, therefore not a good basis for the society's conclusion. We aren't told what kind of film was played last week, but since the policy is to play classics only once per month, the chances are it was a contemporary film, and that the audience didn't include a high percentage of classic film buffs. In any case, perhaps those unhappy about the new policy were less likely to continue to attend, or to respond to a survey if they did attend.

(A) Makes a claim about how members are likely to feel about the new policy in the future, which is well beyond the temporal scope of the question.

(C) As there was no reason for the society to disguise their intent in making the survey, knowledge of the survey's purpose on the part of the attendees is no criticism of the society's conclusion.

(D) in fact would strengthen the society's conclusion, skewing the sample towards those most likely to disagree with the change in policy.

(E) It can't be said that the society failed to acknowledge this, as we have to suppose that this is something the society meant to determine by making the survey.

Explanation: Jones Beats Smith

19. A

Here's another study to ponder, and the stem alerts us to the fact that we need to find a plausible explanation for the statistics cited. That alone suggests that the stats are puzzling or unusual, which is reinforced by the word "however" in the final sentence.

Seventy and ninety are large percentages and a quick glance at such results might lead us to jump to conclusions. Yet it's (A), the sentence beginning "only a small percentage" that is the correct choice. While a large percentage of people who would have otherwise voted for Smith may well have changed their minds on the basis of the advertisement, only 10% of Jones voters had even seen the advertisement. This is not unlike what we've seen previously: what seems like the same groups are actually not.

(B) and (C) can be quickly dismissed as it seems that a very large percentage of voters may well have changed their votes because of the anti-Smith advertisement.

(D) is superficially appealing since we know that only a small percentage of Jones voters had seen the anti-Smith advertisement, but this would be scanty evidence on which to base a claim that these voters were uninformed.

(E) is beyond the scope of the question. Only voters were surveyed; no conclusions concerning likely voters can be made.

Explanation: Measles Immunity

20. A

Were you feeling unchallenged? Probably not, but here's a little twist just in case you were. We're directed in this one to determine the role played not by just any piece of information, but rather by a certain assumption in the argument which is given to us in the stem. Strange!

A 180 test taker rolls with the punches. When he sees something a bit unusual, he relates it to something more familiar. With definite strategies for questions regarding both the role of a statement and assumptions there's no need to panic over a minor deviation.

The first task is to see where the given assumption exists in the argument. The author begins by explaining a paradox: Kids who weren't vaccinated seemed to be immune to measles. This is the only place in the stimulus where the author discusses vaccination, so it must be where the stem's assumption comes in. Indeed, in this first sentence the author does assume that vaccinations give kids immunity, or else the researchers wouldn't have been so surprised by this nonvaccination-based immunity. Now for the question at hand: How does this function in the argument? Well, it helps to set up the unusual situation that the rest of the stimulus will strive to explain or, in other words, the problem that requires a solution provided in the argument. (A) captures this by noting that the first sentence (statement plus assumption) creates the confusion that the researchers then worked to explain.

(B) would tie the assumption into the evidence regarding dihydron-X, but this assumption doesn't come from that part of the passage.

(C) contradicts the passage, which explains how the kids were able to achieve such an immunity. Therefore, such immunity is not impossible.

(D) This assumption is not what the researchers seek to prove; they seek to prove how the kids who *don't* receive the vaccination could get such immunity.

(E) Just because the kids became immune through their formulas, that doesn't overturn the assumption that vaccinations also create immunity. The researchers' conclusion does not contradict or undermine this particular assumption.

PRACTICE SET 5: JUST PLAIN TOUGH

21. Candidates for public office who begin their campaigns early and maintain a continuous barrage of campaign rhetoric have an almost insurmountable advantage over their opponents. Money is the single resource that allows these candidates to mount this sort of sustained effort. Politicians with a personal fortune or wealthy backers have instant access to a wide variety of media. They can even buy access to the most important and influential political tool of all—television. Well-heeled candidates can thus ensure that they are consistently before the public eye whether or not they have done anything newsworthy. Less monied candidates can usually afford a certain amount of media exposure, but they must start their campaigns late. It is an unfortunate fact that money, not merit, is the deciding factor in most elections.

    Which one of the following statements, if true, would most seriously weaken the author's conclusion that money is the deciding factor in most elections?

    (A) Even the most impoverished candidates can afford a minimal amount of television air time.

    (B) Most candidates who cannot afford television exposure can at least afford substantial amounts of radio air time.

    (C) Sometimes less wealthy candidates can acquire great sums of money by election day by collecting a very large number of small contributions.

    (D) Candidates who start their campaigns late are nonetheless as familiar to the voters by election day as those who begin early.

    (E) People often consider such factors as a candidate's stance on the issues and his or her personality before deciding whom to vote for.

22. Professor Hendrix is a specialist in the study of new religious movements, sometimes referred to as "cults." She and two of her students spent a full year undercover in one such cult, posing as converts to the movement, in this particular case a "doomsday cult," or one preparing for the end of the world on a specific date set by the cult leader. Prof. Hendrix has subsequently argued against the prevailing view in her field that when end-of-the-world prophecies fail either cult members lose faith in their leader and leave the cult or else the cult engages in some sort of violence directed towards some institution or group perceived to be a threat to the cult. As she notes in her most recent book, neither of these predicted outcomes came to pass in the cult she and her students infiltrated, leading her to conclude that the prevailing view of doomsday cult relationships is mistaken.

    Which one of the following is an assumption upon which Prof. Hendrix's argument depends?

    (A) Participation in the cult by Dr. Hendrix and her students had no effect on the behavior of the cult as a whole.

    (B) The cult leader's prediction of the end of the world did not in fact come to pass.

    (C) Doomsday cults are historically more prone to violent behavior than other kinds of cults.

    (D) If a cult leader's prophecy does not come to pass, he or she is weakened in the eyes of the cult's members.

    (E) As long as a cult does not engage in violent activity it poses no threat to the psychological well-being of its members.

23. Boz: Scots Gaelic, an ancient and unique language, is now spoken only in a few places in the Western Highlands and in the remoter Scottish islands. It does not have a population base of native speakers sufficient to survive on its own. Unless drastic action is taken to preserve Scots Gaelic, we will probably witness the tragic loss of this distinct and irreplaceable language within the next century.

    Gertrude: You are wrong in considering Scotland only. Scots Gaelic and Irish Gaelic are essentially different dialects of the same language. As long as Irish Gaelic is still spoken in Ireland, it would be inaccurate to say that a language has been lost even if Scots Gaelic ceases to be spoken in Scotland altogether.

    Boz and Gertrude are committed to disagreeing with each other on which one of the following statements?

    (A) The population base currently speaking Scots Gaelic in the Western Highlands and remoter Scottish islands is enough to sustain the language into the future.

    (B) Scots Gaelic is properly considered a separate and distinct language.

    (C) Scots Gaelic is only spoken in a few places in the Western Highlands and in the remoter Scottish islands.

    (D) Without drastic action, the Gaelic language will probably be lost in the next century, because of the shortage of native speakers.

    (E) The population base of Irish Gaelic speakers is enough to sustain that branch of the Gaelic language into the next century without drastic action.

Questions 24-25

Just a passing comparison of today's *New York Times* bestseller list with those of thirty or forty years ago demonstrates a decline in overall literacy in this country. Whereas we once saw books by authors such as Thomas Pynchon and William Styron on this list, today's bestselling authors are more likely to be diet doctors or celebrities than accomplished novelists. If overall literacy means simply being able to read and write, then it matters little what we happen to be reading. But if by literacy we mean our ability to understand and appreciate fine literature, then there can be no doubt that overall literacy has declined precipitously.

24. This argument relies on which one of the following assumptions?

    (A) Bestseller lists in other countries continue to reflect an appreciation of fine literature.

    (B) The ability to read and write is not sufficient for the appreciation of fine literature.

    (C) Books by diet doctors and celebrities are more likely to be published today than they were thirty or forty years ago.

    (D) Degraded ability to understand and appreciate fine literature will lead to degraded ability to read and write.

    (E) *The New York Times* bestseller list is an accurate indication of what people in this country are reading.

25. Which one of the following, if true, most weakens the argument above?

    (A) Thomas Pynchon's latest novel was on the *New York Times* bestseller list.

    (B) Film adaptations of classic novels have become increasingly popular at the box office over the past several years.

    (C) A recent American Library Association study reports that borrowings from literature collections has increased by ten to twenty percent over each of the last four decades.

    (D) Bestsellers by celebrity authors are often ghostwritten by accomplished, professional writers.

    (E) Literacy rates in this country continue to be as high as, if not higher than, those in most other countries.

PRACTICE SET 5: ANSWERS AND EXPLANATIONS

Explanation: Media and Candidates

21. D

In this little tale of media and politics (two popular LSAT topics), the media play an indispensable role in a candidate's bid for office; and access to the mother of all media, television, takes moolah, and lots of it. According to the author, money allows a candidate to mount a sustained media barrage, and gain access to "the most important and influential political tool of all—television." We're asked to find the statement that weakens the claim that money is the deciding factor in elections, which means we need to break down the connection between the two that the author attempts to establish. In simple terms, we're looking for something that, if true, would suggest that money is *not* as important in deciding elections as the author would have us believe. That's about as good a prephrase as we're likely to form.

(A) What good is a minimal amount of air time? The wealthy, who could purchase lots of air time, would still have an "insurmountable advantage" over the poor.

(B) ignores the passage's claim that television is "the most important and influential political tool;" the fact that poor candidates can afford some radio coverage doesn't offset the TV advantage of the rich.

(C) The key to the mistake in this one is the phrase "by election day." The whole argument is based around the notion of using money to begin campaigning *early* and to maintain a "constant barrage of campaign rhetoric." Getting the dough by election day is too late.

(D) is what we want: It strongly suggests that the supposed financial advantage isn't so important after all. If candidates who start their campaigns late are just as familiar to voters by election day as candidates who wage sustained media campaigns, the conclusion that money is the deciding factor (because it buys recognition) is seriously damaged.

(E) is tricky, and perhaps sucked you in because it discusses the importance of nonmonetary concerns such as candidates' views and personalities. But in actuality this plays right into the author's argument: Before the public can judge a candidate's stance or personality, that candidate must be known, and what better way to get known than the author's "money and media barrage" approach?

A 180 test taker sees all angles, and recognizes subtle nuances that others miss.

Explanation: Professor Hendrix

22. A

Here is another question that doesn't fall into any of our major categories, but is difficult nonetheless. Dr. Hendrix and her students infiltrated the group and their presence may have influenced its behavior. Or their "posing as converts" may not have been as successful as she thinks, and the group may have known they were being observed. The assumption that nothing is changed by Dr. Hendrix's participation with her students in the cult is a crucial assumption to her argument. If cult behavior was affected in any way by the participation of people who weren't sincere members of the cult, none of her conclusions can be trusted.

(B) isn't really so much an assumption. If the prediction of the end of the world did come to pass you wouldn't be studying for the LSAT right now.

(C) is not important in any way to the argument, as it does not make claims about behavior in different kinds of cults, just in the doomsday cults.

(D) may well be true, but it's not an assumption on which Dr. Hendrix's conclusion is based. It is in fact part of the hypothesis being tested.

(E) is far beyond the scope of the question. It is only the behavior of the cult and its members that is being studied, not its effects on its members.

A 180 test taker quickly eliminates assumption choices that are simply too broad in their scope to be necessary to the argument in question.

Explanation: The Death of Scots Gaelic

23. B

No, it's not a person, although "Scots Gaelic" would make a mighty fine name. We're talking about the possible death of a language here, or at least Boz and Gertrude are talking about that. Boz predicts the death of Scots Gaelic if "drastic action" isn't taken to preserve it, and he says that the death of Scots Gaelic would constitute the tragic loss of a *distinct* language. Gertrude disagrees with this diagnosis; she takes issue with Boz's focus on Scots Gaelic as a unique language. She says that Scots Gaelic is but one *dialect* of a larger language (i.e., Gaelic); therefore, as long as some type of Gaelic is spoken somewhere (specifically, Irish Gaelic in Ireland), the death of Scots Gaelic would not be the death of a distinct language, but merely that of a dialect. Since Boz insisted that Scots Gaelic is a "unique" and "distinct" language, the two speakers are committed to disagreeing on the proposition set forth in (B).

In this question, Boz describes Scots Gaelic twice, once as "ancient and unique" and again as "distinct and irreplaceable." It's that idea of Scots Gaelic's uniqueness that's the key to the disagreement.

(A) Gertrude never said that the population base currently speaking Scots Gaelic was enough to sustain it, only that the loss of Scots Gaelic wouldn't be the loss of a distinct language.

(C) While Gertrude said that Boz was wrong to limit his focus to Scotland, her point was that *other* types of Gaelic are spoken elsewhere, not that *Scots* Gaelic is spoken elsewhere.

(D) Boz only spoke of Scots Gaelic, so we have no idea what he would make of (D). Similarly, Gertrude never took a firm position as to whether Gaelic as a whole could survive into the next century without drastic action; her point was only that Scots Gaelic is a part of a larger Gaelic world.

(E) Boz never even mentioned the existence of Irish Gaelic, so he's not committed to believing anything about (E). Gertrude also never takes a position on (E), limiting herself to saying that *if* Irish Gaelic survives there will be no loss of language.

A 180 test taker knows that for a choice to be correct on a "point-at-issue" question, it must be a statement on which both speakers have taken clear—and contradictory—positions.

Boz never says *anything* about either Irish Gaelic or Gaelic as a whole, so he hasn't taken a position on (D) or (E), which means that these choices simply cannot be correct.

Explanation: Times Bestsellers

24. E

The author's complaint is that, as demonstrated by the *New York Times* bestseller lists, literacy is declining in America. To reach this conclusion, the author provides a special definition of "literacy"—the ability to understand and appreciate fine literature. Even with this tailored definition, though, the author is making a rather sweeping conclusion—that overall literacy is in decline—on what might or might not be rather scanty evidence. If, but only if, the *New York Times* bestseller list is an accurate indicator of the literary habits of Americans, there may be something to his argument. Moreover, the author is assuming a correlation between buying literature (which is all the bestseller list can show) and both reading and understanding it—a point not tested by this question, but that might have been. Of our choices, only (E) gets to the heart of the matter: the adequacy of the evidence presented.

(A) is well beyond the scope of the author's argument, which clearly makes a claim only about "this country."

(B) The author makes no claims about what is necessary for the appreciation of fine literature, only that this appreciation is necessary to "overall literacy."

(C) is in no way necessary to the author's argument, and, if true, could even be seen to weaken it. If diet and celebrity books were less common forty years ago they were also less likely to be bestsellers.

(D) Could be an assumption of a more general argument about the decline of literacy, but is not needed by this author, who has defined literacy as including an appreciation of fine literature.

25. C

We're asked now to weaken the same argument. To recap: the author concludes that the books listed in the *New York Times* bestseller list prove literacy is declining in America; a special definition of literacy is used.

The right answer in *weaken* questions often focuses on an underlying assumption in the argument, but that's not likely here (because we're focusing only on the hardest questions), since the first question for this stimulus already focused on what assumption or assumptions were made.

The issue here is the adequacy of the author's evidence based only on the *New York Times* bestsellers. If an alternate source, like library statistics, show exactly the opposite of what the author's evidence shows, then his whole argument is thrown into question. (C) points out that the reading habits of Americans may be measured in several ways and that the author's evidence is by no means conclusive.

(A) might seem a tempting choice, but would it in fact weaken the author's argument? The author doesn't say Pyncheon novels never appear on the list, but that they are less likely than diet doctors and celebrities. A single instance is merely an anomaly that isn't precluded by the author's statements.

(B) is irrelevant to an argument about literacy, particularly given the author's definition of literacy. Watching movies based on literature can't improve the ability to read and write, let alone the ability to understand and appreciate fine literature. If anything, these might tend to support the argument.

(D) could weaken the author's argument, but only if we make the further, suspect assumption that ghostwriters produce fine literature no matter what the topic.

(E) Again, a comparison between this country and others is irrelevant. The author states clearly that he is comparing literacy between time periods in this country.

A 180 test taker knows that the two most common ways to weaken an argument are by breaking down the argument's central assumption, and by asserting alternative possibilities relevant to the argument.

What's Next?

This concludes our in-depth look at the five major categories of tough LR questions. In the next chapter we'll look at other structural and logical formulations that present difficulties for LSAT test takers on the Logical Reasoning sections. The concept of "alternative explanations"—nicely highlighted here in "Times Bestsellers"—is among them.

CHAPTER NINE

Other Logical Reasoning Challenges

Aside from the major categories of tough Logical Reasoning questions discussed thus far, there are also a number of other logical elements that appear somewhat regularly on the LSAT and are notorious for giving test takers trouble. These logical features and question types often appear in conjunction with the major categories discussed in chapters 7 and 8—indeed, we've noted *en route* those questions that contain some of these logical nuances. But let's now have a better look at them as challenges to reckon with in their own right. Sink your teeth into the following questions, one at a time, focusing on the distinguishing features of each.

PHILOSOPHERS' CORNER

The difficulty of some Logical Reasoning questions resides in the language of the stimulus. The question below is a long-winded discussion of the nature of good and evil, qualifying it as an example of what we at Kaplan call "Philosophers' Corner"—dense prose concerning esoteric topics and laden with abstraction.

1. There are those, Mr. Hobbes foremost among them, who maintain that before any positive laws were instituted, there could be no distinction between the good and the evil, the just and the unjust. In the state of nature, each had the "right" to lop off the head of any other. This frightening situation prompted those in a state of nature to form a social body and enact positive laws that forbid murder. It was only with the formation of these laws that good and evil were born; and it was only as a result of these laws that murder could be termed evil. This description is inaccurate. If murder was deemed so unfit and unreasonable an act that men entered into contracts to preserve themselves, then murder must have been understood as unfit and unreasonable before such contracts were formed. This being the case, these thinkers' supposition that there is neither "good" nor "evil" antecedent to the institution of law is self-defeating: If the distinction between good and evil is once admitted to exist, then it has always existed.

   The author intends to discredit the view of Mr. Hobbes and similar thinkers by attempting to

   (A) present historical evidence in support of his view
   (B) show that their argument contains circular reasoning
   (C) show that their account of the origin of morality presupposes a contradiction
   (D) point out the unacceptable consequences of their views on morality
   (E) impugn the motives of these thinkers themselves, rather than dealing with their argument

You'll see this category resurface later on in the Reading Comprehension section of this book, and the little morality piece we have here in this question certainly seems much like a mini Reading Comp passage in its own right. Let's see how you did with Hobbes and company.

Explanation: Beyond Good and Evil

Perhaps the philosophically minded among you recognize the title of this question as the title of the famous book by German philosopher Friedrich Nietzsche. Nor is this the last we'll hear from Mr. Nietzsche in this chapter.

The author argues that morality—or the distinction between good and evil—has always existed. This contradicts the claims of Hobbes and others that morality is an effect of law, and that where there is no law, there is neither good nor evil. Hobbes and the others presume that in the state of nature—man's condition before laws—there was no distinction between good and evil. They then claim that men entered into a social contract, and with the formation of the contract, good and evil were born—evil being that which breaks the contract (such as murder), and good being that which upholds the contract. The author's point is that, in order to explain the later prohibition against murder, one must assume that in the state of nature men found murder to be unreasonable, and therefore, evil. Thus, the author believes, thinkers such as Hobbes assume *first*, that the state of nature *is* free of moral judgment, and *second*, that this state is *not* free of moral judgment. Pretty dense stuff, but if we boil it down correctly we see that the author attempts to show that his opponents' view is self-contradictory. A contradiction is presupposed in this line of thinking, according to the author, so (C) is correct.

(A) is incorrect because the author presents no historical evidence. The argument concerns history, as it is an argument about origins, yet no actual history is given as evidence.

(B) is wrong because self-contradiction is not the same as circular reasoning. (We'll discuss what circular reasoning is in just a little bit.) Both are serious flaws, but they are not the same flaw.

(D) While the author likely feels that his opponents' views on morality can have unfavorable consequences, this is not what his argument rests on. He is concerned with refuting their argument on logical grounds, not on moral grounds.

(E) is incorrect because there is no *ad hominem* attack here; that is, a situation in which the author attacks his opponents personally rather than the *views* of his opponents. That's not the method employed here.

A 180 test taker is familiar with all forms of argumentation, valid and not, that are known to appear on the LSAT.

CIRCULAR REASONING

Advertisement: If you plan to go to law school, you should take the Kaplan LSAT course because, all things considered, it is very much in the interest of all aspiring lawyers to enroll in and complete Kaplan's preparation program for the LSAT.

How do you like this reasoning? Now, while there are many good reasons to take the Kaplan LSAT course (excellent teachers, world-class materials, access to every released LSAT question with explanations, killer software, etc.), not one is actually mentioned in the ad.

Disclaimer: Not an actual ad. The Kaplan Marketing department is far more on the ball than this.

In fact, the hypothetical ad above says nothing; or, more precisely, *its conclusion says nothing different from its evidence.* And that's the essence of what's known as "circular reasoning," a type of flawed logic that shows up occasionally on the LSAT. The argument in the ad above essentially boils down to "future law students should take Kaplan's LSAT course because future law students should take Kaplan's LSAT course." Of course, the language is dressed up a bit, and on the LSAT these can actually be quite tricky. Choice (B) in question 1 above wrongly suggests that the author is accusing Hobbes of employing circular reasoning, but Hobbes and the others do not use evidence that mirrors their conclusion, nor do they assume the truth of their conclusion in proving it. But the argument in question 2 below is another story. Practice recognizing Circular Reasoning with this example.

2. Censorship is poor policy and should be abandoned. Those who promote censorship, and there are more than one might believe, simply refuse to see that it is a far worse state of affairs when people are not free to express themselves than it is when they are free to express themselves.

Which one of the following best describes the author's method of argument?

(A) It attempts to establish the validity of an argument by denying the truth of the opposite of that argument.
(B) It appeals to a false authority.
(C) It makes a general conclusion based on one segment of the population.
(D) It employs circular reasoning.
(E) It draws a conclusion about a whole group from evidence about some members of the group.

Did you catch the circularity of the reasoning in this question?

Explanation: Censorship

Not much to say after the discussion above, other than to spell out exactly how the argument is circular, making (D) our correct answer. The argument concludes that censorship is bad because it's much worse when there *is* censorship than when there isn't. Sounds pretty unpersuasive, doesn't it? The reasoning literally goes in a circle, using its own conclusion as evidence: X is a poor policy because it's much better when there's no X than when there is X. But that's the very definition of something that's bad, so the argument essentially says nothing and only winds back on itself. Which is to say, it's circular.

(A) The opposite argument isn't presented—we simply don't know why some people would promote censorship—so the truth of it isn't denied and (A) isn't correct.

(B) The author doesn't use an authority, false or not, to establish credibility, so (B) is out.

(C) and (E) are both incorrect for the same reason. There isn't any generalizing here. Censorship is bad for all people, the author argues, because it's bad for all people. That's a circle, not a generalization.

It's worth noting that circular reasoning shows up more often on the LSAT as a wrong choice than as a right answer, but either way it's important to understand what this faulty kind of reasoning is all about. (Hey, if nothing else, it may help you to point out holes in your friends' arguments. And people just love that kind of thing . . . .)

PRINCIPLE APPLICATION

Principle questions are among the more difficult questions in the Logical Reasoning sections, and of the few different types of Principle questions, the kind that asks you to find the choice among the five that conforms to a given Principle in the stem is probably the most difficult. Applying a principle to specific situations is, of course, a very lawyer-like thing to do, so it's not surprising that the test makers want to test this skill. Most Principle questions come with difficult choices, and this one is no exception.

3. The tenure system is meant to safeguard academic freedom in our universities. Under academic freedom, scholars are free to pursue whatever intellectual lines of inquiry they see fit without external influence from university administrators, politicians, or public opinion. Of course tenure may under some exceptional circumstances be revoked, but never based on what a professor may say or write.

Which one of the following adheres most closely to the principle set forth above?

(A) Under academic freedom, a scholar can publish in any respected journal, but could lose tenure for publishing in journals not recognized by her university.

(B) Without academic freedom, a professor could teach a course on astrology and still keep his tenure.

(C) Without academic freedom, no professor could expect to be granted tenure if she advanced ideas that were contrary to public opinion.

(D) Under academic freedom, a professor could lose tenure for embezzling funds from his university, but not for writing an article critical of the university's fiscal policy.

(E) Under academic freedom, scholars must maintain a high standard of scholarship or else risk losing their tenure.

Did you breeze through the choices to the correct answer, or did you have difficulty relating them back to the principle in question?

Explanation: Academic Freedom

When asked for a situation that conforms to a principle, your best bet is to understand the principle thoroughly and then test the choices against this understanding. The principle of academic freedom outlined here makes a clear distinction between the professors' speech or writing in connection with "intellectual pursuits" and their behavior in any other context. While tenure is meant to protect freedom within the realm of scholarship, it doesn't limit its protection to a professor's specific academic department or field. Note, too, that we are told only about protection of faculty who *have* tenure—not about the conditions for obtaining tenure. (D) best illustrates this: Writing any article falls under the protection of academic freedom; embezzlement obviously would not.

(A) The principle as outlined makes no mention of the recognition of journals as respected. Official sanction by universities of journals could be seen as a violation of the principle of academic freedom.

(B) has it exactly backwards. It is academic freedom that would allow a professor to teach what she sees fit without the threat of lost tenure.

(C) is too strong and out of scope. There's no indication in the passage that the principle of academic freedom is the only thing protecting scholars from the influence of public opinion, and in any case, we know nothing about the conditions for gaining tenure, only for keeping it.

A 180 test taker understands that the right answer must be correct on its own merit, without requiring us to introduce extra information.

(E) Would clearly violate the principle. Although we might infer that there are standards of scholarship enforced in some way in universities there is no mention of these in the outline of this principle.

SCOPE SHIFTS

Have you ever been in an argument in which you just know that your opponent is pulling a fast one, but you can't quite put your finger on the flaw in his argument? Perhaps, somewhere along the way, he subtly changed the direction of the argument. This is a classic argumentative technique; in fact, one that the LSAT test makers are quite fond of. In a number of Logical Reasoning questions, the author introduces a subtle distinction that slightly alters or shifts the scope or focus of the argument, as in the following example:

> Educators have been complaining that salaries are not high enough to draw enough top applicants to teaching jobs at the high school level. This is clearly absurd; there is fierce competition for teaching jobs at all levels, with many candidates vying for each new job that opens up.

Do you see the scope shift? The claim that the author attempts to refute deals with *top* applicants, whereas the evidence that the author provides for her rebuttal involves applicants *in general*. It may seem like a minor difference, applicants vs. *top* applicants, but it opens up a logical chasm. This is exactly the type of subtle distinction the test makers like to exploit. Such distinctions provide great material, especially for Assumption, Weaken the Argument, and Logical Flaw questions. They show up both in passages and choices. We've seen examples above in "Home Births" in chapter 7 and "Mt. Dunmore Lodge" in chapter 8. Now give this question a try:

4. It is mistaken to attribute Zanco's failure to the publicity about the supposedly inhuman working conditions in the foreign factories that furnish Zanco with many of its parts. Zanco's failure has more to do with defects in its products than with any boycott on moral grounds. After all, plenty of other companies are supplied by factories with working conditions just as bad as those in Zanco's suppliers, and the public does not hesitate to buy their products.

The argument in the passage is based on which one of the following assumptions?

(A) People are unlikely to let moral considerations affect what products they decide to purchase.

(B) People who patronize companies supplied by factories where working conditions are as bad as those of Zanco's suppliers are aware of those conditions.

(C) The working conditions in the factories that supply Zanco with parts are not as bad as has been claimed.

(D) Zanco's sales did not dip sharply after the poor working conditions in its suppliers' factories became known.

(E) The poor quality of Zanco's products is not a result of the working conditions in the foreign factories where its parts are manufactured.

Did you catch the scope shift here in "Zanco's Failure"?

Explanation: Zanco's Failure

The assertion that Zanco's failure is not due to publicity about poor working conditions in its suppliers' factories only makes sense if those who buy the products of those other companies are *aware* of those conditions in their suppliers' factories. After all, if people bought products from the other companies without knowing that they too were supplied by sweatshop-style factories, the comparison would be moot and the logic of the argument would go down the drain. The scope shift centers around the word "publicity." The conclusion that Zanco's failure was not due to publicity about bad working conditions is backed up by evidence concerning companies with bad working conditions *that says nothing about publicity*. Publicity is a key feature of the conclusion, but drops off the map in the evidence, and therein lies the scope shift and the necessity of (B).

(A) Even if people are likely to base purchasing decisions on moral considerations, it doesn't weaken the conclusion that people didn't do this in the case of Zanco.

(C) The point isn't that the working conditions of Zanco's suppliers have been unfairly exaggerated, but that these conditions are not a factor in the company's failure. It wouldn't affect the argument if, contrary to (C), working conditions are just as bad as the negative publicity claims.

(D) Even if Zanco's sales did dip sharply after people found out about the poor working conditions, we couldn't conclude that the dip resulted from the public's refusal to buy Zanco's products on moral grounds; the sales dip could have easily resulted from something else and merely coincided with the public's learning of the factory conditions.

(E) It doesn't matter whether or not there's a connection between the poor quality of the products and the lousy working conditions—the existence or lack of such a connection doesn't affect the logic of the argument.

ALTERNATIVE EXPLANATIONS

Perhaps, when arguing in real life, you've used the "Oh yeah? But what about . . ." defense. We look for alternative explanations for situations all the time, to prove our own points or argue against others. This is another common feature of Logical Reasoning questions; for example, take a look at question 25 in chapter 8, "Times Bestsellers" In that one, choice (E) addressed a possibility that the author overlooked, thus weakening the argument. Some arguments are flawed, or can be weakened, because their authors fail to see that a piece of evidence can lead to more than one possible conclusion, or that a situation or result can have more than one possible explanation. See if you can spot the relevant alternative that would weaken the argument below.

5. Historians of wine argue that top winemakers develop unique styles as a result of their vineyard's *terroir*—the soil, weather, and general personality of the terrain—and the influence of the early training they receive in the art of making wines. But when the technical advances in modern winemaking are discounted, it becomes clear that today's best winemakers approach their craft in almost exactly the same manner as did the winemakers of hundreds of years ago. This observation makes clear the fact that there is a universally recognized style of good winemaking.

The argument above is most weakened by which one of the following statements?

(A) Attention to genetics and other scientific aspects of grape-growing have made possible great advances in contemporary winemaking.

(B) Differences in *terroir* are even more pronounced than historians of wine believe.

(C) Today's winemakers are not particularly familiar with the winemaking techniques of past generations.

(D) Today's top winemakers were trained by the top winemakers of past generations.

(E) Advances in winemaking technique have made it possible to compensate for differing weather patterns in a single *terroir*.

Explanation: Terroir

The author begins be describing the view of some historians that winemakers have "unique" styles. After dismissing the effects of purely technological advances, the author argues that current styles are not different from previous styles.

The author's argument is complex in that its primary claim—that there is a universally recognized style of good winemaking—is not articulated until the end of the paragraph. Moreover, the universality of the claim is not even hinted at in the presentation of evidence, and it is the universality part of the claim that is most susceptible to criticism.

Consider the opposite of what the author claims, that there are several good styles of winemaking. How could this be consistent with the author's observation that all of today's best winemakers work in the same way as did the winemakers of the past? The answer is in (D). If today's winemakers are the students of past winemakers it's possible—even likely—that winemaking practice today is much a matter of traditions being handed-down from teachers to students.

(A) has no impact on the author's argument, particularly as he expressly discounts technical advances as irrelevant.

(B) and (C) would strengthen the author's argument, as greater differences in *terroir* and unfamiliarity with past practices would make a universal style of winemaking even less likely.

(E) Again, the author more or less dismisses the effect of technical advances on any changes in winemaking style, making technical claims orthogonal to his argument.

THE "ODD MAN OUT"

Next up in our potpourri of tough questions are questions that ask you to locate the one choice that *doesn't* satisfy a particular requirement; in other words, to find the "odd man out." These are difficult because the right answer may do the opposite of what's required, or may simply be irrelevant to the situation at hand. At the same time, the wrong choices are *all* relevant, and sometimes look and sound the same, lulling us into a state of mind in which every choice, including the bogus right answer, sounds reasonable. Finally, some test takers simply blow past the word "EXCEPT" or "NOT" in the question stem, and blow the question on that account.

These come in a number of varieties. Back in chapter 8's "Ninth Ward Council," question 17, we saw a "Strengthen EXCEPT" question. Later on we'll see a few other types. The following question is of the "which is *not* assumed" variety.

6. A political candidate committed to the principal tenets of a political party may not always explain the implications of his or her party commitment to the voters in full detail. Adele Richardson, for example, is a minor-party candidate in contention for a seat on the school board. She is not likely to inform conservative voters in her district that the national leadership of her party has recently recommended that school curricula be more closely monitored by agencies of the federal government.

Which one of the following is not assumed or implied by the passage above?

(A) A political candidate is likely to be more interested in winning an election than in proselytizing the electorate.

(B) The candidate of any party is likely to support the policy decisions made by the national leadership.

(C) All candidates for such community positions as membership on the school board must have commitments to national parties.

(D) Conservatives in Adele Richardson's district do not support federal intervention in decisions made by community school officials.

(E) Voters in Adele Richardson's district are not fully aware of the policy statements made by the national leadership of her party.

How did you make out?

Explanation: School Board Candidate

Four assumptions means we must be dealing with a pretty shaky, or at least, incomplete, argument. The author states a general point in the first sentence: A candidate who has faith in the beliefs of a party may not find it in her interest to explain those beliefs to voters. Enter Ms. Richardson, school board hopeful. Her party would like to see tight government regulation of school curricula, but in accordance with the claim in the first sentence, the author thinks that she's not likely to explain this to conservative voters. Since there are four assumptions here, our best bet is to go right to the choices, looking for the "odd man out."

(A) If (A) is *not* true, then the argument is weakened, which shows that (A) must be assumed. If a candidate is interested in proselytizing the electorate rather than winning an election, then, contrary to the author's assertion, the candidate would have no reason to conceal her opinions from voters likely to disagree with her.

(B) must be assumed because if a candidate is *not* likely to support the national leadership's policy decisions, then the author's assertion about Richardson makes no sense.

(C) is the only nonassumption here—the argument doesn't depend on candidates for community positions having commitments to national parties. The author addresses only those candidates who *are* committed to a political party's central tenets; he says nothing about what's required to run for community positions. Adele Richardson happens to be committed to a national party, but this needn't be true of all candidates for such positions.

(D) is a fairly obvious assumption: Why would Richardson conceal her party's recommendation from conservatives if conservatives supported it? Instead, she'd be more likely to parade the party recommendation in order to garner conservative votes.

(E) is also assumed: The only way Richardson can conceal her party's recommendation from voters is if they're not fully aware of it already.

TOUGH CHOICES

We've covered all kinds of tough Logical Reasoning questions, but we would be remiss to overlook questions that are difficult simply because they contain tough choices. Tough choices are especially prevalent in Method of Argument and Principle question types—both of which often include choices with general, somewhat abstract descriptions of what's going on in the passage—but there's really nothing stopping tough choices from showing up in any question type. Some of the questions you've seen already contain tough choices, and there's more to come later on. As for the question below, there's nothing inherently difficult about the story told in the stimulus, but the choices are a different matter altogether.

7. Hansen is a major league baseball player who is also very active in charity work. This work takes him all over the world and has made it necessary for him to miss most team workouts in the past two seasons, seasons that have seen his batting average and RBI totals decline. His team has offered him a new contract at a lower salary, reflecting Hansen's decreased production on the field. Hansen's agent has argued that his client's high-profile charity work benefits the team in positive publicity and therefore also in ticket sales. As Hansen's charity work is an economic benefit to the team, argues the agent, his salary ought not to be cut.

    Which of the following principles is NOT supported by the stand taken by Hansen's agent?

    (A) A factor that determines an individual's value in one context should not be used to determine that individual's value in a dissimilar situation.
    (B) Nothing that causes a condition can be used to compensate for the consequences of that condition.
    (C) The overall value of an activity must not be overridden by the negative result of a single aspect of that activity.
    (D) Negotiations affecting the livelihood of an individual must not discount any factor relevant to that negotiation.
    (E) The consequences of an action can only be evaluated with respect to the possible consequences of an opposing alternative action.

Explanation: Hansen's Charity Work

The question stem tells us to focus on the argument made by Hansen's agent, but the author gives us a good deal of background information before we hear about the agent. Apparently, Hansen's charitable activities may have affected his baseball performance, which resulted in his being offered a lower salary. But the agent says Hansen's good publicity for charitable work is good for the team's ticket sales, so his salary shouldn't be cut.

Now remember, we are looking for a principle that opposes this argument.

(A) is more the sort of claim that the agent might make than a principle opposed to his claim. It is exactly by comparison of dissimilar situations that the agent wants his client's value to be determined.

(B) is correct. If this principle is applied, and it is true that it is Hansen's charity work that has led to a decline in his play, then that work, no matter what other good it might have done, cannot compensate for Hansen's loss of value to the team on the field.

(C) The negative results in this case are of one activity upon another, so consideration of the aspects of a single activity have no real impact on the agent's argument.

(D) again is more helpful to the agent than opposed to his position. This choice collapses distinctions between the factors under consideration.

(E) sounds impressive, but says relatively little relevant to Hansen's situation. There is some question here of what the "actions" and "consequences" might be. One supposes that the action would be Hansen's charity work and the consequences his decline in play. This principle might in this case state that had Hansen not devoted so much time to charity work his play would not have declined. But this fails to address the agent's argument that his client's charity work has value to the team independent of anything that happens on the field.

A 180 test taker is adept at matching up the general terms in a tough choice with the specifics of the passage.

NECESSARY AND SUFFICIENT CONDITIONS

If I throw a baseball at the window, the window will break.

Considering the statement above, if I *don't* throw a baseball at the window, can we conclude that the window has *not* broken? No. While the baseball is enough to break the window—that is, is *sufficient* to break the window—nothing in the statement above indicates that the baseball is *necessary* to break the window. The window may break some other way, such as from a sonic boom, or from an egg thrown at it on Halloween.

Questions that test an understanding of the difference between necessary and sufficient conditions are perennial LSAT favorites. The Formal Logic example in chapter 8, "Mondavian Uprising," contains a necessary/sufficient element, and choice (B) in particular was wrong for mistaking one for the other. Questions 4 and 5 in chapter 8, "Railway System," are other Formal Logic questions you've seen earlier that involve necessary and sufficient conditions. In question 4, we say the following for (D) and (E): "We're told that public transport can grow more popular only if the railways are modernized and expanded. This doesn't mean that it *will* grow more popular simply because the railways have been modernized and expanded." What that means in this context is that modernization and expansion are *necessary* for increased popularity, but not *sufficient*. Other factors may need to come into play.

The question below is a complex Formal Logic question that's centered squarely around this notion of necessity vs. sufficiency.

8. In order to justify the merger of two banks, two things must be accomplished: First, the cost of the merger must not exceed one billion dollars; second, the bank created by the merger must retain the two former banks' customers. The newly formed bank cannot keep those customers, however, unless it avoids claims of discrimination by earmarking at least ten billion dollars for loans to low-income customers. If the bank cannot keep its customers, it cannot keep the cost of the merger from exceeding one billion dollars. So, it follows that if the new bank earmarks ten billion dollars in loans, it will keep the cost of the merger from exceeding one billion dollars.

   The reasoning in the argument is not valid because it fails to establish that

   (A) many successfully merged banks have earmarked loan money

   (B) some unsuccessful mergers cost less than one billion dollars

   (C) earmarking loan money is sufficient to guarantee customer loyalty

   (D) earmarking loan money is necessary for guaranteeing customer loyalty

   (E) many merged banks that experienced costly mergers have not earmarked loan money

Explanation: Bank Merger

We hope you noticed the landslide of necessity going on here: Earmarking loan money to low-income customers is *necessary* to retain customer loyalty (earmarking is *necessary* to prevent claims of discrimination, avoiding discrimination claims is *necessary* to customer loyalty), which in turn is *necessary* to keep merger costs from going over the one billion mark.

A 180 test taker can translate complex formal logic constructions such as "cannot . . . unless" into easy-to-work-with statements.

From the introduction above, you can probably see where this is going. Despite these necessary conditions, note the definite nature of the conclusion: If the new bank earmarks ten billion dollars in loans, then it *will* keep the cost of the merger under one billion dollars. What the author fails to consider is that, just because earmarking loan money is *necessary*, that doesn't mean it's *sufficient* to guarantee loyalty. That's choice (C). Nor, for that matter, is it established that maintaining customer loyalty will guarantee that the deal won't cost more than one billion dollars; again, loyalty is *necessary* for this outcome, but we can't conclude that the cost will be kept down simply because loyalty is maintained; other factors may involved.

(A), (B), and (E) all offer useless background information; it's not necessary to the logic of the argument for the author to provide examples of past mergers. Therefore, these choices are all beyond the scope of the argument.

(D), actually, is valid. As noted above, the argument does succeed in establishing this point.

CAUSATION

The great German philosopher, Friedrich Nietzsche, put it perfectly in his 1888 book *Twilight of the Idols*:

> There is no more dangerous error than that *of mistaking the consequence for the cause*: I call it reason's intrinsic form of corruption. (italics Nietzsche's)

LSAT test takers mistake cause and effect at their own risk. Some Logical Reasoning questions even contain precisely the same kind of reasoning as the example Nietzsche furnishes on the same page as the quote.

> Everyone knows the book of the celebrated Cornaro in which he recommends his meager diet as a recipe for a long and happy life—a virtuous one, too . . . I do not doubt that hardly any book . . . has done so much harm, has shortened so many lives, as this curiosity, which was so well meant. The reason: mistaking the consequence for the cause. The worthy Italian saw in his diet the *cause* of his long life: while the prerequisite of long life, an extraordinarily slow metabolism, a small consumption, was the cause of his meager diet. (italics Nietzsche's)

What Nietzsche is saying is that a meager diet didn't cause Cornaro to live long; a necessary condition of long life caused him to eat little. A perfectly LSAT-like example, right down to the name—we certainly wouldn't be surprised to find "Cornaro" in a Logic Game or as a contestant in a Logical Reasoning dialogue debate.

The LSAT test makers are fond of all kinds of causation problems. In some, one causal element is mistaken for another. In others, correlation is mistaken for causation, or occasionally, vice versa. You've already seen a few questions that contain causal elements. See for example "Lisa's Knees," "Ninth Ward Council," and "Times Bestsellers." Later on you'll also see examples in which cause and effect are reversed—that's a popular one.

The following question illustrates another very common and basic way that causation is tested on the LSAT. See what you can make of the reading predicament in Gotham.

9. Reading skills among high school students in Gotham have been steadily declining, which can only be the result of overcrowding in the schools.

   Which one of the following, if true, most seriously weakens the argument expressed above?

   (A) The high school system in Gotham succeeds in giving students a good education at considerably less cost than do most systems.

   (B) Several cities have found that overcrowding in the schools is not always associated with lower reading scores.

   (C) Gotham schools have a greater teacher-to-student ratio than most other school systems.

   (D) Students' reading skills have not declined in other cities where the high schools are just as crowded as those of Gotham.

   (E) Schools are not overcrowded in many cities where high school reading scores have declined more than they have in Gotham.

Explanation: Gotham Reading Skills

The important word in the author's conclusion is the word "only." She states that the problem of declining reading skills can only have one cause—overcrowding. Anything that renders doubtful the causal connection between Gotham's overcrowding and Gotham's declining reading scores will seriously weaken the argument. (E) does this by pointing out a case in which skills have declined, yet there is no overcrowding. So something *other* than overcrowding *can* account for a decline in reading skills. (Notice how this ties in with the notion of Alternative Explanations discussed earlier.)

(A) just tries to make an excuse for Gotham schools by pointing out that they spend less money. While this may furnish a reason for the overcrowding, it does nothing to hurt the argument that the overcrowding causes declining scores.

(B) and (D) point to overcrowding without declining scores. Yet the author didn't say that overcrowding always leads to declines in skills, but rather that declines in skills are always a result of overcrowding. Be careful to keep the causal mechanism straight!

(C), if anything, strengthens the argument by pointing out that the decline in reading scores cannot be attributed to a low teacher-to-student ratio. It must, therefore, be attributed to some other cause (e.g., overcrowding).

What's Next?

You've now heard about five major categories and nine subcategories of the most difficult LSAT Logical Reasoning material. What do you need to reinforce this learning and to match your wits against the conquests presented? More questions, of course. Onward to chapter 10.

CHAPTER TEN

Putting It All Together

By now, you should have a very definite idea of the many kinds of challenges presented in LSAT Logical Reasoning. While we've broken down these challenges into major and minor categories, roughly based on their prevalence on the test, the truth is that difficult questions are often combinations of the various logical elements you've just encountered. In other words, the logical elements and question types presented in chapters 7, 8, and 9 may, and often do, overlap in a single question. And just as in Hybrid Logic Games, the existence of multiple logical elements within questions complicates matters significantly.

In this chapter, you'll get practice with plenty of complex Logical Reasoning questions. Not every question contains more than one logical element, but many do, and we cite in the explanations the distinguishing logical or structural characteristics of each. We've arranged the questions in small groups so that you can learn as you go along and get practice recognizing the logical patterns that recur throughout the Logical Reasoning sections of the test.

PRACTICE SET 1

1. Studies of trauma victims suggest that shock brought on by violent or life-threatening situations causes damage to the hippocampi, structures in the brain that play a crucial role in learning and memory. Researchers found that in combat veterans suffering from post-traumatic stress symptoms, which include nightmares and vivid flashbacks, the hippocampi were eight percent smaller in volume than in combat veterans who suffered no such symptoms. The researchers concluded that the hippocampi had lost cell mass as a result of trauma.

    Which one of the following, if true, would most seriously weaken the researchers' conclusion drawn above?

    (A) In another study, subjects who had experienced the death of a close relative were found to have no reduction in the volume of their hippocampi when compared to those whose close relatives were all still living.

    (B) In the study, the traumatized veterans were compared with other veterans of similar background, body size, and other characteristics that might have a bearing on brain size.

    (C) Some individuals are born with hippocampi whose volume is smaller than average, and this reduced volume makes them more susceptible to post-traumatic stress symptoms.

    (D) Combat veterans who experience post-traumatic stress symptoms perform significantly worse on tests of verbal memory compared with veterans who suffer no such symptoms.

    (E) Further study revealed that veterans who had seen more intense combat and had more severe post-traumatic symptoms exhibited even greater reduction in the volume of their hippocampi.

2. Over the past seven years, private college tuition rates have increased, resulting in a large decrease in private college attendance across the country. Private college revenues, however, have progressively increased in each of the seven years during this period, and researchers predict further increases in the years to come.

    Which one of the following, if true, offers the best explanation for the situation described above?

    (A) Most private colleges increase tuition rates approximately once every two years.

    (B) Attendance at vocational schools generally exceeds attendance at private colleges in most cities.

    (C) The increase in tuition rates at private colleges has influenced many prospective students to seek a state scholarship to attend a public university.

    (D) The decrease in students attending private colleges over the last seven years has been more than offset by the increases in tuition.

    (E) Private colleges gain a larger percentage of their revenue from alumni contributions than do public universities.

3. When attempting to understand the world of art, it is necessary to distinguish between an artist's conception of his or her own particular work and the conception of the public who will experience that work of art. It is true that anyone can ascribe his or her own personal meaning to a work of art. Some art scholars, however, argue that only the artist's own conception of a work of art constitutes the "true" meaning of that work. Furthermore, they believe that only when an individual's conception of a work of art matches the "true" meaning of that work is it possible for an individual to experience art's power of transcendence.

If the views of the art scholars discussed in the passage above are correct, then which one of the following can be properly concluded from the passage?

(A) If an artist has a particular conception of a work of art, then no individual is justified in ascribing a personal meaning to that work.

(B) The stronger the personal meaning an individual ascribes to a work of art, the more likely that individual will experience art's power of transcendence.

(C) Some art scholars believe that an artist's conception of a work of art can never match the conception of individuals experiencing that work of art.

(D) There are some works of art that could never invoke art's power of transcendence.

(E) If art's power of transcendence is realized, then some artist's conception of his or her work matches the conception of some individuals experiencing that work of art.

4. A person should not take an action that involves a serious physical risk to another person unless the person thereby placed at risk is aware of the risk incurred and consents to it, or unless the risk that person faces as a result of the action is likely to be less serious than the risk that person would face if the action were not taken.

Which one of the following actions would most clearly violate the principle expressed above?

(A) In order to avoid a water landing, the pilot of a stricken plane crash lands in a thinly populated community, endangering its inhabitants without their knowledge.

(B) An officer summons an all-volunteer bomb-disposal unit to the front lines to neutralize a minefield.

(C) Following the outbreak of a deadly disease especially threatening to kids, the board of education inoculates school children without their parents' knowledge, despite the danger of painful side effects to some of those inoculated.

(D) A person in charge of a trust fund invests some of the money in risky stocks, without the knowledge or consent of the trustees.

(E) The government raises the tax on cigarette sales in order to curtail tobacco smoking, despite abundant evidence that smokers understand and accept the risks entailed in smoking.

PRACTICE SET 1: ANSWERS AND EXPLANATIONS

Explanation: Trauma Victims

Distinguishing Features: Study, Causation

1. C

Here we have a cause-and-effect argument presented in the context of a study. The trauma of the vets must have caused the loss of hippocampi cell mass, the doctors conclude, because those with stress symptoms had smaller hippocampi than those without the symptoms. We're looking for something that would weaken the argument, and a classic way of attacking cause-and-effect is illustrated by (C), which points out that the cause and effect could actually be working in reverse—it could be that the symptoms are the result of the small hippocampi, rather than vice versa. This should remind you of Nietzsche's Cornaro example presented in chapter 9. When confronted with the proposition that X caused Y, consider the possibility that Y may have caused X; that some third factor, Z, caused both X and Y; or that the two things are merely correlated and not causally related at all.

(A) The argument concerns the effects of "violent or life-threatening" events. The death of a close relative is traumatic, to be sure, but it isn't "violent or life-threatening," as those terms are used here. So (A) is irrelevant.

(B) and (E) do the opposite of what we're looking for here. The very fact that (B) asserts the similarity among all the veterans studied tends to support, rather than weaken, the study's findings. And (E), if anything, strengthens the argument by cementing the connection between trauma and tiny hippocampi.

A 180 test taker does not carelessly choose a strengthener when asked for a weakener, or vice versa.

(D) omits the main issue—the connection between trauma and hippocampi damage—and hence cannot have any effect on the reasoning.

Explanation: Tuition Rates

Distinguishing Feature: Numbers and Statistics

2. D

Here we have a specific, and common kind of number question: an increase/decrease problem. The author discusses two simultaneous trends that might seem to contradict one another. Tuition has increased at private universities, leading to a decrease in enrollment—so far that's logical. However, revenue at these universities has continued to increase despite the decreased enrollment. The correct answer must offer some source of revenue that more than compensates for the decrease in revenues created by the lower enrollment. That's where (D) fits in: If the tuition hikes have brought in more revenue than the loss of enrollment has taken away, then it's easy to see how both trends discussed in the stimulus can simultaneously co-exist.

(A) The frequency with which private schools increase tuition doesn't begin to explain the revenue situation in the stimulus. The relevant fact is that tuitions are increasing, which triggers the rest of argument. In what specific manner they're increasing is irrelevant.

(B) offers an irrelevant distinction between vocational schools and private colleges that doesn't contribute any new information to the stimulus. Vocational schools are outside the scope, which focuses only on the situation related to the decrease in enrollment at private colleges.

(C) tells us what happens to some students who can no longer afford private universities. Their fate, sorry to say, doesn't matter, and again it doesn't add any new information to the scenario. We already know that enrollment decreased; this choice just gives us a human-interest story when we really want to know how it's possible under these circumstances for revenues to actually increase.

(E) is similar to (B) in that it provides another irrelevant distinction. It compares the role of alumni contributions at public and private colleges, while the stimulus does not express any interest in public universities or in alumni contributions. Even if private colleges do get a larger percentage of money from alumni, decreasing enrollment shrinks the number of alumni and would, if anything, seem to decrease revenue even further, deepening the mystery but not explaining it.

> A 180 test taker knows that in explanation questions, his task is to reconcile, not to change, the facts presented in the stimulus.

Explanation: The Meaning of Art

Distinguishing Features: Philosophers' Corner, Formal Logic, Necessary Conditions

3. E

This one is long and complicated, but the key to the right answer comes from two statements of *necessity*: Understanding the "true" meaning of art requires one to have the artist's conception; and experiencing art's power of transcendence requires an understanding of the "true" meaning. Putting these together, we know that if the scholars are right, if transcendence is realized, then someone must understand the true meaning, and therefore someone must have the same conception as the artist. This powerful prephrase is paraphrased in choice (E).

> A 180 test taker uses her Formal Logic skills to provide shortcuts in tough inference questions.

(A) "Justified"? A viewer of art can come up with any meaning he wants. The question is what's necessary for him too experience the transcendental powers of art.

(B) "Personal meaning" is devalued because anyone can ascribe any old meaning to a work. What's important is "true" meaning. No matter how strong "personal meaning" is, transcendence is impossible if one's interpretation doesn't match the artist's conception.

(C) "Never"? There is no evidence here that suggests that there is at least one art scholar who is so pessimistic.

(D) is possible but not inferable. For all we know, the right viewer is out there for every work of art, in which case no work of art would fail to invoke art's power of transcendence.

Explanation: Risk to Others

Distinguishing Feature: Principle Application

4. A

The difficult part about this one is working through the principle and getting it organized in your mind. Once you do, (A) is a pretty clear violation. The pilot crash-landing in the community is placing the people there at risk; moreover, since the landing is taking place "without their knowledge," it can't be true that they are aware of the risk and consent to it. The only question that remains is: Are the people in the community being placed at greater risk by the crash-landing than they otherwise would face? Clearly, yes: it's riskier to have a plane land on your house than it is *not* to have a plane land on your house. The pilot is violating the principle in every way, and we have our answer.

A 180 test taker boils down the principle as much as possible before attempting to find the choice that conforms.

In question 4, that means recognizing a basic rule ("don't place another person at risk") that allows for two specific acceptable exceptions.

(B) Since the bomb-disposal unit is "all volunteer," we can presume that all of its members understand and accept the risks involved in disposing of bombs or mines.

(C) The people placed at risk by the inoculations are the children. Although we're told that the parents are unaware of the procedure, for all we know the children themselves are aware of the risks and consent to them. More importantly, if the students did *not* get the inoculation and risk "painful side-effects," it seems likely that they would be facing a greater risk from the "deadly disease." So (C) is in accordance with the principle; the situation presented represents one of the special cases where placing another person at risk is justified.

(D) contains a scope shift: The principle only concerns placing a person at serious *physical* risk; there's no hint that the unauthorized investments involve a physical risk to the trustees (though there may be some physical risk to the investor when the trustees find out what's going on).

(E) The government's action does not place smokers at physical risk; more likely, the action is motivated by the desire to place them at *less* risk, even without their consent.

PRACTICE SET 2

5. The recent proliferation of newspaper articles in major publications that have been exposed as fabrications serves to bolster the contention that publishers are more interested in selling copy than in printing the truth. Even minor publications have staffs to check such obvious fraud.

The above argument assumes that

(A) newspaper stories of dubious authenticity are a new phenomenon
(B) minor publications do a better job of fact-checking than do major publications
(C) everything a newspaper prints must be factually verifiable
(D) only recently have newspapers admitted to publishing erroneous stories
(E) publishers are ultimately responsible for what is printed in their newspapers

6. For exactly 10 years, it has not been legal to bungee-jump in state A. All of the members of the Rubberband Club must live in state A and have bungee-jumped at least once in the last two years. The Rubberband Club is currently taking applications for new members.

Which one of the following necessarily follows from the information provided above?

(A) Every current member of the Rubberband Club has bungee-jumped outside of state A.
(B) No current applicant to the Rubberband Club has legally bungee-jumped in state A.
(C) The current members of the Rubberband Club have bungee-jumped illegally at least once.
(D) Current members of the Rubberband Club who have never bungee-jumped outside of state A have broken the law in state A.
(E) The Rubberband Club does not include members who have bungee-jumped legally in state A.

7. If 400 or more students are enrolled for the next school year, Shady Creek Junior High School in Washburn county will be able to offer electives in psychology and economics only if additional teachers are hired before the start of the next school year. Proposition 307, if passed, would mandate that all schools in Washburn county hire three to seven additional teachers before the start of the next school year.

Which one of the following can be properly concluded from the statements above?

(A) If Proposition 307 passes, Shady Creek may be exempted from the requirement to hire additional teachers before the start of the next school year.
(B) If Proposition 307 does not pass, hiring additional teachers at Shady Creek before the start of the next school year will not allow Shady Creek to offer electives in psychology and economics during the next school year.
(C) If current students at Shady Creek show no interest in psychology or economics, Shady Creek should not look to hire additional teachers for the next school year.
(D) If fewer than 400 students are enrolled at Shady Creek for the next school year, representatives of Shady Creek should vote against Proposition 307.
(E) The passing of Proposition 307 could ensure that a condition necessary for Shady Creek to offer electives in psychology and economics during the next school year would be met.

8. A team of pediatricians recently announced that dogs are more likely to bite children under age 13 than any other age group. Their finding was based on a study showing that the majority of all dog bites requiring medical attention involved children under 13. The study also found that the dogs most likely to bite are German shepherds, males, and non-neutered dogs.

    Which one of the following, if true, would most weaken the pediatricians' conclusion that dogs are more likely to bite children under age 13 than any other age group?

    (A) More than half of dog bites not requiring medical attention, which exceed the number requiring such attention, involve people aged 13 and older.

    (B) The majority of dog bites resulting in the death of the bitten person involve people aged 65 and older.

    (C) Many serious dog bites affecting children under age 13 are inflicted by female dogs, neutered dogs, and dogs that are not German shepherds.

    (D) Most dog bites of children under age 13 that require medical attention are far less serious than they initially appear.

    (E) Most parents can learn to treat dog bites effectively if they avail themselves of a small amount of medical information.

PRACTICE SET 2: ANSWERS AND EXPLANATIONS

Explanation: Publishers and Fraud

Distinguishing Features: Just Plain Tough, Scope Shift

5. E

The distinguishing features listed above pretty much say it all. The question is just plain tough, although deceptively so—it doesn't really appear to be a difficult argument to follow. The trouble comes from the subtle shift in scope that's introduced as the argument proceeds. If you caught it, then this is a fairly doable question. If not, then you're likely to end up staring at the choices, wondering if there actually is one that's correct. The argument is based on a scope shift: The author concludes that publishers are more interested in selling copy than in printing the truth. The evidence is that many newspaper articles have recently been exposed as frauds. The assumption—that is, the necessary yet unstated premise here—is contained in (E): that publishers *know about*, or must take responsibility for, the truth of every article in their newspapers. If that's not the case, then the author cannot fairly blame publishers for the rash of bogus stories. So (E) must be assumed in order for this argument to stand.

Now, this assumption—and the scope shift that creates the need for it in the argument—may be a bit subtle; you may say, "well, of course publishers are responsible for what is printed in their newspapers."

Even 180 test takers can't be expected to prephrase every right answer, and it's quite possible that even many top test takers would not have come up with this answer on their own. No matter; that's what the choices are on the page for.

A 180 test taker recognizes the validity of an answer choice when she sees it, even if the concept contained in the choice didn't occur to her up front.

Eliminating the wrong choices here may have been more than half the battle. Many people are at least able to get it down to (C) and (E).

(A) and (D) are pretty much out of left field. The conclusion doesn't have anything to do with the relative novelty of inauthentic articles (or admissions thereof), despite the tangential reference in the stimulus to "recent" proliferation.

(B) contains a distortion. Minor publications' fact-checking apparatus is mentioned in order to emphasize that the big publications ought to check too; it's not there as the basis of a quality comparison.

(C) is a popular wrong choice, but is too extreme. "Everything a newspaper prints must be factually verifiable" encompasses the movie clock, the weather forecast, today's horoscope, and *Dilbert*. The author's not peeved because *Beetle Bailey* was inaccurate, but because false stories are appearing without adequate checking. The issue isn't lies, but *willful* lies. If you proved to this author that every one of those bogus stories was thoroughly checked and published in good faith, her complaints would fade away.

Explanation: Bungee-Jumping

Distinguishing Feature: Formal Logic

6. D

This inference question is an exercise in keeping track of the many discrete Formal Logic statements given in the stimulus. Everyone in the Rubberband Club lives in state A. Everyone in the Rubberband Club has bungee-jumped at least once in the past two years. The club's still chugging along, despite the fact that it's been illegal to bungee-jump in state A for the past ten years. Even though it may seem like there's a possible contradiction in the stimulus, don't seek to resolve the seeming discrepancy; rather, remain faithful to the four primary pieces of information while searching for a proper inference.

(A) is too extreme. The stimulus doesn't tell us that they *can't* bungee-jump in state A, but that it's illegal to do so. While each current member must have jumped in the last two years, some of them may have broken the law and jumped away in state A for all that we know.

(B) and (E) take us too far also: It's quite possible that one or more of the current applicants (B) has taken the plunge legally in the state A ten or more years ago, before the ban was enacted. Bungee-jumping has only been illegal in state A for the past ten years, during which it's safe to infer that no member has jumped in the state legally, but current members (E) might have also done so before the prohibitive law went into effect.

(C) is yet another overly extreme option. As mentioned above, while each must have jumped at least once in the last two years, they needn't have jumped in state A; perhaps they're getting all of their kicks in another state where jumping is legal.

> A 180 test taker recognizes statements that are too extreme to fit the scenario. He avoids choices that make overly generalized claims.

(D) is perfect. If they didn't jump outside of state A, then they must have jumped within state A sometime in the last two years to fulfill the club's requirements. And if they did that, then they must have bungee-jumped illegally. There are no unsupported steps in this chain of reasoning, so it's the logical inference we seek.

Explanation: Shady Creek Electives

Distinguishing Features: Formal Logic, Necessary Conditions

7. E

Here's another Formal Logic question; perhaps you were tipped off by the "if...only if" construction in the first sentence. "Only if" usually denotes a necessary condition, and that's what we get here. Like many inference questions, this question doesn't lend itself to prephrasing. Don't worry: You may not know exactly what the right answer will look like, but a strong grasp of the formal logic statements in this stimulus should be all that's needed to recognize the right answer when you see it. We know what the first sentence says; now, what does it *mean*? If the school has more than 400 students, then offering both electives will require hiring more teachers; that is, extra teachers will be necessary for offering the electives under these circumstances.

> A 180 test taker knows that understanding the passage on his own terms is the key to most questions.

A rule like this—and we *can* simply look at it as a rule, just like the kind we find in Logic Games—is very specific; it tells us one thing in particular, and leaves open many possibilities that we simply don't know anything about. For example, can we deduce anything if *fewer* than 400 students are enrolled? No, which incidentally kills (D) right off the bat. We can do the same with the next sentence. If 307 passes, then Shady Creek will hire more teachers. What if it *doesn't* pass? Who knows . . . which means we can chop (B) as well.

At this point, we're better off using our understanding to put the remaining choices through their paces. We've already axed (B) and (D). As for the rest:

(A) 307's passage would lead to the fulfillment of a requirement, not an exemption from that requirement.

(C) "Should"? The stimulus is purely descriptive, and does not go into evaluation or prescription. The stimulus deals with what's required for offering electives, and what's mandated if a proposition passes. What Shady Creek should *look to do* is not inferable here. And that leaves only (E):

(E) If 307 passes, we know that extra teachers will be hired, which means that the necessary condition for offering electives would be satisfied. It may not be as strong a statement as the other choices, but it's a valid inference and therefore gets the point.

Explanation: Dog Bites

Distinguishing Features: Scope Shift, Study, Numbers and Statistics

8. A

There sure are a lot of things going on in this question, which touches on a number of the logical elements we've been discussing. We don't have to look far for the conclusion; it's restated right in the question stem: Dogs are more likely to bite children under age 13 than any other age group. The evidence is found in the second sentence dealing with the findings in the study. The last sentence expands on the study, but essentially adds nothing of value to the logic of the stimulus; it's basically "filler" material.

So what's the scope shift? The conclusion is about dogs biting children under 13, but the evidence is based on dog bites *requiring medical attention.* (A) weakens the argument by addressing this scope shift. It basically says that many dog bites that *don't* require medical attention (bites that are within the scope of the conclusion) happen to people *over* 13. Now, this doesn't *disprove* the argument; it merely weakens the link between the stated evidence and the stated conclusion. The pediatricians counted up all the people bitten by dogs who came in for medical attention, found most of them to be under age 13, and concluded *from this alone* that dogs are more likely to bite children under age 13. This general conclusion is based on evidence about a very specific group. If it's true, as (A) says, that many who don't seek treatment are over 13, then the argument is weakened.

A 180 test taker is sensitive to scope shifts.

(B) We're not concerned with the results of the dog bites, only the frequency of bites by age group. Even if everyone over 65 who's bitten dies, it could still be true that children under 13 are most likely to be bitten.

(C) is a takeoff on the filler sentence—once again, it's the sheer number of bites that's important, not the kinds of dogs inflicting them.

(D) Same thing—the number of bites, not the seriousness of them, is the issue.

(E) is irrelevant; what *can* happen plays no role in the study and the conclusion based on it.

PRACTICE SET 3

9. Gus is the sort of poker player who thrives on high-stakes situations, being less attentive to the game when there are fewer chips on the table. But when there are thousands of dollars riding on a single hand he turns into a human calculator, will bluff with devastating effectiveness, and seems always to draw the right card. The best way, then, to beat Gus at poker is to grind out small win after small win.

Which one of the statements below does NOT reflect an assumption upon which the argument depends?

(A) In order to beat Gus at poker, one must never raise a bet against him.

(B) When the stakes are high in a game of poker, Gus' opponents are in greater danger of losing.

(C) In situations where the stakes are not in the thousands of dollars per hand, Gus is less likely to win.

(D) One's chances against Gus are more favorable when the stakes are low.

(E) An accumulation of small wins could be wiped-out by a single loss at high-stakes.

10. As the public relations agent for a major film star, it is an important part of Valerie's job to minimize the amount of negative coverage her client receives in tabloid magazines. Such coverage can have a negative impact on her client's public image and thereby decrease her box office draw and ability to get high-profile roles in major motion pictures. Yet she finds that when such tabloid coverage decreases it is a good indication of a corresponding if temporary decrease in her client's popularity with the general public and with studio executives.

Which one of the following, if true, most helps to explain the discrepancy noted above?

(A) The tabloids cover most intensively those performers who are at the moment most popular.

(B) Tabloids are often owned by large media conglomerates, which in turn own the studios that produce major motion pictures.

(C) Tabloids often manipulate photographs of celebrities to seemingly place them in situations that never occurred.

(D) Younger actresses often hope to get tabloid coverage as a way of increasing their exposure to the general public.

(E) The tabloid business is highly competitive, with enormous amounts of money at stake.

Questions 11–12

No one who listened to the debates and thought that the Democrat argued more convincingly than the Republican is a registered Republican, but some of them intend to vote for the Republican candidate anyway.

11. If the statements above are true, which one of the statements below must also be true?

(A) No one who thought the Republican argued more convincingly than the Democrat intends to vote for the Republican candidate.

(B) No one who heard the debates is a registered Republican.

(C) Some of those who intend to vote for the Republican candidate thought the Republican argued more convincingly.

(D) Not everyone who intends to vote for the Republican candidate is a registered Republican.

(E) Everyone who thought the Democrat argued more convincingly than the Republican is a registered Democrat.

12. If it is also true that all those who thought the Democrat argued more convincingly than the Republican are registered Democrats, which one of the following must be false?

(A) No registered Republicans intend to vote for the Democrat.

(B) Some registered Republicans intend to vote for the Democrat.

(C) No registered Democrats intend to vote for the Republican.

(D) Some registered Democrats thought the Republican argued more convincingly than the Democrat.

(E) Some of those who thought the Democrat argued more convincingly than the Republican intend to vote for the Democrat.

PRACTICE SET 3: ANSWERS AND EXPLANATIONS

Explanation: Betting Against Gus

Distinguishing Feature: Odd Man Out

9. A

Four valid assumptions in the answer choices? The stem itself prepares us to expect a pretty weak argument. Our job is to locate the statement that's not assumed in the argument. The author concludes that, to win against Gus, you have to play lots of small-stakes games. The evidence: Gus pays little attention when stakes are low, but with thousands of dollars at risk he gets both calculating and lucky. It's not worth the effort to try to prephrase all the assumptions inherent in this, but if a few ideas jumped out at you, great. At the very least, you should go to the answer choices with a clear understanding of the evidence and conclusion.

The tricky thing here is that the correct answer (A) sounds as if it may be true, and it may well be a bad idea ever to raise a bet against Gus, but it is not an assumption of the argument. The key to seeing this is to recognize that the subject of the argument is not playing strategy but the size of wagers. It's possible to raise bets without ever reaching high stakes (thousands of dollars). The other hint here is the extreme nature of the statement: that it is *never* a good idea.

A 180 test taker reads the answer choices extremely carefully and notices even the subtlest inaccuracy.

(B), (C), and (D) are logically equivalent statements of a single assumption: that high stakes games against Gus decrease his opponents' chances against him.

(E) The argument's conclusion is that the method of defeating Gus is to grind out small-stakes wins. If (E) were not true then there would be no necessary cause for avoiding high-stakes at all costs.

Explanation: Valerie's Job

Distinguishing Feature: Just Plain Tough

10. A

Nothing fancy here; just a difficult paradox to resolve. Our first task is to understand the discrepancy. The author tells us that a high volume of negative publicity can hurt her client's popularity. "Yet" (a contrast keyword that signals the discrepancy in the stimulus), a low volume of negative publicity corresponds to temporary reductions in the client's popularity.

Although it's her job to believe otherwise, Valerie understands that in some sense there is no such thing as bad publicity. It's her job to head-off any coverage that might put her client in a bad light. At the same time, she knows that when such coverage decreases it reflects a decrease in general interest in her client. It's for these reasons that (A) is the correct answer, explaining how it is that even harmful publicity can be an indication of popularity.

(B) hints at some sort of conspiratorial tie between tabloid coverage and movie roles. But this explanation can't reconcile the unfavorable and favorable natures of each, and fails to address the issue of popularity with the general public.

(C) doesn't touch on the discrepancy at all. No claims are made in the stimulus about the nature of tabloid coverage beyond the fact that it has a negative impact.

(D) is out of scope and irrelevant. We don't know the age of Valerie's client, so this choice can't help us at all. And it doesn't address the discrepancy, in any case.

(E) also doesn't address the discrepancy. The competition in the tabloid business doesn't explain anything about the seeming paradox of tabloid coverage.

> A 180 test taker identifies the issues involved in complex discrepancy questions, and then searches for a choice that addresses those issues.

Explanation: Democrats and Republicans

Distinguishing Features: Formal Logic, Tough Choices

11. D

Occasionally Formal Logic is tested in particularly nasty ways. In this relatively short blurb we get two formal statements telling us about three groups of people, and it's certainly not easy keeping it all straight. The first group comprises those who found the Democrat more convincing. We're told that not one person in this group falls into the second group, the group of people who are registered Republicans. So far, then, we have those two mutually exclusive groups, with no person overlapping. The third group comprises those who intend to vote for the Republican. We know that some of the people in this group are also members of the first group. That is, there are people who found the Democrat more convincing, and who nonetheless intend to vote for the Republican. And since we know these people are not registered Republicans, we know that (D) is correct: Some who intend to vote for the Republican are not themselves registered Republicans. It's a bit circuitous, but it all adds up to the deduction in (D).

A 180 test taker uses his Logic Games skills in Logical Reasoning Formal Logic questions.

We included this one in the "Tough Choices" category because all of the choices sound alike, which is a common feature in strict Formal Logic questions. Here's how those pan out:

(A) and (C) are out because they draw inferences about those who found the *Republican* more convincing. We are told nothing about such persons, and therefore cannot infer anything about them.

(B) infers that no registered Republicans heard the debates. That's not necessarily true. Many may have heard the debate, just so long as they found the Democrat *less* convincing than, or only *equally* convincing as, the Republican.

(E) is out because although those who were more convinced by the Democrat are not registered Republicans, it does not necessarily follow that they are registered Democrats. They may be independents, or they may not be registered at all.

12. C

As if this Democrat-Republican business isn't bad enough as it is, now the plot thickens.

The second question of the pair adds the new information that all those who found the Democrat more convincing are registered Democrats. This information is added because it is *not* inferable, and seeing it here may have tipped you off to the fact that choice (E) in the previous question was incorrect, had you not thought so earlier.

A 180 test taker, whenever possible, uses information given in questions to help him deal with other questions.

Since most LR questions are independent entities, the opportunity to reuse information from previous questions rarely presents itself in this section, although we do see a case of it in this question. (This strategy applies much more often in the Logic Games and Reading Comprehension sections, since each game and passage is accompanied by a question set, which allows for much greater interplay between questions.)

With this new information included, we're asked to recognize the statement that must be false. Let's take them in order and see which one contradicts the total scenario.

(A) and (B) speak of registered Republicans. (A) concludes that none of them intend to vote for the Democrat, whereas (B) concludes that some intend to vote for the Democrat. Since we don't know whether anyone intends to vote for the Democrat, either could be true.

(C) says that no registered Democrats intend to vote for the Republican, and this is the statement that must be false. Since, according to the question stem, all of those who found the Democrat more convincing are registered Democrats, and some who found the Democrat more convincing intend to vote for the Republican, there must be at least one registered Democrat who intends to vote for the Republican.

(D) suggests some registered Democrats found the Republican more convincing. Perhaps; there's nothing to prevent this from being true.

(E) There's no reason under these circumstances why some who found the Democrat more convincing couldn't intend to vote for the Democrat. All we know for sure regarding voter intentions concerns votes for the Republican.

PRACTICE SET 4

13. Peacocks with spectacular plumage are almost always free of parasites. While the naive might conclude that a brilliant display of feathers somehow provides a defense against parasites, the evidence shows that the peacocks with parasitic infections are rarely capable of maintaining spectacular plumage.

The pattern of reasoning displayed in the argument above is most closely paralleled by that in which one of the following arguments?

(A) Corporations that reimburse employees for educational expenses are almost always profitable. The X Corporation reimburses its employees for educational expenses, but it also produces superior products.

(B) Almost every student in the honors program at Overton High School wears a tie to school each day. Therefore, it is certain that school uniforms enhance academic achievement.

(C) The best-selling cars are almost always reliable and moderately priced. However, since measures to guarantee reliability always increase production costs, the most reliable cars are probably not bestsellers.

(D) Candidates endorsed by the *Post-Dispatch* are almost always elected to office. However, endorsement by the *Post-Dispatch* does not influence the electorate one way or the other, as the *Post-Dispatch* only endorses candidates that are strongly favored to win.

(E) Household electricity use is at its highest in the summer, when there are more daylight hours. While longer days do contribute to increased demand for electricity, the increased use of air conditioners in the summer is known to be a more significant factor.

14. Our conception of our self-interest shapes and influences our behavior, from the sentences we utter to the actions we undertake. As a result, we can see that this self-interest is not the product of ethics, for ethics alone cannot influence our behavior. Our conception of our self-interest necessarily determines our behavior, at least in part, influencing us to act in some way and not in another. Ethics alone, on the other hand, has no such power.

Which one of the following points to an assumption the author makes in the argument above?

(A) If our conception of our self-interest is not the product of ethics, it will have a detrimental influence on our behavior.

(B) If our conception of our self-interest were the product of ethics, then ethics would have some influence on our behavior.

(C) If our conception of our self-interest is not the product of ethics, the standards of proper conduct will be more difficult to derive.

(D) If our conception of our self-interest influences our behavior, it is unreasonable to act on our self-interest.

(E) If ethics influences our behavior, immoral acts would decrease.

Questions 15–16

Dean of students: The number of queries from prospective students about our master's degree program has tripled just this year. This clearly shows that the students in our bachelor's degree program are taking a greater interest in continuing their education.

Director of admissions: Actually, my research would seem to indicate that the opposite is true. If you look at the records in detail, queries from current students in the bachelor's degree program have decreased by 30% over the past year. This would indicate that, contrary to your conclusion, current students' interest in pursuing master's degrees at the university has actually decreased.

15. If the statistics cited by both the dean of students and the director of admissions are correct, which one of the following must be true?

   (A) The master's degree program has had a decrease in enrollment over the past year.
   (B) The quality of education that students receive at the university has improved over the past year.
   (C) The university has received queries about the master's degree program from individuals who are not enrolled in the bachelor's degree program.
   (D) Applications to the master's program have also tripled over the past year.
   (E) Only a small percentage of people who initiate queries about the master's program actually are accepted into and attend the program.

16. Which one of the following, if true, would most seriously weaken the director's argument?

   (A) Several fields of study in the bachelor's degree program do not correspond directly to the fields of study in the master's degree program.
   (B) Over the past year, funding for the university's bachelor's degree program has decreased significantly.
   (C) Enrollment in the master's degree program requires an intensive application and interview process for which most individuals do not have the time.
   (D) Due to the wide availability of program materials in a new campus center, many interested students in the bachelor's degree program do not make formal queries about the master's degree program.
   (E) The admissions standards for the university's master's degree program are relatively relaxed compared to those of other universities in the state.

PRACTICE SET 4: ANSWERS AND EXPLANATIONS

Explanation: Peacock Plumage

Distinguishing Features: Parallel Reasoning, Causation

13. D

The stimulus presents a correlation found in some peacocks: beautiful plumage and being parasite-free. The "naive" believe that the former causes the latter, but the author indicates that only parasite-free peacocks can maintain beautiful plumage. Remind you of the reasoning of someone you know—Cornaro, for instance, in the Nietzsche example back in chapter 9? Same thing. Or how about the weakener to the argument in "Trauma Victims," the first question in this chapter? Yet another example of reversing cause and effect. Here, we can summarize the argument in the stimulus like so: Beautiful plumage doesn't lead to being parasite-free; rather, being parasite-free is a precondition for having beautiful plumage. Which choice mimics this? (D)'s the one: The newspaper's endorsements don't improve anyone's chance of winning. Instead, having a strong chance of winning is a precondition for receiving the endorsement. In all of these arguments, we're forced to confront the possibility that a stated causal relation may actually work the other way around.

(A) proceeds from a general correlation (reimbursement policy and profitability) to a specific case about the specific X Corp. The original did not do so.

(B) proceeds from a correlation (honors program and uniforms) to the claim that the latter cause the former. This is closer to the "naive conclusion" cited in the stimulus than the author's actual logic.

(C) begins with a correlation between three factors: sales, reliability, and price. On that ground alone you can reject it. Plus, (C) goes on to suggest a tradeoff between two factors (reliability and price) which has no parallel in the original.

(E) concedes that the number of daylight hours has a causal impact on electricity use, whereas the original explains why plumage does not cause peacocks to be parasite-free. Also, (E) brings in a supplementary "more significant factor" influencing electricity use, unlike the original, which sticks to parasites and plumage.

> A 180 test taker meticulously analyzes Parallel Reasoning answer choices, and immediately tosses the ones that deviate from the original.

Explanation: Self-interest, Ethics, and Behavior

Distinguishing Features: Philosophers' Corner, Tough Choices

14. B

This one, laden with abstract conceptual issues such as "self-interest" and "ethics," falls squarely into the Philosophers' Corner category. In addition, we can designate the choices as tough since they all sound fairly alike and are all formulated as conditional statements, beginning with the hypothetical "if." Such things in the context of an Assumption question usually make for a difficult time. But Assumption questions are often about connecting the dots, and we can make our task easier by sorting out the evidence from the conclusion and looking for the missing link between them. The argument can be summed up as follows: Self-interest influences our behavior (evidence), and " . . . we can see that" (a strong conclusion signal) this self-interest is not the product of ethics (conclusion). Why not? "For (note the structural signal "for," meaning "because") ethics alone cannot influence our behavior" (evidence).

A 180 test taker uses structural signals to determine the role a statement plays in an argument.

The author continues: Conception of self-interest determines some part of behavior, but ethics does not. This last part is merely intended to reinforce the conclusion that self-interest doesn't come from ethics. But just repeating the evidence for the conclusion doesn't establish it; the case is still not fully made. Just because ethics has no bearing on something (behavior) that self-interest does influence, doesn't mean we can rule out any possible connection between ethics and self-interest. The missing piece that would make the conclusion valid is found in choice (B). The author must assume that if self-interest came from ethics, then ethics would influence behavior, in order to disregard the connection between ethics and self-interest based solely on the fact that ethics does not influence behavior. It's a little roundabout, and made more complex by the factors cited above, but (B) contains the necessary piece of information that completes this puzzle of an argument.

(A) Exactly *how* self-interest influences behavior is beyond the scope of the argument, which is concerned simply with the fact that it does influence behavior. Nothing need be assumed regarding any detrimental, or for that matter, beneficial influence.

(C) How difficult it is to derive proper conduct—presumably, in this context, that means to set ethical standards—is also beyond the scope of the argument, so nothing about that need be assumed here.

(D) The circumstances in which it is proper to act on our self-interest are not discussed in the passage, so (D) need not be assumed in order for this argument to stand.

(E) We're told flat-out that ethics does not influence our behavior, so what the effect on morality would be if they did has nothing to do with the line of reasoning.

A 180 test taker knows that a choice dealing with superfluous issues cannot be an assumption required by the argument.

Explanation: Master's Degree Program

Distinguishing Features: Numbers and Statistics, Alternative Explanation

15. C

Here's a less common use of statistics. Usually, when statistics are used in a two-person dialogue, the question deals with how one or both of the parties misinterpret them. We do see a little of that in the next question, when we're asked to weaken the admissions director's argument. However, in this case, we are told to assume that both the director's and the dean's statistical assertions are correct, so we need to find the choice that must be true based on both facts presented.

Let's have a look at the stats here. Over the past year, the master's degree program has seen an increase in queries from prospective students; the dean says they've tripled. The director of admissions points out, though, that queries from current students have actually decreased by 30% this year. If the overall number of queries has increased, but queries from current students have decreased, what can we infer? (C) provides a logical deduction: The master's program is receiving queries from people who are not enrolled in the bachelor's degree program. Think of it this way: If the program received queries only from students in the bachelor's program, then the statistics cited here would not make sense.

(A) does not necessarily follow from the statistics we're given in the passage. Those stats deal with queries about the master's degree program, not with the size of its enrollment. The data that we've been given about the queries tells us nothing about the enrollment one way or the other.

(B) may look tempting, but it doesn't provide us with the inference we need here. Given the statistics in the passage, we cannot know whether the quality of the university's education has improved or not. We're told that queries about the program have increased, but we can't take this to mean that the cause of the increase is an improvement in the program.

(D) takes us outside the scope of the passage. The focus here is on queries about the program, not applications to it.

(E) is again beyond the limits of what we can infer here. We are told that the number of queries has increased and that the number of queries from current students has decreased—but that's all we're given. This is not enough information to tell us anything about the admissions process; for all we know, every person who makes a query may actually apply, and be accepted, to the program.

A 180 test taker sticks to the facts—just as important as understanding what we can tell from the facts is knowing what we *cannot* tell from them.

---

16. D

Next, we are asked to find a statement that weakens the admissions director's argument. The first step here is to isolate the director's conclusion and evidence. The director concludes that the dean's interpretation is incorrect: students in the bachelor's degree program are less interested in the master's degree program than they were a year ago. She bases this conclusion on one piece of evidence: queries from current students have decreased during this time period.

To weaken the argument, we might find another explanation for why queries from current students are down. (D) provides just such an alternative. If students can pick up information about the master's degree program on campus, then they won't have to submit a query, which could easily explain the 30% decrease. But their interest in the program may remain just the same. (D), if true, would weaken the director's argument considerably.

A 180 test taker thinks of "alternatives and assumptions" when faced with weakening an argument.

(A) doesn't affect the director's argument one way or the other, because it discusses "fields of study" at the university. We don't know how students are distributed within fields, or which students are interested in the master's degree program. This choice provides irrelevant information.

(B) touches on the issue of the bachelor's degree program, but it doesn't tell us anything about those students who would be interested in the master's degree program. Like (A), it neither strengthens nor weakens the director's argument because it doesn't address the reason why queries from current students are down.

(C) might be tempting, because it provides another reason (other than lack of interest) why people might not submit queries about the master's degree program. The problem with (C) is that it addresses individuals in general, and makes no distinction between current students and other candidates for the program. Even if (C) is true, the fact remains that queries from current students are down, and this choice does nothing to weaken the conclusion that the director bases upon that fact.

(E) If anything, this choice might serve to strengthen the director's argument. If the admissions process is not an obstacle, this might reinforce the contention that students aren't asking about the program because they lack interest. Whether this choice helps the director's argument or not, (E) certainly contributes nothing that would damage it.

PRACTICE SET 5

17. Admission to the Bay City Professional Guild is easily obtained by those who have previously had strong professional connections with current guild members. However, one must have worked closely with one or more of the members in order to develop such strong professional connections. People who lack these connections because they have not worked with one or more of the current guild members will therefore find it difficult to gain admission to the guild.

    This argument displays flawed reasoning because it neglects to consider the possibility that

    (A) it is more difficult to develop professional connections with guild members than with non-guild members
    (B) many professionals who worked with guild members did not themselves become members of the guild
    (C) it is more important in the long run to network with non-guild members than to maintain strong connections to current guild members
    (D) some current guild members did not work closely with other members
    (E) one may easily obtain admission into the guild through means other than having strong professional connections with existing guild members

18. Many international correspondents believe that the formation of opposing political parties within country X demonstrates that the president of country X no longer retains absolute control over the government. However, if the president had lost his grip on power, he would no longer be able to censor the local media. Since the media in country X uniformly reflect the views of the president, the president must have retained his power to censor, and thus these international correspondents must be mistaken.

    The argument in the passage proceeds by doing which one of the following?

    (A) Arguing that since censorship of the media is against a state's long-term interests, external action will be required to bring about a revolution in country X
    (B) Concluding that since an event occurred under one set of circumstances, that event can be expected to occur under all similar circumstances
    (C) Arguing that since two sets of circumstances are mutually exclusive and exhaust all possibilities, exactly one must have occurred
    (D) Concluding that since an expected result of an event did not take place, the event itself did not occur
    (E) Arguing that since the evidence supporting a claim is balanced by evidence weakening that claim, more information is required to make a proper judgment

19. A wave of incidents of unusual violence, from murder to acts of self-destruction, plagued the small medieval town for a period of five years, nearly wiping out the population. At the same time, there was an unusual shift in the area's weather pattern. Rainfall was so heavy and continuous that the wheat crop probably fell prey to the ergot fungus. When eaten, grain thus affected can cause ergotism, a condition associated with hallucinations and other disturbing psychological side effects. In the end we can conclude that the violence was the result of freakish weather conditions.

Which one of the following is the most effective rebuttal to the contention made above?

(A) It is based upon a series of plausible suppositions rather than upon contemporary evidence.

(B) No clear distinction is drawn between cause and effect.

(C) Explanations of historical events cannot be convincing when too great a role is assigned to chance or the irrational.

(D) The author makes no distinction between probable occurrence and actual occurrence.

(E) Such crucial terms as "unusual violence" are not adequately defined in regard to the specific historical event.

20. A study found that last year roughly 6,700 homeless people in the United States were admitted to hospitals due to malnutrition. In the same year, a little more than 7,200 nonhomeless people were admitted to hospitals for the same reason. These findings clearly show that the nonhomeless are more likely to suffer from malnutrition than are the homeless.

The answer to which of the following questions would be most likely to point out the illogical nature of the conclusion drawn above?

(A) What is the relative level of severity of the malnutrition suffered by each group cited in the study?

(B) To what extent, on average, are the nonhomeless better off financially than are the homeless?

(C) To what extent are the causes of malnutrition in the nonhomeless related to ignorance of proper dietary habits?

(D) What percentage of each group cited in the study suffered from malnutrition last year?

(E) What effect would a large increase in the number of homeless shelters have on the incidence of malnutrition among the homeless?

PRACTICE SET 5: ANSWERS AND EXPLANATIONS

Explanation: Professional Guild

Distinguishing Features: Formal Logic, Necessary and Sufficient Conditions

17. E

Did you have trouble isolating the logical structure at work here? The formal logic element present is subtle, but is nonetheless the key to the question. The argument begins by describing one way that a professional can gain admission into the exclusive guild. For those lucky individuals who have worked with a current member of the guild and developed a strong professional connection with that person, entrance is easy. People who haven't worked with a guild member in the past can't easily gain admission through this route, but we were never told that this was the *only* way to easily become a member of the guild.

The author concludes that the unconnected individuals will have trouble getting into the guild, but that's only true if the route the author describes is the only possible easy one—and the author never states that it is. (E) thus gets at the possibility the author fails to consider: There might be other ways to easily gain admission to the guild. In terms of "necessary" and "sufficient," the professional connections described here are *sufficient* to easily get a person into the guild, but nowhere does the author state or imply that these connections are actually *necessary*.

(A) The relative difficulty of building these connections has nothing to do with their necessity for membership. This choice also shares with (C) an interest in non-guild members, which the author never mentions.

(B) First, those who worked with guild members are not necessarily the same people who have made strong professional connections with them, so the "many" in this choice may not even be relevant to the argument. Second, even assuming that these people are close professional associates of the guild members, the author argues only about what conditions make for easy entry into the guild. She need not consider the possibility that many former coworkers of its members would choose not to join.

(C) As we saw in (A), association with non-guild members are not relevant to the argument and fall outside of its scope. Additionally, this choice discusses the long-term benefits of these connections; the author is concerned only with entrance into the guild, not with the long-term happiness of its members.

(D) is perfectly consistent with the author's argument—it completely avoids the issue of the ease with which these current members joined the guild in the first place. This choice falls outside of the author's scope, which is about the possibility of getting into the guild with ease. We therefore can't fault the author for neglecting the possible scenario raised here.

> A 180 test taker always pays close attention to an author's topic and scope.

In this question, only (E) addresses the difficulties of obtaining entrance into the guild; most of the other choices fall outside that scope.

Explanation: Presidential Control

Distinguishing Features: Tough Choices, Formal Logic

18. D

While there is a touch of Formal Logic present in this one, it's not crucial to picking up the point. Still, it's good practice to recognize and understand formal logic statements when you see them.

> A 180 test taker sees the LSAT as an integrated whole, and brings all her skills to bear on every question.

The statement "if the president lost control, then he would no longer be able to censor the media" is essentially a simple "if A, then B" statement. The correct implication of this is that if the president is able to censor the media, then he must not have lost control. The last sentence, which contains the author's conclusion, plays off of this logic. Since the media's views are in line with the president's, the author concludes that correspondents who assert that the president has lost power are wrong.

The formal logic element is thus entirely self-contained, and we're not asked about *it*, per se. And here's another difficulty with this question: The argument is actually flawed, but we're not asked about that, either. (Did you catch the flaw? Just because the media reflect the president's views doesn't necessarily establish that he's maintained power of censorship; perhaps they all just think alike.) So there's formal logic in here, but we're not asked to crunch through that. And there's a subtle logical flaw, but recognizing that doesn't get us the point, either.

Rather, we're asked about what the author is *doing* in the argument; that is, about the author's method of argument. And here's where the final difficulty lies—in the choices. They're mostly dense and abstract, consisting of phrases like "one set of circumstances . . . similar circumstances" and "mutually exclusive." But if we hang in there and compare the choices piece by piece to the argument, it's not too bad.

(A) Huh? The state's "long-term interests" are outside the scope.

(B) and (C) start off okay, or at least not obviously wrong, but the reference to "all similar circumstances" in (B) has no relation to the action of the stimulus. And (C) says that *exactly one of two events has occurred*, whereas this conclusion is more definite. That's enough to chop that one.

(D) is the winner. An "event" that may or may not have occurred (the president losing power) is connected to an expected result that would have taken place if the event in question *did* occur (loss of the power to censor the media). Since this expected result didn't happen, the author argues that the event itself didn't happen; that is, that the president did not lose power. (Note that even that is not stated explicitly, but is implied by the conclusion that the commentators are wrong.) It's a little tricky, but it does match the situation in the stimulus.

(E) What balancing evidence? That's just not there.

Explanation: The Case of the Poison Grain

Distinguishing Features: Causation, Scope Shift

19. D

This passage tells a story similar to the anonymous fable of the poison grain, in which all of a kingdom's grain crop is mysteriously poisoned, causing anyone who ate it to go insane. The author describes a wave of unusual violence that swept over a medieval town for a period of five years, characterized by acts ranging from self-destruction to murder. That's followed by a description of a chain of events, beginning with an unusual shift in weather patterns that coincided with the violent period. Due to unusually heavy rainfall, the wheat crop probably fell prey to the ergot fungus, which can cause ergotism, a condition characterized by hallucinations and other psychological abnormalities. The author then concludes that the violence was caused by ("was the result of") the freakish weather conditions. There's the element of causation alluded to above.

> A 180 test taker recognizes causation in the all of the various ways it can be suggested by the wording of arguments.

When presented with a causal argument—especially when looking for a rebuttal to that argument—the first thing to do is check to see that the causal mechanism described is appropriate. The author blames the unusual acts of violence in the town on ergot fungus. However, he doesn't know for a fact that the ergot fungus was present in the town's wheat. He knows conditions were ripe for the formation of the fungus (i.e., lots of rain), and he knows fungus-infected wheat *can* cause psychological disturbances—but the crucial point, the actual presence of the fungus, is mere supposition. (Note how the author says that the wheat crop "probably" fell prey to the fungus.) As (D) points out, the conclusion treats the probable occurrence of the fungus as if it were a certain, actual occurrence. And therein lies the scope shift as well; the author argues from probability in the evidence to a clear-cut, definite statement of actual causation in the conclusion. In arguing against this reasoning, it would be perfectly appropriate to point out that the author misses the distinction described in (D).

(A) Contrary to (A), the argument does use contemporary evidence: the shift in the area's weather patterns at the time of the incidents of violence.

(B) Actually, the author *does* set up a clear chain of cause and effect—rain causing fungus which causes psychological abnormality. The causes and effects are perfectly distinct; the question is whether the causal mechanism described is *valid*.

(C) distorts the argument, since no role at all is assigned to the chance or irrational in causing the psychological disturbances.

(E) The term "unusual violence" is reasonably well defined as involving acts of murder and self-destruction so pervasive as to endanger the town's very survival. We really can't ask for a more comprehensive definition than that.

Explanation: Homeless, Nonhomeless, and Malnutrition

Distinguishing Features: Numbers and Statistics, Study

20. D

The LSAT test makers have an incredible knack for writing short, unassuming arguments that nonetheless pack a major wallop. This one's an example of this type. It's one of the shortest arguments you'll see, and it doesn't even contain any difficult words, but it sure gives people fits—and that's because of the statistics involved. It goes to show that it really doesn't take much more than a few well-placed statistics to, shall we say, liven things up.

The first thing you might have noticed is that the argument contains both numbers and statistics. The 6,700 and 7,200 figures represent actual numbers of people, while the conclusion states what's "more likely" to happen—a clear reference to an element of probability. Knowing from the stem that the argument is fatally flawed, this should have already raised a red flag. Here's the specific lowdown: Since only 6,700 homeless people suffering from malnutrition were admitted to U.S. hospitals last year, compared to 7,200 nonhomeless people, the nonhomeless must be more likely to suffer from malnutrition. Perhaps the argument immediately struck you as a little wacky, as it well should have given the clues in the question stem.

A 180 test taker is suspicious whenever she see in an argument raw numbers side by side with rates, percentages, or probabilities.

We're asked to find a question whose answer would most effectively illuminate the problem with the argument, and, as strongly suggested above, this boils down to a numbers versus percentages game: We cannot figure the odds of suffering from malnutrition solely from the number of malnourished people in each group. We must also know the overall total number of people in each group before we can create ratios and thus figure out the "likelihood" of suffering from this condition.

The only way for this conclusion to be valid is if the total number of homeless people in the United States was close to or greater than the total number of nonhomeless people. Then, the 7,200 hospitalized nonhomeless, as opposed to the 6,700 hospitalized homeless, would suggest that the nonhomeless are more likely to suffer from malnutrition. But this is clearly a ludicrous assumption (at least at the present time)—there's no way the number of homeless comes close to the number of nonhomeless people in the United States. The answer to the question in the correct choice will somehow point this out, thus making the flaw in the reasoning (using raw numbers as the basis for a conclusion about likelihood) plain to see.

Choice (D) provides the question whose answer would provide the information we need to correctly understand the odds. Since the United States has far fewer homeless people than it has people with homes, the 6,700 figure would form a far higher percentage of homeless people who suffer from malnutrition than the percentage of nonhomeless people based on the 7,200 cases of malnutrition among this group. The answer to this question would allow us to see how the raw numbers cited do not support the author's counterintuitive conclusion that the nonhomeless are more susceptible to malnutrition than are the homeless.

(A) goes beyond the scope of the argument. The argument involves the likelihood of suffering from malnutrition, not the relative levels of severity.

(B) also introduces a new issue—finances. No matter how much people with homes are better off financially than are the homeless, the fact remains that more nonhomeless than homeless were hospitalized for malnutrition, and the answer to this question would do nothing to reveal the illogical conclusion that's drawn from this data.

(C) introduces another new issue. The argument draws no conclusion about the causes of malnutrition within these groups, only about the likelihood of malnutrition. Nailing down the precise causes of malnutrition in one of the groups wouldn't change the numbers in the evidence nor point out the problem with the logic.

(E) is irrelevant to the argument as presented: The future possibility of remedying homelessness to some degree does not impact upon these numbers and this particular conclusion drawn from them. The reasoning still seems off, but the answer to the question will not show how the logic goes astray.

PRACTICE SET 6

21. The plastics commonly used in household garbage bags take, on average, 100 years to decompose in landfills. From an environmental standpoint, the plastic bag industry should be forced to switch to newly developed plastics, which begin to decompose after only 20 years.

    Which one of the following pieces of information would be most helpful in evaluating the argument above?

    (A) the rate of growth or decline in sales of plastic garbage bags
    (B) the number of plastic garbage bags sold last year that eventually wound up in landfills
    (C) the feasibility of enforcing legislation that regulates the plastics used in garbage bags
    (D) the length of time it takes the newly developed plastic to fully decompose in landfills.
    (E) a comparison of the production cost of one bag made with the old plastics and of one bag made with the new plastics

22. Superintendent: Teachers in our district must refrain from intervening in student conflicts in order to encourage students to hone their social interaction skills, except for cases in which physical violence is involved.

    Which one of the following is an application of the Superintendent's principle of teacher intervention?

    (A) A gym teacher watches while students break up a fistfight between the players of two teams that was ignited over a disputed call.
    (B) An English teacher takes the side of one student in an argument concerning a school locker, and sends the other student to the principal's office.
    (C) A parent instructs her child who is having difficulty getting along with certain schoolmates to work it out on his own.
    (D) A philosophy teacher instigates a heated debate between students holding radically different opinions on a controversial topic.
    (E) A math teacher allows a group of students to tease another student about her new haircut.

23. A useful philosophy, unless conceived simply as a means of indulging its creator's ego, is incomplete unless it interprets major recent historical events and offers specific prescriptions for the future. Ernesto's philosophy Neo-Futurism is full of advice on how to live in the world of the future, but makes no mention of the invention of atomic energy or the dawning and ramifications of the computer age, two of the most significant events of the twentieth century. Therefore, one can only conclude that Ernesto's philosophy is incomplete.

    Which one of the following is an assumption on which the argument relies?

    (A) The prediction of future events is the central tenet of Ernesto's philosophy.
    (B) Ernesto's philosophy includes no other elements besides discussions of the past and prescriptions for the future.
    (C) Ernesto's prescriptions for the future are unrealistic.
    (D) Ernesto's philosophy was not conceived simply as a means of indulging his ego.
    (E) Ernesto's philosophy includes no interpretations of current trends.

24. Some companies calculate the number of employee vacation days based strictly on the employee's length of service to the company, while other companies use the employee's position in the company hierarchy as the sole basis for determining vacation days. All other companies take both factors into consideration. Since Cathy and Joe have different positions in the hierarchy of CMA Inc., but receive the same number of vacation days per year, CMA Inc. must therefore base its vacation policy partly or fully on length of service.

The pattern of reasoning in which one of the following is most similar to that in the argument above?

(A) In figure skating competitions, a contestant's total score is based on independent scores in the categories of technical merit and artistic expression. For this reason, if two contestants receive different scores in technical merit, yet finish with the same total score, then they must have received different scores in artistic expression.

(B) A company with high revenue may be profitable, and a company with low expenses may be profitable, but the likelihood of profitability increases significantly if a company has both high revenue and low expenses. Therefore, a business seeking to maximize profitability should attempt to increase revenue whenever reducing expenses is impossible.

(C) On days when Sheila has early morning classes, she wakes up at 7 A.M. However, on days when she has only afternoon classes, or no classes at all, she always wakes up at 10 A.M. Since Sheila woke up at 7 A.M. this morning, she must have early morning classes today.

(D) Car rental charges are influenced by either the number of days a car is rented, the distance traveled during the time of rental, or a combination of both. Therefore, if a customer is charged the same amount for two different cars rented from the same car rental agency, yet kept each car for a different number of days, then part if not all of the charge associated with renting a car from that specific agency must be attributed to distance traveled.

(E) The Rapido Shipping Company bases its package delivery prices on at least one, and sometimes both, of two factors: package weight and speed of delivery. Therefore, if the company's shipping foreman quotes identical cost estimates for two packages that have identical weights, it must be because he believes that the amount of time that it will take to deliver the two packages will be the same.

PRACTICE SET 6: ANSWERS AND EXPLANATIONS

Explanation: Landfill Plastics

Distinguishing Feature: Scope Shift

21. D

Some questions test nothing more than whether you've recognized a scope shift, and this one falls into that category. The question stem complicates matters, however, and requires a bit of translation. A piece of information that would help us evaluate the argument is essentially a piece of information that would strengthen or weaken the argument. The right choice will need to have one of those effects in order for us to be able to say that this argument is good or bad. In other words, the operative question one has to ask to test each choice is: "Does this help me pass judgment on the argument?"

Now, if you picked up on the scope shift, then you would have known that the right choice will somehow address it. The shift is subtle, but definite, and perhaps if you didn't see it up front on your own, you would have recognized the shift when you came to correct choice (D). The author argues for the switch to the new plastics, but takes no account of the fact that there's a difference between 100 years *to decompose* and 20 years to *begin* to decompose. The newly developed plastic takes only 20 years to *begin* to decompose, but we need to know how long it takes for it to *fully* decompose in landfills before we can pass judgment on the argument. Only then would we be able to compare the new plastics to the current bags. (D) provides this information and is therefore correct.

(A) and (B) present irrelevant issues. We're trying to evaluate whether the change from one plastic to another is environmentally beneficial. Neither of these pieces of information helps us to differentiate between the environmental impact of the old vs. new bags.

(C) Whether or not the industry will be able to switch over to and legally maintain the new plastic bags is outside the scope. The question is whether or not it *should*.

A 180 test taker knows that in an argument about what "should" be done, whether or not it *can* be done is logically irrelevant.

(E) offers up an irrelevant distinction. The argument is made from an environmental standpoint; the cost per bag has no logical bearing on this.

KAPLAN

Explanation: Teacher Interventions

Distinguishing Feature: Principle Application

22. E

In order to apply a principle, the first step is to have a very strong grasp of the principle as the author originally presents it. The Superintendent argues that teachers should not intervene in student conflicts except when violence is involved. The Superintendent therefore provides a general rule and offers one definite exception to it. The argument also contains a justification of this hands-off policy: it hones student interaction skills. It's pretty much impossible to prephrase an answer to such a question, so once you have a solid grasp of the principle presented, proceed to the answer choices, looking for the one that best conforms. And remember—every element of the correct choice must match up with the tenets of the principle.

(A) presents a hands-off gym teacher, but the teacher's non-involvement contradicts the stimulus' principle by not intervening even though violence is involved. Since violence justifies intervention, the situation in (A) doesn't accord with the principle in the stimulus.

(B) presents a teacher intervening in a dispute that is not clearly defined as violent. We therefore can't tell whether it demonstrates the original principle or not.

(C) is outside of the author's scope, which specifically concerns *teachers'* intervention in student conflicts. Parents have no role in the principle as it is originally presented, so they can't be centrally present in a situation that applies that original principle.

(D) Generating debate in philosophy class seems like a fully justifiable teaching activity. This is not the type of student conflict toward which the principle is geared, especially when it is instigated *by* a teacher. The principle simply doesn't apply to the situation in (D).

(E) While we may pity the student with the new 'do, this is the right choice because it precisely follows the rules of the Superintendent's principle. The teacher does not intervene in a clearly nonviolent (teasing doesn't suggest violence) student conflict situation. Perfect.

> A 180 test taker recognizes that principle questions are similar to inference questions—the right answers are strictly consistent with the information in the original argument.

Explanation: Ernesto's Neo-Futurism

Distinguishing Feature: Formal Logic

23. D

Don't be fooled by the use of the word "philosophy" in the first sentence—this is not a Philosophers' Corner problem, as the stimulus is really not that difficult to understand. Rather, we have a Formal Logic problem on our hands (signaled by the word "unless"), albeit a subtle one at that. A useful philosophy—*unless* conceived simply for ego's sake—is *required* to have two elements.

Ernesto's philosophy has one requirement covered (he's got advice for the future), but comes up short on the second (he neglects important recent historical events). So is his philosophy incomplete? If his philosophy is intended to indulge his ego, then he's excused from the dual requirement, and therefore Neo-Futurism would be off the hook. The problem with the argument, as it stands, is that the conclusion is formulated as if the entire "unless" clause in the beginning didn't exist. So (D) the notion that this philosophy was *not* conceived merely to stroke Ernesto's ego—must be assumed in order for the conclusion "Ernesto's philosophy is incomplete" to stand.

A 180 test taker understands that single words (especially powerful Formal Logic words like "unless") are always important—sometimes the entire point hinges on them.

(A) First of all, "prescriptions for the future" in the stimulus is not the same thing as "predictions of future events" here in (A); the former speaks to what should happen, the latter to what *will* happen. But even if these were the same, there's no requirement that this be the central tenet of the philosophy.

(B) So what if Neo-Futurism is chock full of other meaningful (or not) platitudes? There's no reason to assume that these are the only elements of his philosophy.

(C) Unrealistic? Nothing in the argument touches on the *value* of Ernesto's work, so this needn't be assumed.

(E) is not necessary for this argument to work. Including interpretations of current trends wouldn't damage the argument, since "interpretations of current trends" is different from "interpretations of major recent historical events." In any case, discussing the latest fad wouldn't save Neo-Futurism.

Explanation: Vacation Days

Distinguishing Features: Parallel Reasoning, Scope Shift

24. D

The sheer length makes this one fairly intimidating, but recognizing how the scope shifts between the conclusion in the stimulus and the conclusion of some of the choices helps to eliminate a good number of choices right off the bat.

A 180 test taker does not allow the length of a question to overwhelm him, but rather looks for ways to cut the text down to size.

Let's rephrase the action of the stimulus and put it into general terms. We're told that either one factor (length of service), another factor (hierarchical position), *or a combination of both*, brings about a specific result (number of vacation days). Already, recognizing this "one or the other or both" scenario allows us to eliminate choices that don't contain this same element, and we'll see some choices drop like flies in just a bit.

(D), however, conforms: Number of days rented, distance traveled, *or both* contribute to a car rental charge. The conclusions of the stimulus and (D) match perfectly as well. If two different situations have the same result (Cathy and Joe have the same number of vacation days/two rentals cost the same), but are different according to one of the considerations (different hierarchical positions/different number of days traveled), then the other consideration (length of service/distance traveled) must have been a factor in the result.

(A) lacks the element of "one or the other or both" present in the stimulus. Since all skating scores are influenced by both factors, it's not possible for a skating score to be entirely determined by one factor alone, as opposed to the stimulus, which does allow for this possibility.

(B) can be eliminated solely on the basis that its conclusion concerns what a business *ought* to do in the future, which has no parallel in the original. Also, the stimulus applies a general rule to a specific example, whereas (B) does not.

(C) lacks the element of two factors working in combination. In the case of Sheila, it's either one or the other; she can't possibly wake up at 7 and at 10 on the same day.

(E) has two factors working alone or in combination, but shifts the scope of the conclusion. The original states that one consideration (length of service) must have been a factor in the policy decision, whereas (E) makes a decision concerning what the foreman *believes*, which has no parallel in the original. Also, the conclusion in (E) concerns the particular packages, whereas the conclusion in the original concerns the general policy adopted by the company.

In this case, the scope shifts of the conclusions in (B), (C), and (E) are enough to disqualify these choices.

PRACTICE SET 7

25. If Juanita worked longer hours, she would have an improved attitude about her performance at work and she would be glad that she had made the decision to work longer hours. Her entire perspective about her job would improve. Clearly, then, Juanita's increase in work hours will lead to a better attitude about work.

Which one of the following arguments contains flawed reasoning that most closely parallels the flawed reasoning in the argument above?

(A) If shoppers were to compare prices, they would see that Savings Center is the best grocery store in the city. A recent survey showed that our prices are more than 10% lower than our competitors'. We provide free delivery, and offer a wider variety of ethnic and organic foods than any other market in the city. Clearly, therefore, if shoppers are well-informed they will probably come to Savings Center.

(B) If employees who are experiencing conflict with a coworker turn to mediation, the conflict will probably be resolved to the satisfaction of both parties. Mediation also helps to clear up miscommunications between a supervisor and an employee. Mediation leads to fewer distractions in the workplace. Thus, every workplace should implement a mediation program.

(C) If the wildlife center offered more programs, a wider variety of community members would visit. Expanded programs would bring new populations, such as college students and senior groups, and many visitors who come stay for more than one program or exhibit. Clearly, therefore, a wider variety of programs at the wildlife center will attract a new demographic of visitors.

(D) If parents want their children to be healthier, they should implement a family exercise program. They would show their children how to lead an active, healthy lifestyle, while reaping the benefits of exercise themselves. Therefore, exercising together is the best way for parents to keep their children healthy.

(E) Clearly, we should be more concerned about the effects of improper trash disposal in the city. Not only does trash clog sewers and pollute the ground water, it also attracts wild animals, creating an unsafe environment for children to play in. Therefore, we should impose severe fines on those who allow trash to collect on their property.

26. Kopke: In the past 10 years, most of the new clothes that I have purchased have fallen apart within a few short years. However, all of the clothes that I have purchased at vintage clothing shops are still in excellent condition, despite the fact that they were all over 30 years old at the time that I bought them. Clearly, clothes are not manufactured as well today as they were when those vintage clothes were made.

Which of the following is a weakness in the argument above?

(A) It fails to demonstrate that the clothes manufactured 30 years ago were of higher quality than clothes of all other eras.

(B) It neglects the possibility that the clothes of 30 years ago, when prices are adjusted for inflation, cost more than clothes manufactured today.

(C) It confuses the number of clothing items sold with the proportion of those items that are no longer useful.

(D) It does not explain why clothing manufacturing standards have fallen over time.

(E) It fails to take into account clothes made over 30 years ago that are no longer fit for sale.

27. A man cannot lie unwittingly. He is not properly a liar who, while thinking he speaks truly, utters a falsehood. He may be said to be in error, and this perhaps because his will to know has overstepped the boundary of his reason; yet such a man does not lie, for knowledge of the falsity of one's assertions is essential to the act of lying. Thus, when the ancients propounded ridiculous notions concerning the nature of the heavenly bodies, they did not lie, as a proper understanding of celestial phenomena was not within their grasp.

Which one of the following best describes the argument in the passage above?

(A) The argument attempts to draw a false conclusion from an inaccurate definition by using an analogy.

(B) The argument draws a conclusion about the past from evidence about the present.

(C) The argument denies a proposed effect by first denying its proposed cause.

(D) The argument uses a specific definition as evidence, and draws a conclusion from the definition.

(E) The argument concludes the truth of a general principle from evidence about one instance of the principle.

28. The overall rate of emphysema has declined 15 percent over the last 15 years in region A. During that period, the total cost of care for emphysema sufferers in region A, after accounting for inflation, declined by 2 percent per year until eight years ago, at which time it began increasing by approximately 2 percent per year, so that now the total health care cost for treating emphysema is approximately equal to what it was 15 years ago.

Which one of the following best resolves the apparent discrepancy between the incidence of emphysema in region A and the cost of caring for emphysema sufferers?

(A) The overall cost of health care in region A has increased by 7 percent in the last 15 years, after accounting for inflation.

(B) Improvements in technology have significantly increased both the cost per patient and the success rate of emphysema care in the past 15 years.

(C) About seven years ago, the widespread switch to health maintenance organizations halted overall increases in health care costs in region A, after accounting for inflation.

(D) The money made available for research into the causes and cures of emphysema had been declining for many years until approximately eight years ago, since which time it has shown a modest increase.

(E) Beginning about nine years ago, the most expensive-to-treat advanced cases of emphysema have been decreasing in region A at a rate of about 5 percent per year.

PRACTICE SET 7: ANSWERS AND EXPLANATIONS

Explanation: Juanita's Work Hours

Distinguishing Features: Parallel Reasoning, Circular Reasoning

25. C

Here we're looking not just for a similar argument, but for an argument that is similarly flawed. Since the author is trying to assert that if Juanita worked longer hours, she'd have a better attitude about her job, the evidence should back this up by showing how increased time at work leads to an improved attitude. Instead, the evidence (Juanita feels better about work, and is glad she decided to work longer hours) are effects caused by the better attitude—which, lo and behold, is the conclusion the author is trying to establish.

In other words, the conclusion is being used to set the evidence in motion; the evidence and conclusion are, for all intents and purposes, identical. This is precisely how we described circular reasoning earlier. So, rather than feeling intimidated by this somewhat lengthy Parallel Reasoning question, all we have to do is to look for the choice that also contains circular reasoning. (C) is the winner. If the center expands its programs, more people will come, but the first piece of evidence (new populations) depends on more people visiting the center.

(A) Although this sales pitch may not work on everyone, the reasoning certainly isn't circular. Also, the word "probably" in the last sentence makes the argument more qualified, whereas the conclusion in the original is stated in absolute terms.

(B) is similar to the original in content, dealing as it does with the issue of problems in the workplace. But the reasoning couldn't be more different—in fact, it's not flawed at all. The merits of mediation seem plausible, and the conclusion seems justified, based on the evidence.

A 180 test taker is not fooled by Parallel Reasoning choices written about the same subject matter as the original.

(D) We might say that there's a slight flaw here, in that the evidence doesn't fully support the strongly worded conclusion. But not any flawed choice will do. The correct answer has to be flawed in the same way as the original—in this case, it must be circular. Here, the evidence may be insufficient, but it's not identical to the conclusion.

(E) is also not an example of circular reasoning. It states a problem, discusses the problem's effects, and ends with a specific recommendation for reducing the problem.

Explanation: Kopke's Vintage Clothing

Distinguishing Features: Alternative Explanation, Scope Shift

26. E

The stem alerts us to the fact that there's a flaw afoot, so we should expect something in Kopke's speech to get all fouled up. In more official LSAT lingo, that simply means that the evidence won't adequately support the conclusion. And what is that conclusion? Kopke maintains that clothes manufactured 30 years ago were constructed better than clothes manufactured today. His evidence is that clothes he's purchased within the last 10 years have fallen apart, while the clothes he bought in vintage shops are all in excellent shape despite their age.

This might sound persuasive so far, but we know from the stem that this is a flawed argument. Think about where Kopke's logic goes astray. For one thing, he compares all the clothes he's bought within the last 10 years to only the clothes that have *survived* 30 years before he purchased them. That's a subtle shift, but a shift nonetheless. The correct answer should point out the dubious nature of this comparison, and indeed, choice (E) points out the inappropriateness of this kind of comparison.

The only "vintage" clothes he takes into account are those that have proven to be extremely durable. So it isn't much of a surprise that they're still functional. Kopke doesn't consider the clothes made long ago that have fallen apart, so he can't evaluate the overall standards of that era. Comparing only the extremely durable vintage clothes to all modern clothes is like comparing apples and oranges, so choice (E) gets to the heart of the flaw here. It suggests an alternative explanation for the "favorable" comparison that Kopke relies on in forming his conclusion.

(A) The argument doesn't address all eras, so Kopke doesn't have to compare the clothes made 30 years ago with those of every other era.

(B) Kopke's argument does not address cost at all—just quality. Considering cost would not affect the validity of the argument.

(C) Kopke doesn't take into account vintage clothes that are no longer fit for sale (see choice (E) above), but he never equates the proportion of tattered clothes with the total number of clothing items sold. So choice (C) doesn't describe a weakness in the argument.

(D) The argument doesn't hinge on explaining why standards have fallen, just that they have.

A 180 test taker notes the scope of the argument, and immediately discounts choices that violate it.

Explanation: Liar, Liar

Distinguishing Features: Philosophers' Corner, Tough Choices

27. D

The answer choices in Method of Argument questions are often laden with abstraction, and the subject matter here—a discussion of what constitutes lying—is no picnic, either. The argument begins with a wordy expression of the idea that one cannot lie without being aware that one is lying. In other words, "lying" is defined in such a way that only people who *know* that they are not telling the truth can be considered liars. On the other hand, those who make incorrect statements without knowing that what they say is false are merely in error.

In order to lie, then, you must be aware that you aren't telling the truth. This definition of lying is then used as evidence to draw the conclusion that the "ancients," who said erroneous things about the moon and planets, weren't lying. Why not? Because they couldn't know that what they said was false. Thus the argument uses a specific definition of lying as evidence to draw a conclusion about the ancients. (D) therefore offers the best description of this argument.

(A) is incorrect because irony is never used in the argument. Nor is it acceptable to consider the author's definition "incorrect" or her conclusion "false." (A) is little more than a judgment, and not a very objective one at that.

(B) goes astray in that the author's evidence is a general, presumably timeless, principle. It is not evidence about "the present."

(C) would describe this argument as one dealing with cause and effect. Yet there is no cause and effect at work here. The argument concerns whether or not it is legitimate to consider ancient stargazers "liars." And it proceeds from the *definition* of "lying."

A 180 test taker understands a logical mechanism such as causation to the point of knowing perfectly well when that mechanism is not employed.

(E) has it backwards. The argument uses a general principle (in this case a definition) as *evidence*, not as a conclusion. And the one instance of this principle (the ancient stargazers) is the argument's *conclusion*, not its evidence.

Explanation: Emphysema Rates and Costs

Distinguishing Features: Numbers and Statistics, Alternative Explanation

28. B

On the LSAT, "apparent discrepancy" is just another way of saying "paradox," and here it is: Despite the fact that the rate of emphysema has declined 15 percent within the past 15 years in region A, the cost of caring for emphysema sufferers in the region is now roughly equal to what it was 15 years ago. In other words, the decline in the percentage of emphysema sufferers has not been accompanied by a corresponding decrease in the cost of treating such sufferers. Without trying to predict what might resolve this discrepancy, let's look to the answer choices for some sort of explanation.

> A 180 test taker prephrases answers as much as possible, but knows when it's best to let the choices do some of the work for her.

(A) deals with the overall cost of health care in the region, which goes beyond our concern with one particular category of costs: the money spent on emphysema sufferers. Thus, knowing that the region's overall health care costs have increased doesn't help to explain what's going on with the cost of emphysema care in particular.

(B) addresses both parts of the paradox and does help to explain it. If improved technology has increased the cost of caring for emphysema sufferers, then a decline in sufferers wouldn't necessarily yield a decrease in costs, since the cost per patient would increase. Also, if the technology worked, then there would be fewer sufferers. This technology would thus decrease the overall incidence of emphysema without necessarily decreasing the costs attending such care. A perfect explanation for the passage's surprising result.

(C) tells us that the region's overall health care costs haven't really increased in the past seven years, which, if anything, would only heighten the paradox. After all, the stimulus informs us that the costs of emphysema care *have* increased in the past eight years. After reading this choice, we still don't know what might account for that.

(D) doesn't connect the dots enough to really help. It only contributes to explaining the paradox if we assume that the research funds which have recently increased have actually been used, and then assume that the "modest increase" in such funds would counteract the savings offered by the decline in the rate of emphysema sufferers. (D) doesn't tell us this much.

(E), like (C), would if anything only exacerbate the problem: If the most expensive cases are becoming more rare, why hasn't the cost of caring for emphysema sufferers declined?

PRACTICE SET 8

29. All of the business seminars offered by Speakers-R-Us cost more than $1,000, while all of the personal achievement seminars offered by this company cost less than $1,000. Most of the seminars offered by Speakers-R-Us are over two hours in length. All of the seminars offered by a rival seminar company, Consultant Connection, are under two hours in length and cost less than $1,000. The Brookdale Community Center presents the seminars of these two companies only, and presents only seminars that cost less than $1,000. Last Sunday, The Brookdale Community Center presented the business seminar "Taking Corrective Action."

If the statements above are true, which one of the following must be true on the basis of them?

(A) The Brookdale Community Center does not present seminars on any other topic besides business and personal achievement.

(B) "Taking Corrective Action" is under two hours in length.

(C) "Taking Corrective Action" is a seminar offered by Speakers-R-Us.

(D) The Brookdale Community Center does not offer personal achievement seminars.

(E) All of the seminars offered by Speakers-R-Us are longer than any seminar offered by Consultant Connection.

30. Forest rangers in Crosby State Park implement Red Alert procedures only when weather conditions in or near the park indicate that forest fires may break out suddenly and spread quickly. Red Alert procedures are an extremely rigorous version of the usual safety protocol that must be followed by the rangers, and require that they institute elevated safety measures such as performing more frequent forest surveys (at least once every hour), keeping more detailed logs, and notifying the Parks Service Director of a possible need for additional fire staff.

Which one of the statements below does NOT follow logically from the passage above?

(A) Some park safety measures are less stringent than Red Alert procedures at Crosby State Park.

(B) The implementation of Red Alert procedures does not take place according to a precisely regulated schedule.

(C) The safety procedures that rangers follow in a non-Red Alert situation do not require hourly surveys of the forest.

(D) Some types of emergency safety procedures may remain in place for an indefinite period of time.

(E) In a non-Red Alert situation, the safety procedures that the rangers use are primarily determined by individual rangers.

31. History has shown that severe and sudden political instability strikes country Y roughly once every 50 years. The most recent example was the attempt on the president's life in 1992. The reaction of average investors in country Y to crisis situations in the country cannot be predicted in advance. The government's fiscal affairs department has introduced an electronic protection mechanism into the stock market of country Y in the hopes of avoiding a prolonged large-scale selloff. The mechanism is triggered in specific instances based on estimations of how average investors will react to changes in corporate data and economic indicators.

If the statements above are true, which one of the following conclusions can be drawn regarding the electronic protection mechanism?

(A) Sometime within the next 50 years an attempt on the president's life will trigger the protection mechanism.

(B) Whether the protection mechanism will function appropriately in response to a sudden political event depends on whether the event is seen by investors as positive or negative.

(C) It is unclear how well the protection mechanism would work in the event of a sudden political coup if such an event is partially or wholly unrelated to changes in corporate data and economic indicators.

(D) There would be no way for the protection mechanism to differentiate between market fluctuations resulting from economic factors and those that are caused by political instability.

(E) The protection mechanism would be purposely destroyed by political insurgents if they were able to infiltrate the government's fiscal affairs department.

32. Poor health is best understood as merely a symptom of deeper spiritual problems. Therefore, the only way to improve a patient's physical health is to address that patient's spiritual well-being. While this conclusion has been met with unrelenting criticism from the medical establishment, consider this: Since the only way to remedy poor health is to address spiritual well-being, then other methods relied upon by the medical establishment are useless in promoting good health.

The reasoning in the argument is flawed because it

(A) presupposes what it sets out to prove

(B) overlooks the possibility that some members of the medical establishment might also be practitioners of "alternative medicine"

(C) is based on premises that are inconsistent with each other

(D) bases its conclusion on an attack on the character of members of the medical establishment

(E) relies on experts outside of their area of expertise

PRACTICE SET 8: ANSWERS AND EXPLANATIONS

Explanation: Speakers-R-Us

Distinguishing Feature: Formal Logic

29. B

We're given loads of information on the nature of the seminars offered by two different companies, and then have to figure out the deal with the seminar actually offered at a community center. "All," "most," and "only" give away the formal logic element in this one; there's no doubt that interpreting and combining statements will be the way to go. In fact, this one's almost like a mini Logic Game, with each of the statements in the stimulus representing rules. Our job, accordingly, is to make deductions.

So how did you do? As we've said before, the best place to start a complicated Formal Logic question is with the most concrete piece of information given, which in this case is the fact that the Brookdale Community Center presented a business seminar. ("Taking Corrective Action"? Sounds kind of ominous, no?) What other formal logic statements mention either the BCC or business seminars?

Well, we're told that the BCC presents only seminars from the two companies, and only seminars costing under $1,000. All the business seminars from Speakers-R-Us cost more than $1,000. We can combine these conditions to deduce that "Taking Corrective Action" must have been offered by Consultant Connection. Is that one of the choices? Ha! Maybe in any easier question, but certainly not in the questions contained in this book of challenge material. However, in general, it does pay to look. In Logic Games, top test takers scan the choices as soon as they discover a new deduction, and they do the same in Logical Reasoning questions that structurally resemble Logic Games challenges.

A 180 test taker uses any skills gained in her LSAT preparation wherever they may apply on the rest of the test.

No, we're not there yet, but this deduction certainly leads us to the point. All Consultant Connection seminars are under 2 hours, which brings us squarely to choice (B). It takes a few steps, but you're used to that from Logic Games, right?

(A) is too broad. The BCC is restricted to the two companies mentioned, not to the two topics mentioned.

(C) On the contrary. As we deduced, "Taking Corrective Action" must have been offered by Consultant Connection.

(D) is possible only. Either company could offer personal achievement seminars at the BCC.

(E) would be true if *all* of the Speakers-R-Us seminars are more than 2 hours, but we only know that most are over 2 hours, which leaves open the possibility that some S-R-U seminars are shorter than those of Consultant Connection.

Explanation: Crosby Forest Fires

Distinguishing Features: Odd Man Out, Formal Logic

30. E

Since we need to find the one choice that *isn't* a reasonable inference, we should keep careful track of the boundaries around the argument. That way, we'll be better prepared to spot what isn't there.

The author begins by noting that Red Alert procedures go into effect when weather makes forest fires more likely. The distinctions between Red Alert procedures and the normal daily safety measures for the park are described—understanding them will be key to getting this question right. Red Alert procedures require rangers to survey the forest more often, keep more detailed logs, and consider additional staffing needs. Thus there are three specific ways in which Red Alert procedures are different from standard safety procedures. Let's go to the choices.

(A) The author states that Red Alert procedures are more stringent than regular safety procedures, so (A) must be true. Since we have one example of a less stringent set of procedures, we can rightfully infer that *some* parks have less strict guidelines. A formal logic element is present here, as signified by the word "some" here and in choice (D), as well as the "only" in the stimulus.

> A 180 test taker understands that on the LSAT, the word "some" strictly means "one or more."

(B) The rangers use Red Alert procedures only when weather causes the likelihood of fires to go up; since weather isn't precisely scheduled, the use of these procedures must not be precisely scheduled either. That's a fair inference to make from the information we're given here.

(C) If Red Alert procedures require *more frequent* surveys of the forest, occurring at least once per hour, then non-Red Alert procedures would occur less frequently than once per hour. This choice is therefore also inferable from the passage.

(D) Again, "some" means "one or more," so since Red Alert procedures seem to remain in effect for as long as there is an increased threat of fires, we can say that "some types" of emergency procedures do remain in place indefinitely.

(E) is correct because, even though the author implies that the Red Alert requires compliance with an increased number of procedures, this doesn't mean that the rangers are NOT required to comply with forest procedures in other situations. In fact, the author implies that some procedures (keeping logs, performing surveys of the forest) are present in both Red Alert and non-Red Alert situations. (E) takes us beyond what the passage supports, so it's not a valid inference and is therefore the correct answer here.

> A 180 test taker has a keen eye and ear for distortions of the original text.

Explanation: Market Protection Mechanism

Distinguishing Features: Just Plain Tough

31. C

The president of country Y is sure having a harder time of it than the president of country X in question 18. The president of X has solidified control with the media under his wing, while this one's being shot at. No matter. The real issue here is this electronic market regulation gizmo that's supposed to help the country avoid a major economic disaster. Our job is to draw a conclusion about it.

Once again, there's a lot going on here, so let's recap: Roughly every 50 years, country Y experiences political instability. The reaction of average investors to such crises cannot be predicted. Country Y has created an electronic protection mechanism for its financial market that relies on estimates of how average investors will react to changes in corporate data and economic indicators. The purpose of the mechanism is to avoid a major market selloff. The correct answer will draw an inference that logically connects the different ideas stated in the evidence. It's difficult to prephrase the correct answer here, so your best bet is to test the choices rigorously, looking for the one that absolutely must be true.

(A) goes too far in its inference that an attempt on the president's life will happen within 50 years. The 1992 attempt was only an example of the political instability that occurs roughly every 50 years, and the 50-year period was an average, not an absolute limit. Furthermore, even if there is an attempt on the president's life, it is unclear how investors will react because their behavior in such situations cannot be predicted in advance. For all we know, the market will go up and the mechanism will not be needed.

(B) goes beyond the scope of the argument. Whether investors perceive sudden political events positively or negatively isn't mentioned in the stimulus, so we can't infer that that perception makes any difference to the accuracy of the mechanism.

(C) draws a reasonable conclusion based on the evidence. If political instability involves changes in corporate data and economic indicators, then the mechanism should work the way it is designed to work. But if the incident does not involve those elements, then the way the mechanism will work becomes unclear, because the behavior of investors will be unpredictable.

(D) The statement in (D) goes too far to be inferable here. The mechanism might be able to differentiate between various types of market fluctuations, even though it might not be able to trigger appropriate responses to some of them.

(E) takes the argument far beyond its original scope. Nothing in the stimulus leads to a prediction of what might happen to the protection mechanism in the event of political instability.

Explanation: Poor Health and Spirituality

Distinguishing Feature: Circular Reasoning

32. A

It's funny, isn't it, how an argument can sound persuasive, yet not really say anything at all? To understand why this is an example of circular logic, consider what follows "Consider this": Other methods are ineffective because improving spirituality is the only effective method. In other words, other methods are ineffective because other methods are ineffective. Hello? We are given no independent evidence to the effect that the spiritual approach works and others don't; thus, the author is assuming (instead of providing evidence) that that method works (addressing spiritual well-being is "the only way to remedy poor health") in order to prove that it works. This is what (A) is saying. "Presupposes what it sets out to prove" is just a fancy way of accusing the author of employing circular logic.

(B) "Unrelenting criticism" of alternative treatment still leaves open the possibility that some doctors practice or approve of it, so the author doesn't overlook the possibility in (B). But even if the author *had* overlooked that possibility, (B) wouldn't describe a flaw in the argument. If anything, a crossover between members of the medical establishment and practitioners of alternative medicine would tend to rebut the "unrelenting criticism" from that medical establishment.

(C) Nothing in the argument is self-contradictory. How could it be? The evidence and conclusion are functionally identical.

(D) No doctors are maligned in the course of this argument.

(E) The argument doesn't rely on any outside expertise at all—just on the author's unsupported claims.

A 180 test taker understands that wrong choices in "flaw" questions often wrongly accuse the author of doing something he hasn't done, or wrongly fault the author for failing to do something he isn't logically obligated to do.

PRACTICE SET 9

33. Julia: No one knows exactly how the Russian wheat aphid made its way to the United States, but it has caused tremendous damage to certain crops around the country. If the aphid continues to infest these crops, then this damage will be irreparable.

    Hector: So we can save those crops just by stopping the aphid infestation.

    Which one of the following statements is consistent with Julia's claim but not with Hector's claim?

    (A)   The aphid infestation is stopped and the crops suffer irreparable damage.
    (B)   The aphid infestation continues and the crops suffer irreparable damage.
    (C)   The aphid infestation is stopped and the crops do not suffer irreparable damage.
    (D)   The aphid infestation is kept under control but not stopped and the crops do not suffer irreparable damage.
    (E)   The aphid infestation is kept under control but not stopped and the crops suffer irreparable damage.

34. Catering manager: The head chef has recommended that we prepare Menu 12A for the last-minute wedding party this evening, because once Menu 12A has been put into the oven, it can be ready to serve in a short time, and the price per plate for this dish is lower than any other we serve. However, the entree for Menu 6D is already marinating, and could be prepared at the reception location in a minimal amount of time, whereas Menu 12A would take at least two hours to be mixed and prepared. Since the kitchen at the reception location is open for only a limited time before the dinner, I must overrule the chef's recommendation that we prepare Menu 12A.

    Which one of the following is assumed in the manager's argument?

    (A)   The reception guests' satisfaction with the dinner would be higher if Menu 12A were served than if Menu 6D were served.
    (B)   By the time the chef had begun to prepare Menu 12A, Menu 6D would already have finished cooking.
    (C)   The cost per plate of a catered reception is not a significant consideration when choosing between meal options.
    (D)   It would take longer to prepare any dish besides Menu 6D than it would to prepare Menu 12A.
    (E)   Any time saved in cooking Menu 12A would not offset the additional time required for its preparation.

35. If the fluid levels in a small engine fall below the 30% level, the engine's components can lose lubrication, which invariably leads to increased friction and causes a signal light in the control panel to illuminate. Since the signal light on Farmer Lea's tractor has illuminated seven times in the last month, the fluid levels in her tractor must have fallen below the 30% level.

Which one of the arguments below contains flawed reasoning similar to that in the argument above?

(A) Children who begin speaking before they are a year old are highly likely to begin reading before age five. Rachel did not begin speaking before she was a year old, so she must not be highly likely to begin reading before she turns five.

(B) The handwriting on a manuscript seems identical to that of the well-known playwright Henri St. Philip. However, the date on the manuscript is ten years prior to St. Philip's first known writings. The manuscript must therefore be a forgery.

(C) Mega-Crunch bars are sold in the vending machines at Jefferson Elementary School. Mega-Crunch bars are very popular among children under 12 because of the collectible trading cards that are included in each package. Therefore, the vending machines at Jefferson Elementary must sell more Mega-Crunch bars than any other product.

(D) For many individuals with wheat allergies, reactions to eating wheat can include severe headaches. Sal ate a sandwich on whole grain bread, and later in the afternoon he developed an intense headache. Sal must therefore be allergic to wheat.

(E) If a beta bug tries to make its way inside a house, it can leave distinctive tunneling marks on the wood around the doors and windows. Angelo recently inspected his home and found none of these marks. Clearly, there are no beta bugs in Angelo's neighborhood.

36. Any student who wishes to be appointed to the student activities committee should submit a brief background and qualifications statement to the student life coordinator by Friday. This is in order to give faculty members more information about the interested students, so that they may make informed decision about the appointment. Last year's faculty members explicitly stated that the appointment process favored students about whom something was known over those who were not known to the faculty at all.

Which one of the following statements represents an assumption upon which the argument above depends?

(A) Faculty members will each nominate one student from their classes to be considered for the student activities committee.

(B) If a student submits a brief background and qualifications statement to the student life coordinator by Friday, that student will be appointed to the student activities committee.

(C) In order to be considered for the student activities committee, a student must be enrolled in a class taught by a participating faculty member.

(D) All paperwork for the student activities committee appointments must be submitted to the student life coordinator by the deadline of Friday.

(E) To be appointed to the student activities committee, a student must have submitted the requested background and qualifications information to the student life coordinator.

PRACTICE SET 9: ANSWERS AND EXPLANATIONS

Explanation: The Russian Wheat Aphid

Distinguishing Features: Formal Logic, Necessary and Sufficient Conditions, Tough Choices

33. A

Here's a dialogue question, and both speakers, whether they know it or not, are employing a form of formal logic. And the choices are difficult because they all present various combinations of the same terms—quite easy to confuse if you're not paying careful attention. According to Julia, the mysterious Russian wheat aphid is devastating crops around the country, and here comes the formal logic element: If this infestation continues, soon the damage will be permanent. That's a statement of sufficiency. It means that continuation of the aphid infestation will guarantee that the damage will be irreparable. It's not, however, a statement of necessity—we can't infer that the continuation is necessary to bring about irreparable damage to the crops; perhaps other factors are at work that could completely damage the crops as well. Now, evidently Hector doesn't understand this distinction. He states that the crops can be saved just by eliminating the aphid infestation, but that's not a proper interpretation of Julia's statement. Eliminating the aphid infestation will get rid of a factor that would certainly bring about total ruin of the crop, but we don't know that the crop would be guaranteed survival simply by removing this one factor. Now, what makes the question more difficult is the fact that we're not asked for the flaw in Hector's response, but rather for a statement that's consistent with Julia's claim but not with Hector's. So, with a reasonable understanding of the respective claims, we can proceed confidently to the choices, looking for the one that meets this requirement.

(A) does the trick. As we saw, according to Julia's statement, stopping the infestation is necessary, but not sufficient for halting the damage. While the damage will surely be irreparable if the infestation is not stopped, the fact that it *is* stopped doesn't ensure that the crops won't suffer irreparable damage. So (A) satisfies the first part of the stem—it's consistent with Julia's claim. Seeing that is the tough part; it's a bit easier to see how (A) is inconsistent with Hector's reasoning. He says flat out that stopping the infestation is the only thing needed to save the crops. In (A), however, the infestation is stopped, but the crops bite the dust anyway. So (A)'s the choice we seek.

(B) is perfectly consistent with Julia's argument, but does not contradict Hector's. He speaks only to the issue of what will happen if the infestation is stopped.

(C) The easiest way to eliminate (C) is to recognize that it mirrors Hector's argument precisely. He says that stopping the infestation will save the crops, so this choice is consistent with his claim, and therefore incorrect.

(D) Forget about this "kept under control" business—the key point in (D) is that the infestation is *not stopped*, which, according to Julia, means that the crops are goners. So this one is inconsistent with Julia's claim.

(E) Also discounting the "kept under control" phrase, which essentially adds nothing, (E) is the same as (B), and is therefore wrong for the same reason.

A 180 test taker is familiar with the ways in which the terms "consistent" and "inconsistent" are used on the LSAT.

Explanation: Menu 12A and Menu 6D

Distinguishing Features: Numbers and Statistics, Scope Shift, Alternative Explanation

34. E

This question finds us trying to determine which of two catering menus will better fit the needs of the company for a last-minute reception, and as you can see from the list of distinguishing features above, there are many logical elements present here. While the chef believes that Menu 12A is the right choice because its cooking time is shorter and it falls within the customers' budget, the catering manager orders that the chef prepare Menu 6D instead. She provides one piece of evidence to support her decision: Only Menu 6D can be prepared in the amount of time the staff has available at the reception location.

Someone who argues for one option over another must assume that the benefit provided by the preferred option can be gained only by choosing that option. In other words, the manager must assume that Menu 12A cannot be prepared in the amount of time available. But perhaps that's not the case? The manager says that it would take at least two hours of preparation time before cooking, but she never says that it couldn't be prepared in the time available. Perhaps the shorter cooking time would make up for the longer preparation time. That's a plausible alternative that the catering manager has overlooked. In order for the manager's conclusion to be valid, she must assume (rightly or wrongly) that Menu 12A could not be prepared and served within the specified time. Thus, she assumes that the shorter cooking time required by Menu 12A would not recoup the extra time that it takes to prepare the menu.

This number issue is a common one. The test makers like to create situations in which a decrease in one area is, or may be, made up or even surpassed by an increase in another. One could also see this scenario in terms of a scope shift: The catering manager speaks of the lower price of Menu 12A early on, but then makes her decision based solely on the time factor. Recognizing that shift will help you eliminate at least one incorrect choice here.

A 180 test taker sees situations in Logical Reasoning questions from a number of angles and thinks through problems on multiple levels.

(A) The stimulus never states that one dish is more pleasing than the other; one is simply quicker to prepare. So (A) is not relevant to the manager's decision.

(B) goes too far. The manager never states exactly how much time either item takes from beginning to end, so there's no basis for concluding that 6D would be done before 12A had even been started.

(C) The cost per plate may be a significant consideration in some cases, and the manager doesn't say that it's not significant here; she simply overrides it by making timing a *more* significant consideration, so she need not assume (C) to formulate her recommendation.

(D) focuses on menu options other than 12A and 6D. The manager seems to think that these two are sufficient—they're the only ones discussed. How long it would take to prepare other menu items is irrelevant to the manager's argument.

Explanation: Signal Light

Distinguishing Features: Parallel Reasoning, Causation

35. D

This Parallel Reasoning question lends itself well to algebraic characterization. The question stem itself gives us some critical information: The argument in the stimulus is flawed, and we're looking for the answer choice that is flawed in a similar manner. Since this example contains formal logic statements, we can reduce the action of the stimulus to letters to help us. If the fluid levels in the engine fall below 30%, it can lead to lost lubrication and cause the signal light to illuminate (if X, then possibly Y). Since the signal light on Farmer Lea's tractor has illuminated several times, the fluid levels must have fallen below the specified level (Y, therefore X). This argument makes the mistake of concluding that a "reverse cause and effect" relationship is operating: Because the consequence occurred, the cause must have occurred.

We know from formal logic that we can't simply jump from "if X, then [possibly] Y" to "if Y, then X." All we need to do is find the choice that commits the same error. There's no way to prephrase the content of the right choice, only its structure. Now check the choices.

(A) tells us that if a child begins speaking early, she is likely to begin reading early (if X, then Y). That has the first part of the argument right. But the second sentence tells us that Rachel did not begin speaking early, so she is not likely to begin reading early—"If not X, then not Y." This conclusion simply negates the terms, without switching them around as the original argument does.

(B) and (C) can both be eliminated because neither presents a "reverse cause and effect" argument. In fact, neither choice contains anything that can be translated into a formal logic "if-then" statement. (B) *does* contain a temporal flaw; for all we know, St. Philip started writing much earlier than previously believed. We would need information to indicate otherwise before the conclusion would be valid. The conclusion in (C) is premature as well, but again does not have the same formal logic structure as the original; there's nothing here that can be translated into "if X, then Y."

(D) contains the kind of flaw we're looking for. If people are allergic to wheat, then they may get headaches when they eat it—"if X, then possibly Y." So far, so good. The next sentences tell us that Sal ate a sandwich and got a headache (Y), so he must be allergic to wheat (therefore X). This choice lines up perfectly with all the elements of the original.

(E) deals with cause and effect, but not in the same manner as the stimulus. There is an initial cause: If beta bugs try to get in, they will leave marks on the house ("if X, then Y"). But the second sentence introduces a negative condition—Angelo took a look, and the bugs are *not* trying to get in. Therefore, there are no bugs around. This translates to "not Y, therefore not X," which doesn't parallel the structure of the original.

Explanation: Student Activities Committee

Distinguishing Features: Scope Shift

36. E

The author concludes that students who want to be considered for appointment to the student activities committee should be sure to submit brief statements about themselves for the faculty to consider. The evidence follows: these statements allow faculty to learn more about each student, and the faculty probably won't appoint a student about whom they have no information.

Look back over the evidence and the conclusion, and you'll realize that they're not really talking about the same thing. The conclusion is about what one should do in order to be *appointed* to the committee, and the evidence is about what one should do in order to be *known* to the faculty. That's a classic scope shift. The only way to make these two different subjects relate to one another is to assume that the only way to become known to the faculty is to submit the requested statement. Otherwise, the evidence about faculty learning about students would have no relevance to the conclusion about appointment to the committee. (E) expresses this central assumption well, tying the evidence about the faculty to the conclusion about who they appoint.

A 180 test taker knows that an apparent scope shift can often be bridged by an assumption.

(A) and (C) While the stimulus does state that being known by the faculty is an advantage, it doesn't suggest how students become known or exactly how the appointment process works. (A) also seems to contradict the conclusion in the stimulus; if appointments are based on teachers knowing students from class, then students wouldn't have any need to submit a statement about themselves. (C) has a similar failing; if all students who were eligible for appointment were already known to the faculty, the written statements would be unnecessary.

(B) overstates the link between the two subjects. The argument in the stimulus assumes that submission of a statement is necessary for consideration for the committee, while (B) says that submission of a statement guarantees appointment to the committee. However, the stimulus implies that the submission of a statement simply allows the faculty to make a more informed decision about the appointments.

(D) is too broad to be necessary here. The argument concerns written statements from students, which do need to be submitted by the Friday deadline. But (D) deals with an unspecified amount of "paperwork," and we don't know (nor do we really care) what paperwork besides the statement might be necessary. There may or may not be additional paperwork, but this particular argument doesn't depend on this issue.

PRACTICE SET 10

37. Brendan is concerned about teaching reading appreciation to the students in his second-grade class. He has worked to help students enjoy reading by encouraging them to read their favorite books aloud to the class during an extra reading period each afternoon. But some students have difficulty concentrating on listening to the stories without having a book in front of them. These students become distracted and talk to one another or make noise during the reading period. The noise they create also distracts other students and makes it difficult for all of the members of the class to hear the story that's being read. To ensure that students learn reading appreciation, then, Brendan should separate these noisy students from the rest of the group during the extra reading period.

Which one of the following best describes the logical flaw in the argument above?

(A) Two actions that occur simultaneously are presented as being causally related.

(B) A hypothesis is presented that runs counter to a proposal related to that hypothesis.

(C) A course of action that is proposed to resolve a problem would in actuality resolve only one cause of the problem.

(D) A conclusion is based on evidence that is unrelated to the issue at hand.

(E) A conclusion is supported by evidence that contradicts the conclusion.

38. An international study recently examined the effects of secondhand smoke on health. Surprisingly, although the dosages of harmful chemicals from secondhand smoke are so small that their effect should be negligible, the study found that nonsmoking spouses of smokers displayed an incidence of heart disease that was significantly greater than that of nonsmokers who were not as regularly exposed to secondhand smoke.

Each of the following, if true, could contribute to an explanation of the unexpectedly high incidence of heart disease in smokers' spouses EXCEPT:

(A) A disproportionately high number of people married to smokers are among the older segment of the married population, a group that inherently has a higher-than-average risk of heart disease.

(B) On average, more alcohol and coffee, both of which have been linked to heart disease, are consumed in the homes of smokers than in the homes of nonsmokers.

(C) A disproportionately high number of smokers are married to other smokers, and the risk of heart disease increases in proportion to the number of smokers living in a household.

(D) Smokers generally tend to live in higher-stress environments than do nonsmokers, and stress is a factor associated with above average incidence of heart disease.

(E) A disproportionately high number of smokers live in areas with a high level of industrial pollutants, which have been shown to be a factor in increased risk of heart disease.

PRACTICE SET 10: ANSWERS AND EXPLANATIONS

Explanation: Brendan's Second-Grade Class

Distinguishing Features: Tough Choices, Causation

37. C

Brendan's goal is clear: he wants all of the students in his class to learn to enjoy reading. In order to achieve this goal, he has set up a program where one student at a time reads to the entire group, but this approach isn't working. The problem is that some students become distracted without a book in their hands, and they in turn distract other students, causing a less effective reading experience for the entire class. This is all a long setup for the conclusion, which is that Brendan should separate the distracted students out in order to allow the rest of the class to learn more effectively.

The stem alerts us that the argument is flawed, and that flaw becomes apparent in the recommendation. The problem that Brendan seeks to resolve stems from two causes: some students are distracted during the readings, *and* their noise is making the experience less valuable for everyone else. The recommendation as it stands might prevent the quiet students from getting distracted during the readings, but it doesn't do anything for the kids who are having trouble concentrating on the story. Therefore, the argument is flawed because its conclusion would remedy only one of two factors that create the problem it seeks to resolve. The choices here are a bit cumbersome, but (C) sums up this flaw precisely.

A 180 test taker fights through long, tough choices to locate the idea that he prephrased, or the choice that holds up best under close scrutiny.

(A) Apparently "two actions" refers to the students becoming distracted and then distracting the rest of the class. (A) is most immediately wrong because the author does not suggest that these incidents occur simultaneously. On the contrary, the author presents them sequentially: first one set of students becomes distracted and makes noise, and then the noise causes other students to lose concentration as well. So while there is an element of causation here, the author does not commit the causality flaw described in (A).

(B) is incorrect because there is no hypothesis in this argument and there is no contradiction within the elements of the argument. The conclusion is flawed because it's an incomplete solution to the problem, not because it runs counter to anything.

(D) The evidence we're given here is completely relevant to the conclusion. They are both focused on the same issues, so there's no scope shift here.

(E), like (B), suggests that the elements of the argument contradict one another, but that is not true in this case. Brendan's evidence is consistent with the conclusion—the issue is that the recommendation he comes up with deals with only part of the initial problem.

Explanation: Secondhand Smoke

Distinguishing Features: Study, Causation, Odd Man Out, Alternative Explanation, Scope Shift

38. C

Perusing the list of distinguishing features, you're likely to ask "what's *not* in this one?" This one nearly has it all, and we can take the features in order to describe what's going on. First of all, we're dealing with another study, and you should be fairly familiar by now with the kinds of mishaps, misconceptions, and downright mistakes that can arise when researchers get their hands on things. The study involves the nonsmoking spouses of smokers; that is, people who are presumably in contact with a decent amount of secondhand smoke. While the author contends that secondhand smoke shouldn't really have any effect, the study found that the incidence of heart disease in nonsmokers married to smokers is actually much higher than that of nonsmokers not exposed to secondhand smoke. So while there shouldn't be any causal mechanism at work here, the author implies that the study's finding suggests that there is.

Now, we're asked to evaluate possible explanations, and to choose the one that *wouldn't* contribute to an explanation. So there are the odd man out and alternative explanation features—four of the choices will provide plausible alternative explanations for the surprising results, while the right answer will not. And let's jump right to our Odd Man Out, since it relates to the final feature mentioned above—Scope Shift. As difficult as this question may be for a number of reasons, the right answer is actually quite simple if you noticed the shift that takes place between the scope of the study and the scope of choice (C): The study focuses entirely on nonsmokers married to smokers. Cases in which *smokers* are married to other smokers fall outside of this scope, so (C) has no power to clear up the mystery at hand.

As for the wrong choices—that is, the valid explanations—they all hinge on breaking down the notion of causality in order to show that the study's finding is not so surprising after all. The author is surprised at the finding because, supposedly, secondhand smoke shouldn't cause heart disease. Each wrong choice lessens the surprise by suggesting that some other factor *correlated* with smoking is responsible for the higher incidence of spousal heart disease.

A 180 test taker recognizes the difference between causation and correlation.

(A) If the spouses of smokers tend to be on the old side, and older people are more prone to heart disease, this helps explain the findings in a way that would satisfy the author—in other words, in a way that's consistent with her belief that secondhand smoke, by itself, shouldn't cause the increased incidence of heart disease noted in the study.

(B) Same thing: If smoking homes are generally homes with increased alcohol and coffee intake, and these things are associated with heart disease, then we'd be less surprised by the findings in light of the fact that the effects of secondhand smoke should be negligible.

(D) and (E) Same thing: If smoking is correlated with higher stress and higher pollution levels, both of which are related to heart disease, the mystery would be lessened.

section three

READING COMPREHENSION

CHAPTER ELEVEN

The Reading Comprehension Challenge

See Spot run.

According to the passage, Spot engaged in which one of the following activities?

(A) growling
(B) sleeping
(C) digging
(D) running
(E) eating

Ever since you learned to read, you've been tested on your comprehension of written material, so it's no surprise that Reading Comprehension is the most familiar section in all of standardized testing. Medicine, business, archaeology, psychology, dentistry, teaching, law—the exams that stand at the entrance to study in these and most other fields all have one thing in common: a Reading Comprehension section. No matter what academic area you pursue, you have to make sense of dense, unfamiliar prose. And passages don't get much more dense, difficult, or unfamiliar than those on the LSAT.

As with all LSAT material, Reading Comp passages and question sets run the gamut from cake to killer, and naturally for the purposes of this book we've compiled for your test-taking pleasure a group of the densest, nastiest passages we could find. If you can ace these, it's safe to say you have absolutely nothing to fear from the Reading Comp section come test day.

The following offers some guidelines on how to get the most out of the passages in this book.

USING THE READING COMPREHENSION PASSAGES IN THIS BOOK

The Reading Comp passages in this book are broken up into three categories:

- Just Plain Tough
- Blinded by Science
- Philosophers' Corner

You may wish to build up to the ones in the final category, as these are particularly complex. Here are a few general pointers that should help guide your attack.

Read for the author's purpose and main idea. It's easy to get bogged down in details, especially in difficult passages like the ones in this book. But if you keep the author's purpose—that is, the reason he or she wrote the passage—and main idea in mind, you'll be able to answer many general types of questions immediately, and will know where to find the answers to the others.

Pay attention to passage structure. Many questions ask about how the author strings ideas together to present his or her overall point, or how certain elements function in relation to the passage as a whole. Paying attention to passage structure as you read will give you a leg up on these questions.

Paraphrase the text. You'll be able to process and apply the information in any passage, including these toughies, if you simplify the passage's ideas and translate them into your own words.

A 180 test taker cuts past impressive-sounding text and boils it down to basic ideas.

Observe timing guidelines. Four passages in 35 minutes allows for roughly eight and a half minutes per passage, but considering the difficulty level of the readings in this book, it's reasonable to allow a little extra time. Try, however, not to exceed nine to ten minutes per passage. If you can knock out tough ones like the ones in this book in that amount of time, you should have no problem finishing easier passages in less than the average time allowed per passage.

Read the explanations. Review the key points of each passage, comparing your own synopsis of the passage to ours. Notice whether you are consistently spotting the main idea and focusing on the relevant parts of the passages. As in the Logic Games and Logical Reasoning sections, the thought processes and habits of 180 test takers are highlighted throughout the explanations. Try to make these habits your own.

Have fun. No doubt this advice is easier to take for Logic Games than for Reading Comp. However, it still behooves you to approach the Reading Comp section with enthusiasm and a good-natured appreciation for the challenges presented. Who knows, you may even come across some material that's *interesting* to you.

CHAPTER TWELVE

Just Plain Tough

Technical science and abstract philosophical passages often give test takers trouble, and you'll cut your teeth on examples of these soon enough. But it's important to remember that the difficulties of the Reading Comp section are not confined to these types alone. Passages from any other category commonly represented in LSAT Reading Comp—humanities, social science, law—can pose serious problems for the unsuspecting test taker.

The following four examples epitomize difficult passages that are neither scientific nor particularly philosophical in nature, but nonetheless present their own unique challenges. They are, as the title of this chapter states, just plain tough—and it's up to you to be tougher.

PASSAGE 1

While original U.S. nationality legislation of 1790, 1795, and 1802 limited naturalization eligibility to "free white persons," it did not limit eligibility by sex. But as early as 1804 the law
(5) began to draw distinctions regarding married women in naturalization law. Since that date, and until 1934, when a man filed a declaration of intention to become a citizen but died prior to naturalization, his widow and minor children were
(10) "considered as citizens of the United States" if they/she appeared in court and took the oath of allegiance and renunciation. Thus, among naturalization court records, one could find a record of a woman taking the oath, but find no
(15) corresponding declaration for her, and perhaps no petition.

Unless a woman was single or widowed, she had few reasons to naturalize prior to the twentieth century. Women, foreign-born or native,
(20) could not vote. Until the mid-nineteenth century, women typically did not hold property or appear as "persons" before the law. Under these circumstances, only widows and spinsters would be expected to seek the protections U.S.
(25) citizenship might afford. One might also remember that naturalization involved the payment of court fees. Without any tangible benefit resulting from a woman's naturalization, it is doubtful that many women or their husbands
(30) considered the fees to be money well spent.

New laws of the mid-1800s opened an era when a woman's ability to naturalize became dependent upon her marital status. The act of February 10, 1855, was designed to benefit
(35) immigrant women. Under that act, "[a]ny woman who is now or may hereafter be married to a citizen of the United States, and who might herself be lawfully naturalized, shall be deemed a citizen." Thus alien women generally became U.S.
(40) citizens by marriage to a U.S. citizen or through an alien husband's naturalization. The only women who did not derive citizenship by marriage under this law were those racially ineligible for naturalization and, since 1917, those
(45) women whose marriage to a U.S. citizen occurred suspiciously soon after her arrest for prostitution. The connection between an immigrant woman's nationality and that of her husband convinced many judges that unless the husband of an alien
(50) couple became naturalized, the wife could not become a citizen. While one will find some courts that naturalized the wives of aliens, until 1922 the courts generally held that the alien wife of an alien husband could not herself be naturalized.
(55) In innumerable cases under the 1855 law, an immigrant woman instantly became a U.S. citizen at the moment a judge's order naturalized her immigrant husband. If her husband naturalized prior to September 27, 1906, the woman may or
(60) may not be mentioned on the record which actually granted her citizenship. Her only proof of U.S. citizenship would be a combination of the marriage certificate and her husband's naturalization record. Prior to 1922, this provision
(65) applied to women regardless of their place of residence. Thus if a woman's husband left their home abroad to seek work in America, became a naturalized citizen, then sent for her to join him, that woman might enter the United States for the
(70) first time listed as a U.S. citizen.

1. It can be inferred from the passage that naturalization records between 1855 and 1922 are likely to reflect

    (A) an incomplete account of the population of married women who immigrated to the United States
    (B) an increase in naturalization of women after the new policies of 1855 took effect
    (C) naturalization primarily of single women and widows who needed the protections that came with citizenship
    (D) a large number of widows who took oaths of naturalization
    (E) an increase in marriages of immigrant women to naturalized citizens after 1855

2. A German widow who immigrated to the United States in 1848 after her husband's death in 1842 would NOT

    (A) become naturalized by getting married to a German man who was previously naturalized
    (B) have been able to undergo naturalization before a judge
    (C) be able to file a declaration of intention to become a citizen
    (D) be able to become naturalized without getting married or paying court costs
    (E) be considered a citizen if her husband had filed a declaration of intention to become a citizen prior to his death

3. From the information given in the passage, it can be inferred that

    (A) more women became naturalized through official channels after women won the right to vote
    (B) a Chinese woman who married a naturalized citizen would be ineligible for naturalization in 1856
    (C) fewer single women than widowed women sought to become naturalized citizens
    (D) all "free white persons" who immigrated to the United States after 1802 were naturalized
    (E) women immigrated during the period in question primarily because their husbands were seeking work

4. Which one of the following, if true, would most seriously weaken the author's assertion that only widows and single women would be expected to seek the protection of U.S. citizenship?

    (A) Judges granted naturalization to widows and single women only if a male relative was willing to serve as a sponsor.
    (B) Property laws prevented women from appearing as "persons" before the court until 1922, when the laws were challenged or overturned.
    (C) Naturalization fees were lower for women whose husbands had already been naturalized, as well as for the husband's female relatives.
    (D) Married women were more likely to earn money from doing sewing or laundry work at home, although such jobs were often underpaid.
    (E) An 1844 law provided weekly food rations for impoverished households, but restricted their distribution to those citizens whose names appeared on birth or naturalization records.

5. According to the policies outlined in the passage, which one of the following is not an example of a woman who would have been eligible for U.S. citizenship?

    (A) A foreign-born woman who married a naturalized citizen
    (B) A foreign-born woman who remained in her native country while her husband immigrated and became naturalized
    (C) A foreign-born woman who immigrated between 1855 and 1917 while her husband remained in their native country
    (D) A foreign-born widow whose husband had intended to become a citizen but had died prior to naturalization
    (E) A foreign-born woman whose husband became a naturalized citizen between 1855 and 1906

6. The primary purpose of the passage is to

    (A) reconcile two opposing viewpoints about a policy
    (B) discuss the effects of a policy upon a demographic group
    (C) argue for the reconsideration of a longstanding policy
    (D) support the establishment of one type of policy over another
    (E) assess the authority of a government agency in two situations

7. Which of the following relationships does the author suggest?

    (A) A partial causal link between the nationality of a man and the eligibility of his wife to be naturalized
    (B) A correlation between widow status and likelihood of being naturalized
    (C) A causal relationship between gender and changes in naturalization policy
    (D) A connection between naturalization records and women's rights
    (E) A direct causal link between a woman's nationality and her husband's eligibility to be naturalized

Passage 1: Naturalization of Women

What Makes It Difficult

This passage offers a long and complicated story of legal requirements for naturalization of women until the beginning of the twentieth century—a topic of interest to a few legal scholars and feminists, but a snoozer to many of the rest of us. Twists and turns abound, and the paradoxes of some women's legal status add to the confusion offered by the unfamiliar subject matter. It all adds up to some fairly difficult reading followed by challenging questions. Let's look at the key points.

Key Points of the Passage

Purpose and Main Idea: The author's purpose is to evaluate women's legal status as citizens in America in the nineteenth and early twentieth centuries. The main idea is that national policy, which was determined more by neglect than by deliberation, led to some peculiar results.

Paragraph Structure: The first paragraph tells us that early naturalization laws drew no distinction based on gender, but were quickly interpreted differently for men and women, with some specific detail offered.

Paragraph 2 discusses reasons why women had little incentive to become citizens, the principal reason being that women didn't have the vote.

Paragraph 3 introduces mid-180s laws explicitly tying women's naturalization rights to their marital status, and a few of the (perhaps unintended) results.

In the final paragraph, the author expands her discussion in paragraph 3, showing how issues of proof of citizenship were raised and how some women became citizens before they even came to this country.

Note the strategic use of "thus" and the end of paragraphs 1 and 4 and in the middle of paragraph 3, drawing attention at regular intervals to the author's interest in the results of these laws.

A 180 test taker uses Keywords to follow an author's twists and turns.

Answers and Explanations

1. A   2. D   3. B   4. E   5. C   6. B   7. A

1. A

This inference question asks us to draw a conclusion about what naturalization records from this period would look like, based on the information in the passage. What are we likely to see included in these records? This is discussed in the last paragraph: Many immigrant women had no documents that explicitly naturalized them or declared their citizenship, only documents detailing the naturalization of their husbands. So we can infer that a modern-day look at these naturalization documents would not list every woman who became a naturalized citizen during the period in question. Choice (A) states this pretty well: Records from that time give us an incomplete account of the population of married women who immigrated to the United States.

(B) The passage gives us no evidence as to whether more women were naturalized after the act of 1855. Given the evidence the author presents, however, it actually seems likely that the record would reflect a decrease or no change at all, since while the protection of the law was extended to a new group of women, the records of their naturalizations were still held in their husbands' names, and might not include the women's names at all.

(C) contradicts the passage; the author describes a situation in which most of those going on record as being naturalized were men. So it's not accurate to say that records would reflect "primarily single women and widows"; based on the passage, it seems more likely that records would reflect primarily men. It's possible that *of the women who were recorded as being naturalized*, a majority were single women or widows, but this answer choice fails to make that distinction.

(D) The author gives this scenario as an example of a possible process, but again, we have no evidence upon which to base a conclusion about the *numbers* of women being naturalized. There could have been thirty thousand widows who took oaths of naturalization, or there could have been ten. We can't draw a conclusion from the information we're provided.

(E), like (B), deals with an increase in naturalization of women, this time by marriage, after the new laws of 1855. Again, the question is asking us not what might have happened at that time, but what is likely to be reflected in the naturalization records. The author tells us repeatedly that women usually did not have their own naturalization records, so it follows that if a woman married a citizen who was already naturalized, there would be no record of her naturalization. Perhaps marriage records would reflect such an increase, but that's outside the scope of the question, which asks specifically about naturalization records.

A 180 test taker is not tempted by a choice simply because it contains words or characters that appear in the passage.

---

2. D

This inference question asks us to use the policies outlined in the passage to make a prediction about a specific situation—note that we are being asked which of the choices would NOT be possible for a woman in this situation. To answer the question, we reread the passage and see that single women had two ways of becoming naturalized during the period in question: They could marry a man who was already naturalized, or they could go through the naturalization process on their own. Choice (D) rules out both of these possibilities, so it's the correct answer: A woman in this situation could not become a naturalized citizen without marrying a naturalized citizen or paying to go through the naturalization process herself.

The other choices all describe options that *would* allow a widow to become naturalized. The wives of naturalized citizens were automatically considered to be citizens themselves, so (A) works. A widow could pay to go through the process herself, which rules out (B) and (C). Finally, paragraph 1 of the passage explains that the widows of men who had started the citizenship process during their lives were considered citizens, so choice (E) is also incorrect.

3. B

It's not easy to prephrase an answer to an inference question that's as open-ended as this one. The best strategy here is to go right to the answer choices, looking for the one that follows most logically from the facts we're given in the passage.

(A) The author does list the right to vote as part of an argument about why married women didn't have an incentive to be naturalized themselves. However, it's not given as the sole reason. We can't infer that if women *do* have the right to vote, then they will choose to be naturalized in order to exercise it; this choice reaches too far.

(B) is the correct choice. The author opens the passage by stating that the original naturalization legislation discriminated against nonwhite immigrants, making them ineligible for naturalization. Paragraph 3 tells us, in more detail, that the only women who did not derive automatic naturalization from their husbands' naturalizations were those who were "racially ineligible," or nonwhite.

(C) The author discusses the fact that single and widowed women were more likely than married women to become naturalized in a court. However, we have no evidence to form a conclusion about which groups of women sought naturalization more often.

(D) Paragraph 1 does tell us that only "free white persons" were eligible to be naturalized. But it doesn't follow that *all* free white persons were necessarily naturalized—we can certainly imagine situations in which they would not have been (for instance. if they entered the country illegally), so we can't make such a broad statement.

(E) brings up a detail from the last paragraph of the passage. It certainly is possible that women did immigrate because their husbands needed jobs, but the focus of this passage is on the legalities of their becoming citizens after they immigrated. We can't infer anything about their motivations for doing so.

A 180 test taker quickly dismisses choices that focus on irrelevant parts of the passage.

---

4. E

In order to find the choice that best weakens the author's stance, we must first understand the assertion to which the question refers. We are asked to determine which choice would most weaken the author's assertion that only single or widowed women were likely to seek the protection that naturalization would give. To state it another way, the author is saying that married women had no reason to go through a costly naturalization process, because it held no benefits for them. It follows, then, that to weaken this argument, we're looking for a choice that says that married women *did* benefit from becoming naturalized. Choice (E) does this: If the only way to ensure an extra food ration was to have a woman's name on the naturalization record, and the only way to get her name on the record was to be officially naturalized, then women would have a reason to go through the costly process of naturalization.

(A) does not pertain to married women at all, and the presence of a male relative provides no information about the benefits of naturalization.

(B) We know that this is true; it's included in the second paragraph of the passage. However, it actually serves to strengthen the author's argument; not being able to own property would be yet another reason that married women would have no incentive to undergo naturalization.

(C) comes a little closer, but again, if married women reaped absolutely no benefits from undergoing naturalization, why would they spend any amount of money to do it?

(D) isn't really relevant to the assertion we're dealing with here; there is no clear connection between the likelihood of married women having their own incomes and why they would want to be naturalized.

5. C

"According to the passage" lets us know that we're being asked for something that is found directly in the passage. We need to find an answer choice that is not included as an example of how immigrant women became citizens. These examples are provided throughout the passage, which tells us that for the most part, women were naturalized as a result of their marriages—either by marrying a U.S. citizen, or by immigrating with their husbands, who were then naturalized. (C) is the only choice that doesn't fit within this scope; the passage makes no mention of married women who immigrated without their husbands, only single women and widows.

The other choices can all be found as examples in the passage. (A) is in paragraph 3, as an implication of the 1855 act. The scenario in (B) is detailed in the last sentences of the passage. Paragraph 1 talks about the issue of widows and naturalization, choice (D). Finally, the passage mentions in several places that women became naturalized by way of their husbands' naturalizations (E), notably in paragraphs 2 and 3.

6. B

Your initial reading should have revealed the author's purpose in writing the passage: to talk about nineteenth- and twentieth-century naturalization policy as it pertains to women. Answer choice (B) expresses this purpose in a more general manner, to "discuss the effects of a policy [i.e. naturalization law] upon a demographic group [i.e. women]."

(A) What two viewpoints are reconciled? The author discusses two sets of changes in the policy, but the passage really doesn't incorporate viewpoints *about* the policy.

(C) The author isn't making an argument here; we can't draw any conclusions about her opinion from reading the passage. It is implied that these policies were reconsidered (they were in effect until 1934 and 1922), but that's not the author's intent.

(D) Again, we can't draw any conclusions about the author's opinion, or which type of policy she would be likely to support. The purpose of the passage is to inform readers about the policies, not persuade them to support one or another.

(E) goes a bit beyond the scope of the passage. Presumably a government agency was involved in making decisions about who could be naturalized, but the passage doesn't tell us anything about that agency; in fact, it mentions only judges as the authority figures in these situations.

> A 180 test taker quickly scans the main verbs in each answer choice in questions asking about the author's purpose or attitudes.

7. A

This question requires us to take a closer look at the various connections the author is creating in the passage. The correct choice is (A): In paragraph 3, we see that if a man were ineligible by nationality to be naturalized, then courts usually would find his wife ineligible as well. "Partial causal link" is correct here because there the inverse was not always true; a man who was eligible for naturalization might marry a woman who, for one reason or another, was not.

(B) While the passage gives us several situations in which widowed women became naturalized, we don't have any indication of how widow status would *change a* woman's likelihood of doing so.

(C) It's true that the focus of the passage is the relationship of naturalization laws to women during a specified time period, but the relationship is not one of causation. In order for this choice to be correct, women would have had to have directly *influenced* the policies in question, and that doesn't seem to be the case.

(D) Again, these are two topics from the passage, but it would be a stretch to say that the author implies a connection between them. Women's rights are mentioned only as a reason why women might not become naturalized, but the subject is brought up only in passing, not given as evidence to support a relationship.

(E) There's nothing in the passage that suggests that a woman's nationality would affect her husband's eligibility for naturalization. Paragraph 3 tells us that the reverse might be true, but as a whole, the evidence in the passage seems to support the conclusion that men were deemed eligible for naturalization on their own merits, without consideration of their marital status, while the same was not true for women.

A 180 test taker quickly recognizes choices that shift the scope from the focus of the passage.

What's Next?

Let's move on to our next tough passage. In this one we make the leap from political philosophy to computers and the information revolution.

PASSAGE 2

If since the late 1970s we have been living in and seeing the economic impact of the "computer revolution," then the past few years at least have been the time of most dramatic and rapid change.
(5) Indeed, this period is generally seen as a revolution different enough in kind and in its effects to be given its own name: the "information revolution." The growth of the World Wide Web has had several unintended and unexpected
(10) consequences that have radically changed economies throughout the world and, most dramatically have forced changes in business models, planning, and practices that at least seemed as if they might threaten the old balance
(15) of power. It will undoubtedly be many years before we can judge the true nature and full extent of the impact of the development of the Internet on business and the economy as a whole.

Typically, projections for development during a
(20) period of revolution are made from points of maximum change, and already some predictions look to be grossly overoptimistic or unnecessarily alarming. But there can be no doubt that the Internet has changed the facts of business life
(25) forever.

Throughout the computer revolution, but particularly in the period of the "information revolution," there has been much talk of a "new economy." The claim is that the rules of
(30) economics that were developed during the industrial revolution and that we have come to take for granted are no longer in effect. Kevin Kelly has said that the new economy is "tearing the old laws of wealth apart," that we are
(35) witnessing a revolution in manufacturing and business in general that is incommensurable with any other period in history in terms of the creation of wealth and the conduct of business. Kelly argues that we are in a period of revolution like no
(40) other in history, both in terms of technological innovation in microelectronics and in the discovery of the economic aspects of information.

According to J. Bradford DeLong, it is exactly this rapid technological change and its attendant
(45) effects on the old laws of wealth that the information revolution shares with earlier technological and economic upheavals. DeLong points out that the development of the automobile almost exactly matched the types of changes
(50) wrought by Silicon Valley's innovations. And for this reason he warns against predictions of unending technological advancement in one industry: like the automobile industry, the microelectronics and information industries will
(55) mature and their rates of innovation flatten. Yet

DeLong does see the move from emphasis on technological innovation in microelectronics to emphasis on the economic aspects of information as truly revolutionary. In so far as businesses are
(60) able to focus not so much as they used to on making superior products and instead can focus on convincing consumers to pay for what they use, the business and economic upheaval will be enormous.

1. The author's main point in the passage is reflected most accurately in which one of the following statements?

    (A) Although it has been overstated, the information revolution has affected changes in our economy and in business practices that have yet to be fully understood

    (B) DeLong has disproved Kelly's claims that the information revolution has changed the laws of wealth creation

    (C) The information revolution has had a far greater impact on the economy and on business practice than did the computer revolution

    (D) Predictions about the impact of the information revolution on business are illegitimate because they have been made from points of maximum change

    (E) Despite some superficial disagreement, Kelly and DeLong share a long-term view of what impact the information revolution will have on business

2. Which of these statements would the author say Kelly and DeLong are most likely to disagree on?

    (A) The information revolution is having enormous affects on the ways businesses sell to consumers

    (B) The move from innovation in microelectronics to emphasis on the economic aspects of information is truly revolutionary

    (C) The computer and technological revolutions are unique and without precedent in the history of technological change

    (D) As the microelectronics industry matures, its rate of innovation will flatten

    (E) The full impact of the Internet on manufacturing and on business models cannot be ascertained at this time

3. The passage states which one of the following about DeLong's description of the computer revolution?

    (A) The rate of innovation in earlier technological revolutions is comparable to the rate of innovation in the computer revolution
    (B) Unlike in the automobile industry, the computer industry has the potential for ever-increasing rates of innovation
    (C) Kelly's claims that the computer revolution has overthrown the economic rules in place since the industrial revolution are mistaken
    (D) The move from emphasis on technological innovation to emphasis on the economic aspects of information is necessary for the survival of the computer industry
    (E) Projections for change during the computer revolution have been unreliable because they have been made from points of maximum change

4. Which one of the following best describes the function of the second paragraph in the context of the passage as a whole?

    (A) It argues that projections made from points of maximum change are inevitably misleading
    (B) It introduces the primary topic of contention between Kelly and DeLong
    (C) It challenges the assumption made in the previous paragraph that the World Wide Web has had several unintended and unexpected consequences
    (D) It provides additional support for the claim made in the first paragraph that the past few years have been the period of most rapid change in the computer revolution
    (E) It acknowledges the fact of tremendous change caused by the computer and information revolutions, but introduces some skepticism about the most far-reaching predictions of coming change

5. On which topic are Kelly and DeLong most likely to find themselves in agreement?

    (A) The differences and similarities between the computer revolution and technological changes of the past
    (B) The laws of economics of the industrial revolution
    (C) The impact of the information revolution on rates of technological innovation
    (D) The importance of the economic aspects of information
    (E) The differences and similarities between the microelectronic and automobile industries

6. The author refers to the concept of the "new economy" in the third paragraph in order to

    (A) provide evidence for the impact of the information revolution on economics
    (B) help clarify the difference in nature between the computer and information revolutions
    (C) refute the notion that the laws of economics that held during the industrial revolution are still in force today
    (D) set the stage for a dispute about the impact of the information revolution on economics
    (E) support the claim that it will be many years before we can evaluate the full impact of the Internet on business and the economy

Passage: Computer Revolution

What Makes It Difficult

It's possible, even likely, that you will encounter a reading comprehension passage on a topic about which you have no knowledge or interest. This needn't be a problem and can even be an advantage. If you're not bringing any prejudice to the reading it can be easier to focus on the logical structure of the passage.

What's important to note about this passage is that the author makes few claims of his own, leaving it up to Kelly and DeLong to slug it out over the impact of the information revolution. Even so, we have to be careful, as neither of these authors are literally quoted and, as far as we can tell, do not address one another directly. This will become crucial when we you are asked to identify what Kelly and DeLong would agree or disagree about.

Key Points of the Passage

Purpose and Main Idea: The author's purpose is to contrast a simplistic view of the impact of the information revolution on business and economy with a more considered and sophisticated one. The main idea is that what could be truly revolutionary is an emphasis on the economic aspects of information.

Paragraph Structure: Paragraph 1 sets the time frame for the topic. The computer revolution began in the late 1970s; the information revolution has occurred only in the "past few years." There is a cautionary note: we won't be able to judge the extent of change for many years.

Paragraph 2 amplifies the caution suggested at the end of the first paragraph. Most predictions have been made from points of maximum change and have already been seen to be exaggerated in one direction or the other.

Paragraph 3 introduces Kevin Kelly, clearly one of the people making the sort of hyperbolic predictions we are warned about in paragraph 2. The language used to communicate Kelly's ideas is a strong clue to the author's intentions. The new economy is "tearing ... apart" old understandings of economics; the information revolution is "incommensurable" with other technological revolutions and it is "like no other in history."

Paragraph 4 explains the views of J. Bradford DeLong, which are clearly meant as corrective to those of Kelly. We immediately find a flat contradiction of what Kelly has told us: DeLong says that the computer revolution is in many ways just like the automotive revolution, and that hyperbolic predictions are likely to turn out to be wrong. But in the final sentence we find DeLong on board the revolution in a more nuanced way when he claims that a focus on the the economic aspects of information could be truly revolutionary for business.

A 180 test taker knows that a good "Roadmap" doesn't include every detail of a passage, but recaps the gist of each paragraph.

Answers and Explanations

1. A   2. C   3. A   4. E   5. D   6. D

1. A

While the author may be skeptical of some of the more outsized claims about the impact of computer and information technology on business models and the economy, he is clearly keeping an open mind about the future. His extensive consideration of DeLong is meant to underscore the large economic potential of the information revolution as much as it is meant to counter Kelly's rather larger claims. For these reasons, (A) best reflects the author's main points.

(B) can be quickly dismissed. DeLong does not address Kelly's claim directly, much less disprove it.

(C) may be more easily attributable to DeLong than to the author who quotes his work. But as both this author and DeLong are more interested in the potential of information revolution than on its effects to date it cannot be taken to be either writer's main point.

(D) The author suggests that predictions made from points of maximum change are not likely to be reliable, but to say that they are illegitimate overstates his case. This alone would disqualify (D), but this choice also has too small a scope to be the main point of the passage.

(E) could be the case, but as Kelly's position is hardly considered at all it's difficult to infer much about the extent to which he would agree with DeLong. And as Kelly is quoted hardly at all it is not likely that his beliefs could be part of the main point of this passage.

2. C

The author doesn't give us much to go on as far as Kevin Kelly's beliefs are concerned. Really all we know is that Kelly claims that the computer and information revolutions are unlike any other business or technological revolutions in history. Knowing this, it should be easy to decide on what it is that he and DeLong disagree on.

(A) and (B) are points that Kelly and DeLong are most likely to agree upon. It's made explicit that DeLong believes both of these propositions. We could infer that Kelly would agree. There's certainly no reason to believe that Kelly would disagree.

(C) is the correct answer. Kelly says that these revolutions are unlike any other, while DeLong makes a descriptive comparison between the computer and automotive revolutions.

(D) could very well be a point of disagreement for Kelly and DeLong, but it would be inferring too much from little said on Kelly's part for this to be the correct answer. Kelly's claim is that these revolutions are like no others, not that they will continue at the same revolutionary pace for all time.

(E) is one of those statements so general that it is hard to imagine anyone taking issue with it. As such, it can't be a point of much contention.

3. A

Here we're presented with another detail question, this time regarding DeLong's views. DeLong is discussed in detail in the final paragraph—so now is a good time to return to the passage and examine that paragraph to answer the question.

A 180 test taker returns to the passage to reread text carefully when a question makes it necessary to pick up a point.

(A) DeLong does make the comparison between the rate of innovation in the computer and automotive industries. It's important to note that (A) does not attribute to DeLong any claim that the rates are the same or different, just that he makes the comparison. This is the correct answer.

(B) contradicts what DeLong actually says about rates of innovation in the computer industry: that they will flatten as the industry matures.

(C) can be dismissed immediately. DeLong does not address Kelly directly and there is no suggestion that one is necessarily familiar with the other's claims.

(D) DeLong does locate the most dramatic revolution in the move from manufacturing to the economic aspects of information, but he says nothing about the survival of the industry.

(E) This claim is made, but by the author of the passage. It is not attributed to DeLong.

A 180 test taker can keep multiple theories and views straight in his mind, and doesn't fall for choices that confuse them.

---

4. E

The paragraph in question consists only of two sentences. The first makes the claim that many predictions about the computer revolution already look to be exaggerated. The second, however, concedes that business has been changed forever by the Internet. The author is setting the stage for his comparison of Kelly and DeLong by saying, yes, these changes are real and considerable, yet they're not quite as dramatic as some have led us to believe they have been and will continue to be. And (E) says exactly this: the author concedes the reality of the revolution while maintaining a skeptical eye towards claims about it.

(A) The paragraph suggests that predictions made from points of maximum change may be misleading, but it does not make any claims of inevitability.

(B) It is not clear what the primary topic of contention between Kelly and DeLong might be, since they do not address one another's news.

(C) On the contrary, the second sentence of the paragraph grants that the Internet has changed the facts of business life forever. It is perhaps the case—though almost certainly not—that none of these changes have been unintended or unexpected, but nothing in this paragraph challenges the previous claim or is inconsistent with it.

(D) Again, two claims are made in this paragraph but there are no arguments nor support for arguments. Moreover, there is no mention in this paragraph of any specific period of time.

5. D

Now we're asked to choose a statement about which Kelly and DeLong would be likely to disagree. Rather than attempt to prephrase an answer (the possibilities could be very broad), we should scan the choices to determine the best option.

A 180 test taker knows that, when passages include a number of theories, it is common for wrong choices to reflect the opposite of what the passage, author, or theorist in the passage believes or suggests.

(A) is the first choice to dismiss, as Kelly and DeLong are explicitly at odds on this topic. Kelly's claim is that the computer revolution is like no other in history, while DeLong says that it is much like the automotive revolution.

(B) We have almost nothing to go on as far as this topic is concerned. Neither author says anything specific about laws of economics. Too much would have to be inferred here in order to determine any possible agreement.

(C), like (B), requires far too much inference to determine whether or not Kelly and DeLong would be in agreement. Neither is quoted as saying anything about what impact the information revolution may have had on rates of technological change.

(D) here we have a point of real comparison. We're told that Kelly "argues that we are in a period of revolution like no other in history ... in the discovery of the economic aspects of information," and that DeLong "does see the move from emphasis on technological innovation in microelectronics to emphasis on the economic aspects of information as truly revolutionary." If nothing else, these two agree on the economic importance of information.

(E) We've already seen that Kelly and DeLong disagree on this point. Kelly believes that the computer revolution is like no other; DeLong thinks it's much like the automotive revolution.

6. D

The phrase "new economy" is used to introduce the thoughts of Kevin Kelly about the ways in which the computer and information revolutions are changing the laws of economic life. As such, it's the beginning of the contrast drawn between what he says and DeLong's views. That is, it helps set the stage for the Kelly-DeLong dispute. The correct answer is (D).

(A) (C) and (E) all ask too much of a simple phrase. "New economy" is merely a name given to something that may now exist or may yet come to be. The name alone can't provide evidence, refute, or support anything.

(B) might also be dismissed on the grounds that a name can't clarify anything, but even more strongly on the grounds that what follows the use of the phrase "new economy" seems to conflate the computer and information revolutions rather than make any distinction between them.

What's Next?

Had enough of tackling the global issues of nations and their various political and economic problems? Next up is a topic a little closer to home. But don't get caught napping—just because the concept is bit easier to grasp doesn't mean that the questions are easy.

PASSAGE 3

Are there circumstances under which we may lie without any hesitation? To answer this question we must first say what it means to lie. A
(5) lie is a verbal communication that is at odds with the truth, or at least with our own understanding of the truth. Moreover, it is not enough to merely communicate an untruth. In lying we tell a falsehood with the intention of purposefully misleading. In other words, we must intend to
(10) cause some belief or action in the person to whom we lie. In lying, then, we a) communicate something we know not to be the case, and b) do so in order to create some state of affairs that would not be possible if we were to tell the truth.
(15) The most common form of lying is one in which the liar hopes to make some personal gain. But aside from whatever moral issues may apply to such lies, there are consequences to lying in general that must be considered. Two
(20) consequences are particularly important, and correspond to the two conditions of lying mentioned above. One is that of communication breakdown. When we communicate something that is not the case we create a situation in which
(25) genuine communication has failed. The practice of lying in general makes communication among people problematic, if not completely impossible. Another consequence is that in trying to create a belief for action in a person that would not
(30) otherwise be the case we are using that person as a means. Both of these consequences have considerable impact on society, or community, and it is in this context that we must decide on to whom we may lie and when.
(35) In order to lie to someone we must be prepared to accept both of these social consequences. That is, in lying to someone we are excluding them from any community in which we value communication and cooperation. This may seem
(40) to include everyone, but there are circumstances in which someone may have excluded themselves from our community or may have been excluded from our community, at least temporarily. Those who mean to cause harm to others or themselves
(45) provide one example. A sociopath who, if we were to tell him the truth, would kill or harm someone can be lied to without hesitation. Such a person is self-excluded from our community and so the consequences of lying do not apply.
(50) Similarly, a seriously deranged person may have to be excluded from society in order to avoid harm to himself or to others. Such a person has not chosen to excluded himself from our community, but for the welfare of the community
(55) we may chose to exclude him. Again, the social consequences of lying to such a person do not

apply in the same way as they would to members of our community.

In no case may we lie to someone without
(60) hesitation unless the consequences of telling the truth are more injurious to our community than are the consequences of excluding that person from the community.

1. Which one of the following best expresses the main idea of the passage?

   (A) We may lie without hesitation only when the social consequences of lying are less injurious than those of telling the truth
   (B) A lie is an intentional verbal communication at odds with the truth
   (C) We may exclude from our society those people who are likely to cause harm to themselves or to others
   (D) Lies for personal gain are worse than those which merely exclude someone from our community
   (E) Those who have chosen for whatever reason to exclude themselves from society are free to lie without hesitation

2. Which of the following, if true, would strengthen the author's claim that someone who might kill or harm others is "self-excluded" from our community?

   (A) To be a member of a community entails concern for the welfare of the members of that community
   (B) Murder and other forms of harm are universal moral evils
   (C) Sociopaths cannot be held responsible for their behavior, no matter how extreme or dangerous
   (D) To murder or otherwise cause harm is morally equivalent to lying, and all instances of lying are instances of self-exclusion
   (E) Anyone who might commit murder or other harm must be detained or removed for the welfare of the whole community

3. Which one of the following choices most closely parallels the author's reasoning in the first two sentences of paragraph 3?

   (A) Most cases of preventive detention involve the jailing or otherwise limiting the freedom of a person charged with no crime but who is believed to be a danger to the public in some way. As our constitution specifically forbids this practice, preventive detention is acceptable only under those rare circumstances in which we are willing to suspend constitutional rights, such as in wartime.

   (B) All cases of preventive detention involve the jailing or otherwise limiting the freedom of a person charged with no crime but who is believed to be a danger to the public in some way. As our constitution specifically forbids this practice, preventive detention is acceptable only under those rare circumstances in which we are willing to suspend constitutional rights, such as in wartime.

   (C) All cases of preventive detention involve the jailing or otherwise limiting the freedom of a person charged with no crime but who is believed to be a danger to the public in some way. In those circumstances in which we are willing to suspend constitutional rights, such as in wartime, we must also be willing to practice preventive detention.

   (D) Whenever someone is jailed or otherwise has their freedom limited we call it preventive detention. In wartime or other circumstances in which constitutional rights may be suspended, we are free to practice preventive detention without hesitation.

   (E) All cases of preventive detention involve the jailing or otherwise limiting the freedom of a person charged with no crime but who is believed to be a danger to the public in some way. As our constitution specifically forbids this practice, preventive detention is acceptable only during wartime.

4. The last sentence of paragraph one serves as

   (A) justification for the author's claim that a lie is a verbal communication at odds with the truth

   (B) a distinction between acceptable and unacceptable lies

   (C) the author's definition of what it means to tell a lie

   (D) an illustration of the contrast between types of lies

   (E) evidence that lying leads to a breakdown in community communication

5. Which one of the following can be inferred as beliefs on the author's part from the second consequence of lying?

   (A) That under no circumstances do the ends justify the means

   (B) That genuine communication is necessary for the proper functioning of any community

   (C) That failures in communication and the use of other people as means are equivalently injurious to communities

   (D) That we may use others as means only when we are willing to exclude them from our community

   (E) That it is unacceptable to use another person as a means to something else

6. According to the passage, the author believes that lying

   (A) is sometimes less injurious to communities as a whole than is telling the truth

   (B) is acceptable only under circumstances that are so rare as to be not worth considering

   (C) creates states of affairs that could also be achieved through telling the truth

   (D) always entails the hope of personal gain on the part of the liar

   (E) is acceptable as long as we are not intentionally misleading

7. The author would most likely agree with which one of the following statements?

   (A) Of the two consequences of lying, using others as a means is the greater evil.

   (B) Effective and genuine communication is a good that ought to be preserved.

   (C) Only under very rare circumstances may we lie without hesitation.

   (D) We may lie without hesitation in certain circumstances as long as we have no intention to mislead.

   (E) A lie with which the liar hopes to make some sort of personal gain is the most pernicious sort of lie.

Passage: Lying

What Makes It Difficult

Sometimes it's most difficult to evaluate a passage on a topic so familiar that we cannot help but have strong opinions. This in one such passage. Lying is a topic all of us have had to think about—and have been lectured on—since childhood. We need in a passage like this to put aside our evaluation of the author's definitions and conclusions and focus exclusively on what he or she is saying.

Fortunately, the author here is clear. He or she defines what it means to lie quite explicitly, and just as explicitly states what he believes to be the most problematic consequences of lying. It's important to note that the author places all the definitions and consequences of lying in the context of their effects on community. That is, no universal moral claims are being made here; we're asked instead to evaluate consequences on the basis of the impact they have on communities.

Key Points of the Passage

Purpose and Main Idea: The author's purpose is to define what it means to lie, identify the consequences of lying, and identify the circumstances (if any) under which we may lie. The main idea is that lying is permissible only when we are willing to exclude from our community the person being lied to.

Paragraph Structure: Paragraph 1 asks when it is we may lie and then provides the author's definition of lying. A lie is a verbal communication of something we know not to be the case made with the intention of bringing about a situation that would not be possible if we were to tell the truth.

Paragraph 2 outlines the two consequences of lying of most concern to the author, and it's here that we find that the author will evaluate the morality of lying based on its effect on community. The two consequences are the breakdown of genuine communication and that in lying we use another person as a means to something.

Paragraph 3 begins by explaining a consequence of these consequences. With the breakdown of communication and in using another as a means, we have excluded the person being lied to from our community. This is the ultimate consequence we must accept if we are to accept a lie as permissible. The author then goes on to name some exceptional cases in which we might chose to exclude someone from our community.

Paragraph 4 simply states the author's conclusion. We may lie only when telling the truth would cause more harm to our community.

Answers and Explanations

1. A   2. A   3. B   4. C   5. E   6. A   7. B

1. A

The first question asks the main idea of the passage. If you've properly developed a "Roadmap" of the passage and put some thought into the author's purpose as you read, this question shouldn't pose a problem.

The author makes a summation of the main point of the passage very easy for us by doing this himself in the final paragraph. Although there are some definitions and exceptions along the way this last paragraph summarizes everything preceding it: we may lie without hesitation only when the social consequences of doing so are less injurious than those of telling the truth. (A) is the correct answer.

(B) is a definition. As such it could be the main point of a passage, but is not for this one. It rather serves as a basis for the meat of the passage in paragraphs two and three.

(C) is suggested in the course of the passage, but refers not at all to lying. It's made clear in the introductory and closing passages that the question of when we may lie is the author's main concern.

(D) The author says only that lies for personal gain are common. He makes no judgment about the relative demerits of types of lies.

(E) just confuses the author's argument, which states that we may lie only to those who we exclude from our community or who have excluded themselves.

A 180 test taker avoids choices that are too narrow or too broad when searching for the answer to a "main idea" question.

---

2. A

This "strengthen the argument" question requires that we first understand how the author argues that someone who might kill or harm others is "self-excluded" from our community. This appears in paragraph 3. The author first says that, by lying to someone, we are excluding them, at least temporarily, from our community "in which we value communication and cooperation." So the argument revolves around a specific definition of what the author means by excluding someone from the community.

It doesn't seem much of a stretch to suggest that someone who kills or harms someone else is "self-excluding" him or herself from that community, but only one of these choices will strengthen that claim.

(A) does. It seems counterintuitive to suppose that it's possible to be a member of a community without concern for the welfare of its other members. Making this explicit strengthens the claim of self-exclusion.

(B) and (C) may well be true, but does not help strengthen the claim as it makes to reference to what it means to belong to a community.

(D) Even if it were true that murder and lying were morally equivalent, this statement would be irrelevant to the author's argument. The author's argument is not that lying excludes us from a community, but that in lying we exclude the person being lied to.

(E) refers only to exclusion on the part of the community, not self-exclusion.

3. B

This might seem like a nightmare at first glance, but it's not as hard as it looks. We're asked to identify a pattern of reasoning that most closely approximates that used by the author at the beginning of paragraph 3. We just reviewed that material to answer question 2.

A 180 test taker knows that similar ideas are tested throughout the question set, and that the thought process used in an earlier question can often be reapplied later.

It's helpful to restate exactly what we're looking for in order to eliminate the wrong choices quickly. In the first two sentences of paragraph 3, the author is setting out the conditions under which we may lie. The primary difficulty with lying is that it excludes someone from our community. In order to lie without hesitation, we must be prepared to accept the consequences of excluding from our community (at least temporarily) the person being lied to, as well as possible breakdowns of communication.

The form here is to make clear what is entailed first by the act of lying and then by the consequences of that action. (B) has the same form. First we are told what it means to place someone in preventive detention and then are told the exceptional conditions under which this is acceptable.

(A) is identical to (B) except for the first word. Here we find "most" rather than "all," which makes the forms of the two arguments radically different: the author's claim is universal while this claim is not.

(C) is similar in form to (B) and to the author's argument, but it is stronger, saying that under these circumstances we must practice preventive detention. This would be equivalent to saying that in cases where we are willing to exclude someone from our community we must lie to them.

(D) really has no form at all. The two statements here are separate, without any connection between the practice of preventive detention and constitutional rights.

(E) In the other choices here, wartime is given as an example of a situation under which constitutional rights may be suspended. (E) makes a much more specific claim: that wartime is the only situation under which such rights may be suspended. In the original passage the author points to no one circumstance under which we may choose to exclude someone from our community.

4. C

Now we're asked to determine what function is served by the last sentence in paragraph 1. The last sentence of the first paragraph begins, "In lying, then, we ...," which is clearly setting-up a definition, something underlined by the structure of the sentence, divided as it is into very specific (a) and (b) clauses. These clauses give us the conditions that must be satisfied in order for something to be a lie.

(A) far from being any sort of justification is just a restatement of the (a) condition of the definition.

(B) and (D) are far from the mark, there being nothing in the sentence about what is or is not acceptable, or about more than one type of lie.

(C) is correct. The sentence is a specific, condition-based definition.

(E) The definition suggests how community communication might break down, but no evidence is supplied here. In fact, the breakdown of communication follows logically from the definition.

5. E

First, let's identify the consequences of lying mentioned by the author in this paragraph. The first consequence is the breakdown of communication. The second consequence is that in lying we use the person being lied to as a means. It's not stated explicitly, but it's clear that the author finds neither of these consequences to be desirable. So we're looking for an inference about the use of others as a means to something, an inference that does not attempt to place this practice in a positive light.

(A) can be confusing, as it does refer to means. But the author makes no comparison between means and ends.

(B) has mistaken the two consequences. The consequence of communication breakdown is the first, not the second one mentioned.

(C) takes both consequences together. We are interested only in what can be inferred from the second consequence mentioned.

(D) could perhaps be inferred from the passage as a whole, but the possibility and practice of excluding others from our community is not discussed until the subsequent paragraph.

(E) gets it right. The argument being made is a moral one. The consequence is clearly meant to be a negative consequence and the claim universal. So we can infer that it is morally unacceptable to use someone else as a means.

6. A

The answer to a detail question like this will most likely not directly quote the relevant passage information, but will be a close paraphrase. The author makes it clear in the third paragraph that there are circumstances—specifically those in which lying may prevent community members from being harmed—under which lying is acceptable. In other words, sometimes lying causes less harm than not-lying. (A) is the correct answer.

(B) From the author's description, it sounds as if the conditions under which we may lie without hesitation are quite rare. But he makes no claim or suggestion about the frequency of such situations, and so we are not warranted in drawing any conclusions about this.

(C) states something completely contradictory to what the author states. It is part of his definition of lying that it creates a state of affairs that cannot be created by telling the truth.

(D) No. The author says only that the most common lie is one in which the liar hopes for personal gain.

(E) also contradicts the author's definition of a lie, which states that it must be intentionally misleading on the part of the liar.

7. B

This inference question requires us to determine which statement could most likely be attributed to the author, based on the information presented in the passage. Again, our grasp of the author's purpose in writing the passage comes into play.

(B) is not explicitly stated in the passage, but is easy to infer. The author mentions two consequences of lying that are harmful to communities. One is the breakdown of communication. It follows easily that the author believes this to be a good that ought to be preserved.

(A) It's clear that the author finds the use of others as a means to be morally wrong, but there's no comparison anywhere in the passage of the wrongs that may be committed in lying.

(C) Again, as we know from question 6, it sure sounds like the conditions under which we may lie are quite rare, but the author makes no claims or suggestions about their frequency.

(D) contradicts the author's definition of lying, in which all lies include the intent to mislead.

(E) We're told explicitly that the lie for personal gain is the most common sort of lie. No comparison of severity of lies is made.

What's Next?

How's it going so far? Next up we present one more legal-minded author to contend with before moving on to the more specialized and esoteric material. We call this one "Law and Liberty." Do what you can with it and then check out the explanation.

PASSAGE 4

In the nineteenth century, legal and political philosophers were agreed that the end of the legal order, the purpose of political organization and purpose of lawmaking, were to secure and
(5) maintain individual liberty. The historian found in history the unfolding of this idea in human experience. The philosophical jurist postulated free will as the fundamental principle and deduced from there an ideal system of principles
(10) of liberty to which law ought to conform. The utilitarian legislator took individual liberty for the one sure means of producing human happiness and so made it the goal of all lawmaking. Mill's treatise "On Liberty" is the best example of a
(15) thoroughgoing exposition of this nineteenth-century idea of abstract liberty. Moreover, it is much more tempered and reasonable in its attitude toward what we now call social legislation, so far as it restrains an abstract liberty of action whereby
(20) under pressure the weak barter away their actual liberty, than most contemporary or even subsequent writing from the same standpoint.

Today the social-philosophical school has given us a new conception of the end of the legal
(25) order. Instead of the maximum of individual self-assertion consistent with a like self-assertion by all others, we are now putting as the end the maximum satisfaction of human wants, of which self-assertion is only one, even if a very important
(30) one. Hence juristic and political theory today thinks of interests, that is of claims which a human being may make, and of securing or protecting the greatest number of these interests possible with the least sacrifice of other interests.
(35) Moreover there are public interests, or claims which the organized political society may make, and social interests, or claims of society at large. Ultimately all interests, individual and public, are secured and maintained because of a social
(40) interest in so doing. But this does not mean that individual interests, the details of which the nineteenth century worked out so well, are to be ignored.

On the contrary, the greatest of social interests
(45) is the moral and social life of the individual, and thus individual interests become largely identical with a social interest. In securing them because of the social interest in the moral and social life of the individual, however, and in recognizing that
(50) individual self-assertion is only one human want, which must be weighed with others in a finite world where all wants cannot be satisfied, a governmental paternalism or even maternalism may become proper, which would have seemed
(55) intolerable to thinkers in the last century. In this connection, Mill on Liberty has a permanent value, despite the entire change in our views as to the end of law and of the state. Just as in the seventeenth century an undue insistence upon
(60) public interests, thought of as the interests of the sovereign, defeated the moral and social life of the individual and required the assertion of individual interests in Bills of Rights and Declarations of Rights, there is a like danger that
(65) certain social interests will be unduly emphasized and that governmental maternalism will become an end rather than a means and will defeat the real purposes of the legal order. Hence, although we think socially, we must still think of individual
(70) interests, and of that greatest of all claims which a human being may make, the claim to assert his individuality.

1. The primary purpose of the passage is to

   (A) advocate a socially conscious model of law
   (B) explain two models of law and determine which is more appropriate
   (C) describe two models of law and compare their approach to individual liberty
   (D) discuss the development of legal theory from the seventeenth century to today
   (E) distinguish between two facets of a legal model

2. The author states that the nineteenth-century idea of liberty was

   (A) impractical as a foundation for law
   (B) difficult to translate into law
   (C) unrealistic in practice
   (D) susceptible to extremism
   (E) incompatible with the public interest

3. The author refers to Mill in order to

   (A) reveal the failures of the nineteenth-century legal model
   (B) support the view that liberty is an unreasonable abstraction
   (C) show that liberty is an outmoded ideal
   (D) warn against the perils of unrestrained liberty
   (E) suggest one of the limitations of the nineteenth-century ideal of liberty

4. The author would probably express sympathy with which of the following statements?

    (A) It is necessary to sacrifice some personal freedom to maintain the greatest liberty for all.
    (B) The goal of law today is to protect the public interest.
    (C) Individual wants must be subordinated to the social interest.
    (D) Self-assertion is unimportant in the context of the social-philosophical school of thought.
    (E) Today's legal model is not vulnerable to the same sort of extremism that plagued the seventeenth-century and nineteenth-century legal models.

5. The author states all of the following points about today's legal model EXCEPT that it

    (A) aims to satisfy the greatest number of interests with the least sacrifice
    (B) secures and maintains interests because of the social interest in so doing
    (C) considers public and social interests in addition to individual interests
    (D) downplays the interests of the individual in favor of the greater social good
    (E) weighs the want of individual self-assertion against all the other human wants

6. It can be inferred that which of the following is the most appropriate example of government maternalism?

    (A) A state-wide sales tax
    (B) A government-run postal service
    (C) A guarantee of freedom of the press
    (D) A restriction on the use of public land
    (E) A pledge of religious tolerance

7. The author would most likely describe the assertion that preserving individual liberty is less important than upholding the social interest as

    (A) accurate
    (B) misguided
    (C) brilliant
    (D) debatable
    (E) tragic

Passage 4: Law and Liberty

What Makes It Difficult

The passage is an abstract discussion of the relation of liberty to the law, with the emphasis on abstract. The author does not give any real world examples to elucidate the models of the law presented in the passage. The author does provide as an example the work of John Stuart Mill, referred to simply as "Mill," but assumes that readers will be familiar with his work *On Liberty*. This casual reference to a work of philosophy, with no explanation of its contents, adds to the seeming impenetrability of the passage. However, although it would help to have a rudimentary understanding of Mill, it is not essential to unraveling the author's argument. The reader's task is further complicated because the author fails to define a number of key terms such as "social legislation," "social-philosophical school," and "governmental maternalism." However, neither of these terms is essential to understanding the author's main argument and their meaning can be gathered from the context of the passage. As usual, we can paraphrase the main ideas and break the passage down into manageable chunks. Here are the key points:

Key Points of the Passage

Purpose and Main Idea: The main purpose of the passage is to contrast the nineteenth-century model of the law with today's, particularly as it relates to the concept of liberty. Essentially the author asserts that in the nineteenth century the purpose of law was to preserve individual liberty and today the purpose of law is to satisfy social interests. However, the author concludes that individual liberty is the most important social interest.

Paragraph Structure: Paragraph 1 describes the nineteenth-century model of law and liberty. In fact, the author does this in the first sentence. A good first step is to paraphrase the first sentence in plain language: "In the nineteenth century," "the end," or purpose, of "the legal order," or law, was "to secure and maintain individual liberty." The rest of the paragraph elaborates on this idea, discussing how the goal of individual liberty was expressed by historians; "philosophical jurists," of legal theorists; and "utilitarian legislators," or politicians. Mill's work *On Liberty* is cited as best example of the nineteenth-century idea of "abstract liberty."

Paragraph 2 expresses today's model, which can also be called the "social-philosophical" model, of law and liberty. The author introduces the term "the social-philosophical school" in the first sentence, but does not use the term again rather referring to the model as "today's." Unlike the nineteenth-century model, the sole aim of which was to maximize individual liberty, the law today strives to satisfy the maximum number of human wants. While "self-assertion," or individual liberty, is still an important human "want," it is now weighed against other wants, including social and public interests.

The passage essentially describes a paradigm shift (as suggested by the line "the entire change of our views as to the end of law") in the perceived goal of the law. Paragraph 3 discusses how this paradigm shift affects individual liberty. In the first sentence, the author states that because "the moral and social life of the individual" is the greatest of all social interests, individual and social interests are largely the same. Put another way, as a society we have determined that what we want most is to preserve our individual freedom. However, in order to satisfy the most people, some limits must be placed in individual freedom through government "maternalism." Although this term is not defined, one can assume that the author means that the government takes on a nurturing or caretaking role in society. The author closes the passage with a warning that government maternalism should not supplant the goal of maximizing social interest, or prevent people from asserting their individuality.

Answers and Explanations

1. C   2. D   3. E   4. A   5. D   6. D   7. B

1. C

We are looking for the primary purpose so let's quickly review the structure of the passage: paragraph 1 describes the nineteenth-century model of law and liberty and paragraph 2 describes today's model, explaining how it differs from that of the nineteenth-century. Paragraph 3 discusses how the new model of law affects the ideal of individual liberty. Choice (C) sums up the author's approach: two models of law are described and each model's approach to individual liberty is compared. Keywords indicating that the author is comparing the two models include "Instead" and "On the contrary." Also, (C) is the only choice that mentions liberty, which is the main focus of the passage.

(A) While today's model does consider "social interests" and so could be called "socially conscious," there is nothing in the author's language to suggest that he is advocating this model. Only in the last sentence does the author attempt to convince his reader of a particular view ("we must still think…"), and in this sentence he is advocating for the importance of individual interests.

(B) also suggests that the author is making a judgment about one model, but in fact the passage does not contain language that suggests advocacy of one model over the other. The language is descriptive and dispassionate. The author does not discuss the success or failure of either the nineteenth-century or today's model. The only model that the author discredits is the seventeenth-century mode, which placed "an undue insistence upon public interests" and "defeated the moral and social life of the individual."

(D) is too broad. The author discusses two models of the law with respect to liberty not broad trends in legal theory. The reference to the seventeenth century should alert you that this answer choice is too broad as it is only mentioned in passing in the last paragraph.

(E) suggests that only one model of law is discussed, when the passage is about two distinct model, not two sides of the same model.

2. D

A scan of the answer choices tells you that the question is asking for a negative aspect of the nineteenth-century ideal of liberty, which is primarily discussed in the first paragraph. The best approach is to read each choice, as some can be quickly rejected.

(A) "impractical" cannot be the answer because nowhere does the author discuss the practicality of either model.

(B) contradicts the fourth sentence of paragraph 1, which states that legislators made liberty the goal of all lawmaking.

(C) again, the author does not discuss the practicality of either model, or consider how each works "in practice."

(D) The discussion of Mill at the end of the first paragraph does indicate that the nineteenth-century ideal of liberty, which the author calls "abstract liberty," needed to be restrained, and suggests that without restraint, or taken to the extreme, it could deprive the weak of their "actual liberty."

(E) is not supported by the passage; the author does not discuss how the nineteenth-century idea of liberty related to the public interest.

A 180 test taker reads only as much as is necessary to eliminate a choice.

---

3. E

Considering the answer to question 2 has prepared you to tackle this question. Mill is introduced as "the best example…of this nineteenth-century idea of abstract liberty." The author then states that "On Liberty" is "tempered and reasonable in its attitude toward…social legislation" and "restrains…abstract liberty." From this discussion the author transitions to the new model of law, and the shift away from "individual self-assertion" to "social interest."

(A) is incorrect because the discussion of Mill does not concern the legal model, only the idea of liberty.

(B) although the use of "abstraction" might catch your eye, this choice contradicts the author's assertion throughout the passage that individual liberty is the most important social interest. Nowhere does the author contend that liberty is "unreasonable."

(C) is too broad. The discussion of Mill is about a particular idea of liberty, not about liberty itself.

(D) is a tempting answer as it mentions "unrestrained liberty," which is included in the discussion of Mill. However, "warn" misstates the author's purpose.

(E) is correct because Mill is offered as the best example of the nineteenth-century idea of liberty and then the author suggests that "On Liberty" "restrains abstract liberty." This raises a limitation, or weakness, of the nineteenth-century idea.

4. A

This question asks you to make a very general inference about a view with which the author is most likely to agree. The best approach is to keep in mind what you already know about the author's opinion while testing the answer choices.

A 180 test taker knows what the author does think, as explained in the passage, before speculating about what the author might think.

Although the passage is not persuasive in tone, the author does express an opinion. Most important, the author stresses that individual liberty is central to today's legal model. However, the social model of law, which weighs individual wants against all other wants, requires some sacrifice of individual liberty. This sentiment is most clearly expressed in the third sentence of paragraph 2 and the second sentence of paragraph 3. (A) is an apt summary of this opinion.

(B) is too narrow. According to the author, the goal of law is "the maximum satisfaction of human wants" of which the public interest is only one.

(C) contradicts the idea that individual liberty is the most important human want.

(D) goes against the author's opinion that self-assertion "is only one want, if a very important one."

(E) misstates the opinion expressed at the end of paragraph 3, which states that "there is a danger that social interests will be unduly emphasized."

5. D

We have no choice but to try out the choices and test them against the author's statements about today's legal model. A quick scan of the choices shows that all address the relationship between individual interests and social interests.

(A) is quite true, and in fact is a summary of the author's definition of the goal of today's legal model.

(B) is almost a direct quote of the second-to-last sentence of paragraph 2.

(C) is another summary of the definition of today's legal model, which weighs all human wants, rather than just individual wants.

(D) "downplays" is the Keyword that makes this answer correct. The author states throughout the passage that "individual wants" are the most important human want. The aim of today's legal model is satisfy the most wants, of which individual wants are the most important, with the least sacrifice.

(E) correctly states a key component of today's model, the need to weigh wants against one another.

> A 180 test taker gets stronger as she proceeds through the question set due to better and better assimilation of the author's ideas.

---

6. D

Whether the question asks about a term as familiar as public interest or as obscure as government maternalism, it is a good strategy to locate the term in the passage and see what the author has to say about the subject. Toward the beginning of paragraph 3 we learn that government maternalism can be proper when self-assertion, or individual wants, must be weighed against other wants, which cannot all be satisfied. We can infer from this information that government maternalism involves protecting certain interests that are in conflict with other interests. (D) is the only choice that involves restricting rights, or protecting the interests of one group, say environmentalists, over the competing interests of another, say loggers.

(A) is imposed equally on all shoppers and merchants, so does not involve competing interests.

(B) is a government service that does not restrict the rights of individuals or groups.

(C) and (E) are both guarantees of individual liberty that do not necessitate restricting the interests of a competing group.

7. B

This question should be fairly straightforward as it addresses one of the basic premises of the passage. The author talks a great deal about individual liberty, or wants, in relation to the social interest. In paragraph 2, he asserts that individual interests are secured, or preserved, because of the social interest in doing so. This could be interpreted as saying that individual wants are less important than the social interest, but the author quickly states that individual interests are not to be ignored. Rather, they are the greatest social interest. Perhaps the most important sentences are the final two of the passage in which the author asserts that social interests should never be unduly emphasized, or made too important, and individual interests, or liberty, are the greatest claim which a human being may make. In this context, the author can only view the idea that individual liberty is less important than the social interest as (B) misguided, or wrong. He would not view the statement as either (A) accurate or (C) brilliant. Nor would he consider it a point up for debate (D). While (E) tragic, does express a negative opinion about the statement, it makes an inference about the author's views that is not supported by the passage.

What's Next?

Still there? Good. In the next chapter we'll explore the wonderful world of science. You don't have to be Einstein to handle these.

CHAPTER THIRTEEN

Blinded by Science

This Reading Comprehension category could also be called "It's Not Brain Surgery—It's Rocket Science." Actually, neither brain surgery nor rocket science would be an unusual topic for the LSAT Reading Comp section. Nor, for that matter, would esoteric, mind-numbingly technical topics such as MRI technology, mitochondria, symbiotic stars, or plate tectonics—the very subjects of the passages that follow.

We at Kaplan designate these as "hard" science passages, not in the sense of being difficult (although they certainly are that), but rather to distinguish these technical science passages from "soft" science passages, which view scientific topics from other angles such as the history or social repercussions of scientific findings. There's not always a "hard" science passage on the test, but when they appear, they often give test takers fits—especially those coming to law from a nontechnical background such as humanities or social science. The key to successfully tackling science passages is to not allow yourself to be overwhelmed by the technical terms and processes described.

A 180 test taker notes the location and purpose of details, but doesn't attempt to memorize or even fully understand those details unless a question specifically asks about them.

Focus on the author's purpose and main idea, using the mass of details to fill in the big picture rather than to learn everything about the topics presented. You should dig deeper only when a point is at stake. Follow these keys, and when someone asks you how hard the science passages are on the LSAT Reading Comp section, you'll be able to proudly state, "hey, it's not *brain surgery*"—even when it is.

PASSAGE 5

The newfound appreciation of the dynamic nature of the teen brain is emerging from MRI (magnetic resonance imaging) studies that scan a child's brain every two years, as he or she grows
(5) up. Individual brains differ enough that only broad generalizations can be made from comparisons of different individuals at different ages. But following the same brains as they mature allows scientists a much finer-grained view into
(10) developmental changes. In the first such longitudinal study of 145 children and adolescents, reported in 1999, Dr. Judith Rapoport of the National Institute for Mental Health (NIMH) and colleagues were surprised to discover
(15) a second wave of overproduction of gray matter, the thinking part of the brain—neurons and their branch-like extensions—just prior to puberty. Possibly related to the influence of surging sex hormones, this thickening peaks at around age 11
(20) in girls, 12 in boys, after which the gray matter actually thins some.

Prior to this study, research had shown that the brain overproduced gray matter for a brief period in early development—in the womb and for about
(25) the first 18 months of life—and then underwent just one bout of pruning. Researchers are now confronted with structural changes that occur much later in adolescence. The teen's gray matter waxes and wanes in different functional brain
(30) areas at different times in development. For example, the gray matter growth spurt just prior to puberty predominates in the frontal lobe, the seat of "executive functions"—planning, impulse control and reasoning. In teens affected by a rare,
(35) childhood onset form of schizophrenia that impairs these functions, the MRI scans revealed four times as much gray matter loss in the frontal lobe as normally occurs. Unlike gray matter, the brain's white matter—wire-like fibers that
(40) establish neurons' long-distance connections between brain regions—thickens progressively from birth in humans. A layer of insulation called myelin progressively envelops these nerve fibers, making them more efficient, just like insulation on
(45) electric wires improves their conductivity.

Advancements in MRI image analysis are providing new insights into how the brain develops. UCLA's Dr. Arthur Toga and colleagues turned the NIMH team's MRI scan data into 4-D
(50) time-lapse animations of children's brains morphing as they grow up—the 4th dimension being rate-of-change. Researchers report a wave of white matter growth that begins at the front of the brain in early childhood, moves rearward, and
(55) then subsides after puberty. Striking growth spurts can be seen from ages 6 to 13 in areas connecting brain regions specialized for language and understanding spatial relations, the temporal and parietal lobes. This growth drops off sharply after
(60) age 12, coinciding with the end of a critical period for learning languages.

1. The passage suggests that which of the following can be inferred about growth of gray matter in the brain?

    (A) Amounts of gray and white matter in the brain increase progressively from birth, helping to develop reasoning and planning skills.
    (B) Children under age 6 possess a greater amount of gray matter than do children older than age 12.
    (C) Significant dissipation of gray matter in the frontal lobes of the brain is a primary cause of childhood-onset schizophrenia.
    (D) Myelin fibers strengthen during adolescence, improving connections between gray and white matter.
    (E) The rate of gray matter growth is overtaken by the rate of white matter growth in the average human brain after age 12.

2. Which one of the following provides the best description of the organization of the passage?

    (A) A technology is introduced, and its benefits and side effects are described in greater detail.
    (B) A problem is defined, its potential causes are discussed, and a possible solution is critiqued.
    (C) A process is outlined, its consequences are explained, and predictions are made.
    (D) A technology is described, its effects are discussed, and another aspect of the technology is introduced.
    (E) A process is critiqued, and several of its benefits are considered and generalized.

3. The author states in the second paragraph that the frontal lobe controls the "executive functions" primarily in order to

   (A) explain a newly discovered link between a mental condition and a physical deterioration of the corresponding area of the brain

   (B) refute a commonly held belief about the development of white matter during adolescence

   (C) show how growth in the frontal lobe of the brain affects the aptitude for language acquisition and spatial relations understanding

   (D) prove that slow growth of gray matter prior to adolescence is a harbinger of childhood-onset schizophrenia

   (E) supply new background information relevant to an explanation of white matter growth processes in the frontal lobe

4. The passage suggests that new imaging processes and technologies

   (A) will help physicians repair frontal lobe damage associated with childhood-onset schizophrenia

   (B) can help to prevent loss of gray matter in the frontal lobe during childhood

   (C) may show that the production of gray matter accelerates steadily until puberty

   (D) will help physicians make more accurate predictions about the brain development of individual adolescents

   (E) show that early overproduction of gray matter leads to structural changes in the brain during adolescence

5. Which of the following is not mentioned in the passage as a step in brain development that occurs during or just before adolescence?

   (A) Gray matter is pruned from the frontal lobe, preparing the brain for an increase in growth.

   (B) A wave of white matter growth moves toward the back of the brain.

   (C) The brain's temporal and parietal lobes connect, improving understanding of spatial relations.

   (D) A surge of overproduction of gray matter occurs in the brain.

   (E) Growth in the areas of the brain that specialize in language acquisition decreases abruptly.

6. The author is primarily interested in discussing

   (A) an effect of the growth of white matter in the brain during adolescence

   (B) advances in adolescent brain research that have been made possible by a new imaging technology

   (C) development of gray matter in the frontal, temporal, and parietal lobes during adolescence

   (D) advances in the study of mental illness and abnormal brain development in children under age thirteen

   (E) the relationship between two types of brain matter in humans during a critical period of growth

What Makes It Difficult

A common thread in most science passages is the use of jargon—technical terms and phrases peppered throughout the passage that serve to scare off, or at least befuddle, the unsophisticated test taker.

This passage is no exception, introducing us to things like "magnetic resonance imaging" and a "longitudinal study," acronyms like NIMH and MRI, and "white matter" and "gray matter" (which you may have heard of, but probably can't explain). We have to ask: is that really necessary? But the jargon here isn't even as thick as in some of the others that follow. The problem in this passage is keeping track of the various processes at work. Lots of details, lots of brain structures, lots of terminology to keep on top of—that's the challenge. But if you keep each of the structures clear in your mind, it's not so hard to handle. The passage is, after all, mostly descriptive.

Key Points of the Passage

Purpose and Main Idea: The author's purpose is to explore some new insights into how the brain develops. The main idea is that MRI technology has shed new light on the way brains develop in adolescence.

Paragraph Structure: Paragraph 1 introduces the fact that there are unusual brain development during adolescence, discovered through MRI. Note that the author doesn't consider this just "more scientific data," but refers to a "newfound appreciation of the dynamic nature of the teen brain." The study that produced this data is described.

Paragraph 2 describes what was believed prior to the new study, including information about prenatal and infant brain development, then details the new information, including the important distinctions between white and gray matter, and their differing development patterns.

Paragraph 3 summarizes the newly discovered pattern of brain development as a work-in-progress—"Advancements in MRI image analysis are providing new insights."

Answers and Explanations

1. E   2. D   3. A   4. D   5. A   6. B

1. E

This inference question addresses the subject of gray matter growth, which comes up many times in the passage. It's not easy to pinpoint immediately which part of the passage we should review to answer the question, so the best strategy here is to evaluate each answer choice, looking back at the passage to verify or discredit information.

> A 180 test taker knows how to identify an open-ended question and allow the answer choices to guide her to the relevant parts of the text.

We're told in paragraphs 1 and 2 that the white matter of the brain thickens progressively from birth, while the gray matter stops thickening, and actually thins to a degree, after age 12, making (E) the best inference here.

(A) On the contrary, the passage tells us that the amount of gray matter in the brain grows in spurts until about age 12, and then decreases slightly. It's the white matter in the brain that grows progressively from birth. The passage also tells us that the frontal lobe's primary growth in the adolescent years is comprised of gray matter.

(B) We aren't given enough information about the amounts of gray matter in the brain to make this inference. The passage does say that the amount of gray matter decreases slightly after age 12, but there's no basis for comparison to the amount of gray matter a 6-year-old's brain would contain.

(C) might be tempting, but while the passage correlates schizophrenia and gray matter loss in the brain's frontal lobe, there is no suggestion that the relationship between the two is one of causation. For all we know from the passage, schizophrenia could be brought on by an external cause, and frontal lobe loss could be one of the effects of the disease.

(D) Like (A), this choice relies on a careless reading of the text. True, myelin does grow throughout adolescence (from birth). However, paragraph 2 tells us that myelin binds only white matter, not gray; there is no mention of how, or whether, the two are connected.

2. D

The next question asks about the general organization of the passage. Hopefully, you took time to make a note of the passage's structure, which will help you to create a prephrase. Although the details might be a bit complex, the basic structure of the passage isn't too complicated, and (D) provides a good summary: A technology (MRI imaging to monitor gray matter growth) is introduced, then its effects (scientists reconsider when gray matter growth occurs) are discussed; finally, another aspect of the technology (four-dimensional animations) is introduced.

> A 180 test taker is able to form and recognize general paraphrases of the specific action occurring in the passage.

(A) looks good initially, but while the passage might be said to discuss the benefits of MRI technology (new understanding of gray and white matter growth), no information about side effects of the technology is provided.

(B) This choice can be ruled out quickly, since the author discusses a new technology and its effects, not a particular problem or solution.

(C) The author does discuss the collection of MRI images over several years, so it's probably all right to say that a "process" is taking place. The problem here comes at the end, as it did in (A); the author does not make any predictions about the technology.

> A 180 test taker doesn't fall for half-right, half-wrong choices that start off well, but go awry.

(E) is incorrect because the author doesn't provide any critique of the technology that's being discussed here.

3. A

This question ends with the words "in order to," which tells us that we need to determine the purpose of a piece of information—in other words, how does a certain statement function in the context of the section in which it appears? In this case, why does the author mention that the frontal lobe of the brain controls the "executive functions"? You might have prephrased the answer and scanned the choices for it. We read on, and see that that information is used in the next sentence, where the author explains that the loss of gray matter in this area is linked with a mental illness that impairs these functions. Choice (A) summarizes this connection well.

If you weren't able to prephrase this answer, you needed to evaluate the answer choices to eliminate the ones that don't represent the purpose of this detail.

(B) can be ruled out quickly, because while the author does contrast new research with previously held beliefs about brain development, she isn't attempting to refute any theories in this passage.

(C) On the contrary, the passage tells us that the parietal and temporal lobes, not the frontal lobe, are the centers for language acquisition and spatial relations understanding.

(D) is tricky because the author does suggest a connection between low levels of gray matter in the frontal lobe and childhood-onset schizophrenia, but a closer reading makes it clear that her intent is not to prove that one causes the other. This information fits into a larger context: The author is giving us one example of the advances made possible by the MRI technology that is the subject of the passage.

(E) might look pretty good initially, but a more careful look shows us that there's a detail out of place. In the relevant portion of the passage, the author is discussing the growth of gray matter, not white matter, in the frontal lobe.

4. D

Here we have another inference question, identified by the word "suggests." What does the author suggest about new imaging processes and technologies? The most significant effect she discusses is that MRI imaging is giving doctors new insight into the way that the human brain develops, particularly during the teenage years. We're told in paragraph 1 that taking repeated images from the same person over time yields a fuller picture of the brain's growth. That would certainly help physicians to make predictions about patients' development, as choice (D) indicates.

(A) No, the passage does say that MRI has allowed doctors to detect irregularities in the frontal lobe, but it gives us no indication that the new technologies provide any methods for repairing the damage.

(B) is incorrect because the author makes no suggestion that there is a way to stop the loss of gray matter before puberty—or even that this would be a desirable thing. Paragraph 1 makes it sound as if some pruning of gray matter in childhood is normal and healthy.

(C) On the contrary, paragraph 2 tells us that MRI technology has shown exactly the opposite: Gray matter growth during adolescence occurs in irregular bursts, and can't be said to occur "steadily" at all.

(E) is incorrect because it creates a connection that isn't in the passage. The author does mention an early surge of overproduction of gray matter and later structural changes that occur in adolescence, but she doesn't make any effort to suggest a relationship between the two.

5. A

Here's a detail question that asks you to look for a fact that was NOT included in the passage—a bit harder than the traditional detail question. (A) is the only choice that's not mentioned; it brings in a point from the text (pruning of gray matter), but a careful reading tells us that no information is given about when the pruning occurs.

Each of the other choices repeats information from the passage. Paragraph 3 tells us that a wave of white matter growth moves backward in the brain and stops after puberty, so this eliminates (B). In the same paragraph, we see that the temporal and parietal lobes connect between ages 6 and 13, eliminating (C). Paragraph 1 helps us eliminate (D), since it tells us that a second wave of overproduction does occur. Finally, choice (E) can be eliminated by paragraph 3, which states that a critical period for learning languages ends after age 12, when growth in the temporal and parietal lobes drops off sharply.

6. B

The stem itself gives away the fact that the author's purpose is "to discuss" something, so there's no need to choose among various verbs (argue, refute, etc.)—but what is she interested in discussing? The author's main concern should be firmly planted in your mind by now: She's simply interested in discussing the ways in which MRI technology has enabled doctors to learn more about the way teenagers' brains develop. Choice (B) comes very close to this prephrase, merely substituting "a new imaging technology" for "MRI."

Each of the four other choices picks out details from the passage, but none of them comes close to describing what the passage as a whole is really about. (A) picks up some of the terminology from the passage, but looking back, we see that the effects of white matter growth aren't even addressed until the last paragraph, and then only briefly.

(C) likewise uses terms we see in the passage, but again, the development of the various parts of the brain isn't the author's primary concern here.

(D) looks good at first, since the passage does talk about new advances, but its scope is too limited; for the most part, the development discussed in the article is typical and not specific to mentally ill patients.

Finally, (E) draws a connection that the author hasn't made. The article does talk about white and gray brain matter, but it never discusses the relationship between the two, so this is certainly not the author's goal.

What's Next?

Not so bad, huh? Well, of course, we're just getting started, and not surprisingly, things do get a bit worse. "Mitochondria," the next passage in our little group of nightmares, raises the bar, both in the density of the material and in technical jargon. We'll get back to you in the explanation.

THE NEXT READING COMPREHENSION PASSAGE
BEGINS ON THE FOLLOWING PAGE

PASSAGE 6

Some one and a half or two billion years ago, when the Earth was still poor in oxygen, a primitive bacterium that made a precarious living from the anaerobic fermentation of organic
(5) molecules engulfed a smaller cell that had somehow evolved the ability to respire. The event was a turning point in organic evolution. Respiration liberates far more energy than fermentation, and the growing abundance of
(10) oxygen in the atmosphere must have been the driving force behind a symbiotic relation that developed between the two cells, with the aerobic cell generating energy in return for shelter and nutrients from its larger host.

(15) In time the engulfed cell and others like it were to become subcellular organelles, passed on by host cells to their progeny. Eventually the host cells themselves changed, developing other subcellular structures and internal membranes and
(20) segregating their genetic material in chromosomes within a nucleus. These cells were the ancestors of all modern eukaryotic (nucleated) cells: protozoans and algae and the individual cells of fungi, plants, and animals. The present-day
(25) descendants of those ancient symbiotic respiring bacteria are the mitochondria, the power plants of the eukaryotic cell.

Mitochondria are oval or worm-shaped organelles, about half a micrometer in diameter
(30) and from two to five micrometers long; this is roughly the size of many modern bacteria. The mitochondrion has an outer membrane and an extensively folded inner membrane that encloses a fluid matrix. The organelle is the site of oxidative
(35) phosphorylation, the primary source of cellular energy. In the fluid matrix, organic molecules derived from the breakdown of foodstuffs are oxidized in a series of chemical reactions known as the citric acid cycle. Electrons removed in the
(40) course of oxidation are passed along a chain of respiratory-enzyme complexes arrayed in the inner membrane, driving the phosphorylation of adenosine diphosphate to form adenosine triphosphate (ATP), the universal energy carrier of
(45) cells. The cytoplasm of eukaryotic cells (the region outside the nucleus) contains a few mitochondria to many hundreds; the greater the energy demands placed on the cell, the more mitochondria it has.

(50) Perhaps because they are descendants of a free-living bacteria, mitochondria have their own genetic material and the machinery to express it. The possibility that the organelles might have their own genes, distinct from the genome in the
(55) cell nucleus, was raised as early as 1949, when

Boris Ephrussi found that the ability of baker's yeast to carry out oxidative phosphorylation seemed to be controlled by some factor in the cytoplasm rather than in the nucleus. It was only
(60) in 1966, however, that the first vertebrate mitochondrial DNA (that of the chick) was isolated and characterized. Since then the mitochondrial DNAs of many organisms have been under intensive study.

1. Which one of the following titles best reflects the content of the passage?

    (A) The Structural Complexity of Eukaryotic Cells
    (B) The Evolution and Significance of Mitochondria
    (C) Reverse Evolution: From Cell to Subcellular Organelle
    (D) Fermentation vs. Respiration: Which is More Efficient?
    (E) The Origin and Role of Mitochondrial DNA

2. The author of the passage would most likely agree with which one of the following statements about the "symbiotic relation" in line 11?

    (A) The new cell that developed out of the symbiotic relation between anaerobic and aerobic cells has not changed over the last one-and-a-half billion years.
    (B) Neither anaerobic nor aerobic cells had a specific function to perform in the new cell.
    (C) Anaerobic and aerobic cells combined to create a new cell because neither type of cell was capable of surviving for long on its own.
    (D) Anaerobic and aerobic cells could not have joined to form a new cell in the absence of the proper atmospheric conditions.
    (E) The chromosomes of eukaryotic cells were originally located in aerobic cells before aerobic cells combined with anaerobic cells to form a new cell.

3. The passage suggests which one of the following about "anaerobic fermentation" (line 4)?

    (A)   It occurs in the mitochondria located in cells' cytoplasm.
    (B)   It causes the breakdown of organic molecules during the citric acid cycle.
    (C)   It is the basis of energy production in modern eukaryotic cells.
    (D)   It can only be carried on by primitive bacteria in an oxygen-poor environment.
    (E)   It is not the most efficient way for cells to produce energy.

4. According to the passage, the energy released by a eukaryotic cell is

    (A)   generated by the mitochondria contained in its cytoplasm
    (B)   dependent on the transformation of adenosine triphosphate into adenosine diphosphate
    (C)   caused by chemical reactions that take place outside of the mitochondrion's inner membrane
    (D)   related to the number of chromosomes in the cell nucleus
    (E)   incorporated into the mitochondrion's genetic material

5. According to the passage, which one of the following occurs during the citric acid cycle?

    (A)   Organic molecules that are derived from food penetrate the mitochondrion's outer membrane.
    (B)   Electrons help to transform adenosine diphosphate into adenosine triphosphate.
    (C)   Mitochondria from a eukaryotic cell's cytoplasm are transported to the cell's nucleus.
    (D)   Eukaryotic cells develop subcellular structures, internal membranes and nuclei.
    (E)   The fluid matrix enclosed by the mitochondrion's inner membrane is transformed into organic molecules that are later broken down in a series of chemical reactions.

6. The author of the passage mentions Boris Ephrussi in the fourth paragraph most probably in order to

    (A)   demonstrate that eukaryotic cells have genetic material in both the nuclei and mitochondria
    (B)   suggest that genetic research has only just begun to understand how cells reproduce
    (C)   point out the historical roots of more recent research on the genetic composition of mitochondrial DNA
    (D)   prove that subcellular structures like mitochondria contain genetic material
    (E)   illustrate the difficulties involved in isolating vertebrate mitochondrial DNA

Passage 6: Mitochondria

What Makes It Difficult

Well, we were just talking about jargon in the previous passage, and this one is chock full of it. It's quite a chore to simply chop through the heavy biology in the beginning to get a sense of where this author is going. In fact, it takes a good long while before the main character, mitochondria, even hits the stage. By the time we recognize that the details in the beginning are presented to shed light on the evolution of mitochondria, the focus shifts to a complex discussion of the characteristics and function of mitochondria, laden with complicated terms and descriptions of heavy-duty processes. As if digesting all this were not bad enough, the focus shifts *again* in paragraph 4 to mitochondrial DNA, with the introduction of a new character (Boris Ephrussi) and further findings.

Now, sometimes dense complicated passages are followed by easy questions, and these really aren't as bad as they could be. However, every question except for the first plays off the technical terms and complex mechanisms described in the passage. Recognizing the following key passage points will help, but you'll also have to go back to the passage at points to pick up a few of the details.

Key Points of the Passage

Purpose and Main Idea: The author's purpose is to describe the evolution of mitochondria and its function in present-day organisms. The passage is purely descriptive, and so there is no main idea, per se.

Paragraph Structure: Paragraph 1 describes a turning point in organic evolution, the coming together of a host cell with a smaller respiring cell. The author speculates on how this may have occurred (increase in atmospheric oxygen), and describes the benefit to each of the participating cells. The passage is still pretty wide open at this point; there's no telling where it might go.

> A 180 test taker constantly interrogates the passage and the author, asking "where are you going with all this?"

Paragraph 2 continues the saga of "the little cells that could": The engulfed cell evolved into specialized subcellular organelles, and the host evolved other structures within a nucleus. The hosts are the forebears of modern eukaryotic cells, and the present-day version of the respiring symbiotic duo are the mitochondria.

Is the author going to settle down to one concept here, or what? Thankfully, yes. Paragraph 3 describes mitochondria in great detail—its size, its structure, its function. The latter is the key, although you don't have to take in the mess of technical details just yet; we'll return to those when necessary (and unfortunately, it does become necessary). The main thing is to see is that mitochondria supply cells with energy.

Paragraph 4, as we said, shifts the scope yet again, discussing mitochondrial DNA; specifically, the notion that mitochondria might contain genes distinct from the nucleus. Boris Ephrussi raised this possibility in the middle of the 20th century after observing the behavior of baker's yeast, but it wasn't until 17 years later that real evidence began to support the theory. You may as well notice what's here, but don't let it distract you from the gist of the passage. If a Boris/DNA question arises (and of course, one does), you'll know where to look.

Answers and Explanations

1. B   2. D   3. E   4. A   5. B   6. C

1. B

A "best title" question is just another way for the test makers to ask about the author's purpose in writing the passage. The point of a title (at least so far as academic prose is concerned) is to summarize in a few words what the author intends to convey in the text.

A 180 test taker knows all of the variations of questions that the test makers might throw at her.

It takes a while to come to the forefront, but mitochondria is the star of this show, so any choice without at least that word in the title would be incomplete. That kills (A) and (C), which focus on details from paragraph 2. (D) is worse yet: Not only doesn't it include the word *mitochondria*, but its topic is raised and dropped in paragraph 1. (E) may be tempting, because "origin and role" seems very much to capture the scope of the passage. However, the other half of (E) is wrong— mitochondrial DNA is mentioned only in paragraph 4. Heck, mitochondrial DNA (in vertebrates, anyway) was isolated only in 1966; the events of the passage go back billions of years before that. Only (B) is broad enough to fully cover the passage's topic, scope, and purpose.

2. D

We're asked to infer something about the symbiotic relationship mentioned in paragraph 1, and there's a bunch of material relating to that early on, so we have no idea specifically what the test makers are after here. In other words, as is common in inference questions, prephrasing an answer is not a good option, so we should go right to the choices, looking to confirm or negate each based on the information in the passage.

(A) and (B) are both flatly contradicted by the passage: The new cell *did* evolve quite a bit, and each partner cell in the original symbiotic relation *did* have a specific function.

(C) Presumably, the cells managed pretty well on their own before the atmosphere became oxygen-rich, so there's no way we can infer that the combination occurred because the cells were in danger of dying out.

(D) is the winner: The reasonable implication of oxygen being the "driving force" is that, absent all of that oxygen, the symbiotic relation that led to the formation of the new cell would have been difficult if not impossible.

(E) not only distorts information in the passage—information in paragraph 2—but the information it plays on is located far from the cited lines.

A 180 test taker knows that the correct answer to questions containing a line reference usually won't be very far from that line.

---

3. E

The line reference brings us right to the concept in question, so it's best to quickly review what's said about anaerobic fermentation. And it's what comes a bit later that's really the key to the question; we're told that "respiration liberates far more energy than fermentation," which is just another way of saying that anaerobic fermentation isn't the most efficient way for cells to produce energy. (E) is therefore inferable here.

(A), (B), and (C) are all far removed from the detail in question. They misrepresent matters, anyway.

(D) might be tempting—after all, we're told that primitive bacterium in an oxygen-poor environment did employ anaerobic fermentation. But it's not valid to deduce from this that *only* primitive bacterium in an oxygen-poor environment can carry on anaerobic fermentation. Perhaps you put (D) on hold until you reached (E)—but we really have to work much harder to justify (D) than to justify (E).

4. A

"According to the passage" signifies a detail question, and we had to expect at least a few of those to make our lives somewhat miserable. But it's not that bad, really, as long as we find the subject in question and focus on what's said about it. The striking term that appears in this question is "eukaryotic cell," which appears only in lines 21–24 and then again in line 45. These references tell us a few major things: Mitochondria are located in the cytoplasm of eukaryotic cells, and they power these cells. And that's really all we need to know to answer the question—(A) paraphrases that very closely.

(B) and (C) both contradict the passage: ADP is transformed into ATP, and the chemical reactions, according to information in paragraph 3, take place in the fluid matrix, which is *enclosed* by the mitochondrion's inner membrane.

(D) and (E) distort details taken from the wrong paragraphs—(D) a detail in paragraph 2 and (E) a detail in paragraph 4. Of the two, (D) is likely to be more tempting, since paragraph 4 makes no mention of eukaryotic cells. But neither is directly related to the energy released by a eukaryotic cell.

5. B

The detail "citric acid cycle" is even easier to skim for than the detail from the previous question—it shows up only in the middle of paragraph 3. There we see that the citrus acid cycle is a set of chemical reactions that oxidize molecules derived from food. If we keep reading, we sees that the oxidation moves the electrons along to turn ADP into ATP, just as (B) says. (B)'s wording is no mystery and no real challenge. The challenge lies in figuring out where the answer is going to come from, and translating the relevant text once found into simpler words.

A 180 test taker often asks himself "where is the answer likely to come from?"

(A), like a few choices in the previous question, gets it backwards. The citric acid cycle takes place in the fluid matrix, which is part of the mitochondrion's *inner* membrane.

(C) and (E) distort information in the passage. The citric acid cycle is a process that takes place within the mitochondrion; it has nothing to do with the movement of a mitochondrion from one part of the cell to another (C). Nor does the citric acid cycle result in the transformation of the fluid matrix (E); rather, a transformation (of organic molecules) occurs *within* the fluid matrix during the citric acid cycle.

(D) plays on an irrelevant detail from paragraph 2. There's no reason why we should look at paragraph 2 in a question about the citric acid cycle.

6. C

As promised above, here's our cameo by Boris Ephrussi, and it certainly isn't hard to track him down. The purpose of paragraph 4 is to discuss the history of scientific research on mitochondrial DNA, and Boris Ephrussi is identified as the father of such research. (C)'s notion of "historical roots" is therefore on target.

(A) and (D) both focus on the substance of the detail rather than why the author has included it. Mentioning Boris doesn't demonstrate or prove anything regarding the possibility Boris himself investigated; that is, whether or not mitochondria actually contains genes. The reference is simply there to tell us when and how this idea was first formulated.

(B) is way too broad to be the reason Ephrussi was mentioned. In the fourth paragraph, the author limits himself to a discussion of mitochondria, while (B) deals with the scope of genetic research in general and whether the field is in its infancy. Nothing about the Boris reference relates to that.

(E) distorts the situation: We can't infer that isolating the DNA didn't happen until '66 because it was so difficult. For all we know, 17 years is an incredibly short time to advance from Ephrussi's original insights to the accomplishment of 1966. Nothing about the Boris reference speaks to this issue of "difficulties."

What's Next?

We now move from one type of symbiosis to another. Having finished with microscopic biological symbiotic partners—the cells in the first paragraph that came together to eventually produce mitochondria—we journey to the other side of the spectrum and out into the universe to find "Symbiotic Stars."

All this helping out, both cells and stars working together so well; it's really very touching, isn't it?

PASSAGE 7

Among the several hundred million binary
systems estimated to lie within 3,000 light-years
of the solar system, and thus to be theoretically
detectable on sky-survey photographs, a tiny
(5)   fraction, no more than a few hundred, belong to a
curious subclass whose radiation has a wavelength
distribution so peculiar that it long defied
explanation. Such systems radiate strongly in the
visible region of the spectrum, but some of them
(10)   do so even more strongly at both shorter and
longer wavelengths: in the ultraviolet region and
in the infrared and radio regions.

This odd distribution of radiation is best
explained by the pairing of a cool red-giant star
(15)   and an intensely hot small star that is virtually in
contact with its larger companion as the two travel
around a common center. Such objects have
become known as symbiotic stars. On
photographic plates only the giant star can be
(20)   discerned, but evidence for the existence of the
hot companion has now been supplied by satellite-
borne instruments capable of detecting ultraviolet
radiation at wavelengths that are absorbed by the
earth's atmosphere (and therefore cannot be
(25)   detected by instruments on the ground). Recently
two symbiotic-star systems, the first to be
detected outside our galaxy, have been observed
in the Large Cloud of Magellan, one of the
satellite galaxies associated with ours.

(30)   The spectra of symbiotic stars indicate that the
cool red giant is surrounded by a very hot ionized
gas. The existence of the ionized gas marked such
objects as being peculiar several decades before
satellite observations finally identified the
(35)   ionizing source as the radiation from an invisible
hot companion. Symbiotic stars also flared up in
outbursts indicating the ejection of material in the
form of a shell or a ring, reminiscent of the
recurrent outbursts of a nova. Symbiotic stars may
(40)   therefore represent a transitory phase in the
evolution of certain types of binary systems in
which there is a substantial transfer of matter
from the larger partner to the smaller.

The exact evolutionary course that turns a
(45)   binary system into a symbiotic one is a matter of
conjecture. The comparatively small number of
known symbiotics in our galaxy suggests that if
all binaries of modest mass normally pass through
a symbiotic phase in their evolution, the phase
(50)   must be extremely brief, perhaps as short as a
million years. It is suspected that the evolutionary
course of a binary system is predetermined by the
initial mass and angular momentum of the gas
cloud within which binary stars are born. Since
(55)   red giants and Mira variables are thought to be

stars with a mass of one or two suns, it seems
plausible that the original cloud from which a
symbiotic system is formed can consist of no
more than a few solar masses of gas.

1. The passage implies that symbiotic star systems
    differ from other binary systems in which one of the
    following ways?

    (A) Symbiotically paired stars emit a radiation
         pattern different from that of most binary
         stars.
    (B) In symbiotic star systems, one star is the
         center of the other's orbit.
    (C) Symbiotically paired stars are the only binary
         stars which are capable of exchanging
         matter.
    (D) Symbiotic star systems are more common
         than other binary systems.
    (E) Symbiotic star systems are the only binary
         systems that can be detected by satellite-
         borne instruments.

2. According to the passage, which one of the
    following is true about symbiotic star systems?

    (A) The majority of binary systems are symbiotic.
    (B) Most symbiotic systems lie outside our
         galaxy.
    (C) Evidence for the existence of each distinct
         partner in such systems is gathered via
         independent mechanisms.
    (D) Only symbiotic star systems are formed from
         clouds of gas.
    (E) The Large Cloud of Magellan obscures the
         view of most symbiotic stars.

3. The primary purpose of the passage is to

    (A) argue that a great percentage of binary star
         systems are symbiotic
    (B) criticize the theory of symbiotic stars as
         overly speculative
    (C) describe symbiotic stars as a distinct type of
         binary system
    (D) present evidence that binary star systems have
         evolved from gas clouds
    (E) compare symbiotic stars to red giants and
         Mira variables

4. According to the passage, the radiation emitted by symbiotic stars is distinctive in that it

   (A) is visible on photographic plates
   (B) consists partly of visible waves
   (C) cannot be detected by satellite-borne instruments
   (D) is strongest at the extreme ends of the spectrum
   (E) emanates primarily from the larger star

5. The author suggests that

   (A) the detection of radiation from an invisible hot companion star prompted scientists to investigate the peculiar ionized gas surrounding cool red giants
   (B) small hot stars attach to cool red giants because red giants have a mass of one or two suns
   (C) a million years is a brief period of time for the occurrence of many solar events
   (D) the only symbiotic star systems to be detected outside of our galaxy are in the Large Cloud of Magellan
   (E) if binary stars of modest mass passed through symbiotic phases lasting much more than a million years, it is likely that more of them would have been detected

6. The existence of which one of the following would weaken a hypothesis stated in the passage concerning a mechanism by which symbiotic stars evolve?

   (A) A cool red giant, involved in a symbiotic relation, that loses mass over time
   (B) A small hot star, involved in a symbiotic relation, that loses mass over time
   (C) Millions of star systems that passed through symbiotic phases lasting one million years
   (D) Stars that absorb matter emitted by a surrounding gas cloud
   (E) Solar phenomena other than symbiotic stars that emit odd radiation distributions

7. The passage as a whole can be considered an answer to which one of the following questions?

   (A) How do binary star systems evolve into symbiotic systems?
   (B) Why are symbiotic stars surrounded by ionized gas?
   (C) What percentage of the binary star systems detected to date are symbiotic pairs?
   (D) Why are red giants usually accompanied by intensely hot, small stars?
   (E) Why do certain binary stars emit unusual radiation patterns?

Passage 7: Symbiotic Stars

What Makes It Difficult

This one has a structure common to many LSAT science passages: it introduces a mystery that has puzzled scientists for some time, and then proceeds to document various findings supporting a theory meant to explain the mystery. This passage holds together a little better than does "Mitochondria"; the structure is a bit more coherent. The author states the mystery up front, and then methodically presents the theory of symbiotic stars as a possible solution. But the theory contains a ton of details, which, of course, the test makers exploit in the questions. In passages in which the details are so technical and abstract, so difficult to connect to everyday experience, you have to pay extra careful attention to the reason why the author includes the details she provides. As always, it behooves you to break down the passage into its key elements.

Key Points of the Passage

Purpose and Main Idea: The author's purpose is to describe the phenomenon of symbiotic star systems; namely, their characteristics and possible origin. The passage is mainly descriptive, but if we had to settle on a main idea, it would sound something like this: The nature of symbiotic stars helps explain certain strange radiation distribution patterns that have long puzzled scientists.

Paragraph Structure: Paragraph 1 introduces a mystery that had "long defied explanation": certain binary star systems exhibiting quirky radiation patterns stronger on the extreme sides of the spectrum.

Paragraph 2 gets right to the explanation. Evidently, this pattern can be explained by the pairing of a cool big star and a hot little star. These two types of stars are attached to one another through a common center; hence, the notion of symbiosis. The paragraph goes on to explain how the big and small stars are detected, and where a few of these things have been found.

A 180 test taker paraphrases the author's ideas in simple terms.

Paragraph 3 throws in some more details about this partnership, and suggests that symbiotic stars represent a phase in the evolution of certain binary systems. There's no need to assimilate every detail just yet. You should simply mark this paragraph as the place where some of the mechanisms of these star systems are laid out.

In the last paragraph, the author continues this speculation as to the evolution of symbiotic stars, employing a good deal of scientific terminology in the process. Again, not to panic—get the gist and you'll know where to return to reread if a question demands it.

Answers and Explanations

1. A   2. C   3. C   4. D   5. E   6. B   7. E

1. A

Paragraph 1 states that symbiotic stars are distinctive from other binary star systems in the pattern of radiation that they emit. In fact, this is the basis of the whole mystery, right? So (A) must be true. It goes to show that sometimes the first few questions on even a difficult passage are very straightforward.

(B) The second paragraph specifically mentions that both stars in a symbiotic system travel around a common center, so (B) is wrong.

(C) and (E) are way too broad; neither one is implied by anything in the passage, which doesn't speculate on the case out there in the universe in general.

(D) contradicts the first paragraph, where we're told that symbiotic stars make up a tiny fraction of binary systems.

2. C

In the middle of the second paragraph, the author states that only the cool red giant stars show up in photographs, and that it took satellite technology to eventually produce evidence about the small hot invisible partners. (C) may be a bit wordy, but it's right on the money: Independent mechanisms are employed to supply evidence of these distinct partners.

(A) As we saw in choice (D) above, paragraph 1 explicitly states that symbiotic systems represent a very small percentage of all binary systems.

> A 180 test taker uses the thought process employed in one question to help with similar choices in later questions.

(B) Paragraph 2 mentions that two symbiotic star systems have recently been detected outside our galaxy, but the passage supplies no information that allows us to conclude where *most* such systems exist.

(D) Paragraph 4 states that all binary stars originate in gas clouds, so (D) contradicts the passage.

(E) distorts a detail found in the second paragraph: Nothing suggests that the Large Cloud of Magellan obscures the view of symbiotic stars.

3. C

Since the gist of the passage is that symbiotic stars represent a special type of binary star system—one with a bizarre radiation pattern—choice (C) is correct. And the neutral verb "describe" fits the author's method to a T. The same, however, can't be said of choices (A) and (B), which we can dismiss on the basis of their verbs alone. The author doesn't "argue" or "criticize" anything in this passage: he or she simply describes a phenomenon.

> A 180 test taker pays careful attention to the verbs in answer choices, especially in "Primary Purpose" or "Method of Argument" questions.

(D) The theory that binary stars are born in gas clouds is a detail from the last paragraph. It's certainly not the passage's main point, so (D) cannot describe the primary purpose of this passage. Notice how it doesn't even mention the main concept of the passage, symbiotic stars. It's very hard to describe the author's purpose without a reference to the passage's central character.

(E)'s out because the author doesn't even tell us what Mira variables are, let alone compare them to symbiotic stars.

4. D

Next up is a detail question that relates to the main idea. The last sentence of the first paragraph states that the type of binary system later defined as symbiotic radiates "even more strongly at both shorter and longer wavelengths" than in the middle of the spectrum. Choice (D) is a near perfect paraphrase of this.

(A) We know that only one star of the symbiotic pair shows up in photographs, and we aren't told whether radiation emitted by nonsymbiotic stars is visible on photographic plates, so there's no basis to choose (A).

(B) Although some of the radiation from symbiotic systems is visible, that's not what makes these systems' radiation patterns "distinctive," so (B) cannot be correct.

(C) contradicts information presented in the second paragraph about evidence provided by satellite-borne instruments. At least one partner in the symbiotic pair can be detected by satellites.

(E) The passage never suggests that the radiation primarily emanates from the larger star, and even if we somehow made this leap, it would still be incorrect to say that this is what makes their radiation distinctive. None of this is hinted at in the passage.

5. E

Next up is an open-ended inference question with no clues as to what the test makers are after, so we have no choice but to wade into the choices, looking for the one that's supported by the hard facts of the passage.

(A) bollixes up the order of things; in fact, pretty much gets it backwards. In paragraph 3 we learn that the ionized gas surrounding the cool red giant looked weird to scientists for decades before radiation from the invisible hot companion was discovered, so it can't be the detection of radiation that prompted scientists to look into the matter.

(B) tries to fashion a causal relationship out of two facts of the passage. True, the small hot stars attach to the big cool ones, and yes, we're told in paragraph 4 that red giants have a mass of one or two suns. But what has one thing to do with the other? Nothing, as far as the passage suggests, so (B) is out.

> A 180 test taker is suspicious of choices that attempt to tie together two or more elements from different parts of the passage.

(C) A million years may not seem so "brief" to us, but according to the passage, that's a relatively short period of time for a symbiotic phase. Regardless, other solar events are outside the scope of the passage, so there's no way we can judge from the material at hand the time it takes for these to occur. For all we know, a million years is a long time for most solar events; all we know about is symbiotic stars.

(D) erroneously plays off the Magellan detail in paragraph 2. Just because a few symbiotics *were* found over there doesn't in any way suggest that the *only* symbiotic stars outside our galaxy are in the Large Cloud of Magellan.

(E) That leaves (E), which must be correct. In paragraph 4, the author says that the small number of symbiotics detected in our galaxy suggests that the symbiotic phase is brief—"perhaps as short as a million years." Evidently, the author sees a link between the length of the phase and our ability to detect symbiotic stars. Therefore, it's reasonable to infer that if these phases were much longer, we'd probably detect more of them.

6. B

There seem to be a number of hypotheses in the passage regarding the mechanisms of symbiotic stars, so it's not likely we'll be able to paraphrase this weakenener off the top of our heads. Let's therefore move right to the choices, looking for the one that contradicts some mechanism described in the passage.

(A) Does a cool red giant losing mass over time contradict, support, or have no effect on some hypothesis in the passage? In fact, it directly supports the notion, discussed at the end of paragraph 3, that symbiotic stars represent an evolution of star system in which matter goes from the big star to the small one. That means that the larger star, the red giant, loses mass while the small, hot companion gets bigger. The existence of a cool red giant that's in such a relationship and getting smaller over time would certainly supports this. The star in the next choice, however, would not.

(B) According to the same hypothesis just cited in (A), a small hot star involved in a symbiotic relationship would get bigger in time, as matter was transferred to it from the red giant. The existence of the shrinking small star in (B) would not bode well for the theory at the end of paragraph 3, so (B) is the weakener we seek.

(C) Nothing in the passage is blatantly overturned by the fact that millions of systems go through "brief" symbiotic phases. A million years, remember, is not always long enough to allow us to detect these, so there's nothing here in (C) that would weaken any claim in the passage.

(D) We're told that binary stars originate in gas clouds, so nothing in (D) seems to damage any theory in the passage.

(E) There's nothing in the passage that precludes the existence of other solar phenomena besides symbiotic stars emitting odd radiation patterns. Perhaps these other distributions are odd but have always been explainable. Perhaps they aren't odd in the same way as the patterns emitted from what turned out to be symbiotics. The facts in the first paragraph don't conclusively establish symbiotic stars as the only solar phenomenon ever to emit strange radiation.

A 180 test taker avoids unwarranted conclusions.

7. E

We need to keep the passage's main idea in mind in answering this question, which itself deals with the passage as an answer *to* a question. Interesting . . . Well, we merely have to return to the question that was set out in the beginning, namely: How can the odd distribution of radiation put out by some star systems be explained? According to the passage, symbiotic star systems provide the best explanation of the previously puzzling observation that some binary systems emit extremely unusual patterns of radiation. The author spends most of the passage presenting theories regarding the mechanisms of these systems, and yet never loses sight of the original question. Therefore, (E), dealing with the unusual phenomenon introduced in the beginning, is the question that can best be answered by information in the passage.

(A) Since the first sentence of paragraph 4 says that the way in which a binary star system evolves into a symbiotic system is conjecture, (A) can hardly be answered by the passage.

(B) First of all, the red giant is specifically surrounded by ionized gas, but even if we allow "symbiotic star" to substitute for red giant here, the passage as a whole isn't structured to answer this question, since this is merely one detail in the story of symbiotic stars.

(C) We know only that few binary star systems are symbiotic—the passage doesn't address the precise percentage here.

(D) While paragraph 2 states that symbiotic stars involve a pairing of red giants and small hot stars, the passage never suggests *why* these two stars pair up, so (D) is wrong.

What's Next?

Three science passages down, and one to go. This next passage, "Plate Tectonics," takes as its scope entire continents. More excitement for the geologically minded among you. Have fun.

THE NEXT READING COMPREHENSION PASSAGE
BEGINS ON THE FOLLOWING PAGE

PASSAGE 8

The basic theory of plate tectonics recognizes two ways continental margins can grow seaward. Where two plates such as the African plate and the South American plate are moving away from a

(5) mid-ocean rift that separates them, the continental margins on those plates are said to be passive, or rifted. Such continental margins grow slowly from the accumulation of riverborne sediments and of the carbonate skeletons of marine organisms,

(10) which are deposited as limestone. Suites—unbroken sequences—of such accretions, consisting of nearly flat strata, are called miogeoclinal deposits. Since most miogeoclinal deposits are undeformed and exhibit an unbroken

(15) history, it is evident that passive margins are generally not associated with mountain building.

Along active, or convergent, margins, such as those that ring most of the Pacific basin, continents tend to grow much faster. At an active

(20) margin an oceanic plate plunges under a continental plate, with the continental plate scraping off deep-ocean sediments and fragments of basaltic crust that then adhere to the continental margin. Simultaneously the plate plunging under

(25) the continental margin heats up and partially melts, triggering extensive volcanism and mountain-building. A classic example is the Andes of the west coast of South America.

In the original plate-tectonic model western

(30) North America was described as being a passive margin through the late Paleozoic and early Mesozoic eras (roughly 350 to 210 million years ago) after which it became an active margin. It was assumed that the continent grew to a limited

(35) extent along this margin as sedimentary and igneous rocks of oceanic origin were accreted in a few places, as in the Coast Ranges of California. The model was successful in explaining such disparate features as the Franciscan rocks of the

(40) California Coast Ranges, formed by local subduction processes, and the granite rocks of the Sierra Nevada, farther to the east, which clearly originated as the roots of volcanoes similar to those of the Andes.

(45) The basic plate-tectonic reconstruction of the geologic history of western North America remains unchanged in the light of microplate tectonics (the process by which the edge of a continent is modified by the transport, accretion

(50) and rotation of large crystal blocks called terranes), but the details are radically changed. It is now clear that much more crust was added to North America in the Mesozoic era (248 to 65 million years ago) than can be accounted for by

(55) volcanism along island arcs and by the simple

accretion of sediments from the ocean floor. It has also become evident that some terranes lying side by side today are not genetically related, as would be expected from simple plate tectonics, but

(60) almost certainly have traveled great distances from entirely different parts of the world.

1. Which one of the following best expresses the main idea of the passage?

   (A) The margin of the west coast of North America developed through a combination of active and passive mechanisms.
   (B) The growth of continental margins is only partially explained by the basic theory of plate tectonics.
   (C) Continental margins can grow seaward in two ways, through sedimentation or volcanism.
   (D) The introduction of microplate tectonics poses a fundamental challenge to the existing theory of how continental margins are formed.
   (E) Continental margins grow more rapidly along active margins than along passive margins.

2. The passage supplies information for answering all of the following questions regarding continental margins EXCEPT:

   (A) How have marine organisms contributed to the formation of passive continental margins?
   (B) What were some of the processes by which the continental margin of the west coast of North America was formed?
   (C) Are miogeoclinal deposits associated with mountain building along continental margins?
   (D) Were the continental margins of the east and west coasts of South America formed by similar processes?
   (E) How much crust added to North America in the Mesozoic era can be accounted for by the accretion of sediments from the ocean floor?

3. According to the passage, which one of the following is true about the formation of the Sierra Nevada Mountains?

   (A)   They developed through the deposition of terranes.
   (B)   They were formed during the Paleozoic era.
   (C)   Their geologic origin is analogous to that of the Andes.
   (D)   Their history can be traced back to the accretion of miogeoclinal deposits.
   (E)   They are similar in structure to the California Coast Ranges.

4. The author mentions the Franciscan rocks of the California Coast Ranges in order to make which one of the following points?

   (A)   The basic theory of plate tectonics accounts for a wide variety of geologic features.
   (B)   The original plate tectonic model falls short of explaining such features.
   (C)   Subduction processes are responsible for the majority of the geologic features found along the west coast of North America.
   (D)   Passive margins can take on many geologic forms.
   (E)   The concept of microplate tectonics was first introduced to account for such phenomena.

5. Which one of the following does the author mention as evidence for the inadequacy of the original plate tectonic model to describe the formation of continental margins?

   (A)   Nearly flat, undeformed crystal blocks have been found along some continental margins where there are mountains further inland.
   (B)   Sediments and fragments from the depths of the ocean accumulate along continental margins.
   (C)   Large pieces of the Earth's crust that appear to be completely unrelated are found in the same area today.
   (D)   Undeformed miogeoclinal deposits are usually not linked to mountain building.
   (E)   Oceanic plates drop beneath continental plates along active margins.

6. According to the passage, a passive margin is more likely than an active margin to be characterized by which one of the following?

   (A)   Rapid growth
   (B)   Mountain-building
   (C)   The aggregation of oceanic rocks
   (D)   Carbonate deposits
   (E)   The accretion of terranes

7. The author seems to regard the basic theory of plate tectonics as

   (A)   outdated
   (B)   unassailable
   (C)   insufficient
   (D)   revolutionary
   (E)   unlikely

Passage 8: Plate Tectonics

What Makes It Difficult

There's not much to say about the difficulty of this final science passage that hasn't already been said about the others preceding it. We're faced with the same challenges: An esoteric, difficult topic containing its own unique lingo. A mass of technical details, and questions to test your understanding of them. As always, you're best served by getting the basic gist of the passage, noting where specific details occur so you can return to them as needed. Here are the key points:

Key Points of the Passage

Purpose and Main Idea: The author's purpose is to describe the basic theory of plate tectonics. The main idea is that the theory ultimately falls short of explaining all the phenomena of growing continental margins.

Paragraph Structure: Paragraph 1 introduces the basic theory of plate tectonics, which posits that there are two ways in which continental margins can grow seaward. The paragraph goes on to describe one of those ways, a mechanism known as passive margins. Details regarding passive margins abound, but it's best to let those pass for now and see where the author's going with all this. As always, we'll return to this material if a question demands it.

Paragraph 2 describes the other way continental margins can grow, and that's along active margins. A simple distinction is presented which is worth noting; continents grow faster along active margins.

> A 180 test taker pays careful attention to distinctions in passages that compare two or more people, theories, or phenomena.

Again, details are plentiful, as we'd expect in a science passage. We're told what actually happens at active margins, the results of such activity (volcanoes and mountains), and an example of these results (the Andes). Take in what you can, but again, there's no need to obsess over the particulars. All you really need to note is that this paragraph contains a process, some results, and an example.

Paragraph 3 applies the model to a concrete example (western North America), illustrating how the concepts of passive and active margins, taken together, can accurately describe the growth of a continental margin and successfully explain various specific continental features.

Things are humming along quite well until we get to paragraph 4, which introduces something new—the concept of microplate tectonics. Here, with the aid of specific examples, the author shows how this new theory helps to explain certain phenomena that "simple" or "basic" plate tectonics cannot account for. While remaining in general accordance with the story told by basic plate tectonics, microplate tectonics "radically" changes some of the details. Much of the paragraph is given over to examples of how this is so.

Answers and Explanations

1. B   2. E   3. C   4 A   5. C   6. D   7. C

1. B

First up is a main idea question, and we looked into that issue above while getting the passage squared away. While the basic theory of plate tectonics explains much about the growth of continental margins, the fourth paragraph suggests that it cannot fully explain certain geologic details. (B) captures this, and is the correct answer.

A 180 test taker understands that the author's full main idea may not emerge until the end of the passage, and stays alert throughout.

(A) and (E) both represent true statements, but they're details from the passage, not the passage's main idea.

(C) distorts the notion of the two ways that continental margins can grow. Though the first paragraph mentions sedimentation as an example of passive margins, and paragraph 2 states that volcanism often results from active margin growth, the author never goes so far as to say that sedimentation and volcanism are the two ways that continental margins grow. And even if this could be inferred, it's still not big enough to be the main point of the passage.

(D) is incorrect because the first sentence of paragraph 4 states that the basic plate tectonic theory remains unchanged in the light of microplate tectonics; it's the *details* that are radically changed, not the basic theory.

2. E

This is an unusually worded detail question, but it does force us to focus on the details nonetheless. The question in each wrong choice is one that can be answered by the information in the passage, while the right answer is one that goes unanswered by the author. Let's check the choices.

(A) is covered in the first paragraph, which describes the growth of passive margins. There, the author says that passive margins grow, in part, through the accumulation of the carbonate skeletons of marine organisms.

(B) is the subject of the paragraph 3—the continental margin of the west coast of North America grew at first as a passive margin, and then as an active margin.

(C) is answered in the last sentence of paragraph 1: Miogeoclinal deposits are associated with passive margins and are "generally not associated with mountain building."

(D) We have to search a bit for the answer to the question posed in choice (D): Paragraph 1 suggests that the eastern edge of the South American plate is a passive margin, while the last sentence of the second paragraph says that the west coast of South America is an active margin.

(E) That leaves (E), which must be correct. In fact, if you had full confidence eliminating the other four choices, you could choose (E) without much fanfare and move on.

Indeed, the question in (E) cannot be answered by information contained in the passage. Microplate tectonics has revealed that much more crust was added to North America in the Mesozoic period than was added from volcanism and the accretion of sediments, but that doesn't tell us precisely how much crust the accretion of sediments accounts for in the grand scheme of things.

3. C

To answer this detail question, we focus on the third paragraph, since that's where the author mentions the Sierra Nevada mountains. The end of that paragraph states that the Sierra Nevada mountains "clearly originated as the roots of volcanoes similar to those of the Andes." This is correctly paraphrased in answer choice (C).

(A) There is no mention of terranes in reference to the Sierra Nevada Mountains.

(B) contradicts the author's statement that the Sierra Nevada Mountains originated as the roots of volcanoes, formed by the processes of active continental margins *after* the Paleozoic era.

(D) Miogeoclinal deposits are associated with passive continental margins, whereas the Sierra Nevada Mountains were formed while the west coast was an active margin.

(E) is wrong because the author states in the third paragraph that the Coast Ranges and the Sierra Nevada Mountains are "disparate features," formed by two different processes.

4. A

The Coast Ranges of California are introduced in paragraph 3 to provide an example of the variety of geologic features that the original plate-tectonic model could successfully explain: the Franciscan Rocks, formed by local subduction, and the granite rocks of the Sierra Nevada, formed by volcanic action. (A) therefore represents the best account of why this detail was mentioned.

(B) is wrong because the problems with the basic plate tectonic model are discussed in paragraph 4, a paragraph in which the California Coast Ranges are never mentioned.

(C) is a distortion of the facts. We don't know if subduction processes are responsible for the *majority* of the west coast's geologic features—we're only told that they are responsible for some, such as the Coast Ranges.

(D) is wrong because the Coast Ranges were formed by local subduction processes, according to paragraph 3, not by the actions of passive margins.

(E) The concept of microplate tectonics was introduced to account for phenomena that the basic, or original, plate-tectonic model could not adequately explain. But the Coast Ranges are features that the basic model *can* account for, so (E) is incorrect.

5. C

The inadequacy of the plate tectonic model is introduced in the final paragraph of the passage. There we're told that genetically distinct pieces of the Earth's crust are found in the same area, a fact which the original plate tectonic model cannot explain. (C) gets at this issue.

(A) The original plate tectonic model can account for (A)—see the third and fourth paragraphs.

(B), (D), and (E) are true statements—see the first and second paragraphs—but none of these statements has a direct bearing on the issue of the inadequacy of the original plate tectonic model.

> A 180 test taker is not tempted by a choice simply because it contains a true statement. It must, first and foremost, answer the question.

6. D

We're looking in this one for something that distinguishes passive from active margins. (D) correctly states a likely characteristic of passive margins which we hear nothing about in regards to active margins—carbonate deposits—as stated in the third sentence of the first paragraph.

(A) and (B) state characteristics more likely to be associated with active margins. In the first sentence of the second paragraph, the author states that active margins tend to grow much faster than passive ones. And the second to last sentence of that paragraph characterizes active margins as associated with mountain building, while the last sentence of paragraph 1 states that passive margins are "generally not associated with mountain building."

(C), (E) The aggregation of oceanic rocks (C) is something that microplate tectonics is involved with, as mentioned in the first sentence of the last paragraph, while (E) is also incorrect because it states a phenomenon associated with microplate tectonics, not with passive or active margins.

7. C

This final question asks you to identify the author's attitude toward the basic theory of plate tectonics. The passage as a whole suggests that the basic theory of plate tectonics is useful in that it adequately describes certain geological features, and even remains valid in its basic formulation in the light of the more advanced theory, microplate tectonics. However, by now we're certainly familiar with the author's beef with the basic model, as described in the final paragraph: It botches some of the details of the geologic history it attempts to explain, and it leaves other things (such as non-genetically related terranes) unexplained. All this points to a view that the basic plate tectonics theory is useful but not complete. Choice (C), "insufficient," therefore best captures the author's attitude toward the basic theory.

> A 180 test taker gauges the author's tone early on, and is prepared in advance for general "attitude" questions.

(A) The author never suggests that the basic theory of plate tectonics is outdated, just that it's incomplete. This is verified by the fact that the author believes the basic theory generally remains unchanged in the light of microplate tectonics. Such a thing would not likely be said about a theory the author considers "outdated."

(B) "Unassailable" means something that is incapable of being disputed or disproven, but the author clearly does think that there are minor problems with the basic theory of plate tectonics, so (B) is too strong to represent the author's attitude here.

(D) The author never suggests that the basic theory of plate tectonics is revolutionary. It's simply presented as a theory with some explanatory power, and some defects as well. If anything's revolutionary, it's the theory of microplate tectonics, since that theory calls certain details of the basic theory into question.

(E) Although the author thinks that the basic theory does not sufficiently explain certain phenomena, it is presented as a sound theory capable of explaining many features, not an unlikely theory, as (E) suggests.

What's Next?

Enough of science, you say? Good—let's move on. Maybe the more science-phobic among you will welcome with open arms the philosophical passages in the next chapter, while those adept at science who breezed through this chapter will be in for a rude awakening. That's the marvelous thing about the LSAT—there's something for everyone.

CHAPTER FOURTEEN

Philosopher's Corner

You probably think you've already seen some pretty dense material, so what's the deal with this special chapter entitled "Philosophers' Corner"? What's the difference between these passages and the ones, say, found in the "Just Plain Tough" category? Surely there's a certain amount of subjectivity in this kind of classification; the demarcation isn't fully clear-cut, and there's no doubt that these are all difficult passages.

What distinguishes the passages in this chapter, however, is the sheer level of abstraction inherent in their actual topics. The meaning of community and communication, or the nondidactic performative essence of virtue (the subjects of two of the upcoming passages), for example. These are themselves philosophical subjects, and not just complex, philosophical treatments of real-life, easy to grasp phenomena. As the author of the "Teaching Virtue" passage states: "Knowing what virtue is, is not the same as knowing what some kind of object is, because virtue is not an object." Precisely. And therein lies the difficulty of dealing with inherently philosophical material: These are abstract (to many, even obscure) concepts. Many find these to be even harder than science passages. Despite the technical terms, processes, and mass of details used to describe a star or a cell, physical things are still easier for many to get their hands around than abstractions such as virtue or a theory of morality.

So buckle up for these final few. It may turn out to be a bumpy ride.

PASSAGE 9

Persons do not become a society by living in physical proximity, any more than a man ceases to be socially influenced by being so many feet or miles removed from others. A book or a letter
(5) may institute a more intimate association between human beings separated thousands of miles from each other than exists between dwellers under the same roof. Individuals do not even compose a social group because they all work for a common
(10) end. The parts of a machine work with a maximum of cooperativeness for a common result, but they do not form a community. If, however, they were all cognizant of the common end and all interested in it so that they regulated
(15) their specific activity in view of it, then they would form a community. But this would involve communication. Each would have to know what the other was about and would have to have some way of keeping the other informed as to his own
(20) purpose and progress. Consensus demands communication.

We are thus compelled to recognize that within even the most social group there are many relations which are not as yet social. A large
(25) number of human relationships in any social group are still upon the machine-like plane. Individuals use one another so as to get desired results, without reference to the emotional and intellectual disposition and consent of those used.
(30) Such uses express physical superiority, or superiority of position, skill, technical ability, and command of tools, mechanical or fiscal. So far as the relations of parent and child, teacher and pupil, employer and employee, governor and
(35) governed, remain upon this level, they form no true social group, no matter how closely their respective activities touch one another. Giving and taking of orders modifies action and results, but does not of itself effect a sharing of purposes, a
(40) communication of interests.

Not only is social life identical with communication, but all communication (and hence all genuine social life) is educative. To be a recipient of a communication is to have an
(45) enlarged and changed experience. One shares in what another has thought and felt and in so far, meagerly or amply, has his own attitude modified. Nor is the one who communicates left unaffected. Try the experiment of communicating, with
(50) fullness and accuracy, some experience to another, especially if it be somewhat complicated, and you will find your own attitude toward your experience changing; otherwise you resort to expletives and ejaculations. The experience has to
(55) be formulated in order to be communicated. To

formulate requires getting outside of it, seeing it as another would see it, considering what points of contact it has with the life of another so that it may be got into such form that he can appreciate
(60) its meaning. Except in dealing with commonplaces and catch phrases one has to assimilate, imaginatively, something of another's experience in order to tell him intelligently of one's own experience. All communication is like
(65) art. It may fairly be said, therefore, that any social arrangement that remains vitally social, or vitally shared, is educative to those who participate in it. Only when it becomes cast in a mold and runs in a routine way does it lose its educative power.

1. Which one of the following best expresses the main idea of the passage?

    (A) In order for communication to be educative, it must convey the experiences of all the parties who are involved in it.
    (B) Effective communication serves to build community, to educate, and to help individuals to articulate their experiences.
    (C) In a successful community, individuals must work together, paying no heed to relationships of power.
    (D) Communication, like art, gives individuals a new frame of reference through which to articulate their thoughts.
    (E) Teachers must take into account the experiences of their students in order to facilitate learning and manage a classroom effectively.

2. Based on the information in the passage, which of the following statements would the author LEAST likely agree?

    (A) People of similar experience and ideals are more likely to form a community than are people who are located close to one another.
    (B) Strong relationships are based not on family, professional, or social connections, but on shared thoughts and beliefs.
    (C) The act of speaking about one's experiences renders those experiences more meaningful to the speaker.
    (D) Highly educated individuals are more likely to be effective communicators than are those who have had little or no formal education.
    (E) Social situations outside of the classroom may be equally or more educative than time spent inside the classroom.

3. The primary purpose of the passage is to

(A) discuss and reconcile two differing views of a topic
(B) present and test a hypothesis
(C) resolve a debate over a widely held theory
(D) argue against a commonly held belief and present new evidence
(E) interpret a term and discuss its implications

4. According to the passage, which of the following best expresses the author's views on communication in relationships within social groups?

(A) In order for communication to be successful, it must begin with the intent to educate other individuals within the group.
(B) Individuals within a group must be motivated by an interest in one another's beliefs and purposes.
(C) Successful relationships within a social group must be founded on a shared ability or skill.
(D) The members of a group must communicate with each other in order to accomplish a shared goal.
(E) Effective relationships will develop among individuals who are socially influenced by their surroundings.

5. Which one of the following best describes the author's overall organization of the passage?

(A) A concept is described and then connected to a process.
(B) Two processes are defined and then their steps are explained in greater detail.
(C) An explanation is put forth and then rejected in favor of a second explanation.
(D) A hypothesis is advanced and then strengthened through empirical testing.
(E) An argument is put forth and then negated by the presentation of conflicting evidence.

6. Which one of the following is mentioned in the passage as evidence for the assertion that all communication is like art?

(A) Art requires the artist to look outside of her own experiences to create, whereas communication allows the speaker to share her views by meditating on her own experience.
(B) A letter or book sent from a distance may create a greater sense of community than is present between a group of people in the same location.
(C) An effective communicator must use his imagination to speculate about others' experiences, using the new perspective to inform his own expression.
(D) The distinction between art and communication parallels the distinction between a social group and a community.
(E) Any social arrangement that is engaging and shared, creating a sense of community with a common purpose, is educative to its participants.

7. The author presents a comparison between humans and machines primarily in order to

(A) explain the means by which individuals who are thousands of miles apart can maintain effective communication
(B) argue that the increase of mechanization has caused a rift in communication within social groups
(C) create a parallel between the parts of a machine working together and a group of people interacting in order to educate one another
(D) persuade the reader that technology is an essential part of community building
(E) draw a distinction between communication which is based upon a shared interest or design and that which is designed to produce a desired result for the communicator

Passage 9: Society and Communication

What Makes It Difficult

Here we have a tract, excerpted from *Democracy and Education* by John Dewey, about what constitutes a society. A definition of "social" is given in the first paragraph. Though he doesn't specifically cite a "traditional" definition, Dewey is clearly posing a definition of "social" that we are expected to find unusual—"a book or a letter may institute a more intimate association between human beings separated thousands of miles from each other than exists between dwellers under the same roof." This kind of distinction may be common fare for philosophy majors, but for many of us it's pretty deep stuff. The questions are long and complex, matching perfectly in this respect the tone and style of the passage. Let's, as always, break the passage down to see if we can make it a bit more user-friendly.

Key points of the Passages

Purpose and Main Idea: The author's purpose is to make an argument regarding the nature of society and social relationships. The main idea is that communication, as defined by Dewey, is essential to—in fact, "identical with" society and social life. The author interprets a term—"communication"—and discusses related topics, community and education.

Paragraph Structure: Paragraph 1 presents a definition of "society" and "social" that explains why communication is essential to that concept. While unstated, the paragraph clearly intends to challenge conventional views of society.

A 180 test taker recognizes challenges to traditional theories and perspectives in reading passages.

Given this starting point, we might expect the following paragraphs to show us how and why Dewey's views of "society" are complicated. This is exactly what happens. Paragraph 2 notes that even within clearly "social" relationships there are, therefore, non-social relations that can involve cooperation without considering "emotional and intellectual disposition and consent."

Paragraph 3 further develops the nature of communication, which affects both the giver and recipient of the communication. This effect is defined as "educative," and its antithesis is "routine."

Answers and Explanations

1. B   2. D   3. E   4. B   5. A   6. C   7. E

1. B

This question asks us for the main idea of the passage. The author is defining "communication" and discussing its relevance to society and social life. His thesis is laid out at the end of the third paragraph, where he tells us: "any social arrangement that remains vitally social, or vitally shared, is educative to those who participate in it." Choice (B) sums this up nicely.

(A) takes a point from the passage, but presents it in a distorted way. The author does suggest in paragraph 3 that for people to communicate well, they must imagine other people's experiences and use this imagination to express their own, but he never says that the communication itself needs to convey all of these experiences.

(C) This choice comes a little closer to the message of the passage, but it brings in only information from paragraphs 1 and 2. The missing information is how communication becomes educative, a key piece of the author's argument.

(D) The author does liken communication to art, but that's not the main message he's trying to get across. The passage as a whole seeks to give a definition of communication, and explain how communication and social relationships can be educative.

(E) goes outside the scope of the author's argument. The passage is concerned with the ways that communication can be educative in a social setting, not in a classroom setting.

A 180 test taker relates all of the content in a passage back to its main idea.

---

2. D

It's difficult to prephrase an answer to such an open-ended inference question as this, so we must proceed to the choices to see which one most directly contradicts the point of view expressed in the passage. (Note that the question asks you to choose the view with which the author would most likely disagree.) (D) is the only choice that has no supporting evidence in the passage. The author never says that good communicators must be highly educated; he says only that effective communication requires participation, imagination, and shared interests.

(A) This choice echoes the author's sentiments from paragraph 1, which states that community does not come from physical proximity but from communication.

(B) reiterates paragraphs 1 and 2: The author tells us that true communication puts all of its participants on the same level, with no regard to status or power relationship

(C) In paragraph 3, the author states that the process of formulating an experience into words allows an individual to gain a new perspective on it.

(E) simply restates points from paragraph 3: The author believes that any social situation involves communication, and that all communication is educative. Thus, the potential for learning is no greater in a classroom than in a social situation outside of school.

3. E

Since this passage focuses on the idea of communication and its applications, the correct answer will indicate that a concept and its related topics are discussed. (E) is the only choice that does this; the author is interpreting a term, communication, and discussing related topics, community and education.

(A) and (D) are too far-reaching; the author presents only one perspective, and doesn't seek to discuss or argue against other points of view. It could be said that the author is presenting a hypothesis, but there is no information about testing here, so (B) is not correct. The passage gives us no indication of whether the argument here is part of a debate, so we can't choose (C) as the correct answer.

4. B

The phrase "according to the passage" here clues us in that we can expect the author to draw on a specific detail from the passage. Which paragraph discusses relationships within a social group? Exactly—paragraph 3. The phrase "a sharing of purposes, a communication of interests" is the one that best captures the author's formula for successful relationships. Choice (B) stands out as the best paraphrase of this.

(A) While the author does say that education is the product of successful communication, the issue of intent that's raised here is not one we see in the passage. The passage tells us only that education is the result, not that it must be the communicator's intent.

(C) also ascribes a meaning to the author's words that isn't there. The passage does say that "superiority of...skill" or ability on the part of one party is one thing that can prevent successful communication. It doesn't follow, though, that successful communication would require all of the parties involved to have the same skills.

(D) is almost a direct quote from the passage, but if we look at it in context, we see that it's actually talking about what relationships should not be; the author says in paragraph 1 that working together toward a common end is not enough to form a community.

(E) uses language from the passage as well, but it's vaguely worded and is an incomplete explanation of the author's position. For successful relationships to develop, more is needed than just people who are socially influenced; we're looking here for the idea of an interchange of thoughts or ideas between the parties.

5. A

Next up we're asked for the structure of the passage, and hopefully your work on the passage to this point has helped you to prephrase an answer, or at least quickly eliminate choices that stray beyond your conception of the passage as a whole. We know that the concept of communication is the subject of this passage, and that the author links communication with the act of education. This fits with the gist of choice (A): The concept of communication is described from several angles, and in the last paragraph, the author connects this definition of communication with the process of education.

(B) We could probably say that the author views communication and education as "processes." However, the passage doesn't contain detailed descriptions of the steps in both of the processes, so we must reject this choice.

(C) The author does put forth an explanation, but nowhere in the passage does he reject his initial thoughts in favor of a second explanation.

(D) This choice tries the same trick we saw in question 3. Again, no hypothesis is presented here and no testing is accomplished.

A 180 test taker is not tempted by terms such as "hypothesis" and "empirical testing" that sound impressive and official but don't apply to the passage at all.

(E) Similar to (C), this choice states that the author presents information and then negates it. On the contrary, he reaffirms his views throughout the passage.

6. C

The first step here is to locate the assertion that "all communication is like art." A quick review shows us that this point is raised in paragraph 3, where the author discusses the ways in which communication is educative. This detail question asks for evidence specifically mentioned in the passage that supports the comparison in the stem, and we see it just before the comparison itself: "one has to assimilate, imaginatively, something of another's experience in order to tell him intelligently of one's own experience." The author is creating a link between art and communication: imagination. (C) describes this connection perfectly.

(A) reflects the opposite of what is stated in the passage, distorting the author's comparison. This choice says that artists use imagination and communicators do not; the author is saying that both parties do use imagination.

(B) and (E) bring up ideas raised in the passage, but neither one of these statements presents information that's relevant to the comparison in question. The idea that distance does not prevent feelings of community is discussed in the passage, but only in paragraph 1. We're looking for information given in paragraph 3. The idea that all social situations are educative is also raised in paragraph 3, but not in relation to the connection between communication and art.

(D) claims that the author draws a distinction between art and communication, but on the contrary, this comparison attempts to say that the two things are alike. Additionally, there is no parallel between this relationship and the author's distinction between social groups and communities.

7. E

This last questions asks why the author compares humans to machines. Reviewing paragraph 1, we see that the comparison is not a favorable one: the actions of a machine are compared to those of a group of people who are working toward a common goal but not communicating with each other. What's the purpose of the comparison? It shows us the difference between social and machine-like (non-communicative) types of interaction. Choice (E) describes this reason well.

(A) pulls in a point from earlier in paragraph 1, but the author doesn't make a connection between this part of the paragraph and the mention of machinery.

(B) and (D) both use terminology from the passage, but it really isn't relevant to the author's message. His argument has nothing to do with how mechanization affects communication, and there is no mention of the way technology can affect community building.

(C) might be tempting, since it does incorporate two actions that are occurring in the passage. However, on careful examination, we see that this choice draws a false parallel. The author is comparing the workings of a machine not to a group of people educating one another, but to a group of people who are not communicating effectively. It's that crucial distinction that prevents this choice from being correct.

What's Next?

The writing in this one is fairly dense, but you won't find any relief from the wordiness and abstraction in the next passage.

THE NEXT READING COMPREHENSION PASSAGE
BEGINS ON THE FOLLOWING PAGE

PASSAGE 10

Virtue is not so much a matter of learning specific rules or principles or maxims as it is one of developing the knack of exercising one's capacity for right action. Since "virtue" can mean
(5) both "moral goodness" and "successful or excellent action," comments regarding the teaching of virtue must apply to both senses or uses of the term, narrow and broad. Both are matters of human action or activity and, as such,
(10) are taught nondidactically, performatively.

That virtue is taught (and learned) performatively has something to do with the ineluctably normative quality of human action or activity. Norms are ways of doing something,
(15) getting something done; these ways of acting are taught by doing and showing how to do. Being normative, however, human actions can go wrong. They can be done wrong, or be wrongly done. As Stanley Cavell wrote: "The most characteristic
(20) fact about actions is that they can—in various specific ways—go wrong, that they can be performed incorrectly. This is not, in any restricted sense, a moral assertion, though it points the moral of intelligent activity. And it is as
(25) true of describing as it is of calculating or of promising or plotting or warning or asserting or defining . . . These are actions which we perform, and our successful performance of them depends upon our adopting and following the ways in
(30) which the action in question is done, upon what is normative for it." Thus, in talking about virtue, we are talking about normative matters, matters taught and learned in terms of successful or unsuccessful human action. As such, we are
(35) speaking about the cultivation of human skills and practices, human ways of acting (or ways of acting humanly) in this world.

Whether virtue is narrowly or broadly understood, the teaching of virtue is the teaching
(40) of a skill within a practice or form of life, the training of a capacity, not the memorization or indoctrination of rules or guidelines. The latter may indeed play some part in teaching a skill within a practice, but it is not all, or even most, of
(45) what I understand the teaching of virtue to be. Virtue is embodied in action; accordingly, our knowledge of virtue is a kind of performative knowledge—both knowledge acquired through action and knowledge expressed or revealed in
(50) action, in performing a task. Our knowledge of virtue is not, then, a matter of *propositional* knowledge, but rather a matter of performative knowledge. This helps account for our relative inability to define or say what virtue is with any
(55) confidence or assurance. Knowing what virtue is,

is not the same as knowing what some kind of object is, because virtue is not an object. And since so much of Western thought uses our knowledge of objects as *the* paradigm of
(60) knowledge, any kind of knowledge that does not fit the model is apt to seem not quite or fully knowledge at all. In this respect, virtue is like language. Both are taught by example. Hence, an inability to articulate the meaning of virtue is not
(65) a sign of the lack of knowledge of virtue, contrary to Socrates (or Plato). Instead, it is a part of the grammar of virtue: it shows what kind of thing virtue is.

1. The primary purpose of the passage is to

   (A) urge that students consult teachers when pursuing knowledge
   (B) reveal different attitudes toward virtue in the history of Western thought
   (C) argue that most teachers approach the teaching of virtue incorrectly
   (D) insist on the value of cultural norms as guidelines for human behavior
   (E) argue that the teaching of virtue is best understood as the training of a capacity

2. According to the passage, which one of the following distinguishes the broad definition of virtue from the narrow definition?

   (A) The broad definition does not include physical activities.
   (B) The narrow definition was not recognized by Plato or Socrates.
   (C) The broad definition deals with cultural norms.
   (D) The broad definition involves the teaching of a skill.
   (E) The broad definition encompasses more than simple moral rectitude.

3. The author would be most likely to agree with which one of the following statements about norms?

   (A) They are derived from specific maxims that define different aspects of virtue.
   (B) Only by faithfully following behavioral norms can virtue be acquired.
   (C) Many norms are simply the correct way of performing a certain action.
   (D) They are the product of didactic teaching.
   (E) They do not evolve, but rather come into being spontaneously.

4. According to the passage, a person who is unable to define virtue

   (A) cannot successfully teach virtue to others
   (B) may impart knowledge of excellent action but not of moral goodness
   (C) can teach didactically but not performatively
   (D) cannot perform virtuous actions
   (E) may still have a knowledge of virtue

5. The author contends that teachers of virtue strive primarily to impart

   (A) skills
   (B) principles
   (C) maxims
   (D) moral goodness
   (E) definitions

6. The author would characterize the view that some human actions are non-normative as

   (A) profoundly mistaken
   (B) controversial and possibly untrue
   (C) reasonable and easily supported
   (D) ambiguous and misleading
   (E) logically persuasive

7. Which one of the following would serve as an example of the "*propositional* knowledge" referred to in lines 51–52?

   (A) Experiments conducted on a trial and error basis
   (B) Practicing virtue by imitating moral actions
   (C) Learning a language in conversational classes
   (D) Memorizing various philosophical definitions of virtue
   (E) Advancing an argument based on insufficient evidence

Passage 10: Teaching Virtue

What Makes It Difficult

Abstract subject matter aside, the writing in this one is just plain difficult. Check out these terms and concepts: "nondidactically," "performatively," "ineluctably normative quality," "propositional knowledge." As if that's not bad enough, the author employs confusing word plays for what seems to be dramatic effect: "They (human actions) can be done wrong, or be wrongly done." Huh? Is there some subtle difference here we're supposed to pick up on? How about: " As such, we are speaking about . . . human ways of acting (or ways of acting humanly) in this world." If you need a further example of the high-minded complexity in this passage, note how the passage ends with a metaphor of an abstraction: "the grammar of virtue."

But really, how bad can it be? After all, the author is talking about learning how to be virtuous, which we can take to mean acting well in the world, to use her wording. By simplifying the material through paraphrasing, you have a much better shot at the questions. Here's how you may have understood the passage on your own terms.

Key Points of the Passage

Purpose and Main Idea: The author's purpose is to describe how virtue is taught. The main idea is that virtue is taught by doing—by example, by showing how to be virtuous—and not by abstract explanations of what virtue is.

Paragraph Structure: Paragraph 1 hits on the main point right at the end, noting that virtue is taught "nondidactically, performatively." For many, these terms are somewhat foreign, but not to worry; the rest of the passage essentially explains what this means.

> A 180 test taker knows that if an obscure term or concept is introduced, the author must clarify it if a question is to test it.

As for the rest of the first paragraph, perhaps the most important concept, which ties in with the main point, is that according to the author, virtue has something to do with developing one's ability to act right.

In the long second paragraph, the author argues that human action is "normative." The detailed argument here is a lot less important than realizing what the author is doing: basically, expanding on the idea that virtue is taught "performatively." But to summarize briefly: The author says actions involve "norms," which are "ways of doing something" and are "taught by doing and showing how to do." All actions, the author says with an assist from Stanley Cavell, have this normative quality. So—getting back to virtue—virtue like anything else involves teaching by doing and showing.

Paragraph 3, equally lengthy and off-putting, expands on this same idea: The teaching of virtue is the teaching of a skill (a "way of doing something"), not "memorization or indoctrination of rules." At the end the author draws one more lesson from the central idea: Since virtue is taught and known through actions, being unable to define it doesn't mean you do not know what it is. The implication: If you recognize virtue and can act with virtue, then you know what virtue is.

Answers and Explanations

1. E   2. E   3. C   4. E   5. A   6. A   7. D

1. E

The primary purpose question focuses right in on the "main idea." As expressed at the end of paragraph 1, this was that virtue is taught "nondidactically, performatively." In the rest of the passage, the author distinguishes between teaching of "rules or guidelines," "propositional knowledge," etc., and the kind of teaching he or she means: teaching "by doing and showing how to do" (paragraph 2), "matters taught and learned in terms of . . . action" (end of paragraph 2), "the teaching of a skill," the "training of a capacity" (paragraph 3). That last phrase is used in correct choice (E), but even if the phrase were not drawn from the passage, you should recognize it as a paraphrase of the recurring theme of the passage. Since the author basically does nothing in the passage except elaborate this one idea, (E) is the best choice.

(A) is an idea never expressed; the author's focus is on how to teach, not what students should do.

(B) tries to fool us with the tiny reference to Plato and Socrates at the very end; other than this, no "attitude toward virtue" besides the author's is ever mentioned.

(C) The idea in (C) is a possible inference—the author wouldn't care so much about how virtue should be taught if most teachers were doing a good job. But that's only an implication; the author never argues the point.

(D), finally, uses the word "norms" in one of its more common meanings—cultural norms—but not in the way the author uses it, to refer to "ways of doing something" and not to "rules or guidelines."

2. E

This question focuses on a subordinate point in paragraph 1. The author refers to virtue as meaning both "moral goodness" and "successful or excellent action," and then refers to these as the "narrow and broad" senses of the term. It's reasonable to assume that the author is keeping the terms in their original order—"narrow" refers to the first sense mentioned, "broad" to the second. Indeed, "successful or excellent action" can be seen as a broader, less specific meaning of "virtue" than "moral goodness." (E) rephrases "moral goodness" as "moral rectitude" and correctly states that the broad definition "encompasses more" than this.

(A) Physical activities are never mentioned, but if anything, they would be included, not excluded, under the broad definition.

(B) The single sentence about Plato and Socrates does not indicate whether they would have included or excluded either sense of "virtue."

(C) drags in "cultural norms" again; remember, to the author, "norms" are ways of doing things, and "cultural norms," in the familiar, everyday sense, are not mentioned in relation to either meaning of virtue.

A 180 test taker keeps everyday definitions at bay if the author has provided a more specific meaning for a word or concept.

(D) is definitely a true statement, but to the author, the narrow sense ("moral goodness") also involves the teaching of a skill, so this is not a distinction between the broad and narrow definitions.

3. C

This next question focuses squarely on the author's curious usage of "norms." As we've stressed already, for our author, norms are "ways of doing something, getting something done" (paragraph 2); this idea is paraphrased in (C).

In (A), "maxims" and "define" should have raised a red flag. Maxims are related to the dreaded "rules or guidelines" in paragraph 3, while "define" recalls the equally dreaded "propositional knowledge." In fact, the author talks about our inability to define what virtue is, so most of the wording in this choice should have clunked against your ear.

(B) Behavioral norms are never mentioned.

(D) "Didactic teaching," like "maxims" and "define" in (A), should be a red flag. Sentence 2 of paragraph 2 says norms "are taught by doing and showing how to do"—not by didactic methods.

(E) is one of those "from absolutely nowhere" choices; nothing in the passage remotely suggests the idea of evolution versus spontaneity.

4. E

The challenge here is mainly locating the right material to work with; from there, the answer comes from a fairly simple paraphrase.

The author's thoughts on the inability to define virtue appear in paragraph 3. If we add together the question stem and choice (E), we'd have a straightforward paraphrase of the sentence about Socrates, and it all stems from a point we've already discussed: the notion that being able to define or articulate what virtue is isn't a prerequisite for knowing it when you see or partake in it. It's stated very directly at the end of the passage: "An inability to articulate the meaning of virtue is not a sign of the lack of knowledge of virtue."

(A) The issue in (A) is not specifically mentioned; but since virtue is taught by "doing and showing how to do," probably someone who knew virtue but couldn't define it could teach it. At least, we can't say for sure that he or she couldn't teach it.

(B) makes a distinction the passage won't support. Whatever is true of the person who can't define virtue—whether he or she can or can't teach it—would presumably apply to teaching virtue in both senses, not just one.

(C) makes exactly the wrong distinction. Someone who can't define the subject matter can't teach didactically, where the main teaching method is to repeat definitions and explanations.

(D) is somewhat absurd, if you think about it—if this were true, only very learned philosophers could act virtuously.

5. A

It's right there in the first sentence of paragraph 3: "The teaching of virtue is the teaching of a skill . . . the training of a capacity." (A) is correct.

(B), (C), and (E) are all part of the "didactic" aspect of teaching. The author does admit, a little later in paragraph 3, that these "may indeed play some part in teaching a skill," but contends that this "is not all, or even most, of what I understand the teaching of virtue to be"; so they are not what teachers of virtue strive primarily to impart, as the question asks.

> A 180 test taker knows that even a single missed word can jeopardize her understanding of the question.

(D) is a misstatement: The author would say a teacher of virtue strives to teach moral goodness through imparting ways of doing, imparting skills. It also makes a false distinction; the teacher would strive to teach "excellent action" as much as "moral goodness."

6. A

Back to paragraph 2. The author refers to "the ineluctably [inevitably] normative quality of human action"; he or she states, "being normative . . . human actions can go wrong." And in the quote, Stanley Cavell includes a list of actions clearly meant to be as broad as possible, all of which are said to be normative. The author clearly views all human actions as normative, and hence would think the opposite view profoundly mistaken, choice (A).

Once you realize that the stem states the direct contrary of the author's view, (A) is easy to select, and the others easy to reject. (B) and (D) are critical of the idea in the stem, but not nearly critical enough; (C) and (E) are approving, and thus are wrong altogether.

7. D

Reading the context here, the key thing to realize is that the "propositional knowledge" discussed is contrasted with the author's main theme—the correct way to teach virtue. From this standpoint, we can rule out choices (A) through (C), since they all fit the author's definition of "performative knowledge": "knowledge acquired through action and knowledge expressed or revealed in action, through performing a task." Conducting experiments, imitating moral actions and learning a language are all ways of learning from actions—learning by example.

Choice (D), on the other hand, exemplifies the type of didactic learning the author contrasts with teaching virtue. We can infer then, that memorizing definitions of virtue is an example of "propositional knowledge."

(E) Advancing arguments without sufficient evidence may play on the word "proposition," but isn't supported in the passage at all.

What's Next?

Philosophical conjecture is not the sole province of professional philosophers or social scientists; literary stars often get into philosophizing mode as well. For example, some consider Fyodor Dostoyevsky to be not only one of Russia's premiere novelists, but also one of its foremost philosophers *and* psychologists. Another such multitalented thinker is Virginia Woolf, who is about to regale us with her philosophy of literary criticism, relying on the works of Dostoyevsky's contemporary (and sometimes rival) Ivan Turgenev for support.

PASSAGE 11

The critical essays of Virginia Woolf, when examined carefully, reveal a thematic and technical complexity that rivals her fiction. Although her fiction also focuses on the
(5) problematical relationship between the reader's experience of the text and the original authorial presence, the problem of interpretation is more sharply visible in her criticism.

Some of her most rigorous essays suggest that
(10) the personality of the author can be fixed if sufficient evidence can be amassed and if its logical implications are followed. In "The Novels of Turgenev," Woolf pursues the problem of interpretation by providing a detailed report of her
(15) own response to Turgenev. She does this in order to make possible the question that leaps the gap between reader and text. That question—"what principles guided Turgenev?"—focuses on the fictional strategies that must have been in
(20) operation in order to have produced her experience. Thus Woolf accounts for her experience of the novel by reconstructing Turgenev's method. But she pushes farther: the method must be a sign of a deeper informing
(25) power, the mind of Turgenev itself. In other words, the gap between reader and writer may be eliminated in the reader's achievement of what Woolf calls the author's "perspective." This distance can be traversed by interpretation, Woolf
(30) argues, because writers like Turgenev achieve a level of personality beneath the surface distinctions among individuals—a level at which all human beings are united. Her greatest examples of this impersonal power are Jane
(35) Austen and Shakespeare. We are allowed by their art to make contact with what is most deeply personal, and therefore most widely human in them.

But one of the riches of Woolf's essays is that
(40) they critique the very possibility of closing the gap between reader and writer. This critique takes the form of Woolf's awareness of the contemporary artist's self-consciousness, that is, the artist's entrapment in superficial, alienating
(45) distinctions among people. Self-consciousness is the enemy of human contact and knowing. It is present, Woolf argues, in the anger of writers who increase our awareness of the division between he sexes, in writers too aware of their nationality, in
(50) authors who can never write without class consciousness, and in realistic writers whose methods emphasize the external at the expense of the deeply human interior. There seem to be so many barriers on the road to the deepest level of
(55) self that the journey is impossible. In fact, Woolf

asserts that it *is* impossible for the modern writer. In "How It Strikes a Contemporary," Woolf contrasts writers of the past—Chaucer is her most powerful example—who believed wholeheartedly
(60) in an atemporal order verified by the entire culture, with modern writers who have lost this advantage. Woolf suggests that, if, for writer and reader, no way to a shared, universal level of experience is available, the very ground of the
(65) interpretive enterprise is removed.

1. According to the passage, Woolf views a belief in an atemporal world order as

   (A) defining the literary customs of modern writers
   (B) being inadequate to the task of eliminating divisions in human society
   (C) having evolved from a belief in a temporal world order
   (D) supporting the values and priorities of modern culture
   (E) contributing to the distinctiveness of past literature

2. The author is mainly concerned with

   (A) revising an interpretation of Woolf's criticism
   (B) analyzing Woolf's interpretation of Turgenev
   (C) comparing Woolf's fiction to her criticism
   (D) examining a theme of Woolf's criticism
   (E) investigating a paradox in Woolf's criticism

3. According to the passage, Woolf believes that, compared to modern writers, writers of the past were

   (A) more interested in personal issues
   (B) more concerned with timeless themes
   (C) more self-absorbed
   (D) less impersonal
   (E) less objective

4. The passage implies that, in her essay "The Novels of Turgenev," Woolf assumes that

   (A) stable and defining qualities of an author's personality are discernible in his or her fiction
   (B) interpretation involves a compromise between the reader's perspective and the perspective of the author
   (C) a reader's experience of a novel's text is determined by a standard set of fictional principles
   (D) making contact with an author's mind requires the use of critical reasoning more than intuition
   (E) an author's achievement of the impersonal involves a renunciation of the personal in his or her fiction

5. The passage suggests that Woolf believes that self-consciousness among contemporary artists is

   (A) liberating for certain artists
   (B) a temporary deviation
   (C) a pervasive phenomenon
   (D) negligible in its effects
   (E) a hopeful sign

6. The passage refers to common themes of contemporary writers in the third paragraph in order to

   (A) exemplify a contemporary preoccupation with separateness
   (B) identify sources of contemporary cultural patterns
   (C) suggest parallels between past and present literature
   (D) refute the idea that self-consciousness is an affliction
   (E) point out a strong contemporary desire to experiment

7. The passage suggests that Woolf would be most likely to agree with which one of the following statements?

   (A) Literary works seldom reflect the period in which they were written.
   (B) Literary criticism should focus on the work rather than the artist.
   (C) Literary criticism should emphasize plot over structure.
   (D) Literary works are the product of an author's unique experiences.
   (E) Literary criticism seldom reveals the biases of the critic.

Passage 11: Woolf on Literary Interpretation

What Makes It Difficult

We're presented with a description of an intellectual's theory on a relatively complex subject. This one deals with the possibility of bridging the gap between the minds of novelist and reader—pretty esoteric stuff. And it deals largely with abstractions such as perspective, interpretation, self-consciousness, and universal experience. As always, summarizing the purpose and main idea, and breaking it down into its structural elements, will help us handle the questions.

Key Points of the Passage

Purpose and Main Idea: The author's purpose is to discuss Virginia Woolf's philosophy regarding a reader's ability to "interpret" a writer. The main idea is that it's possible for readers to gain "perspective" on authors of previous periods because these writers capture a deep universal human experience in their work, but the gap between readers and modern writers is more difficult to traverse because these writers emphasize in their work that which separates people and do not provide a way "to a shared, universal level of experience."

Paragraph Structure: Paragraph 1 simply establishes the fact that Woolf is concerned in her critical essays with the problem of interpretation. We have to wait for the next paragraph for the author to get into what this really means.

Paragraph 2 outlines the argument Woolf makes in her essay "The Novels of Turgenev." She asserts that the central problem for the reader (or the critic) is understanding or *interpreting* Turgenev. As the passage explains it, Woolf believes that there are two stages in the interpretive process: first, understanding Turgenev's fictional strategies—his "method"; second (and more basic), gaining an understanding of Turgenev's mind and personality—his "perspective." Getting a deeper sense of the author's personality is a reader's fundamental goal, because it's at this level that essential human bonds can be established between author and reader. At the end of the paragraph the author generalizes: Woolf believes that Turgenev, Austen, and Shakespeare are great writers because their most personal concerns can be interpreted, understood—shared—by readers everywhere.

Paragraph 3 sets up a key contrast: Woolf argues in other essays (including "How It Strikes a Contemporary") that contemporary writers have abandoned the universal themes favored by past writers. According to Woolf, writers today are preoccupied with social differences and personal uniqueness—their own separateness as people. The result, according to Woolf, is the erecting of impenetrable barriers which jeopardize the traditional interpretive process.

Now, these ideas really aren't that tough. For instance, you probably already know about the universality of Shakespeare, Austen, etc. No surprise there. Woolf's argument about modern writers, their separateness and so on, is more provocative, perhaps even open to question, but it's not such a tough idea, either, if you keep your test-taking cool.

A 180 test taker uses his own knowledge to help him understand an author's ideas, but never replaces the author's ideas with his own.

Answers and Explanations

1. E   2. D   3. B   4. A   5. C   6. A   7. D

1. E

The belief in an atemporal world order relates directly to the concern of past writers for universal themes. The point is made explicitly at the end of the passage. Writers of the past like Chaucer believed "wholeheartedly in an atemporal world order," which is something that distinguishes the work of past masters from contemporary writers. Thus it can be said that this belief contributes to the distinctiveness of past literature, choice (E).

All the wrong choices fly in the face of the passage:

(A) and (D) are nearly synonymous: They falsely suggest a link between belief in an atemporal order and *modern* writers. In paragraph 3, the author explicitly states that this is not the case.

(B) contradicts Woolf: She argues that the older, universal values were healing, and that we moderns are worse off for their absence from modern literature.

(C) A "temporal world order" is never explicitly defined, but we can assume that we're living in it now. We're never given a hint as to the precursor of the belief in an atemporal order.

A 180 test taker is not fooled by concepts that sound familiar but are found nowhere in the passage.

---

2. D

Next up is a straightforward main idea question. The whole passage, all three paragraphs, takes a look at one theme—the problem of interpreting an author—of some of Woolf's criticism. (D) states the author's concern in general terms.

(A) is out because of its verb. The author's not revising anything.

(B) focuses too narrowly on Woolf's Turgenev essay. Sure, this plays a large role in the passage, but it's there to support the larger issue of Woolf's general philosophy of interpretation.

(C) is plain wrong; in paragraph 1 the author makes a brief comparison of Woolf's criticism to her fiction, but it's by no means the author's main concern.

(E) doesn't work because the author never refers to any paradox in Woolf's work.

3. B

Another question focusing on the contrast between past and present writers. As is clear in both paragraph 2 and the passage's last couple of sentences, writers of the past were preoccupied with universal, timeless themes. Again, the wrong choices all contradict the passage. It's modern writers who focus on personal issues (A), are more self-absorbed (C), are less impersonal (D), and who are less objective (E).

4. A

This question is looking for an idea (an "assumption") that's clearly at work in Woolf's essay on Turgenev. We're therefore looking for an idea that's required in order for Woolf's discussion of Turgenev to make sense. (A) goes right to the heart of the passage: According to sentence 1 of paragraph 2, Woolf believes that, through a careful reading of the fictional work, a reader/critic can identify the personality of the author. (A) is a simple paraphrase of this idea. If, contrary to (A), the personality of a writer was *not* discernible from his or her fiction, Woolf would not be able to claim that "the personality of the author can be fixed" if only certain evidence were amassed and its implications observed.

A 180 test taker knows assumptions are most common in Logical Reasoning, but uses the skills developed in that section when one shows up elsewhere.

(B) Nowhere is it suggested that interpretation involves any "compromise" between reader and author.

(C) distorts things by suggesting that there is one "standard" set of principles at work in all fictional works.

(D) Nowhere is it suggested that intuition is less important than critical reasoning in fictional interpretation. In fact, getting a sense of an author's "perspective" or personality would seem to be a highly intuitive (and informed) process.

(E) distorts the generalization at the end of the paragraph: Woolf suggests that Turgenev achieves an impersonal quality as he reveals that part of himself with which his readers can identify. But he is *not* renouncing himself in doing so.

5. C

Here we're being asked about a key point of the last paragraph. We're told there that Woolf believes that self-consciousness—self-absorption—is rampant among today's artists. She is suggesting that it's a pervasive problem, really a blight. (C) gets the point.

As for the wrong choices, there's no talk of self-consciousness being "liberating" (A), "temporary" (B), unimportant (D), or a good thing (E). These choices ignore the intensity of Woolf's apprehension.

6. A

A question that asks why an author has done something we call a "logic" question, which, like most of these other questions, harks back to one of the key points in the passage. These typical contemporary themes are examples Woolf gives of the kinds of issues that today's writers are concerned with: issues of separateness, dividedness, or alienation. (A) is the choice that corresponds.

(B) may be the most tempting wrong choice, but it misses the point. It's illogical to think of the cited themes as "sources" of today's cultural patterns.

(C) and (D) are both inconsistent with the passage. The themes of contemporary writers are cited to show divisions, not parallels, between past and present writers. And the author cites these themes to illustrate how Woolf finds self-consciousness to be a barrier to literary interpretation, so *refuting* the idea that self-consciousness is a bad thing simply doesn't make sense in this context.

(E) The notion of experimentation is outside the scope of the discussion in the final paragraph, but if anything, we'd have to guess that contemporary horizons for writers are fairly restrictive, limited to issues of alienation and separateness. In any case, the contemporary themes cited aren't there to point toward an experimental vein in contemporary literature.

7. D

The last question is looking for the choice that's *consistent* with Woolf's ideas, and the winner is (D). Consider her essay on Turgenev. She believes that, even though his themes are universal, Turgenev's personality lies at the root of his novels. And Woolf would also apparently agree that contemporary fiction, bound by self-consciousness, is also the product of an author's special experiences.

(A) makes no sense. It's clearly not true of today's fiction, and Woolf never suggests that Turgenev's novels could have been written, say, in Shakespeare's time.

(B) contradicts Woolf: her critical method involves analysis of work and artist.

(C) Woolf is concerned with the "fictional strategies" and methods that must have been employed in order for her to experience a novel as she did. How this relates to plot and structure is unclear. Nowhere is it specified which of these elements is better represented in an author's methods and strategies, so we can't attribute this belief to Woolf.

(E) simply sounds unlikely and inconsistent with Woolf. The idea of a reader/critic establishing contact with an author clearly involves a personal, subjective response. If anything, it would seem that biases would be inevitable.

What's Next?

One more passage to go, and it's a whopper, for sure. What did you find to be the most difficult game in the Logic Games section? Maybe one of the process games such as "Children's Questions"? Well, many feel that this next passage is the Reading Comp equivalent of those, at least as far as brutality is concerned.

PASSAGE 12

A group of problems that assumes great prominence in the literature of philosophy is called the theory of knowledge. Although of all philosophical inquiries this may seem at first
(5) glance most artificial and academic, a little reflection will reveal its crucial importance. Suppose, for example, that it is a question of the finality of science, or the legitimacy of faith. The question can be answered only by examining the
(10) methods of science in order to discover whether there is anything arbitrary in them that limits the scope of the results. And one must inquire what constitutes genuine knowledge, or when a thing is finally explained, or whether there be things that
(15) necessarily lie beyond the reach of human faculties, or whether it be proper to allow aspirations and ideals to affect one's conclusions.

Bacon and Descartes, the founders of modern philosophy, devoted themselves primarily to such
(20) questions, so that all thought since their time has taken these questions as the point of departure. Furthermore, philosophy has called attention to a very peculiar predicament in which the human thinker finds himself. He seems compelled to
(25) begin with himself. When Descartes sought to reduce knowledge to a primal and indubitable certainty he found that certainty to be the knowledge that each thinker has of his own existence, and of the existence of his own ideas.
(30) And if a thinker begins with this nucleus, how is he ever to add anything to it; how is he ever to be sure of the existence of anything which is not himself or his ideas? On the other hand, while my knowledge is most certainly of and within myself,
(35) yet it can scarcely be knowledge unless it takes me beyond myself. This has become the central difficulty of philosophy. It is a genuine difficulty, and yet everybody neglects it except the philosopher.
(40) Berkeley was led by an examination of this difficulty to conclude that if reality is to be assumed to be knowable, then it can be composed of nothing but thinkers and their ideas. And in this conclusion Berkeley has been followed by the
(45) whole school of the idealists, the school which has numbered among its members the most eminent thinkers of later times, and has inspired notable movements in German and English literature. Other schools have been led by an
(50) examination of the same difficulty to quite different conclusions. But this difficulty has been the crux of modern thought, and no one can hope to debate fundamental issues at all without meeting it.
(55) Such, then, are some of the matters that at once come under discussion when one attempts to think radically and fundamentally. Philosophy is brought to these and like problems because it expresses the profound restlessness of the mind, a
(60) dissatisfaction with ready-made, habitual, or conventional opinions, a free and unbounded curiosity, and the need of rounding up the world and judging it for the purposes of life.

1. The passage is primarily concerned with

   (A) illustrating a philosophical debate by comparing two theories
   (B) debunking a misconception about a philosophical school
   (C) demonstrating the importance of one branch of philosophy
   (D) considering the practical application of the theory of knowledge
   (E) explaining the history of a school of philosophy

2. The author suggests which of the following about the theory of knowledge?

   (A) The theory of knowledge introduces an important paradox.
   (B) The theory of knowledge leads us to conclude that reality is subjective.
   (C) The theory of knowledge resolves the central difficulty of philosophy.
   (D) The theory of knowledge questions the legitimacy of faith.
   (E) The theory of knowledge denies the certainty of the self.

3. The passage implies that philosophy is important because

   (A) it explains the nature of reality
   (B) it is the only means for exploring fundamental questions about the human experience
   (C) it is capable of determining what knowledge is genuine
   (D) it raises a problem that is central to modern thought
   (E) it is an academic discipline that exercises the mind

4. According to the passage, Descartes's conclusion that the only certain knowledge is of one's existence and the existence of one's ideas has which of the following consequences?

 (A) Each thinker is left isolated in his thoughts, unsure of the world around him.
 (B) Reality becomes unknowable.
 (C) All knowledge becomes theoretical.
 (D) The thinker is freed from the constraints of conventional opinion.
 (E) The quest for knowledge becomes a circular conundrum.

5. The passage suggests that Berkeley would argue that reality is

 (A) a figment of the human imagination
 (B) a product of the human intellect
 (C) essentially unknowable
 (D) a question of faith
 (E) a hollow concept

6. Suppose that an astronomer develops a theory about the nature of black holes based on data retrieved from a radio telescope. According to the author, in order to test the legitimacy of her findings, the scientist must

 (A) check that the telescope is functioning properly
 (B) consider alternate theories to see if they also fit the data
 (C) question the nature of reality
 (D) confirm that the data does not include any errors
 (E) determine if her assumptions are beyond question

7. The primary purpose of the last paragraph of the passage is to

 (A) suggest that radicalism is a necessary force in modern thought
 (B) express the transformational power of philosophy
 (C) decry the modern adherence to conventional opinion
 (D) describe the properties of philosophy that make it fundamental to modern thought
 (E) identify why the theory of knowledge allows for unconventional thinking

8. The passage suggests that the author would be most likely to agree with which of the following statements?

 (A) The theory of knowledge is a radical philosophical inquiry.
 (B) The predicament raised by the theory of knowledge is widely studied.
 (C) Philosophy is a systematic mode of inquiry that relies on established patterns of thought.
 (D) Berkeley's conclusion regarding the dilemma raised by Descartes is the foundation of modern thought.
 (E) Questions of faith are beyond the scope of philosophical inquiry.

Passage 12: The Theory of Knowledge

What Makes It Difficult

The author says right up front that his topic is "artificial and academic." The theory of knowledge is perhaps the most esoteric branch of philosophy, and many test takers will find this subject matter daunting. The author also suffers from the name-dropping problem: he introduces philosophers—Bacon, Descartes, and Berkeley—as if his readers will already be familiar with their work.

This passage is tough on several counts: an abstract, academic topic; complicated prose; and undefined terms. Then, there are eight demanding questions, including four inference questions—which are especially hard to handle when the material is so abstract—and a question that asks us to apply the theory of knowledge to a specific problem. Knowledge might seem like just a theory when you try to tackle this one. How did you fare recognizing the key points?

Key Points of the Passage

Purpose and Main Idea: The purpose of the passage is to persuade the reader of the importance of philosophy, particularly the theory of knowledge. The main idea is that the problem introduced by this school of thought--namely that all knowledge originates with the self, and, if this is the case, how can this be called knowledge--is central to all modern thought.

Paragraph Structure: Paragraph 1 introduces the term theory of knowledge and makes the first case for its importance. The author gives the example of questions of science or faith, and asserts that one has to examine the methods used to gain knowledge in order to determine if the knowledge is "genuine." To put another way, the question is "how do we know that what we know is true."

Paragraph 2 focuses on the work of Descartes, perhaps best known for the aphorism, "I think therefore I am." The author explains this central concept, the foundation of the theory of knowledge. Descartes found that the only certainty is the knowledge that each thinker has of his own existence and his ideas. This raises the "central difficulty of philosophy": if the only certainty is the self and one's ideas, how does one know anything outside of one's self?

Paragraph 3 tells us that a whole school of thought has devoted itself to this problem, and that this difficulty is the "crux of modern thought." The author tells us that one school of thought has come to a completely different conclusion about the problem raised by Descartes than that proposed by the first school.

In paragraph 4, the author makes his final case for the importance of philosophy. The author states that philosophy is particularly suited to the problem of "how do we know what we know" because it is not satisfied with conventional opinion but expresses "unbounded curiosity" and the need to look at the world and judge it for the "purposes of life."

Answers and Explanations

1. C   2. A   3. D   4. A   5. B   6. E   7. D   8. A

1. C

This overall purpose question is a good one to prephrase based on our analysis above. The author's purpose is to "persuade the readers of the importance of philosophy, particularly the theory of knowledge." Choice (C) most closely sums up this statement, as the author is demonstrating the importance of one branch of philosophy.

(A) is incorrect because the author only considers one theory

(B) is too narrow. Although the author does address the misconception that the theory of knowledge is "artificial and academic" in the second sentence this is not the primary purpose of the passage, as he does not touch upon this issue again.

A 180 test taker knows that the answer to a primary purpose question must apply to the entire passage, not just one part.

(D) is also too narrow. And, while the author does discuss the application of the theory of knowledge to science and questions of faith in paragraph 1, the word "practical" does not really apply to the intellectual inquiry described.

(E) is too broad. The author does mention some of the key philosophers, but he does not give enough information to justify calling the passage a history.

2. A

In this question we are asked to draw an inference, as indicated by the word "suggests." An inference question is too broad to prephrase, so it's best to evaluate each answer choice, eliminating the obviously incorrect ones. Each question describes what the theory of knowledge does, so we can start with the verb following "The theory of knowledge" and see if we can eliminate any choices.

(B), (C), and (E) cannot be correct because they suggest that the theory of knowledge reaches a certain conclusion. We know from paragraph 3 that the theory does not "lead us to conclude," "resolve," or "deny" any point of view, in fact it accommodates two completely different solutions to the same problem.

This leaves (A) and (D). (A) is certainly correct; One of the author's main points is that the theory of knowledge raises an important question. (D) is incorrect because paragraph 1 suggests that the theory of knowledge can be applied to questions of faith, but does not suggest that the theory comes to any conclusion about faith.

3. D

Another inference question, this time about the broader subject of philosophy. We know that the purpose of the passage is to persuade the reader that philosophy is important. This asks us why the author thinks philosophy is important. Again, the best approach is to compare each of the choices against what we have learned about philosophy from the passage. According to the author, philosophy raises important questions about what constitutes knowledge, which are essential to debating fundamental issues. The last paragraph also describes philosophy's ability look at the world with an open curiosity free from conventional opinion.

(A) is almost an inverse of what the author suggests about philosophy. Philosophy does not explain reality but offers a means of questioning what is real.

(B) is too finite. The author does not say that philosophy is the only way to think about human experience.

(C) misconstrues the author's argument. The author does not suggest that philosophy provides answers, only that is raises important questions.

(D) aptly summarizes the author's argument

(E) contradicts the author's assertion that philosophy is not an "artificial and academic" inquiry, but something fundamental to modern thought

---

A 180 test taker is aware that often one question will test the same concept as another question in the set.

---

4. A

Here is a question that starts out with the words "According to the passage." That let's us know that we are being asked for a specific detail from the passage. Where does the passage discuss the results of Decartes's conclusion? Toward the end of paragraph 2, the author explains that if a thinker is only certain of himself and his ideas, he cannot add to this knowledge or be certain of anything outside of himself and his ideas. The author also questions if knowledge of the self can really be called knowledge if it does not take "me beyond myself." This conundrum is correctly expressed in choice (A).

(B) is an inference that could perhaps be drawn from the passage, but "reality" is not directly discussed in relation to Descartes

(C) is incorrect because, according to Descartes, we can be certain in the knowledge of ourselves and our ideas

(D) expresses an advantage of philosophy according to the author, but has nothing to do with the problem raised by Descartes

(E) is tricky because it has some components of the correct answer, but the conundrum cannot be called circular

5. B

This question asks for an inference based on Berkeley's views as they are presented in the passage, "reality" is the key term that should jump out at you from the stem. What does the passage tell us about Berkeley and reality? The first sentence of paragraph 3 states that Berkeley concluded that if we consider reality to be knowable it can be made only of thinkers and their ideas. Choice (B) expresses this idea perfectly. It is made, or is a product, of thinkers and their ideas, or the human intellect.

(A) takes Berkeley's idea too far. Berkeley starts with the assumption that reality may be knowable, so he does not consider it to be imaginary.

(C) contradicts the passage. Berkeley may question if reality is knowable, but he does not declare it unknowable.

(D) and (E) are inferences that, while potentially correct, are not supported by the passage.

6. E

This "application" question asks us to take information from the passage and apply it to a situation not presented in the passage.

A 180 test taker focuses on "buzzwords" in the question stem that strongly suggest the place in the passage that the answer will be found.

Paragraph 1 discusses the application of the theory of knowledge to the question of the finality, or fundamental fact, of science, and the situation presented in the stem is about testing a scientific finding. The author states that in order to determine if science is fact we have to look at the scientific methods used and determine if there is anything arbitrary. In other words, the scientist must consider her methods and make sure that they are based on fundamental truths, and are not dependent on her individual discretion. (E) is correct because every scientist accepts certain assumptions as fact, and these assumptions are the starting point of the scientific method. Even if you did not connect "assumptions" with the scientific methods mentioned in the passage, the key words are "beyond question," which is the opposite of "arbitrary."

(A) a telescope is a tool, not a method, so does not apply to the theory of knowledge

(B) is too specific. While this may be one way of checking if her methods are arbitrary, the author is talking about a more fundamental inquiry into the foundation of science.

(C) does not address how the theory of knowledge is applicable to science

(D) errors are not the result of arbitrary methods, but of human or mechanical failure

---

A 180 test taker is adept with questions that require her to apply ideas from the passage to alternative scenarios not raised in the passage.

---

7. D

Finally, another "gimme" (hey, we deserve at least one or two even on tough passages, right?). As the question asks for the primary purpose of the last paragraph, this is another good question to prephrase an answer for. We can return to our analysis of the passage. The author "makes his final case for the importance and philosophy," and explains why philosophy is especially suited to the problem of "how do we know what we know," which the author identified earlier in the passage as "the crux of modern thought." (D) most accurately states this purpose of the last paragraph.

(A) is tempting because the author does mention thinking "radically." However, this is not the main idea addressed in the paragraph.

(B) is not supported by the passage. The author does not discuss philosophy's ability to transform.

(C) decry implies an impassioned argument, which does not fit the tone of the passage

(E) is too narrow. The author is talking about philosophy in general, and its relevance to the problems raised by the theory of knowledge

8. A

With which one of the answer choices would the author most likely agree? Well, we know enough about the author's point of view to answer a specific question, but this is a broad question that asks us to think like the author. We've got no choice but to read the options and see which one fits.

(A) This one fits, all right. Paragraph 3 states that the questions raised by the theory of knowledge come under discussion when one thinks "radically and fundamentally."

(B) contradicts the author's assertion at the end of paragraph 2 that "everybody neglects" the problem raised by the theory of knowledge "except philosophers"

(C) is the opposite of what the author says about philosophy in the last paragraph

(D) misconstrues the information given in paragraph 3. Berkeley comes to one, influential, conclusion about the paradox raised by the theory of knowledge, but it is the paradox itself, not Berkeley's conclusion, that the author declares is the "crux of modern thought."

(E) goes against the author's statement in paragraph 1 that philosophical inquiries can be applied to questions of faith.

A Special Note for International Students

In recent years, U.S. law schools have experienced an increase in inquiries from non-U.S. citizens, some of whom are already practicing lawyers in their own countries. This surge of interest in the U.S. legal system has been attributed to the spread of the global economy. When business people from outside the United States do business with Americans, they often find themselves doing business under the American legal system. Gaining insight into how the American legal system works is of great interest around the world.

This new international interest in the U.S. legal system is having an effect on law schools. Many schools have developed special programs to accommodate the needs of this special population of lawyers and students from around the globe. If you are an international student or lawyer interested in learning more about the American legal system, or if you are considering attending law school in the United States, Kaplan can help you explore your options.

Getting into a U.S. law school can be especially challenging for students from other countries. If you are not from the United States, but are considering attending law school in the United States, here is what you'll need to get started.

- If English is not your first language, you'll probably need to take the TOEFL® (Test of English as a Foreign Language), or provide some other evidence that you are proficient in English. Most law schools require a minimum computer TOEFL score of 250 (600 on the paper-based TOEFL) or better.
- Depending on the program to which you are applying, you may also need to take the LSAT (Law School Admissions Test). All law schools in the United States require the LSAT® for their J.D. programs. LL.M. programs usually do not require the LSAT. Kaplan will help you determine if you need to take the LSAT. If you must take the LSAT, Kaplan can help you prepare for it.
- Since admission to law school is quite competitive, you may want to select three or four programs and complete applications for each school.

- You should begin the process of applying to law schools or special legal studies programs at least eighteen months before the fall of the year you plan to start your studies. Most programs will have only September start dates.
- In addition, you will need to obtain an I-20 Certificate of Eligibility from the school you plan to attend if you intend to apply for an F-1 Student Visa to study in the United States.

KAPLAN ENGLISH PROGRAMS*

If you need more help with the complex process of law school admissions, assistance preparing for the LSAT or TOEFL, or help building your English language skills in general, you may be interested in Kaplan's programs for international students.

Kaplan English Programs were designed to help students and professionals from outside the United States meet their educational and career goals. At locations throughout the United States, international students take advantage of Kaplan's programs to help them improve their academic and conversational English skills, raise their scores on the TOEFL, LSAT, and other standardized exams, and gain admission to the schools of their choice. Our staff and instructors give international students the individualized attention they need to succeed. Here is a brief description of some of Kaplan's programs for international students:

General Intensive English

Kaplan's General Intensive English classes are designed to help you improve your skills in all areas of English and to increase your fluency in spoken and written English. Classes are available for beginning to advanced students, and the average class size is 12 students.

TOEFL and Academic English

This course provides you with the skills you need to improve your TOEFL score and succeed in an American university or graduate program. It includes advanced reading, writing, listening, grammar and conversational English. You will also receive training for the TOEFL, updated for the TOEFL iBT, using Kaplan's exclusive computer-based practice materials.

LSAT Test-Preparation Course

The LSAT is a crucial admission criterion for law schools in the United States. A high score can help you stand out from other applicants. This course includes the skills you need to succeed on each section of the LSAT, as well as access to Kaplan's exclusive practice materials.

Other Kaplan Programs

Since 1938, more than 3 million students have come to Kaplan to advance their studies, prepare for entry to American universities, and further their careers. In addition to the above programs, Kaplan offers courses to prepare for the SAT®, GMAT®, GRE®, MCAT®, DAT®, USMLE®, NCLEX®, and other standardized exams at locations throughout the United States.

APPLYING TO KAPLAN ENGLISH PROGRAMS

To get more information, or to apply for admission to any of Kaplan's programs for international students and professionals, contact us at:

Kaplan English Programs
700 South Flower Street, Suite 2900
Los Angeles, CA 90017
Phone: If calling from outside the U.S.: (213) 452-5800
Phone: If calling from within the U.S.: (800) 818-9128
Fax: (213) 892-1364
Email: world@kaplan.com
Web: www.kaplanenglish.com

FREE Services for International Students

Kaplan now offers international students many services online—*free of charge*! Students may assess their TOEFL skills and gain valuable feedback on their English language proficiency in just a few hours with Kaplan's TOEFL Skills Assessment. Log onto www.kaplanenglish.com today.

---

*Kaplan is authorized under federal law to enroll nonimmigrant alien students.Kaplan is accredited by ACCET (Accrediting Council for Continuing Education and Training) and is a member of FIYTO and ALTO.

NOTES

NOTES

NOTES

NOTES

NOTES

NOTES

NOTES

NOTES

NOTES

NOTES

NOTES

NOTES

NOTES

Also Available